Antitrust and the Digital Economy

Legal Standards, Presumptions, and Key Challenges

Editor

Yannis Katsoulacos

Foreword by

Krisztian Katona

Introduction by

Richard Whish

106 West 32nd Street, Suite 144 New York, NY, 10001, USA
www.concurrences.com
book@concurrences.com

First Printing, May 2023
978-1-954750-09-8 (Hardcover)
Library of Congress Control Number: 2023938382

Cover Design: Yves Buliard, www.yvesbuliard.fr
Book Design and Layout implementation: Nord Compo

Concurrences Books

Tributes

Eleanor M. Fox – Antitrust Ambassador to the World, *2021*

Herbert Hovenkamp – The Dean of American Antitrust Law, *2021*

Frédéric Jenny – Standing Up for Convergence and Relevance in Antitrust, (Vol. I & II), *2019 & 2021*

Albert Foer – A Consumer Voice in the Antitrust Arena, *2020*

Richard Whish – Taking Competition Law Outside the Box, *2020*

Douglas H. Ginsburg – An Antitrust Professor on the Bench (Vol. I & II), *2018 & 2020*

Wang Xiaoye – The Pioneer of Competition Law in China, *A. Emch, W. Ng (eds.), 2019*

Ian S. Forrester – A Scot without Borders (Vol. I & II), *A. Komninos (eds.), 2015*

William E. Kovacic – An Antitrust Tribute (Vol. I & II), *2013 & 2014*

Practical Books

Global Dictionary of Competition Law, *D. Healey, W. Kovacic, P. Trevisan, R. Whish, Forthcoming 2023*

Antitrust in Life Sciences, *M. Cowie, G. Gordon M. Thill-Tayara, Forthcoming 2023*

State Aid & the Energy Transition, *D. Buschle, L. Hancher, M.-T. Richter-Kuhnert (eds.), Forthcoming 2023 (in collaboration with the Energy Community)*

State Aid & National Enforcement, *J. Derenne, D. Jouve, C. Lemaire, F. Martucci (eds.), Forthcoming 2023*

Competition Law Treatment of Joint Ventures, *B. Bleicher, N. Campbell, A. Hamilton, N. Hukkinen, A. Khan, A. Mordaunt (eds.), 2022 (in collaboration with the IBA)*

Information Exchange & Related Risks, *Z. Marosi, M. Soares (eds.), 2022 (in collaboration with the IBA)*

Rulemaking Authority of the US Federal Trade Commission, *D. Crane (ed.), 2022*

The International Competition Network at Twenty, *D. Anderson & P. Lugard (eds.), 2022*

Competition Case Law Digest – 5th Edition, *F. Jenny, N. Charbit (eds.), 2022*

Competition Inspections in 21 Jurisdictions – A Practitioner's Guide, *N. Jalabert-Doury (ed.), 2022*

Perspectives on Antitrust Compliance, *A. Riley, A. Stephan, A. Tubbs (eds.), 2022 (in collaboration with the ICC)*

Turkish Competition Law, *G. Gürkaynak, 2021*

Competition Law – Climate Change & Environmental Sustainability, *S. Holmes, D. Middelschulte, M. Snoep (eds.), 2021*

Merger Control in Latin America – A Jurisdictional Guide, *P. Burnier da Silveira, P. Sittenfeld (eds.), 2020*

Competition Inspections under EU Law – A Practitioner's Guide, *N. Jalabert-Doury, 2020*

Gun Jumping in Merger Control – A Jurisdictional Guide, *C. Hatton, Y. Comtois, A. Hamilton (eds.), 2019 (in collaboration with the IBA)*

Choice – A New Standard for Competition Analysis? *P. Nihoul (ed.), 2016*

PhD Theses

Abuse of Platform Power, *F. Bostoen, Forthcoming 2023*

Bargaining Power, Competition and Innovation, *M. Guignard, Forthcoming 2023*

Reform of Chinese State-Owned Enterprises, *X. Bai, Forthcoming 2023*

Competition & Regulation in Network Industries – Essays in Industrial Organization, *J-M. Zogheib, 2021*

The Role of Media Pluralism in the Enforcement of EU Competition Law, *K. Bania, 2019*

Buyer Power, *I. Herrera Anchustegui, 2017*

General Interest

Women and Antitrust – Voices from the Field (Vol I & II), *E. Kurgonaite & K. Nordlander, 2020*

Conference Proceedings

Antitrust in Emerging and Developing Countries – (Vol I & II), *E. Fox, H. First, 2013 & 2016*

Global Antitrust Law – Current Issues in Antitrust Law and Economics, *D. Ginsburg, J. Wright, (eds.) 2015*

Competition Law on the Global Stage – David Gerber's Global Competition Law in Perspective, *D. Gerber, 2014*

e-Book versions available for **Concurrences+** subscribers

Contributors

Svetlana Avdasheva
National Research University Higher School of Economics (HSE University) Russia

Thembalethu Buthelezi
Competition Commission of South Africa

Luiz Carlos Delorme Prado
Federal University of Rio de Janeiro

Diandra C. de Oliveira Vieira da Rocha
Federal University of Rio de Janeiro

Eleanor M. Fox
New York University School of Law

Svetlana Golovanova
National Research University Higher School of Economics (HSE University) Russia

James Hodge
Competition Commission of South Africa

Herbert Hovenkamp
University of Pennsylvania Carey Law School & Wharton School

Frédéric Jenny
ESSEC Business School & OECD

Yannis Katsoulacos
Athens University of Economics and Business, Jiangxi University of Finance and Economics (China) & CRESSE

William Kovacic
George Washington University

Ping Lin
Shandong University

Camila C. Pires-Alves
Federal University of Rio de Janeiro

Eduardo P. Ribeiro
Federal University of Rio de Janeiro

Howard Shelanski
Georgetown Law

Mpumelelo Tshabalala
Competition Tribunal of South Africa

Clare G. Ye
Shandong University

Preface

YANNIS KATSOULACOS
Athens University of Economics and Business | Jiangxi University of Finance and Economics (China) | CRESSE

The idea for a book on Antitrust and the Digital Economy – Legal Standards, Presumptions, and Key Challenges arose when thinking to organise a Policy Session on Legal Standards (LS) with emphasis on the Digital Economy, during the 16th Annual CRESSE conference of 2022. As it turned out, a number of prominent economist and legal experts agreed to participate in the session on 2 July 2022, in Agia Pelagia, Crete. They then also agreed to contribute a chapter to a book. They were joined by some more contributors, in order to also provide an international perspective by discussing developments in Brazil, China, Russia and South Africa.

CRESSE (www.cresse.info), is an international network of academics and other professionals, with an interest in Competition Policy and Sectoral Regulation. Every year CRESSE organizes an international conference in Greece that is now widely recognized as one of the top academic conferences in the economics of competition policy and regulation worldwide. In the last two years, Conference Keynote Speakers have included Jean Tirole, Herbert Hovenkamp, Ariel Ezrachi, Volker Nocke, Nancy Rose and William Kovacic. An important feature of the annual CRESSE Conference is the organization of a number of Special Policy Sessions in which important topical issues of competition policy are discussed between academics (economists and lawyers), policy makers / enforcers and practitioners.

I would like to thank very warmly all those writing chapters for this book for their excellent contributions and for delivering promptly in a short period of time. I also would like to thank Richard Whish and Krisztian Katona for agreeing to foreword the volume. I acknowledge financial support from the Greek Foundation for Research and Innovation (ELIDEK) research project on "Optimal Design of Competition Policy Enforcement" (ODeCPE – HFRI – FM17 – 1314). Last, but not least, I want to thank Nicolas Charbit and Sonia Ahmad and the other Concurrences staff for the excellent and very efficient collaboration.

Foreword

Krisztian Katona
Computer & Communications Industry Association (CCIA)

Antitrust enforcement and policy perhaps have never been more hotly debated than these days. In recent years, the global antitrust discussion has called into question some of the most basic tenets regarding the direction, scope, and objectives of competition law and enforcement, and much of the dialogue has focused on the opportunities and challenges raised by the digital economy. As part of this ongoing debate, legal standards and presumptions used in competition enforcement have become a particularly important topic. Taking stock of the current thinking and positions regarding antitrust standards and presumptions is a formidable task, yet *Antitrust and the Digital Economy – Legal Standards, Presumptions, and Key Challenges* succeeds in providing a timely and extensive analysis of these rapidly evolving issues.

Antitrust enforcement and policy have long been focused on the prevention of anticompetitive conduct. However, as antitrust enforcement involves the application of relatively general and fairly broad laws and terms to a wide variety of complex and highly nuanced economic scenarios and business models, there is an inherent risk of potentially misapplying the law leading to over or under-enforcement. Competition authorities worldwide face the ongoing challenge of ensuring that their enforcement decisions are correct and that the antitrust apparatus and procedures to arrive at those correct decisions are not overly lengthy or costly. Meanwhile, in recent years rapid digital transformation throughout the economy has raised additional questions and challenges for enforcement agencies.

Over time antitrust standards and presumptions have become increasingly important in guiding the interpretation and enforcement of competition laws around the world. But these standards and presumptions have also been the subject of constant reflection and debate. Much of the historical discussion on the appropriate level of antitrust enforcement has focused on Type I (false positive) versus Type II (false negative) errors. In particular, there has been a general understanding among enforcers and practitioners regarding concerns about the overenforcement of the competition rules, as incorrect findings of antitrust liability regarding procompetitive conduct can result in wasted resources, harm to businesses, and reduced competition in the market. At the same time, underenforcement that can result in higher prices, reduced quality, and less innovation in the market, has been a growing concern for competition authorities. Importantly, in today's increasingly interconnected and global antitrust landscape, incorrect enforcement findings may have a significant impact as they could quickly be mirrored in other jurisdictions and spread globally.

From a business perspective, antitrust standards and presumptions can make enforcement more predictable, contribute to compliance, and may enable competition agencies to focus on cases that merit an analysis of their actual economic effects. However, as the use of presumptions has a profound impact on the allocation of the burden of proof and may result in false positive findings of antitrust liability, presumptions should be subject to the principles of necessity, proportionality, and predictability. In addition, standards and presumptions should be firmly based on sound economic analysis and supported by consistent jurisprudence in the courts. As such, presumptions of illegality may be less appropriate for novel and more complex business conduct and economic scenarios, in particular in the digital economy.

Finding the appropriate level of enforcement remains an ongoing challenge for antitrust agencies and policymakers. Ultimately, the enforcement decision will depend on the specific facts and circumstances of each case. The rapid pace of technological development may create challenges for antitrust enforcers, as well as important opportunities for innovation and growth. While competition policy has an ability to adapt to new market dynamics and circumstances, it is prudent to review regularly all the relevant policy tools and adjust them, as necessary, reflecting sound economics and empirical evidence.

Antitrust and the Digital Economy – Legal Standards, Presumptions, and Key Challenges has been written at a time of unprecedentedly complex and multifaceted debate across the global antitrust community about the role and appropriateness of standards and presumptions in competition enforcement in digital markets. The discussion raises a number of important questions. Are the current legal standards, burdens of proof, and presumptions appropriately fulfilling their role in competition enforcement and policy? Do they need to be adjusted in light of current market realities? Does the digital transformation provide new challenges for the application of these standards and presumptions? If so, what are they and how should antitrust agencies address them? How should developed and developing antitrust regimes apply legal standards and presumptions in digital markets? With chapters addressing these and other relevant questions, *Antitrust and the Digital Economy – Legal Standards, Presumptions, and Key Challenges* informs the debate and provides an important contribution to this discussion.

This publication provides a comprehensive overview of antitrust standards and presumptions, with a focus on US, European, and global perspectives. It examines how antitrust standards and presumptions have evolved over time, and how they are currently applied to address the broader economy in general and digital markets in particular. The book covers important enforcement and policy developments regarding the formulation of presumptions and the role of courts and antitrust enforcement agencies in this area. In addition, it explores the approaches to antitrust standards and presumptions in developed and developing countries, including chapters focusing on Brazil, China, Russia, and South Africa. Companies doing business and their counsel should carefully consider the impact of legal standards and presumptions in light of increasing competition enforcement activity globally, with an eye to identifying and minimizing antitrust risks.

The authors of this book are leading experts in antitrust law and policy, with deep knowledge of the legal, economic, and political factors that shape antitrust enforcement around the world. They provide insightful analysis, global perspectives, and practical guidance on the most pressing issues and questions facing antitrust enforcers and policymakers today.

Antitrust and the Digital Economy – Legal Standards, Presumptions, and Key Challenges is essential reading for anyone interested in competition law and policy, including international antitrust practitioners, enforcers, and scholars. I am confident that this book will be a valuable resource for anyone seeking to understand and navigate the complex and quickly evolving global antitrust landscape in the digital age.

Introduction

Richard Whish
King's College London

Competition law and policy are endlessly fascinating. New challenges present themselves at frequent intervals: in recent times competition authorities have had to decide how to respond to the financial crisis of the late noughties, the pandemic, war in Ukraine, the growth of political and economic nationalism and the horrendous environmental problems that threaten our planet. Throughout my career I have said to students that competition law 'today' (in 1980, 1990, 2000, 2010, 2020 …) has never been so interesting or important as it is now. But as I compose this Foreword, on 17 April 2023, I feel confident in saying that 'Competition law has never been so interesting or important as it is today'!

The rise of 'GAFAM' or 'AAMAM' (choose your preferred acronym) has been astonishing: the world has been changed by the brilliance of these companies' products, and everyone – from the richest to the very poorest, in every part of the world – has benefitted from the services that they provide. Our lives have been changed profoundly and irreversibly, just as our ancestors' lives were changed by the wheel, the printing press, the telephone, the railways and other technological innovations. As big tech firms developed – at astonishing speed – governments, policy-makers, public authorities, the markets and citizens watched with awe. In particular competition authorities tended to refrain from intervention, both in antitrust and in merger control, anxious not to 'chill innovation', and not entirely certain what intervention was called for. However the perception then arose that perhaps the proverbial horse had bolted from the stable: GAFAM rapidly established themselves in commanding positions of influence over our lives and accumulated unimaginable amounts of wealth in excess of the GDP of nation states, indeed entire continents – in multi-sided markets, in which economies of scale and scope were vast, network effects enormous and non-public, big data easily acquired by virtue of their business models. Policy papers began to emerge – *Crémer, de Montjoye and Schweitzer*, *Furman*, the *Stigler Center* and many others – identifying areas of competition concern. For the public at large the availability of 'free' services such as search, shopping, chatting and dating could hardly be seen as objectionable, but perhaps the *Facebook/Cambridge Analytica* affair will come to be seen as a moment when at least some members of the public began to wonder if the world of 'free' services was quite as enchanted as it appeared to be.

But what of competition law? As I have said, competition authorities tended in the 'early' days (by which I mean ten or so years ago – time accelerates) to refrain from intervention. In particular antitrust enforcement was sporadic and acquisitions by GAFAM were for the most part cleared. During the last decade, however, the dial began to move: no doubt influenced by the reports referred to above, various competition authorities adopted a more sceptical approach to the activities of powerful digital platforms, and there was a considerable increase worldwide in enforcement, both in antitrust and merger control. The European Commission became particularly active, with its three *Google* decisions and a range of other cases; various national competition authorities within the EU, notably in France, Italy and Germany, also took action. There have been many high-profile cases in Asia and elsewhere, although it is taking longer for enforcement in the US to lead to final outcomes.

GAFAM and other platforms have radically changed markets, and we have all derived numerous benefits from their innovation and technical brilliance. There are many powerful advocates for the platforms who argue that regulation (including competition law) must not be applied in such a way that the incentive to innovate will be chilled. Some would eschew any intervention at all: the market is ultimately the best determinant of the goods and services that consumers want. Newly dominant firms fiercely resist findings that they are 'dominant' or a 'monopolist', and deploy vast resources fighting antitrust and merger control decisions that they consider to be unfair or simply wrong. However Shakespeare, clearly anticipating the problem of digital platforms, did say (through Isabella in *Measure for Measure*) that:

> O, it is excellent
>
> To have a giant's strength, but it is tyrannous to use it like a giant.

Everyone in the global competition village is grappling with the question of how best to prevent giants from using their power tyrannously. In particular, leaving to one side merger control and the specific issue of 'killer acquisitions', those with an interest in EU competition law are trying to decide whether Article 102 TFEU in its current avatar is 'fit for purpose', and, if not, what can be done to improve the current toolkit of competition and regulatory authorities faced with the theories of harm associated with digital platforms. For a long time I was of the belief that the flexibility of Article 102, which over many decades had proved to be highly adaptable, would be sufficient for these purposes; in due course, however, I came to the view that bespoke regulation was needed. The Digital Markets Act is now with us; German law has been widened to provide broader application than the German version of

Article 102; and in the UK we await publication of the Government's Digital Markets, Competition and Consumer Bill which will propose a system similar to, but not identical to, the DMA.

Quite apart from its application in the digital platform sector, Article 102 is at an important point in its evolution. The move from a form to an effects-based approach to abuse has been under way for many years. The Court of Justice's judgment in *Intel* was a crucial moment: at paragraph 138 of the judgment, the Court 'further clarified' the law on loyalty rebates derived from *Hoffmann-la Roche*, by requiring the Commission/General Court to conduct an effects analysis in circumstances where the defendant dominant firm had presented one of its own: this clarification, to my mind, was a polite overruling of *Hoffmann-la Roche*. More 'clarification' has recently been provided by the Court's *Unilever* judgment of 2023, which completes the circle of requiring effects analysis, in that case for exclusivity agreements. However, now that the effects genie is fully out of the bottle, we are left with many questions. What do we mean by effects? We know that potential effects may be sufficient, but how potential? What evidence is required of actual or potential effects? What is the appropriate standard of proof for a competition authority? When should the 'as efficient competitor' test be applied? What exactly is the as efficient competitor test? If, as seems to be the case, the AEC test does not require price-cost analysis in every case, what other kind of analysis may be sufficient? These are *enormous* questions to which we have some, but by no means all, answers.

In the EU system the answers must come ultimately from the Court of Justice, meaning that we are dependent on the cases that reach it on appeal from the Commission or under Article 267 TFEU. Different Chambers of the Court may provide answers that are subtly, or not so subtly, different from one another. We have had 50 years of jurisprudence on Article 102 and yet we do not have fully satisfactory answers to the questions I have posed, and there are plenty of others I could have suggested. The scope for errors in decision-making in these circumstances – both false positives and false negatives – is obvious. In the meantime Article 102 cases get longer and more complicated: 'quick' cases may take nearer to ten than five years to complete: for example the *Google Shopping* decision of 2017 is still on appeal to the Court of Justice. The European Commission has hesitated to adopt interim measures decisions in abuse of dominance cases, *Broadcom* being the only recent example. Vast amounts of time and resources must be deployed in Article 102 cases on market definition and dominance, before the issue of abuse is even addressed. (On this point I would point out that courts in London, in private business to business litigation on Article 102 and its domestic equivalent, have often held a trial on the issue of abuse in principle as a preliminary matter, reserving the question of dominance to a later stage). When a competition authority such as the Commission does get to the question of abuse, there may be no obvious precedent in the jurisprudence of the Court of Justice to fit the theory of harm in question. Even if the Commission explains why it considers that conduct – for example self-preferencing, as in *Google Shopping* – is abusive, it is inevitable that 'domco' will appeal this to the Courts.

All of this makes Article 102 difficult to apply in practice: to all sectors, but even more so to some of the digital platforms that have arisen so quickly, with their particular set of characteristics (multi-sidedness, 'free' services, economies of scale and scope, network effects, data effects, the tendency of markets to tip, the switching inertia (or complacency, or foolishness) of consumers). The vast rewards that GAFAM and others can derive from their products mean that the available budgets, for lawyers, economists and lobbyists, are vast. Lawyers are endlessly imaginative in devising stratagems to complicate the task of competition authorities, which is what caused me to ask the question 'Do Competition Lawyers Harm Welfare?' in a piece I wrote for *Concurrentialiste* in May 2020. If I were a young academic searching for a good research project today I would be very tempted to try to examine the fees charged by professional service firms to GAFAM in relation to matters of competition policy over the last decade; but of course I would embark on the research knowing that this would be very difficult information to obtain.

The European Commission announced on 27 March that it was changing its 2008 *Guidance on Article 102 Enforcement Priorities* and that it was embarking on a process that would lead, in 2025, to the publication of *Guidelines on Article 102*. I recall the intense debate, over many years, that led to the 2008 *Guidance*, and I anticipate that the debate will be even more intense this time. The very fact of these initiatives on the Commission's part indicates that we are at an inflection point in the life of Article 102, with many complex matters requiring further clarity. If the Commission feels that a sharper understanding of abuse of dominance is required, and perhaps that Article 102 is becoming too complicated to enforce, it is not difficult to imagine the problems that newer, smaller and less well-resourced competition authorities experience in this area.

My own conclusion, in relation to digital platforms, is that *ex ante* regulation is required. I am not persuaded that the Court of Justice could refine its jurisprudence on Article 102, in particular by introducing new presumptions of harm, or by nuancing the law in its application to digital platforms, in a timely manner to address problems that already exist. I also consider that the lengthy and complex process of defining markets and establishing dominance is inappropriate where 'gatekeepers' occupy such powerful positions within their ecosystems: the DMA eliminates this exercise from the process of enforcement, which will lead to quicker decision-making. One can debate what kind of, and how much, regulation is required, and it is probably helpful for countries considering whether to legislate to have the EU, German and proposed UK models (as well as others) to compare. Whatever system is put in place to address the phenomenon of gatekeeper platforms will result in error costs: 'extreme' effects analysis and 'extreme' *per se* rules can each result in false positives and false negatives. I see carefully drafted *ex ante* regulatory rules as in important supplement to Article 102; Article 102 (and its domestic analogues) will continue to be of major importance in the scrutiny of digital platforms, but I do not consider them to be capable of bearing the entire burden of the subject.

This book makes an excellent contribution to this fascinating debate, fascinating not only because of its immense academic interest but also because of its fundamental importance to the way in which we, as citizens, live our lives in a world in which digital platforms play such a dominant role.

Overview

PART II

Legal Standards in Brazil, China, Russia and South Africa

PART I

Legal Standards, Presumptions and Antitrust Enforcement

Economic and Legal Principles and the Cases of EU and US

Simple Rules for Antitrust

ELEANOR M. FOX*
New York University School of Law

Abstract

Antitrust rules and standards are too complex. They require litigants to plow nearly endless paths, wasting human capital and financial resources and subverting public policy. This chapter proposes two solutions, the first being specifically for the United States in view of its body of conservative antitrust law: setting the clock back to the caselaw just before its sharp turn to the right. For the world, with respect to specific abusive conduct, working backwards. Starting with specified conduct and asking, why not proscribe it? The chapter presents examples of simple rules that potentially would work to capture conduct harmful to competition much more efficiently. A critical mass of competition authorities is sympathetic to condemning specific conduct by the Big Tech firms, and a dialog focused on consensus simple rules can contribute to formation of world antitrust norms and thus to global reach of antitrust through convergent national enforcement.

---

* Eleanor Fox is Professor Emerita at New York University School of Law. The author thanks Professor Yannis Katsoulacos for his helpful comments.

I. Introduction

Antitrust rules and standards are very complex. This is so across jurisdictions. It is so even though simpler rules are likely to be more efficient.[1] It is so even in developing countries,[2] which typically face severe shortages of human and financial resources, and could especially benefit from simpler rules.

Assessing what is "anticompetitive" under excessively complex standards wastes billions of euros/dollars (often to the gain of lawyers and economists),[3] attenuates the time to final judgment, weakens constraints on violators, undermines the effectiveness of markets, and impairs the opportunity and livelihood of entrepreneurs who would otherwise be better positioned to contest markets efficiently.

If rules can be devised that proscribe anticompetitive behavior with sufficient precision and without unnecessary overbreadth, why do we not have them, and is there a path to get them?

This chapter argues that the complexity we observe is a triumph of conservatism,[4] particularly in the United States. It argues that the abuses by the Big Tech firms have highlighted the problem. The chapter proposes two partial solutions. The first is particular to the United States and involves a legislative solution to reset the compass, pinpointing a time just before the hard right turn of the Supreme Court jurisprudence. The second is working backwards. This idea is inspired by particular behaviors of the Big Tech firms that have caught the attention of antitrust authorities and policymakers around the world and appear to be the subject of a growing consensus that specific strategies they practice are wrong; that they are inconsistent with free and open markets driven by competition on the merits, and they should not be tolerated. Yet the quest to stop the conduct is filled with obstacles and delays and in the end uncertainty as to the fate of the antitrust challenge. This chapter suggests that the antitrust authorities identify the anticompetitive or abusive conduct that should be prohibited and, depending on their own law, find the way to prohibit it (allowing for justifications where

---

1 *See* Yannis Katsoulacos, *Why Should Legal Standards in Antitrust Enforcement be Different in Developing Than in Mature Jurisdictions: A decision-theoretic approach*, 3 BRICS J. Econ. 63 (2022), arguing that, particularly in the tech area, per se or presumption-based standards are more likely to yield optimal results than full effects analysis, and that this is especially so in developing countries); Giorgio Monti, *The Boundaries of Antitrust in the European Union*, in Oles Andriychuk, Antitrust and the Bounds of Power – 25 Years On (2023) ("the concern remains that the Commission has swallowed more economics than is necessary" in adjudicating abuse of dominance, at p. 56). *See also*, in this volume, Yannis Katsoulacos, *Could a Move to More Presumption-Based Legal Standards Be Justified, for the Big-Tech Digital Markets, on Error-Cost-Minimizing Grounds?* (2023).

2 *See* Thembalethu Buthelezi, James Hodge and Mpumelelo Tshabalala, *Appropriate Legal Standards in Competition Law: A South African Perspective*, in this volume (2023); Eleanor Fox, *Outsider Antitrust: 'Making Markets Work for People' as a Post-Millennium Development Goal*, in T. Bonakele, E. Fox & L. Mncube, Competition Policy for the New Era: Insights from the BRICS Countries (2017).

3 *See* Richard Whish, *Do Competition Lawyers Harm Welfare?*, Concurrentialiste, (May 11, 2020), https://www.networklawreview.org/richard-whish-welfare/.

4 *See* Gabriel Kolko, The Triumph of Conservatism: A Reinterpretation of American History, 1900–1916 (1963).

appropriate). That is, work backwards from the now notorious troublesome conduct rather than forward from market definition and monopoly/dominant power. The European Union and the United Kingdom are on their way to doing just that for offenses in the digital economy by the most powerful firms. The United States is far behind. The world would profit from a multi-jurisdictional coordination on what conduct by firms with significant power fits the category of facially abusive conduct (with a view towards national implementation). The effort could provide a path for greater coherence of enforcement against abuses of power in global markets.

This chapter concentrates on US antitrust law while referencing also the law and policy of other jurisdictions. It limits its focus to unilateral conduct and agreements. It proceeds by: 1 examining the history and evolution of the US Sherman Act from a time of simpler rules to the present; 2 considering insights from around the world, particularly Europe; and 3 reflecting on how the United States might – or might not – be able to break through the thicket to simple rules and whether there is a path forward for the world.

II. A History of Simple Rules in US Antitrust Law

In the 1960s, the United States had simple antitrust rules. They did not derive directly from the language of Sherman Antitrust Act, for the language of the Act is exceedingly general. It prohibits monopolization and agreements that restrain trade (now called "anticompetitive" agreements). The major simple rule is derived from early case law and has held firm ever since. In *Addyston Pipe and Steel*,[5] Judge Taft (later President Taft and still later Chief Justice Taft) decided that the midwest cast-iron pipe makers' price-fixing ring was per se illegal, and then went on to show that, analyzing all of the facts, one would logically conclude that the agreement raised prices and was an unreasonable restraint of trade.

The US courts proceeded to formulate more simple rules, especially in the 1960s in the era of the Warren Court.[6] The Supreme Court enlarged the category of "price-fixing illegal per se". It expanded per se treatment to agreements fixing other terms of trade.[7] From as far back as *Dr. Miles* in 1911, the law forbade buyer-seller pairs to agree to resale prices.[8] It later became illegal to divide markets[9] and to boycott,[10]

5 85 Fed. 271 (6th Cir. 1898), *aff'd*, 175 U.S. 211 (1899).

6 The US Supreme Court is often named for its Chief Justice. Earl Warren was Chief Justice from 1953 to 1969. The Warren Court is known for its liberal decisions, spanning civil rights, human rights, and antitrust.

7 Catalano Inc. v. Target Sales, Inc., 446 U.S. 643 (1980).

8 Dr. Miles Medical Co. v. John D. Park & Sons Co., 220 U.S. 373 (1911), *rev'd*, Leegin Creative Leather Products, Inc. v. PSKS, Inc., 551 U.S. 877 (2007).

9 United States v. Arnold, Schwinn & Co., 388 U.S. 365 (1967), *rev'd*, Continental TV, Inc. v. GTE Sylvania, Inc., 433 U.S. 36 (1977).

10 Klor's v. Broadway-Hale Stores, 359 U.S. 207 (1959).

whether horizontal or vertical. It became illegal to agree to certain behaviour that would chill price competition, such as: not to provide price quotes or to advertise low prices.[11] In concentrated markets, competitors' exchange of sensitive information was illegal.[12] Tying two products by firms with market power was illegal.[13] Moreover, fact questions about whether putative violators actually had an agreement and whether a seemingly dominant firm had monopoly power were usually not difficult to resolve; agreement and sufficient power were readily implied from basic facts and contexts.[14] Antitrust plaintiffs frequently won summary judgment.[15]

But, beginning in the late 1970s with a change in the Supreme Court constituency, and surging in the 1980s with the Reagan Revolution,[16] the tide turned. The (new) Supreme Court set itself on a mission to scale back what it saw as overreach of the Warren Court, which had given short shrift to firms' claims of efficiencies,[17] and the court began a decades-long crusade to reverse antitrust precedents of the Warren age and earlier. The scaling-back project is now substantially complete.[18] The big nails in the coffin were *Verizon Communications v. Law Offices of Curtis V. Trinko*[19] and its progeny and *Ohio v. American Express Co.*,[20] which anchored the libertarian perspective that markets and business firms are to be trusted, that power is evanescent and hard to get, and that, beyond cartel enforcement, antitrust intervention may destroy America's efficient and innovative economy. "Agreement" and "monopoly power" became very hard to prove,[21] and summary judgment for plaintiffs became very rare.[22]

The move from suspicion of corporate power to suspicion of antitrust itself led to increasing burdens of proof on plaintiffs and sympathy for defendants' arguments that their conduct did not cause antitrust harm and indeed was efficient.

---

11 National Society of Professional Engineers v. United States, 435 U.S. 679 (1978).

12 United States v. Container Corporation of America, 393 U.S. 333 (1969).

13 International Salt Co. v. United States, 332 U.S. 392 (1947).

14 United States v. Parke, Davis & Co. 362 U.S. 29 (1960). United States v. Grinnell Corp., 384 U.S. 563 (1966).

15 *See, e.g.*, Arizona v. Maricopa County Medical Society, 457 U.S. 332 (1982).

16 *See* Eleanor Fox, *The Modernization of Antitrust: A New Equilibrium*, 66 Cornell L. Rev. 1140 (1981).

17 *See, e.g.*, FTC v. Procter & Gamble Co., 386 U.S. 568 (1967).

18 *See* Illinois Tool Works Inc. v. Independent Ink, Inc., 547 U.S. 28 (2006), reversing the court's one-time strong disapproval of tying agreements. The qualified per se rule against tying is tottering. Apart from the remaining strong rule against cartels, the other per se rules have all been reversed.

19 540 U.S. 398 (2004).

20 585 U.S. _ (2018).

21 For proof of agreement, *see* Matsushita Electric Industrial Co. v. Zenith Radio Corp., 475 U.S. 574 (1986) (Japanese electronics); District of Columbia v. Amazon.com, Inc., case no. 2021 CA 001775 B, Washington, (D.C. Superior Court, March 18, 2022). For proof of monopoly, *see* FTC v. Facebook, Inc., 2021 WL 2643627 (D.D.C. June 28, 2021), and FTC v. Facebook, Inc., 2022 WL 103308 (D.D.C. Jan. 11, 2022), appeal pending; Epic Games, Inc. v. Apple Inc., 493 F. Supp. 3d 817 (N.D. Cal. 2020), appeal pending.

22 *See, e.g.*, Matsushita Electric Industrial Co. v. Zenith Radio Corp., 475 U.S. 574 (1986); Bell Atlantic Corp. v. Twombly, 550 U.S. 544 (2007). *See* Edward Brunet, *Antitrust Summary Judgment and the Quick Look Approach*, 62 SMU L. Rev. 493 (2009).

The new deference to business and its complex arguments on market effects and efficiencies led to the need for the offices of the competition authorities to be well staffed with PhD economists and the need for the antitrust authorities to retain expensive outside experts, costing many millions of dollars per litigated case. It produced formulations of law requiring much more complex decision-making than necessary to determine whether particular conduct is good or bad for the market. While in the 1980s and '90s there was an emerging "quick look" approach, allowing courts to quickly size up conduct as anticompetitive (or not),[23] this move was undercut by the Supreme Court in *California Dental Ass'n v. FTC*,[24] when a strikingly anticompetitive restriction on dentists (don't advertise price discounts)[25] was seriously examined for procompetitive qualities, and the prohibition was remanded.

Big Tech cases have flashed a spotlight on the problem. Being a monopoly (having monopoly power) is the first necessary condition before applying section 2 of the Sherman Act to reprehend unilateral conduct that is anticompetitive. But are the Big Tech gatekeepers "monopolies"? One court threw out a case against Apple because – after a contentious consideration of bounds of the relevant market – it could not quite find Apple to be a monopoly.[26] In the Federal Trade Commission (FTC)'s case against Facebook, the court threw out the first complaint on grounds among others that the complaint did not plausibly allege that Facebook is a monopoly (explicitly, even if most of the world thinks it is).[27] Facebook's attempt to dismiss the amended complaint was not successful, but the court warned the FTC that the task to prove that Facebook is a monopoly may not be easy.[28] Google, the most convincing monopoly of all the GAFAs, asserts in defense of every section 2 case against it that it has no market power; the competition is a click away. It might well win this argument in any one of the many cases against it, in all of which the litigants will have fresh bites at the apple: What is the relevant market? Does Google have monopoly power? And, did Google harm competition?

The next step in a Sherman Act section 2 case is to identify llegedly offending conduct and prove it is anticompetitive of the sort that should be prohibited. In its *Facebook* complaint, the FTC challenged Facebook's conduct for squeezing meritorious rivals off its platform. The court threw out these allegations – "not premised on the view that [these acts] are incapable of harming competition; they may 'indeed' have that effect";[29] but because US antitrust law embeds a

23 FTC v. Indiana Federation of Dentists, 476 U.S. 447 (1986).

24 526 U.S. 756 (1999).

25 The rule prohibited discount advertising unless so much information was provided that it would not make sense to advertise the discounts.

26 Epic Games v. Apple, 493 F. Supp. 3d 817 (N.D. Cal. 2020).

27 Facebook, Inc., 2021 WL 2643627 (D.D.C. June 28, 2021).

28 Facebook, Inc., 2022 WL 103308 (D.D.C. Jan. 11, 2022).

29 Facebook, Inc., 2021 WL 2643627, slip op. at 35.

prophylactic no-duty-to-deal rule. It does so for three reasons: 1 so as not to deter firms from investing and innovating; 2 to prevent courts from becoming central planners; and 3 to prevent "forced sharing" from facilitating antitrust's prime evil – collusion.[30] In so holding, the Facebook court faithfully channeled *Trinko*.[31]

A consumer class action against Amazon challenged Amazon's most favored nations' clauses, which prevented businesses on Amazon's retail commerce platform from selling at a lower price anywhere else. The court threw out the case on grounds that Amazon's prices were not monopolistic; therefore the MFNs could not harm competition.[32] In Epic's case against Apple, the court dismissed the Sherman Act claim that Apple's gag order on game developers not to tell users how they could buy premium products from the developer and avoid Apple's surcharge, even while recognizing that the conduct was anticompetitive. The court prohibited the conduct under California's Unfair Competition Act.[33]

These holdings reveal a pretty limited domain for US antitrust law to catch behavior of Big Tech that most leading competition authorities believe should not be tolerated.[34] What are the stumbling blocks under US law?

1. Definition of the market, which is often controversial even among the experts. The line-drawing is often artificial even though it may be outcome-determinative. The court can often define the market one way or the other without fear of reversal.
2. Assessment of whether the firm qualifies as a monopoly. Proof of dominance is not enough. Under US law, the requirement that a defendant is a monopoly can be preclusive even though the defendant has substantial market power.
3. Assessment of whether the conduct is anticompetitive *and* is such that it ought to be proscribed.

There is a very high bar in the US after *Trinko*. Leveraging is not an offense.[35] Not dealing or dealing discriminatorily is not an offense. The essential facility doctrine has all but been written out of the law, and there is no concept of

30 *Id.* citing 540 U.S. 398 (2004) and progeny.

31 540 U.S. 398 (2004).

32 Frame-Wilson v. Amazon.com, 2:20-cv-00424-RAJ (W.D. Wash. Mar. 11, 2022). *See* also District of Columbia v. Amazon.com, Inc., case no. 2021 CA 001775 B, Washington, (D.C. Superior Court, March 18, 2022), similarly dismissing the District of Columbia's suit against Amazon for Amazon's agreement with merchant partners providing for price-parity, "fair pricing," and minimum margins.

33 Epic v. Apple, 493 F. Supp. 3d 817 (N.D. Cal. 2020).

34 *See* ICN UCWG draft report, Report on the Results of the ICN Survey on the Analysis of Theories of Harm and the Design of Remedies Concerning Unilateral Conduct With Dominance/Substantial Market Power in Digital Markets, summarizing questionnaire answer. The Report is expected to be presented at the UCWG workshop on March 7 and 8, 2023, Tokyo.

35 540 U.S. 398 (2004), note 4.

"akin to essential facility" that would relax the no-duty principle. There is no special-responsibility rule. There is no antitrust violation for exploitation[36] where there is not also exclusionary conduct that harms consumers. It is unclear whether and when there is a violation for exclusionary practices that harm the competitive process but may not limit output. Yet leveraging, exploitation, and self-preferencing are at the heart of most of the conduct of the Big Tech firms spot-lighted by the rest of the world and by the current US enforcers and many policymakers as well.[37]

III. Other Jurisdictions

Most nations and regions are not handicapped like the United States because they do not have a monopoly threshold and do not have the *Trinko* caselaw and its progeny. The competition law of the European Union and most of the rest of the world has leveraging violations and exploitation violations. It has a dominance threshold rather than a monopoly threshold and is somewhat flexible in finding dominance. And it has a rule of special responsibilities of dominant firms that hold sway over rivals who do business on their platforms. Yet even the EU and the rest of the world face serious challenges in condemning abuses expeditiously. This is especially clear in the case of Big Tech.

The European Union is the prime example. The Treaty on the Functioning of the European Union, Article 102, prohibits abuse of a dominant position. EU law does offer some simple rules; at least simpler than US law. The Directorate-General for Competition (DG COMP) has brought several cases against Google and is investigating conduct of the other GAFA.[38] Commission decisions in two of the *Google* cases have been largely upheld by the General Court; they are on appeal to the European Court of Justice.[39] The General Court has applied some relatively simple rules of improper favoring and down-grading by a super-dominant gatekeeper of rivals on its platform, and has condemned contract clauses requiring preinstallation of Google Search on Android devices that significantly raised barriers to rivals and were not objectively justified. The European Commission is in front of the world in examining the conduct of the Big Tech gatekeepers, identifying abusive conduct that distorts the market and sets back meritorious competition by upstarts and challengers.

---

36 *Id.*

37 *See* ICN UCWG draft report, *supra* note 35, U.S. House of Representatives, Judiciary Committee, Investigation of Competition in the Digital Marketplace: Committee Report and Recommendations, staff report adopted by Judiciary Committee April 2021.

38 The GAFA are Google, Apple, Facebook (now Meta) and Amazon. The Competition Directorate settled a case against Amazon by accepting commitments. https://ec.europa.eu/commission/presscorner/detail/en/ip_22_7777

39 Google and Alphabet v. Commission (Google Shopping), Case T–612/17, ECLI:EU:T:2021:763, on appeal, C–48/22 P; Google and Alphabet v. Commission (Google Android), Case T–604/18, ECLI:EU:T:2022:541, on appeal, C–738/22 P.

Despite its victories so far, the DG COMP and European Commission officials have observed the problems of case-by-case adjudication: it takes too long; final resolution is uncertain; there is a need for simpler rules condemning specific practices so that the same facts and issues do not have to be adjudicated time and again. Moreover, antitrust law might not catch all offensive conduct. The conduct might be unfair (to a meritorious competitor) rather than damaging competition across the whole market. It might block access to platforms or to data necessary to compete. To by-pass these problems of attenuated procedures and boundaries of the law, the European Commission has adopted the Digital Markets Act (DMA).[40] The DMA prohibits certain specified conduct of and imposes duties on the big gatekeepers on grounds of fairness and market contestability, not antitrust.

The DMA imposes eighteen obligations and duties on the covered big digital platforms. For example, the big gatekeepers:

1. may not prefer their own products;
2. may not use the data they derive from firms on their platform to compete against them;
3. must allow use of third party apps on their platforms;
4. must give fair, nondiscriminatory treatment to ranking (e.g., as in Google Search results);
5. may not prevent users from switching platforms;
6. must allow users to port their own data to other platforms; and
7. must give third party search engines access to the gatekeepers' ranking, query, view and click data.

The Act allows no efficiency defense, having taken efficiencies into account in formulating the rules.

The UK's Competition and Markets Authority contemplates a somewhat similar scheme but its rules and standards are more flexible. They will be tailored to the business models of the covered platforms, which will be subject to an enforceable code of conduct.[41]

Germany addressed Big Tech/Big Data abuses not only by case adjudication but also by amending its Competition Act to allow the Federal Cartel Office to

---

40 Regulation 2022/1925 of the European Parliament and of the Council of 14 September 2022 on contestable and fair markets in the digital sector and amending Directives 2019/1937 and 2020/1828 (Digital Markets Act) [2022] OJ L265/1.

41 *See* description on the UK Government website, https://www.gov.uk/government/collections/digital-markets-unit#documents. Legislation is awaited. *See*, for comparison of regulatory designs, Damien Geradin & Dimitrios Katsifis, *Selecting the right regulatory design for pro-competitive digital regulation: An analysis of the EU, UK, and US approaches*, (Nov. 24, 2021), https://ssrn.com/abstract=4025419.

designate firms of paramount significance to competition across markets and to control the behavior of the firms so identified.[42]

The International Competition Network's (ICN) Unilateral Conduct Working Group (UCWG) has launched a multi-year project to explore developments in digital economies and gather information on how the competition authorities are addressing anticompetitive practices, especially by the large digital platforms.[43]

IV. US Initiatives to Join the World

In the United States, legislators have introduced bills that would condemn specified conduct by covered platforms.[44] The specified conduct partly tracks the list of behavior condemned by the DMA. However, the legislative process is complicated and passage of legislation is uncertain. Meanwhile, the antitrust authorities of the Biden Administration are aggressively on the track of challenging abuses especially of the Big Tech firms. The agencies have sued Google and Facebook, almost all states of the United States and private parties have sued some or all of the GAFA. The FTC has issued a major policy statement announcing an expanded scope for enforcement under section 5 of the Federal Trade Commission Act to prohibit unfair methods of competition, and has begun a rule-making procedure under its antitrust powers to prohibit covenants not to compete.[45] While the caselaw interpreting the Sherman Act law remains conservative, the US enforcers have joined the world conversation of how to control the power of Big Tech.

V. Proposals: Rules and Principles

This chapter makes proposals along two lines. First, resetting the compass for US antitrust law, and, second, crafting rules by working backwards from offensive conduct that is now well known.

1. Resetting the Compass

Reforming and modernizing US antitrust law is a big challenge. Legislation was introduced by Senator Klobuchar into the last session of Congress that would have reset the compass towards a greater recognition of corporate power and its

42 Competition Act (Gesetz gegen Wettbewerbsbeschränkungen – GWB), section 19a, added July 19, 2022.

43 *See* ICN UCWG, Work Plan 2022–2025, https://www.internationalcompetitionnetwork.org/working-groups/unilateral-conduct/.

44 S. 2992, American Innovation and Choice Online Act 117th Cong., 2d sess. (2021–2022); S. 2710, Open App Markets Act 117th Cong., 2d sess. (2021–2022).

45 *See* Fed. Trade Comm'n, Notice of Proposed Rulemaking, Non-Compete Clause Rule, RIN No. 3084-AB74, (Jan. 5, 2023), 16 CFR Part 910.

abuse.[46] This bill, however, was not among the few that seemed to have some traction in Congress. Moreover, the bill would create new concepts and introduce some ambiguities; it was not necessarily a route to simpler rules. The FTC's policy statement of November 10, 2022, regarding the scope of its authority to condemn Unfair Methods of Competition is a sharp move away from the narrowness of the Sherman Act. According to the statement, section 5 of the Federal Trade Commission Act reaches "unfair conduct that tends to negatively affect competitive conditions".[47] Application of section 5 under this broad conception would go far to counter the conservatism of the Sherman Act, but it would not satisfy the need for simple rules and might even complicate that quest. Finally, the FTC could in theory do antitrust rulemaking and adopt a set of clear simple rules.[48] The rule-making solution is an attractive partial solution, as discussed below.

But rulemaking is appropriate only for conduct that can be fairly well identified and fairly confidently prohibited. It does not solve the problem of a basic wrong direction of the law; we cannot use laissez faire premises to solve persistently disregarded market power problems. I have suggested elsewhere a legislative solution for US antitrust law complementary to rulemaking.[49] This solution recognizes the great difficulty of changing the direction of antitrust law by black-letter legislation especially in a common-law jurisdiction, for the development of antitrust rules and principles is a common-law type of reiterative fact/law process. For all but the rather narrow category for which rules will work, antitrust law does not lend itself to black-letter rules. The compass of the Sherman Act must be reset. This can be done by legislative repeal of the Supreme Court's path-changing decisions that made a sharp turn to the right, just before the turn of the last century, and reinstating the opinions that were the law at that moment in time before the turn. Repeal would befall the set of cases that closed the law's eyes to anticompetitive conduct, added undue burdens on plaintiffs, and unnecessarily complicated proof of the case; for example: *Trinko*,[50] *Leegin Creative Leather Products, Inc. v. PSKS, Inc.*,[51] *Ohio v. American Express*,[52]

46 S. 225, Competition and Antitrust Law Enforcement Reform Act of 2021 117th Cong., 2d sess. (2021–2022), addressing standards for mergers and conduct.

47 *See* 2022 FTC Policy Statement Regarding the Scope of Unfair Methods of Competition, https://www.ftc.gov/system/files/ftc_gov/pdf/P221202Section5PolicyStatement.pdf.

48 Several problems attend FTC rulemaking. The FTC's power to do antitrust rulemaking is being contested. Moreover, the FTC lacks the power to impose penalties and therefore firms have a diminished incentive to follow FTC rules.

49 *See* Eleanor Fox, *The Decline, Fall, and Renewal of U.S. Leadership in Antitrust Law and Policy, Competition Policy International*, (April 12, 2022), https://papers.ssrn.com/sol3/papers.cfm?abstract_id=4097141.

50 540 U.S. 398 (2004).

51 551 U.S. 877 (2007).

Leegin is a more nuanced example than the others. It reversed the per se rule against resale price maintenance. It is included here not because resale price maintenance is never justified but because of the contrast in analysis between the majority opinion of Justice Kennedy, which introduces complexity and ambiguity, and the dissenting opinion of Justice Breyer, who would simplify the law without threat to efficiency.

52 585 U.S._(2018).

and *California Dental Ass'n.*[53] US antitrust would explicitly return to the line of *Eastman Kodak Co. v. Image Technical Servs., Inc.*,[54] *Aspen Skiing Co. v. Aspen Highlands Skiing Corp.*,[55] and related opinions, which together comprise a coherent narrative of market power and its abuse. In three of the referenced "complicating" cases – *Leegin*, *American Express*, and *California Dental Ass'n* – Justice Stephen Breyer wrote clear dissenting or concurring opinions that pinpointed the harm to competition and the flimsiness of the pro-competitive/efficiency justifications. In this world in which legislation could reset the stage without interfering with the iterative fact/law process, the Breyer opinions would become the beacon of the law.[56]

2. Rules – Working Backwards

The second solution – for qualifying conduct – is working backwards. By working backwards, we start by specifying conduct that, in the interest of robust markets and an environment friendly to competition on the merits, should not happen. We would first identify a level of market power for unilateral abuses, perhaps drawing from the EU, UK or Germany; e.g., "significant market status (SMS)" or "paramount significance for competition across markets". We would then develop a list, guided by what is most likely to command consensus in the jurisdiction and around the world.

For example, platforms with significant market status:

1. may not prevent their users from switching platforms;
2. must allow users to port their own data to other platforms;
3. must not restrain contract parties from giving truthful information to their users such as: *Here is how you can pay me [Fortnite] for [V-Bucks] at a price lower than the platform app charges*; and
4. must not block the route of rivals on the platform for reasons not on the merits; e.g., because they pose a competitive threat.

Prohibitions 1 and 2 would prohibit restraints on interoperability and data portability, which are the two biggest obstructions to competitive platform markets. Prohibition 3 is a market process requirement where antitrust and freedom of speech converge; information facilitates competition and is a vital check against exploitative pricing and other coercive behavior. Prohibition 4 recalls Facebook's conduct: for example, Vine launched an app for creating very short videos that

53 526 U.S. 756 (1999).

54 504 U.S. 451 (1992).

55 472 U.S. 585 (1985).

56 In the fourth referenced case, *Trinko*, the opinion of the US Court of Appeals for the Second Circuit, 305 F.3d 89 (2d Cir. 2002), reversed by the Supreme Court, would be reinstated as part of the body of law that forms the modern narrative.

users could send instantly to friends on Facebook. On the same day, a Facebook executive discovered it and proposed to shut it down, to which Facebook CEO Mark Zuckerberg responded: "Yup, go for it."[57] – thus sabotaging an innovation that posed a threat to Facebook. This incident is invoked in the FTC's claim[58] in *FTC v. Facebook*. Judge Boasberg declared the conduct consistent with the Sherman Act on grounds of the strong US principle of no duty to deal.[59] Conservative US law notwithstanding, Facebook's conduct to Vine is a good candidate for conduct that the world tends to single out for condemnation, without regard to whether Facebook is a monopoly, whether output of social media was restricted, or whether consumers faced higher prices.

The reader will note that, of the seven selected DMA obligations listed above, only two are listed above as examples for the first step in working backwards. The first step examples include only numbers[60] five and six – interoperability and data portability. Why? The other prohibitions have merit but create controversy or are commonly placed in the silo of unfair competition, not antitrust. Rivals' access to the ranking data of a platform is controversial, for the platform is being asked to give up something it created. The prohibition against using a firm's data to compete against the firm falls in the realm of unfair competition. So, too, discriminatory treatment may be unfair and not anticompetitive; whether it harms competition requires a complicated analysis. While, to many analysts and policymakers, a major gatekeeper's preferring its own product on its own platform is the original sin of Big Tech, this proposition is heatedly challenged by those who hold "freedom to deal" as a first principle for a dynamic and innovative economy. The scheme is to start small and continually test consensus on the margins, and to do so in world conversation; for example, within working groups in the ICN or meetings of the OECD or UNCTAD.

As mentioned, Big Tech is not a hermetically sealed corner of antitrust. The abuses spun out in Big Tech arenas have helped identify arbitrary limits of traditional antitrust (such as the threshold of market power for intervention, and what is missed by a narrow consumer welfare paradigm) and have heightened the costs of attenuation of antitrust proceedings. Candidates for the first-step list of facially abusive conduct can go beyond Big Tech. For example, all of the four starting examples can be generalized to non-tech markets. The important point is: certain

---

57 See Adi Robertson, Mark Zuckerberg personally approved cutting off Vine's friend-finding feature, The Verge, Dec. 5, 2018.

58 Facebook, Inc., 2021 WL 2643627 (D.D.C. June 28, 2021). The claim is that Facebook adopted platform policies that prevented interoperability with applications that Facebook viewed as nascent threats against it, and that the platform policies, along with acquisitions of nascent competitors, constituted anticompetitive acts of monopoly maintenance within section 2 of the Sherman Act.

59 The court found that the Vine incident did not get the benefit of the *Aspen* exception to *Trinko* because Vine was a newcomer in the Facebook ecosystem. The court dismissed the platform policies' count also on grounds that the cut-offs by Facebook were old, Facebook had abandoned its platform policy against hosting competitors, and the acts were not shown to be likely to recur.

60 These are arbitrary numbers, not the numbers in the DMA.

specific conduct is abusive or anticompetitive and we should be able to prohibit it without churning up the full heavy and expensive machinery of antitrust. Firms should know (be told that) the conduct is illegal and should not do it. If we start with simple liability rules where simple rules are warranted, and the rules are enforced with sufficient penalties to deter, we can expect a more competitive environment, huge savings of time and money, and more legitimacy for antitrust.

VI. Can We Get Simple Rules? Can We Nudge World Coherence?

Is it possible to get the simple rules?

The European Union is well along the path, but with the DMA, which is regulation and is not antitrust. The DMA will soon be implemented. Implementation will face many complications.[61] We must wait to see if the DMA meets the occasion with simple rules that are not overbroad and that can be enforced efficiently, and whether the covered platforms will internalize the rules in general in their business models. For other jurisdictions such as the UK and Germany, we must also wait and compare.

For the United States, the task is not easy; neither the task to reset the compass nor the task of adopting specific simple rules. Ironically, the United States may find itself a law-taker, not a law-maker, if "its" businesses find that, as a practical matter, they must comply with European rules in their global business.

For the world, the competition authorities today are fairly well aligned in appreciating both the abuses of Big Tech and the weak underbelly of the various administrative and judicial systems that are judging and will judge the claimed abuses.[62] The competition family of the world is "in conversation" – seeking better practices to control Big Tech. For conversations among the competition authorities, working backwards may do good work. Do we want Facebook to be able to destroy Vine because Vine is too good? Do we want Google to block the paths for search challengers by clogging the best routes to market and forbidding innovation from open source code?[63] Do we want commissions, tribunals and courts to relitigate a dozen times whether Facebook or Google has sufficient market power every time it invents a new restrictive practice? On these questions, we may see significant consensus. The next step will be for each jurisdiction to take up the task of implementation as much as possible within its own law, learning from one another as we go along.

---

61 *See* Alexandre de Streel *et al.*, Effective and Proportionate Implementation of the DMA, CERRE January 2023.

62 *See* UCWG ICN draft Report, *supra* note 35.

63 *See* Google Android's "no fork" policy, withholding licences to pre-install Google Search to manufacturers that ran unapproved versions of the Android operating system. This was ruled illegal by the EU General Court. Google and Alphabet v. Commission, *supra* note 39.

VII. Conclusion

Antitrust rules and standards are too complex. They require litigants to plow nearly endless paths and to build bridges to nowhere. What ought to be simple inquiries have become complicated ones. Millions of dollars/euros and hundreds of days are spent unnecessarily, depleting the coffers of the competition authorities and thus limiting their capacities.

This chapter has proposed two solutions. For the US caselaw, setting the clock back to the caselaw just before the sharp turn to the right. For the world, for qualifying conduct such as the worst abuses by Big Tech – working backwards. Starting with specified conduct and asking, why not proscribe it? With what defenses? The chapter presents examples of simple rules that would qualify for this methodology.

We must wait to see the success of – and the difficulties to be overcome by – the new regimes in Europe. Meanwhile, we may expect two positive effects. One, the United States and other nations may enjoy positive spill-over effects of the European rules, if wisely applied and if the covered platforms choose to follow them worldwide. Two, the DMA's lists of dos and don'ts, and like formulations by other nations, may provide a rallying point for discussion in the world. A critical mass of competition authorities seems to be on board in condemning or at least seriously questioning certain specific conduct by the Big Tech firms. The sympathetic dialog of the competition authorities and other policymakers is likely to contribute to the formation of world antitrust norms and to global reach of antitrust through convergent national enforcement.

In sum, undue complexity is counter-productive; simpler rules are needed; and simple rules are hard to get. This chapter has offered a roadmap to pursue them.

Making Antitrust Decisions about Digital Platforms

Herbert Hovenkamp*

University of Pennsylvania Carey Law School and the Wharton School

Abstract

Antitrust litigation often involves situations where important relevant information is limited or costly to obtain, behavior is complex and can have multiple explanations, or theory is not particularly well developed. As a result, legal and factual presumptions, evidentiary shortcuts, and assignment of the burden of proof can be critical and often decisive. This situation is common across all types of antitrust actions, including unilateral and collaborative conduct, as well as mergers. In general, the more complex an issue is or the market in which it occurs, the more valuable evidentiary shortcuts become, provided that they point us in the right direction. This paper considers how these constraints should be applied to large digital platform markets.

Uniquely harsh treatment threatens an error that antitrust policy has made before, which is excessive management of a part of the economy that is in fact notable for its superior performance. The need for and nature of presumptions or other evidentiary shortcuts should be partly based on our overall assessment of performance. If we believe that the markets dominated by large digital platforms are performing poorly, with a great deal of monopoly and low customer satisfaction, then stronger evidentiary biases against them might be warranted. However, if we think they are performing relatively well, then perhaps such presumptions should be weakened or not employed at all.

---

* James G. Dinan University Professor, University of Pennsylvania Carey Law School and the Wharton School. I appreciate research assistance from Tyler Gruttadauria.

At the same time, however, the digital economy contains unique features that serve both to differentiate and to complicate antitrust analysis. Further, the opportunities for engaging in harmful exercises of market power are numerous. Large tech firms trade heavily, although not exclusively, in digital content; they have different cost structures than most traditional firms; they often operate on "two-sided" markets; and they are heavily involved in distribution with both direct and indirect network effects.

I. Introduction

Antitrust litigation often involves situations where important relevant information is limited or costly to obtain, behavior is complex and can have multiple explanations, or theory is not particularly well developed. As a result, legal and factual presumptions, evidentiary shortcuts, and assignment of the burden of proof can be critical and often decisive. This situation is common across all types of antitrust actions, including unilateral and collaborative conduct, as well as mergers.[1]

Is antitrust analysis of the practices of large digital platforms exceptional in this respect? In a speech given in September, 2022 Margrethe Vestager of the European Commission suggested that it should not be. She said:

> We are long past the point where "digital" refers to a particular sector of the economy. And our recent case practice reflects this. As core digital services become more and more vital to the everyday life of our citizens, any possible market concentration poses greater risks for consumers, in terms of less choice, worse services and higher prices. With today's rising prices, that concerns us more than ever.[2]

If it is correct that digital platforms are unexceptional, that could be a good thing. It might blunt the sharp focus that the press, the public, and some law makers have had on large digital platforms as the source of all things anti-competitive. In fact, that focus recalls a phenomenon that has occurred in antitrust before, which is that it singles out for severe treatment a sector of the economy that is experiencing a high degree of growth and innovation.

At the same time, however, the digital economy contains unique features that serve both to differentiate and to complicate antitrust analysis. Large tech firms trade heavily, although not exclusively, in digital content; they have different cost structures than most traditional firms; they often operate on "two-sided" markets; and they are heavily involved in distribution with both direct and indirect network effects.

---

1 *See* Phillip E. Areeda & Herbert Hovenkamp, Antitrust Law ¶¶1504–1507 (5th ed. 2023) (in press) (discussing role of presumptions in antitrust litigation).

2 Margrethe Vestager, EU Comm'r for Comp., Antitrust for the Digital Age (Sep. 16, 2022), https://ec.europa.eu/commission/presscorner/detail/en/SPEECH_22_5590.

If high tech digital markets are in fact more complex or novel, should we address them differently? More specifically, should litigation that involves them be more dependent on evidentiary shortcuts, or should burdens of proof be different? Often the problem with digital platforms is that at present we know less about them than we know about traditional markets – that is, about how they function and what are the competitive effects of their behavior. An evidentiary shortcut must be better than a coin toss. That is, there must be some reason for deciding an issue a certain way even though not all of the information for a full analysis is available.

Rules that are formulated too hastily can cause trouble down the road. A good example is the Supreme Court's poorly considered conclusion in the *AmEx* case, stating categorically that two-sided markets competed only with other two-sided markets.[3] The range of product market competition is of course a question of fact, and in this case the Court clearly got it wrong. Amazon certainly does compete for transactions with brick-and-mortar sellers, just as Uber competes with traditional taxicabs.[4] However, that misstatement has already forced one court to decide that a merger between an internet-based airline reservation system and a more traditional system could not be horizontal because the parties were not competitors.[5]

Another example of such a categorical misstatement was Justice Frankfurter's declaration in the *Standard Stations* case that tying arrangements "serve hardly any purpose beyond the suppression of competition…."[6] Today it is pretty clear, that nothing could be further from the truth, particularly in high tech markets. That is not to say, of course, that tying cannot be a vehicle for anticompetitive behavior. Often it is. But it cannot be inferred from the mere fact of tying. For that reason the courts have spent decades backing away from the implications of Justice Frankfurter's statement.

If there are to be evidentiary biases for large digital platforms, which way should they cut? Clearly, they have provoked a great deal of attention in the press, aroused some public opinion, and have been the subject of legislation and legislative proposals from a number of jurisdictions. Most of this attention has been hostile and has suggested that some kind of special intervention is in order.

---

3 Ohio v. American Express Co., 138 S. Ct. 2274, 2289 (2018), ("only other two-sided platforms can compete with a two-sided platform for transactions."), *see* Natalie Hayes & Carrie C. Mahan, *The US Supreme Court rejects government antitrust challenge against anti-steering provisions of a credit-card network company (American Express)*, E-COMPETITIONS June 2018, art. No. 88732.

4 Phila. Taxi Ass'n, Inc. v. Uber Techs., Inc., 886 F.3d 332 (3d Cir. 2018), *cert. denied*, 139 S. Ct. 211 (2018), *see* Allison Holt, *The US Court of Appeals for the Third Circuit finds that the entry of ride-sharing firms into the local taxi market increased rather than decreased competition (Philadelphia Taxi Association / Uber)*, E-COMPETITIONS March 2018, art. No. 89345.

5 United States v. Sabre Corp., 452 F. Supp. 3d 97 (D. Del. Apr. 7, 2020), *vacated*, 2020 WL 49115824 (3d Cir. 2020) (District Court relied on *AmEx* to conclude as a matter of law that a two-sided platform making airline reservations did not compete with a more traditional reservation service; thus the merger was not horizontal; Third Circuit vacated judgment after parties abandoned the transactions for non-antitrust reasons), *see* Randy Stutz, *USA: We've seen enough – It is time to abandon Amex and start over on two-sided markets*, CONCURRENCES No. 3-2020, art. No. 95410.

6 Standard Oil Co. of Calif., 337 U.S. 293, 305 (1949).

The other side of the story, however, is that the digital platforms both large and small represent one of the fastest growing parts of the economy,[7] leading one to wonder if we are simply repeating a mistake that antitrust policy has made too often in the past, which is killing the goose that laid the golden egg. For example, the Robinson-Patman Act[8] went aggressively after chain stores in the 1930s, just as chain stores were on the way in and traditional single-store sellers were on the way out. The dominant factor in this transition was consumer choice. In fact, consumer preferences were so overwhelming that both multi-store retailers and, a little later, business franchises proceeded apace even after the Robinson-Patman Act was passed.[9]

The ultimate question in most antitrust litigation is whether a firm is using its assets anticompetitively. For antitrust purposes a digital platform should be thought of as an "asset," not as a "market" or a "firm." They are not generally "markets" in the antitrust sense because a priori we do not know the extent of competition between them and the productive assets held by other firms. For example, a firm such as American Express operates on a digital platform, but it is one player in a market probably best described as general-purpose credit cards. The U.S. Supreme Court refused to find sufficient market power after concluding that Amex competed with other digital platforms including Visa and MasterCard.[10]

The large digital platforms are also not necessarily "firms." A firm such as Alphabet (Google) may operate on several different digital platforms. A single firm, Match Group, owns several different and discrete dating sites, each one on its own digital platform.[11] The same thing is true of Time, Inc., which owns roughly 90 different magazines.[12] Each of these has its own website for subscriptions and other management issues as well as content.[13] Often these diverse assets are separately incorporated subsidiaries, but that does not change the fact that they are owned by a single firm.

The need for and nature of presumptions or other evidentiary shortcuts should be partly based on our overall assessment of performance. If we believe that the markets dominated by large digital platforms are performing poorly, with a great deal of

---

7 *See* U.S. Econ Analysis, New and Revised Statistics of the U.S. Digital Economy, 2005–2020 (2022), https://www.bea.gov/system/files/2022-05/New%20and%20Revised%20Statistics%20of%20the%20U.S.%20Digital%20Economy%202005-2020.pdf.

8 15 U.S.C. § 13 (2018).

9 *See* Herbert Hovenkamp, *The Slogans and Goals of Antitrust Law,* NYU J. Legis. & Public Pol'y (*forthcoming* 2023), https://papers.ssrn.com/sol3/papers.cfm?abstract_id=4121866.

10 Ohio v. Am. Express Co., 138 S. Ct. 2274, 2288 (2018) (holding that AMEX is not shown to have sufficient market power when it was in competition with Visa, MasterCard, and others).

11 *See* Match Group, Dating Site Reviews (July 16, 2022), https://www.datingsitesreviews.com/index.php?topic=match-group (showing Match Group owns 45 dating sites).

12 Time, Inc., Crunchbase (July 16, 2022), https://www.crunchbase.com/organization/time.

13 Time Holdings Inc. includes: https://www.si.com/ (sports illustrated); https://people.com/; and https://www.foodandwine.com/.

monopoly and low customer satisfaction, then stronger evidentiary biases against them might be warranted. However, if we think they are performing relatively well, then perhaps such presumptions should be weakened or not employed at all.

Our thinking about any evidentiary bias depends on the extent to which we believe the market in question has characteristics that make it more or less prone to non-competitive outcomes. A good example is the *High Fructose Corn Syrup* price-fixing case. Judge Posner observed that the market in question, which was for a fungible product with high fixed costs and a history of suspicious conduct, justified proceeding to trial with less compelling evidence than in a case where the market was less conducive to price fixing. "More evidence is required the less plausible the charge of collusive conduct."[14] This was both a paraphrase and a reverse application of the Supreme Court's own conclusion in the *Matsushita* case that more evidence of predatory pricing would be required in a case where the structure of the market made predatory pricing highly implausible.[15] Arguing with the current of structural and behavioral evidence should be easier than arguing against it.

Today we have different modes of antitrust analysis for different types of conduct. For example, naked price fixing among competitors is unlawful per se because the chances of a false positive are very small and we have good theory and data indicating that cartels result in higher prices and lower output.[16] As a result, the per se rule, or condemnation by object under EU law, has permitted fairly severe evidentiary shortcuts in which proof of market power is either eliminated or severely truncated, as is proof of actual price/output effects.

What Judge Posner did in the *HFCS* case, which is having different types of antitrust analysis for different industries, is also rational decision-making behavior. Some industries are much more prone to price fixing than others. Unlike agency regulation, antitrust is not sector specific. It purports to apply the same rules to all industries within its reach. That simple conclusion in fact belies some complexities about differences in markets. Some are more conducive to collusion, depending on the number of firms, extent of product differentiation, or prominence of fixed costs. In some, such as networked computer and digital technologies, tying arrangements have more benign explanations than they do in other markets. Some markets have higher entry barriers than others. So while antitrust applies the same nominal rules everywhere they often lead to different results in different markets.

In general, the more complex an issue is or the market in which it occurs, the more valuable evidentiary shortcuts become, provided that they point us in the right direction. Of course, that is not the same thing as saying that a court

14 *In re* High Fructose Corn Syrup Antitrust Litigation, 295 F. 3d 651, 661 (7th Cir. 2002).

15 Matsushita Elect. Indus. Co. v. Zenith Radio Corp., 475 U.S. 574, 588 (1986).

16 *See* Areeda & Hovenkamp, *supra* note 1, at ¶1509.

should adopt any particular evidentiary shortcut. They are valuable only to the extent that they are reasonably predictive. Further, this issue of "difficulty" is quite different from the issue of plausibility, in the sense that difficulty is prima facie neutral: we simply do not have a sufficient understanding for good knowledge about competitive effects.

For example, when the affected asset is a digital platform, market power can be more difficult to assess, but prima facie it is neither more nor less likely to occur when the firm in question is a digital platform. Digital content makes price/cost relationships harder to measure, and a high degree of product differentiation makes market shares less meaningful. Both of these are common characteristics of digital platforms.

The same thing is true of alleged exclusionary practices that occur on two-sided platforms. To the extent that two-sidedness makes our assessment more difficult, the legal system might be tempted to develop more shortcuts in proof. The fact that the products offered by digital platforms are often (but not always) themselves digital complicates questions about the measurement of costs and the identification of competitive baselines. For example, while we say that competition in tactile products drives prices to marginal cost, that concept can be more difficult both to identify and to measure when we are talking about digital output.[17] This particularly affects claims of predatory pricing or discounting, such as have often been leveled against Amazon.[18] Lack of appreciation of market two-sidedness may also explain the government's allegation of predatory pricing of internet explorer in the *Microsoft* case, which the Court of Appeals rejected.[19]

Questions about network effects raise significant problems as well. On the one hand, network effects give large networks a decisive advantage over smaller networks. That has provoked some hostility against them, as well as suggestions that they more-or-less automatically have significant market power. On the other hand, most of the advantage accrues from the fact that consumers like larger networks because that maximizes their own satisfaction from engaging with a particular network. All else equal, consumers tend to prefer things like ride-hailing apps, dating services, or communications networks when they can contact a larger number of participants on the other side. So here, a preference for smallness may cut sharply against consumer interests. Further, many two-sided markets compete robustly against one another and even with brick-and-mortar sellers. Amazon may have significant market power, but what about eBay, which also sells merchandise on a two-sided platform, along with many other internet retailers.

---

17 *See* Herbert Hovenkamp, *Antitrust and Information Technologies*, 68 Fla. L. Rev. 419 (2016), https://scholarship.law.ufl.edu/flr/vol68/iss2/9/.

18 *See* S'comm. on Antitrust, Com. and Admin. Law of the Comm. on the Judiciary, The Investigation of Competition in Digital Markets, at 297 (2020), https://fm.cnbc.com/applications/cnbc.com/resources/editorialfiles/2020/10/06/investigation_of_competition_in_digital_markets_majority_staff_report_and_recommendations.pdf.

19 *See* United States v. Microsoft corp. 253 F. 3d 34, 68 (D.C. Cir. 2001).

The question of decisional biases for two-sided digital platforms then breaks down into two issues. *First*, how should complexities in proving specific issues affect the adoption of presumptions or other evidentiary shortcuts. Second, should there be a general bias either for or against intervention? In general, the adoption of a presumption is justified only when we have established a reasonably strong link between a certain piece of evidence and a particular legal conclusion. In the present state of our knowledge of digital platforms, it seems to be too early to adopt very many categorical presumptions in either direction.

II. Decisional Biases and the Rule of Reason

Antitrust's rule of reason itself is built on factual presumptions, which United States law requires to appear in a plaintiff's complaint.[20] One is a requirement of market power, which is an essential prerequisite for condemnation under the antitrust laws. The other is the presumption of a link between harm to competition and market wide output. Thus in a rule of reason complaint a plaintiff must ordinarily allege that the plaintiff has market power, typically but not necessarily by alleging a relevant market and a market share. Second, it must allege one or more practices whose effect is to injure competition. We ordinarily associate "competition" with higher prices or lower output, occasionally evidenced more indirectly by things like reduced innovation.

In fact, market power is an economic requirement for all antitrust violations, even those under the per se rule, such as price fixing. However, for per se situations the market power is presumed from the characterization of a particular practice. That is, once we have characterized a practice as "naked price fixing," we do not properly say that market power is irrelevant. Clearly it is relevant to the success of a cartel, which could not succeed without it.[21] Rather, what we are saying is that as an evidentiary matter market power is conclusively presumed and the court will not entertain further litigation about it. As a practical matter this often means that the broader issues are litigated in fact, but the litigation shows up in the dispute over how the practice is to be characterized. For example, US decisions such as *Broadcast Music*,[22] *Engineers*,[23] and the 1984 *NCAA*[24] case

20 Bell Atl. Corp. v. Twombly, 550 U.S. 544, 556 (2007), *see* Max Huffman, *The US Supreme Court affirms the necessity of pleading elements in private antitrust conspiracy claims (Bell Atlantic / Twombly)*, E-COMPETITIONS May 2007, art. No. 47313.

21 *See* AREEDA & HOVENKAMP, *supra* note 1 ¶1906 (4th ed. 2020).

22 Broad. Music, Inc. v. Columbia Broad. Sys., Inc., 441 U.S. 1, 9 (1979).

23 Nat'l Soc. of Pro. Engineers v. United States, 435 U.S. 679, 692 (1978), *see* Jarod Bona, *The US Supreme Court rejects the attempt to justify a restrictive practice on the basis of the potential threat that competition poses to the public safety and the professional ethics (National Society of Professional Engineers)*, E-COMPETITIONS April 1978, art. No. 65451.

24 Nat'l Collegiate Athletic Ass'n v. Bd. of Regents of Univ. of Oklahoma, 468 U.S. 85, 100 (1984), *see* Katherine Whitehead Miller, *The US Supreme Court prohibits an association from imposing conditions on its members' televised events as such conditions violate antitrust laws in the market for college football (NCAA / Board of Regents of the University of Oklahoma)*, E-COMPETITIONS June 1984, art. No. 62474.

all entertained disputes about whether the practice at issue properly fell within the per se rule. *Actavis*, which involved a naked pay-for-delay settlement, also adopted a rule of reason.[25] Justice Breyer concluded that, at least at the time of that decision, there was as yet too little experience with pay-for-delay settlements to warrant a per se characterization.[26]

By contrast, once we conclude that the rule of reason applies, then the conduct will be condemned only if it is proven in the particular case to be anticompetitive. Justice Brandeis' influential formulation of the rule of reason in the 1918 *Chicago Board of Trade* decision contemplated a severely open-ended approach with few or no presumptions. The case literally involved a form of "price-fixing." The defendants were buyers and sellers of commodities futures in grain and other products who were both shareholders and self-employed traders on the Chicago Board of trade. During the trading day prices were set by competition among the numerous buyers and sellers and it appeared that this competition was intense. Under the "call rule" that the Board adopted, however, price-making stopped with the last trade made on the floor before the market closed. Trading could continue "after hours," but all trades had to be made at that last closing price. This continued until the next market day, when the first transaction made on the floor once again opened the market to competitive bidding.[27]

In determining whether this after-hours price fix was anticompetitive, Brandeis rejected any simple formulation that would have inferred a violation from the simple fact that the traders were competitors with one another and that they had "fixed" prices. Rather, he required examination of evidence about every aspect of the defendant's business, its history, and the effect of the challenged practice. Justice Brandeis' often quoted statement of the rule of reason was that:

> The true test of legality is whether the restraint imposed is such as merely regulates and perhaps thereby promotes competition or whether it is such as may suppress or even destroy competition. To determine that question the court must ordinarily consider the facts peculiar to the business to which the restraint is applied; its condition before and after the restraint was imposed; the nature of the restraint and its effect, actual or probable.[28]

---

25 FTC v. Actavis, Inc., 570 U.S. 136 (2013), *see* Richard G. Parker et al., *The US Supreme Court holds that reverse-payment in patent settlements should be reviewed under the antitrust rule of reason (Actavis)*, E-COMPETITIONS June 2013, art. No. 52995.

26 *Id.* at 159 (observing that a more presumptive rule would be "appropriate only where "an observer with even a rudimentary understanding of economics could conclude that the arrangements in question would have an anticompetitive effect on customers and markets.").

27 Bd. of Trade of City of Chicago v. United States, 246 U.S. 231, 237 (1918).

28 *Id.* at 237.

That test sent courts off on virtually unlimited expeditions in search of the true effects of a challenged practice. Not only did Brandeis' test make nearly everything relevant, it also failed to describe exactly what makes conduct anticompetitive, other than the distinction between "promoting" and "suppressing" competition. The *Chicago Board* decision never discussed the effect of the call rule on market output. It also never mentioned the market power of the defendants, although there is one fleeting suggestion that the purpose of the challenged price restraint was to break up a "monopoly" of warehousemen in the grain trade.[29] Today we might decide the *Chicago Board* case much more quickly, simply by observing that no inference could be drawn that the call rule as the court described it did anything to make output lower or prices higher.

The eventual result of *Chicago Board* was unbelievably complex cases, requiring discovery that in some cases lasted a decade.[30] It even confronted courts with the possibility that cases could become so complex that juries could not decide them rationally – placing the right to a fair trial under the Fifth Amendment of the US Constitution in conflict with the right to a jury trial, guaranteed for damages actions by the Seventh Amendment.[31]

One of the most important achievements in the law of antitrust decision-making was a more presumptions-based approach to the rule of reason. Under that approach a plaintiff must prove a prima facie case, identifying with some particularity a particular practice, and why it represents an anticompetitive exercise of market power. At that point the burden of proof shifts to the defendant to offer a procompetitive justification for its restraint. If it fails to do so the plaintiff wins. If the defendant succeeds in showing a justification the burden shifts back to the defendant, who can then show that the same or similar benefits could have been achieved by means of a less restrictive alternative.[32] The test is designed in such a way as to avoid "balancing" of pro- and anti-competitive effects.[33]

This basic approach has been applied to agreements among competitors, vertical agreements, unilateral conduct, and mergers. The terminology used in cases involving these various types of practices differs somewhat, but the fundamental queries are similar.

---

29 *Id.*

30 For example, *see* John S. Kingdon, *The "Big Antitrust Case": Thoughts on Procedural Reform*, 37 WASH. & LEE L. REV. 25 (1980) (focusing mainly on the IBM litigation).

31 *See e.g.*, Thomas M. Jorde, *The Seventh Amendment Right to Jury trial of Antitrust Issues*, 69 CALIF. L. REV. 1 (1981).

32 For a more technical formulation, *see* PHILLIP E. AREEDA & HERBERT HOVENKAMP, ANTITRUST LAW ¶1507 (5th ed., *forthcoming* 2023). For a briefer exposition, *see* HERBERT HOVENKAMP, FEDERAL ANTITRUST POLICY: THE LAW OF COMPETITION AND ITS PRACTICE § 5.6c (6th ed. 2020).

33 On the need to avoid balancing, *see Id.* ¶1507d; in analysis of horizontal restraints under the rule of reason, *see* 11 *Id.* ¶1912i (5th ed. 2017).

In fact, this formulation has not worked as intended. It was very largely undermined when the Supreme Court loaded too many requirements into the first step. Most seriously, in *California Dental Ass'n v. F.T.C.* the Court refused to find that a dental association controlled by dentists' severe restrictions on price and quality advertising even met the standard for a prima facie case.[34] That decision virtually proved to be the death knell for rational rule of reason administration. The Court effectively required the FTC to establish the entirety of its case before the initial burden even shifted to the defendant to provide an explanation.

The thing that made the *California Dental* case so pernicious was that the agreements at issue pertained to price and quality advertising two practices that go to the heart of the competitive system. Further, what was at issue was the rules of an association composed of practicing dentists that placed these limitations on their own members, who were competitors. That should have been an easy case for the first stage of the rule of reason. Unlike *Chicago Board*, the facts here created a clear inference of the power to keep prices up. At that point the burden should have shifted to the defendant to justify its rules, and the FTC's record suggested that they would have had a difficult time doing so.

The approach taken by the Supreme Court virtually guaranteed that future rule of reason cases would fail, and the proof was in *NCAA v. Alston* in 2021,[35] when the Court was finally wiling to apply the rule of reason so as to condemn what amounted to a full-on cartel of NCAA universities to suppress the compensation of student athletes. In the process, however, it conceded that plaintiffs lost virtually all rule of reason cases.[36]

Of course, that raises the question of what types of proof should be sufficient to establish a primary facie case of harm. Here, the level of proof should be something like market power plus "probable cause" – something like the standard of proof that police officers have to meet in order to qualify for a search warrant or an on-site search without a warrant. The point of the warrant is to find out what the defendant actually has. At the onset the plaintiff needs to have only enough to justify the search. Here a crucial point is that the defendant is virtually always the creator of its own restraints, as was true in the *California Dental* case, and thus in the best position to provide an explanation and show the evidence that supports it. As a result, much less must be expected of plaintiffs as part of the initial case.

---

34 California Dental Ass'n v. F.T.C., 526 U.S. 756, 781 (1999) ("a less quick look was required for the initial assessment of the tendency of these professional advertising restrictions.").

35 Nat'l Collegiate Athletic Ass'n v. Alston, 141 S. Ct. 2141, 2959 (2021). *See* Herbert Hovenkamp, *A Miser's Rule of Reason: Student Athlete Compensation and the Alston Antitrust Case*, 78 NYU Ann. Surv. Am. L. 1 (2022), https://papers.ssrn.com/sol3/papers.cfm?abstract_id=3879580. *See* Robert E. Connolly, *The US Supreme Court prohibits a sports professional association from imposing conditions on its members as it violates antitrust law through "naked" wage-fixing of student-athletes (NCAA / Alston)*, E-COMPETITIONS June 2021, art. No. 101328.

36 *Alston*, 141 S. Ct. at 2161 ("[C]ourts have disposed of nearly all rule of reason cases in the last 45 years on the ground that the plaintiff failed to show a substantial anticompetitive effect.").

In *Alston* the Supreme Court noted this problem, citing evidence that very few plaintiffs in rule of reason cases are ever able to cross the initial threshold of getting the burden to shift to the defendant.[37]

This critique of the rule of reason cuts broadly across all antitrust cases, not simply those that involve digital platforms. Nevertheless, the same criteria should apply there. Someone challenging a restraint by a large digital platform needs to show the requisite degree of power for that particular offense and a reasonable suspicion of competitive effects. Since the defendant initiated the restraint it should then be well placed to provide a precompetitive explanation or suffer the consequences.

One impact of this process if it is properly applied is that we do *not* need to know everything there is to know about the defendant's market and business, as Justice Brandeis implied. Properly formulated, the rule of reason permits a court to focus on the particular practice, its likely output effects, and its necessity or not for the defendant's legitimate business.

III. Error-Costs

The antitrust theory of error-cost analysis is that decisions made under uncertainty should be guided by presumptions or other evidentiary shortcuts so as to limit the costs of errors. In some cases the cost of a false positive (recognizing antitrust harm when none exists) and that of a false negative (refusing to recognize antitrust harm when it does exist) may be in equipoise. In that case the goal of the tribunal should be to get the right answer and consider only whether a presumption is reasonably calculated to do that.

By contrast, if the impact of bad decisions is lopsided, then decisions may have to be biased in order to correct that balance. For example, if we believe that false positives will be socially costly and take a long time to correct because judicial rules resist change, but false negatives will quickly be corrected by competition-reinforcing market movements, then we should err on the side of non-enforcement. Of course, in order to make such a principle workable we need to have some reason for thinking that false positives are a bigger problem than false negatives, or vice-versa. In the absence of a conclusion on that issue the best approach is simply to attempt to get it right, minimizing bias in both directions.

Judge Easterbrook took an argument about errors-costs from the law and economics literature on predatory pricing and other areas and applied it to

37 *Id.* at 2160; On the broad acceptance of these burden-shifting requirements in rule of reason antitrust cases, *see* Michael A. Carrier, *The Real Rule of Reason: Bridging the Disconnect*, BYU L. Rev. 1265, 1268–69 (1999); Michael A. Carrier, *The Rule of Reason: An Empirical Update for the 21st Century*, 16 Geo. Mason L. Rev. 827, 834–35 (2009).

antitrust in the 1980s.[38] He argued that courts had developed a great many overly aggressive legal antitrust rules and that they were reluctant to change them. By contrast markets moved more naturally from situations of less to situations of greater competition. In that setting underdeterrent rules would be less socially costly than overdeterrent ones.

Easterbrook's twin assumptions were that: (1) markets can generally be trusted to correct themselves from positions of monopoly to positions of greater competition; but (2) overly aggressive antitrust rules condemning competitively harmless conduct tend to linger. These assumptions were very influential during the later 1980s and after, when neoliberal antitrust policy was ascendant. For people such as Robert H. Bork, less antitrust was almost always better.[39]

Easterbrook's first position had already become obsolete as a matter of economic theory by the time he was writing. His own economic backdrop had been a Chicago-induced model of perfect competition, championed principally by George J. Stigler, which saw oligopoly as inherently unstable and monopolistic competition as incoherent. Rather, if left unmolested market forces could generally be trusted to move markets toward greater amounts of competition.[40] Stigler's views were substantially based on his own caricatures of those economic models. For example, he treated oligopoly not as a non-cooperative theory of games, as most of the literature had treated it, but rather as a set of rules about what it takes to engage successfully in collusion.[41] For monopolistic competition he began largely with the premise that the theory is meaningless because it makes the concept of a market equilibrium impossible; you have only the decision-making of each individual firm.[42]

Milton Friedman restated this view, largely as a problem in verification. He argued that monopolistic competition theory obliterated the distinction between markets and firms. Under product differentiation you have many different firms, but no market – in his words, "no stopping place between the firm at one extreme and general equilibrium at the other."[43] Left to run its course it would have threatened the existence of microeconomics as a distinct discipline, because microeconomics depends on the ability to speak of "markets" of competing products, located at a point in between the individual firm and the economy as a whole.

---

38 Frank H. Easterbrook, *The Limits of Antitrust*, 63 Tex. L. Rev. 1 (1984). Within antitrust, some of the earlier literature applying error-cost analysis concerned predatory pricing. *See e.g.*, Paul L. Joskow & Alvin K. Klevorick, *A Framework for Analyzing Predatory Pricing Policy*, 89 Yale L.J. 213 (1979); *See also* Alan A. Fisher & Robert H. Lande, *Efficiency Considerations in Merger Enforcement*, 71 Cal. L. Rev. 1580 (1983); Charles J. Goetz & Robert E. Scott, *Enforcing Promises: An Examination of the Basis of Contract*, 89 Yale L.J. 1261 (1981).

39 *See e.g.*, Robert H. Bork, The Antitrust Paradox: A Policy at War With Itself (1978).

40 *See* Herbert Hovenkamp, *Antitrust Error Costs*, 24 Univ. Pa. J. Bus. L. 293 (2022), https://papers.ssrn.com/sol3/papers.cfm?abstract_id=3853282.

41 George J. Stigler, *A Theory of Oligopoly*, 72 J. Pol. Econ. 44 (1964).

42 George J. Stigler, *Monopolistic Competition in Retrospect*, *in* Five Lectures on Economic Problems (1949).

43 Milton Friedman, *The Methodology of Positive Economics*, *reprinted in* Milton Friedman, Essays in Positive Economics 39 (1953).

Today the existence of equilibria in differentiated markets is largely conceded.[44] Further, the theory of product differentiation has been completely internalized into economic studies of markets. Indeed, most structural antitrust enforcement activity occurs in differentiated product spaces. Right down to the point of market definition and power assessment, we have been able to internalize product differentiation. For example, most studies of markets for antitrust purposes do not assume infinitely high elasticity of substitution between products in the same market. Rather, a price change in one induces a particular rate of change, depending on the size of the change and the amount of distance in product space. The hypothetical monopolist test for market definition and the theory of unilateral effects for mergers both follow such methodologies.

Beginning in the 1970s an empirical revolution in industrial economics provided broad support for models of imperfect competition, while largely making perfect competition models untenable everywhere except some unconcentrated markets for fungible commodities.[45] The theories of oligopoly and monopolistic competition became blended into a set of models of imperfect competition that are dominant in industrial economics today.[46]

There is also no general reason for thinking that markets are working themselves pure. To the contrary, evidence based on both market concentration data and growing price-cost margins strongly suggest that markets overall have become less competitive since the 1980s. To be sure, this evidence is controversial.[47] In part it is based on assumptions about market concentration that seem vulnerable to methodological issues, including determination of the "markets" whose concentration is to be measured. Today, direct econometric measures of price cost margins seem to be a superior tool for this purpose, but they are of more recent vintage and have not yet attained as wide acceptance.

In any event, the "indirect" evidence from market concentration and the "direct" evidence from monopoly markups points in the same direction. Since the 1980s markets have become more concentrated and price-cost margins have increased.[48] Today there is no general reason to assume that markets will naturally work

---

44 *See e.g.*, John Beath & Yannis Katsoulacos, The Economic Theory of Product Differentiation (1991).

45 *See* Timothy F. Bresnahan & Richard Schmalensee, *The Empirical Renaissance in Industrial Economics: An Overview*, 35 J. Indus. Econ. 371, 371 (1987). On the previous debate, *see* Jan Horst Keppler, *The Genesis of "Positive Economics" and the Rejection of Monopolistic Competition Theory: A Methodological Debate*, 22 Cambridge J. Econ. 261, 264 (1998).

46 *See* Hovenkamp, *supra* note 40, 23 Univ. Pa. J. Bus. L. at 318.

47 On the history of the controversies, *see* Herbert Hovenkamp, *The Invention of Antitrust*, 95 S. Cal. L. Rev. (forthcoming 2023), available at https://papers.ssrn.com/sol3/papers.cfm?abstract_id=3995502.

48 *See* Robert E. Hall, *Using Empirical Marginal Cost to Measure Market Power in the US Economy* (Nat'l Bureau of Econ. Rsch., Working Paper No. 25251, 2018), https://www.nber.org/papers/w25251; Robert E. Hall, *Potential Competition, Limit Pricing, and Price Elevation from Exclusionary Conduct*, *in* Issues on Competition Law and Policy (ABA Section of Antitrust Law 2008), https://web.stanford.edu/~rehall/PotentialCompetition.pdf. For a more qualified view, *see* Susanto Basu, *Are Price-Cost Markups Rising in the United States? A Discussion of the Evidence*, 33 J. Econ. Persp. 3 (2019).

themselves from positions of lesser to positions of greater competition, and at least some reason for thinking that they will do just the opposite.

The other error-cost assumption was that needlessly aggressive judge made antitrust rules, such as per se rules against competitively harmless practices, would linger for long periods, frustrating firms' attempts to operate more efficiently. In the mid-1980s antitrust encompassed several anticompetitive per se rules, such as per se illegality for both minimum[49] and maximum[50] resale price maintenance, as well as overly aggressive merger rules[51] and decisional rules favoring jury trials.[52]

Already by the time of Easterbrook's 1984 article, however, the courts had begun moving antitrust policy away from the more aggressive enforcement positions.[53] In 1974 the U.S. government lost a big merger challenge, bringing to an end a period in which government challenges almost always succeeded, even on the flimsiest of theories.[54] In 1977 the Supreme Court overruled the *Schwinn* rule, which had made vertically imposed territorial restraints on dealers unlawful per se.[55] At the time the *Schwinn* rule was only ten years old. In 1977 the Justice Department issued its scathing *Report on the Robinson-Patman Act*, pronouncing its overall effects to be anticompetitive,[56] and all but announcing that it would no longer enforce the statute.[57] The *Report's* conclusions limited enforcement to situations that present "a substantial risk of immediate, adverse impact on market structure," something that the text of the Robinson-Patman Act itself did not require.[58]

---

49 Dr. Miles Med. Co. v. John D. Park & Sons Co., 220 U.S. 373, 394 (1911), *see* Barbara Bruckmann, *The US Supreme Court holds it is per se illegal for a manufacturer to set minimum resale prices in agreements with independent resellers (Dr. Miles Medical / John D. Park & Sons)*, e-Competitions April 1911, art. No. 52947. *Overruled by* Leegin Creative Leather Prod., Inc. v. PSKS, Inc., 551 U.S. 877 (2007), *see* Peter J. Carney & Kristen J. McAhren, *The US Supreme Court overturns its long-standing prohibition against vertical agreements between manufacturers and their dealers setting minimum resale prices (Leegin Creative)*, e-Competitions June 2007, art. No. 38050.

50 Albrecht v. Herald Co., 390 U.S. 145, 149 (1968), overruled by State Oil Co. v. Khan, 522 U.S. 3 (1997), *see* Victor D. Vital & Elizabeth Wirmani, *The US Supreme Court overrules 30-year-old precedent and declares maximum resale price maintenance agreements should be reviewed under the rule of reason in a case against a gasoline wholesaler (State Oil / Khan)*, e-Competitions November 1997, art. No. 52952.

51 *See e.g.*, Brown Shoe Co. v. United States, 370 U.S. 294 (1962).

52 Poller v. Columbia Broad. Sys., Inc., 368 U.S. 464 (1962).

53 *See* Herbert Hovenkamp, *A Posner-Stigler Smoking Gun*, *Promarket*, (Univ. of Chicago Booth Stigler Center, Apr. 29, 2022), https://www.promarket.org/2022/04/29/a-posner-stigler-smoking-gun/.

54 United States v. General Dynamics Corp., 415 U.S. 486 (1974).

55 Continental TV, Inc. v. GTE Sylvania, Inc., 433 U.S. 36, 58 (1977), *overruling* United States v. Arnold, Schwinn & Co., 388 U.S. 365 (1967).

56 U.S. Dep't of Just., Report on the Robinson-Patman Act (1977). *See* 260:
… [T]he evidence is that the Act promotes high prices, restricted entry, and inefficiency in the distribution of goods; and it has encouraged the creation of illegal pricing exchanges by competing manufacturers. The fact that the Act does not apply at all to the offering of services a growing sector in which small business is especially significant – reinforces the conclusion that the Robinson – Patman Act is not a key factor in preserving efficient small businesses.

57 *See id.* at 254:
The simple truth is that Robinson-Patman is a false promise: it provides little, long-run protection to small businessmen. It is jut not possible to legislate equality in a free market system. The basic force in changing the structure of the American marketplace is the consumer.

58 *Id.* at 305.

The Court had already held in the 1970s that only direct purchasers from a cartel or overcharging monopolist could bring an antitrust action for damages.[59] While the merits of that rule remain controversial, there is every reason today to think that it went too far and may leave many cartels underenforced. Roughly half of the states have deviated in their own antitrust provisions.[60] *Illinois Brick* presents the case of a lingering (nearly fifty-year-old) antitrust rule that is *under* deterrent but nevertheless persists. The same thing is true of the Supreme Court's 1993 *Brooke Group* decision, which placed overly severe limitations on predatory pricing claims.[61]

Today, it is hard to make a strong categorical case in either direction for a bias in error-cost analysis. In that case, the best route is to get it right. Errors in both directions are bad, but there is no general reason for assuming that the cost of false positives is either greater or less than the cost of false negatives.

IV. Error-Costs and the Digital Economy

Should the error-cost presumption differ when the particular market in question seems to be functioning quite well? For example, the large digital platforms operate in a new economy market that has a growth rate approximately four times higher than that of the economy overall.[62] Further, as noted earlier, many practices are more difficult to understand when they occur on two-sided digital markets. Should these facts suggest either an exaggerated or an understated error-cost bias in our analysis of competition issues on digital platforms?

That question suggests a broader issue, which is how much should what we sometimes think of as macroeconomic conclusions about economic growth affect antitrust decision-making? This particular question is in fact "microeconomic," in the sense that it focuses on a particular set of markets. However, it relies on evidence about comparative economic growth across all markets.

The question is not as novel as first appears. We use presumptions about market structure all the time. For example, we presume that industries with high fixed costs are more prone to collusion, or that monopoly is unlikely to occur in

59 Illinois Brick Co. v. Illinois, 431 U.S. 720, 733 (1977).

60 *See* Phillip E. Areeda & Herbert Hovenkamp, Antitrust Law ¶346i (5th ed. 2021) (lack of federal preemption), *id.* ¶2412 (4th ed. 2020) (state indirect purchaser provisions).

61 Brooke Group, Ltd. V. Brown & Williamson Tobacco Corp., 509 U.S. 209 (1993). *See* Steven J. Cernak, *The US Supreme Court establishes a test for proving the existence of predatory pricing (Brooke Group)*, e-Competitions June 1993, art. No. 98743. *See* William Rogerson and Howard Shelanski, *Antitrust Enforcement, Regulation, and Digital Platforms*, 168 U. Pa. L. Rev. 1911, 1923 (2020): [T]he *Brooke Group* decision has led to underenforcement. The potential case-by-case advantages of adjudication are lost where judicial precedent renders important facts and circumstances irrelevant. In such cases, the relatively slow process of doctrinal correction through common law evolution is harmful to sound antitrust enforcement.").

62 *See* Jessica R. Nicholson, *New Digital Economy Estimates* (Nat'l Bureau of Econ. Analysis (BEA)) (data covering 2015–2018 indicating 6.8% growth, compared to 1.7% growth in overall economy), https://www.bea.gov/system/files/2020-08/New-Digital-Economy-Estimates-August-2020.pdf.

industries where all important costs are variable. More generally, expansion of market wide output is at least a weak sign of competitive performance, while contraction is the opposite.

In this particular case, the fact that the digital platforms are economically so high performing suggests two things: (1) antitrust policy must be cautious, making sure that it understands both the effects of a particular practice as well as the effects of any remedy; and (2) statutes that *categorically* segregate the large digital platforms for adverse treatment are perverse to the extent that they are punishing the best performing firms.

For example, the proposed American Innovation and Choice Online Act (AICOA)[63] identifies large digital platforms but not equally large traditional retailers for harsh treatment. This is reminiscent of the Robinson-Patman Act, which targeted chain stores for the protection of traditional single-store retailers at great cost to consumers and the overall economy.[64] AICOA in its present form is both underinclusive and overinclusive. First, by identifying only very large digital platforms for its coverage it ignores the very same competitive issues when they occur on small digital platforms or in the more general non-digital market. For example, Amazon is a smaller digital video streamer than Netflix,[65] but Netflix is not covered by AICOA because it is a smaller firm overall. As a result, Amazon's policies, but not Netflix's, will be covered by AICOA rules. Further, this application restriction is perverse to the extent that it targets for restrictive treatment the better performing portion of the economy rather than the one that is not performing as well.

Second, within a covered platform as defined by the AICOA every product and service is covered regardless of the competitive position of that particular product. For example, Amazon is a very large digital retailer, but it sells only about 2.5% of groceries sold in the United States.[66] At the other extreme, it has a significant position in ebooks, assuming that ebooks constitute a relevant market. For most other products its shares lie somewhere in between. A practice such as self-preferencing might be anticompetitive when it denies consumers reasonable alternatives, but that query is very heavily driven by market share in the particular product. If Amazon engages in self-preferencing of grocery items where its market share is roughly 2% consumers have ample avenues of escape.

So the AICOA is a poorly designed piece of legislation. At the same time, however, large digital platforms should not get a free pass. When they do anticompetitive things – and they do – then they should be subject to antitrust

63 S. 2992, 117th Cong., 2d sess. (2021–2022). For a critique, see Herbert Hovenkamp, Gatekeeper Antitrust Policy, Mich. Tech. L. Rev. (forthcoming, 2023), https://papers.ssrn.com/sol3/papers.cfm?abstract_id=4347768.

64 15 U.S.C. § 13 (2018); Hovenkamp, *supra* note 9.

65 *See* https://www.statista.com/statistics/496011/usa-svod-to-tv-streaming-usage/ (2020).

66 *See* Annie Palmer, *Amazon's Sprawling Grocery Business has Become an "Expensive Hobby" with a Cloudy Future*, CNBC (Feb. 19, 2022), https://www.cnbc.com/2022/02/19/amazons-sprawling-grocery-business-has-become-an-expensive-hobby.html.

discipline. Nevertheless, in the current state of our knowledge there is no good reason for applying a decisional bias one way or the other when addressing problems on large digital platforms. This is in fact a version of a proposition that the Supreme Court has recognized, which is that application of the per se rule is appropriate only after there has been considerable judicial experience with a certain type of restraint.[67] The fact is that for a wide variety of issues involving large digital platforms we are not there yet.

This conclusion cuts in both directions, however. The principal thing it means is that when antitrust is dealing with relatively novel circumstances it must be open to a wider variety of possibilities, with no bias one way or the other in addressing them. That may require more deliberate and thus more costly fact-finding and analysis.

The balance of this discussion looks at two very prominent examples. First is the question whether two-sided digital platforms are winner-take-all markets. The second is the extent to which mergers involving large digital platforms should be treated differently from mergers more generally.

1. Digital Platforms as Winner-Take-All Markets

Several writers have suggested that large digital platforms are "winner-take-all" markets, or natural monopolies.[68] That conclusion is understandable for several reasons. First of all, digital content is subject to extreme economies of scale: once it is produced it can usually be reproduced an infinite number of times at very low incremental cost. This can give an enormous advantage to first movers in an area, particularly if their own product has intellectual property rights that prevent copying.

In addition, digital platforms usually benefit from significant network effects, both direct and indirect. Network effects, or economies of scale in use rather than production, generally entail that a platform is more valuable (or cheaper per user) as the number of users increases. Indirect effects entail that a platform becomes more valuable to users on one side as the number of users on the other side increases. A good example is Uber, which is a digital app that people can install on their smart phones in order to hail a taxi. In general, the Uber app becomes more valuable to prospective passengers as the number of drivers increases, because that improves their chances of getting a suitable taxi in a short amount of time. Looking in the other direction, however, the app becomes

67 *See* 11 Herbert Hovenkamp, Antitrust Law ¶1909b (4th ed. 2020).

68 Nikolas Guggenberger, *Essential Platforms*, 24 Stan. Tech. L. Rev. 237 (2021); David S. Evans, *The Antitrust Economics of Multi-Sided Platform Markets*, 20 Yale J. Rev. 325 (2003); David S. Evans, *Antitrust Issues Raised by the Emerging Global Internet Economy*, 102 Nw. Univ. L. Rev. Coll. 285 (2008); Ben Bloodstein, *Amazon and Platform Antitrust*, 88 Fordham L. Rev. 187 (2019); Des Traynor, *Surviving and Thriving in Two-Sided Markets*, Inside Intercom (Aug. 14, 2012); Thomas Eisenmann, Geoffrey Parker & Marshall W. Van Alystyne, *Strategies for Two-Sided Markets*, 10 Harv. Bus. Rev. 84 (2006).

more valuable to drivers as the number of potential customers increases. So a larger Uber-style app should have considerable advantages over a smaller competitor.

Today it seems clear that the early jump to the conclusion that large digital apps are winner-take-all markets was premature. The important missing ingredient was product differentiation. Historically the economic theory of natural monopoly grew out of observations made about public utilities, highways and other forms of transportation.[69] One attribute of these is that fixed costs were very high and as a result average costs declined as output increased. If that decline occurs all the way to the point that a firm controls more than half of the market, then the equilibrium number of firms in that market is one. Necessarily, a second firm offering an identical product would have higher costs because its sales would be less than 50 percent, assuming of course that it used the same technology and was equally efficient.

Offsetting this, however, is the existence and extent of product differentiation.[70] Here, both the theory and the empirical evidence are becoming more ample. First, if the question were whether a Facebook (FB) clone could enter the social network market in competition with FB, the answer is almost certainly no. FB would have an enormous head start in both recognition and users.

In fact, however, social networking sites have entered the market subsequent to FB (2004), and will very likely continue to do so. These include Snapchat (2011), Twitter (2013) and TikTok (2016). Facebook itself entered after Myspace (2003) and LinkedIn (2003) were already established.

So FB's market looks less like a monopoly but more like a fairly concentrated industry with a number of rivals and – perhaps – one dominant firm.[71] However, a defining characteristic of these products is their distinctiveness.

The more serious question is one of magnitudes. For example, dating sites and magazines both operate on two-sided digital platforms that experience strong network effects. Yet there are hundreds of them and new ones enter continuously. By contrast, operating systems for small computers and consumer search engines are far fewer in number, although neither market is a true monopoly. This suggests one of two things. First, as is probably true of search engines, meaningful product differentiation may be difficult to develop and maintain. As a result, other search engines are very largely competing for the same product space.

---

69 *See e.g.,* William W. Sharkey, The Theory of Natural Monopoly (1983); William Baumol, John C. Panzar & Robert D. Willig, *Contestable Markets and the Theory of Industry Structures* (1982); Alan T. Peacock & Charles K. Rowley, *Welfare Economics and the Public Regulation of Natural Monopoly*, 1 J. Pub. Econ. 227 (1972).

70 Avner Shaked & John Sutton, *Product differentiation and Industrial Structure*, 2 J. Indus. Econ. 131 (1987); Avner Shaked & John Sutton, *Relaxing Price Competition Through Product Differentiation*, 49 Rev. Econ. Stud. 3 (1982); Avner Shaked & John Sutton, *Natural Oligopolies*, 51 Econometrica 1469 (1983).

71 *See* https://gs.statcounter.com/social-media-stats (showing market shares as of Aug. 2022): FB, 74.65%; Twitter, 8.22%; Instagram 7.01%, Pinterest 5.06%, YouTube 3.59%, Reddit, .82%. Facebooks owns Instagram.

Second, and possibly true of operating systems, is that they are tied to hardware and have a high need for data exchange with other users. This serves to make both the production costs and the transaction costs of a large number of operating systems very high. If so, a new OS would have to offer sufficiently unique and desirable features in order to succeed in the market.

2. Mergers

A. *The Problem of Nonhorizontal and Potential Competition Mergers*

Another issue affecting large digital firms is the analysis of nonhorizontal mergers. This category includes vertical mergers, which the United States enforcement agencies are starting to take more seriously.[72] It also includes mergers that mainly involve complementary products, or situations in which a firm uses an acquisition to enlarge or extend its range of operations. Historically these were termed "product extension" and "market extension" mergers. The first involved situations in which a firm used a merger to add a product to its line, such as Procter & Gamble's acquisition of Clorox, which was intended to enable P&G to add laundry bleach to its line of household products.[73] By contrast, a "market extension" merger is one in which a firm acquires product assets located in a different geographic area. For example, the *Von's Grocery* decision,[74] which was treated by the majority as involving a merger of competitors, was one in which a grocer operating in one geographic portion of Los Angeles attempted to acquire stores located in a different portion.[75]

Digital platforms have modified this taxonomy. First, the use of digital tech mergers to extend operations into new *geographic* territories is relatively uncommon. Second, many digital platform acquisitions are not "product" expansion as such, but rather acquisition of technology that enables them to perform differently or that adds another feature to their performance. For example, Facebook's acquisition of WhatsApp was intended at least in part to improve its performance in texting for handhelds.[76] There are exceptions, of course. For example, Amazon's acquisition of Whole Foods added a chain of brick-and-mortar stores to its grocery business, which could be viewed as a product market expansion.

---

72 *See* U.S. Dep't of Justice & Fed. Trade Comm'n, *Vertical Merger Guidelines* (2020) (*withdrawn* by FTC (2021)), https://www.ftc.gov/system/files/documents/reports/us-department-justice-federal-trade-commission-vertical-merger-guidelines/vertical_merger_guidelines_6-30-20.pdf. and *see* Herbert Hovenkamp & Carl Shapiro, *How Will the FTC Evaluate Vertical Mergers? Promarket*, (Chicago Stigler Center, Sep. 23, 2021), https://www.promarket.org/2021/09/23/ftc-vertical-mergers-antitrust-shapiro-hovenkamp/.

73 FTC v. Procter & Gamble Co., 386 U.S. 568, 570 (1967).

74 United States v. Von's Grocery Co., 384 U.S. 270, 272 (1966).

75 *Id.* at 295 (J. Stewart dissenting) (observing "market-extension" effect of the merger).

76 *See* John Herman, *Why Facebook Had to Have WhatsApp*, Buzzfeed (Jan. 19, 2014), https://www.buzzfeednews.com/article/jwherrman/why-facebook-was-so-terrified-of-whatsapp.

In any event, the Supreme Court very largely killed the law of nonhorizontal mergers in the 1970s.[77] While the theories under which such mergers had been challenged were excessively speculative and flawed, the fact is that potential competition mergers remain a significant threat to competition.[78] They just need to be analyzed differently than we looked at them 50 years ago.

The traditional law of nonhorizontal mergers focused on variations of the "potential competition" or "potential entrant" doctrine. The most robust of these was called the "perceived potential entrant" doctrine, in which an established firm acquired a firm who was objectively perceived as an entrant into the acquirer's market.[79] The theory was that this firm would have developed into a rival of the acquiring firm, but the latter then cut off that policy by purchasing that firm (or its threatening assets) instead. One component in the theory was that the threat of entry had required the acquiring firm to keep its own price relatively low for fear that higher margins would induce the entry. Once the acquisition had occurred, however, that threat was removed. As the Supreme Court stated it in the *Penn-Olin Chemical* case,

> The existence of an aggressive, well equipped and well financed corporation engaged in the same or related lines of commerce waiting anxiously to enter an oligopolistic market would be a substantial incentive to competition which cannot be underestimated.[80]

In *Falstaff Brewing*[81] the government's theory was that Falstaff would have entered a new geographic area as an additional competitor, but for the fact that it acquired the largest specialty regional brewer in that area. The theory was criticized for inviting excessive speculation about whether the acquiring firm would have entered but for the acquisition, as well as why other firms could not just as easily enter as well.

The Procter & Gamble bleach acquisition was based on a somewhat different theory, which was that P&G would have entered the bleach market on its own, increasing competition there. Instead, however, it purchased Clorox, which was already established and dominant in that market. At the time P&G made a variety of household chemicals but not bleach, which meant that the additional of bleach was a naturally expected expansion of its business.

The potential entrant theory faced a great deal of skepticism because it was thought to require excessive speculation about how "likely" it was that the perceived entrant would actually have entered, how effective the perception of

77 United States v. Marine Bancorporation, Inc., 418 U.S. 602 (1974).

78 *See* Scott Hemphill & Tim Wu, *Nascent Competitors*, 168 U. Pa. L. Rev. 1879 (2020); *see also* 5 Phillip E. Areeda & Herbert Hovenkamp, Antitrust Law ¶¶1121–1142 (4th ed. 2016).

79 *Id.* ¶1127.

80 United States v. Penn-Olin Chemical Co., 378 U.S. 158, 174 (1964).

81 United States v. Falstaff Brewing Corp., 410 U.S. 526 (1973).

its threatened entry really was in reducing prices, and the like. Suffice it to say, he theory of potential competition mergers depended more on long run considerations than the general theory of coordination-facilitating horizontal mergers.

Without going into any detail, a new approach to potential competition mergers should be more econometric, just as the analysis of "unilateral" effects horizontal mergers. These are mergers that occur in product-differentiated markets. Their real difference from potential competition mergers lies in the degree of differentiation and perhaps the amount of time that we want to consider. Further, as noted below, many potential competition mergers are best addressed for their exclusionary effects rather than their short-run effects on output or price.

Offsetting the longer and more speculative time horizon is that we are – or should be – speaking of dominant firms in the affected markets. That is, one component of this strategy is that it is part of a long-run process under which a dominant firm protects its turf from potential entrant.

B. *Exclusionary Mergers*

The currently existing Horizontal Merger Guidelines (2010)[82] are concerned with mergers that increase prices in the relatively short term. That is true of the general theory that a merger that increases market concentration can threaten higher market-wide prices, and also of the "unilateral effects" theory that a merger of two firms who make relatively "adjacent" products in a differentiated market can effect a price increase over their own output.

Treating mergers as exclusionary practices rests on a somewhat different footing. Implicitly it deals with longer run concerns than an immediate price increase. Rather, its focus is on preventing competition that might emerge down the road if the acquired firm should grow into a significant rival. Here, the competitive threat is significantly larger than it was for the various producers of tactile products and services that were responsible for the law of potential competition mergers in the 1960s and 1970s. Digital firms can grow very rapidly and quickly expand into new markets when they have the technology to do so. For example, while Instagram was actually a very small firm when Facebook acquired it, FB's management feared that it would grow into a substantial rival, and no obvious capacity constraints prevented it from doing so.[83] In that case the most profitable

82 *See* U.S. Dep't of Justice & Fed. Trade Comm'n, *Horizontal Merger Guidelines* (2010), https://www.justice.gov/atr/horizontal-merger-guidelines-08192010.

83 *See* Complaint, *FTC v. Facebook, Inc.*, 560 F. Supp. 3d 1 (D.D.C. 2021) (No. 20-cv-3590), 2021 U.S. DIST. CT. MOTIONS LEXIS 154 ("Facebook founder and CEO Mark Zuckerberg described Instagram as 'a large and viable competitor' presenting 'a big strategic risk for us.'"), *see* Fed. Trade Comm'n, *The US FTC files an amended complaint against a social media company alleging it resorted to an illegal buy-or-bury scheme to crush competition after a string of failed attempts to innovate (Facebook)*, E-COMPETITIONS August 2021, art. No. 102162.

solution for FB (now Meta) was to purchase Instagram and eliminate it as a competitive threat. In 2022, Instagram had roughly a billion active users who log in at least once a month.[84] Forcing FB to divest Instagram could present it with a substantial rival.

A merger can thus be said to be exclusionary when its principal purpose or effect is not a price increase in the relatively short term, but rather elimination of an entry or expansion possibility that might occur in the future.

One important feature about such acquisitions, particularly by the large dominant platforms, is that the threat is *more* formidable as the targeted firm is differentiated from the acquirer. In a situation such as Facebook, for example, FB would very likely have little to fear from a simple clone that was attempting to enter its market. Given the severe size disadvantages such a firm would almost certainly fail on its own. The very fact that Instagram was somewhat differentiated from FB is what made its threat more plausible. More recently, FB has lost substantial ground to Tik-Tok, whose rapid growth in the United States relies mainly on the fact that it appeals to a demographic that has become less enamored of FB.[85] This might seem odd and counterintuitive, but the fact is that Tik-Tok is a more strenuous competitor with FB because it is different.

In any event, the current merger standards, which are much more aggressive for horizontal mergers than for those that are non-horizontal, need to be revisited when the feared competitive threat is exclusion rather than coordinated interaction.

At the same time, the differentiation point should not be pushed too far. Before a merger can qualify as an exclusionary practice it must be an effort to keep a potential competitor out of the market. Here, the real question is what is the firm's potential to grow into a significant rival of the acquiring firm?

The FTC did not challenge the Facebook/Instagram acquisition under section 7 of the Clayton Act, which governs mergers. Rather the challenge was under the principles of section 2 of the Sherman Act.[86] This gives added weight to the idea that this is an exclusionary practice. According to the FTC's complaint, FB already has a dominant position in the market, and the acquisition tends to prolong that by eliminating a potential entrant.

Of course, efficiencies must still be considered, as we discuss below.

---

84 *See* https://backlinko.com/instagram-users.

85 *See* Cal Newport, *TikTok and the Fall of the Social-Media Giants*, The New Yorker (July 28, 2022), https://www.newyorker.com/culture/cultural-comment/tiktok-and-the-fall-of-the-social-media-giants; Shannon Bond, *Facebook is making radical changes to keep up with TikTok*, NPR, 16:46 (July 26, 2022), https://www.npr.org/2022/07/26/1113724820/facebook-is-making-radical-changes-to-keep-up-with-tiktok.

86 Complaint, *supra* note 83.

C. *Efficiencies and Non-exclusive Licenses*

While merger law today contemplates a nonstatutory "efficiencies" defense, efficiencies rarely show up in the law in that way. Defendants have had very little success in establishing efficiencies that would rebut a prima facie case that a merger was likely to cause reduced output ad higher prices. This does not mean that efficiencies are irrelevant, but only that they show up in the exercise of prosecutorial discretion or production of a prima facie case against a merger. For example, the HHI standards in the 2010 Merger Guidelines seem excessively tolerant toward mergers creating significant increases in concentration, except on the premise that efficiency offsets are included in the prediction. The same thing is true of econometric methods for predicting post-acquisition price increases, which can be applied to both traditional concentration-increasing mergers and to those challenged under the theory of unilateral effects: an adjustment for "synergies," or cost reductions, is built into the formulas that are used to apply them.[87] One important question is whether these automatic adjustments are calibrated correctly, or even whether they should be used at all.

One important thing to ask when examining an acquisition by a large digital platform is: what is it that the acquiring firm wants? The answer here can be much more complex than it is with respect to a traditional producer or retailer. It is typically not more production capacity or more stores.

Indeed, for a sizeable number of platform acquisitions of small firms the target firm's hardware is not all that valuable, nor even its physical production facilities. There can be exceptions, of course, such as Amazon's acquisition of Whole Foods, where Amazon clearly wanted Whole Foods' stores in order to give itself a physical footprint.[88] For many dominant platform acquisitions of small startups, however, what the acquiring firm really wants is access to the dominant firm's business method, intellectual property (IP) or in some cases its human capital.

Acquisitions of IP rights should get a particularly close look because frequently a non-exclusive license will operate as a preferable solution. A non-exclusive license gives the acquiring firm full access to the acquired firm's intellectual property for its own use, just not the right to prevent other people from having access as well.

Patents give the original patentee the power to exclude. However, patents are also "assets" covered by the merger laws. Finally, patents can be seen as creating a production or integration right and an exclusion right. A transfer or assignment

---

87 *See e.g.*, Carl Shapiro, *Unilateral Effects Calculations*, (2010), https://faculty.haas.berkeley.edu/shapiro/unilateral.pdf; Tommaso Valetti & Hans Zenger, *Mergers with Differentiated Products: Where Do We Stand?* 58 Rev. Ind. Org. 179 (2021); Jerry Hausman, Gregory Leonard & J. Douglas Zona, *Competitive Analysis with Differentiated Products*, *in* Annales d'Economie et de Statistique, No. 34, 159 (1994), https://www.jstor.org/stable/20075951#metadata_info_tab_contents.

88 Lisa Eadicicco, *5 Reasons Why Amazon Bought Whole Foods*, Time, 11:44 (June 16, 2017), https://time.com/4821387/amazon-buying-whole-foods-analysis/.

of a patent moves all these rights to the acquirer. By contrast, an otherwise unrestricted non-exclusive license transfers the integration right, but not the exclusion right.

The question in a merger case is whether the right to transfer a patent, which is explicitly created in the United States Patent Act,[89] always includes both the production/integration right and the exclusion right, or can the antitrust laws provide limitations? On the one hand, the Patent Act grants patentees the power to assign their patents. On the other, the mergers laws forbid mergers whose effect may be substantially to lessen competition, or in the case of section 2 of the Sherman Act, create or threaten to create a monopoly. It is also worth noting that the "monopoly" which is the concern of the antitrust laws is a market monopoly, while the patent laws create no such right. The right they confer on the original patentee is merely one to prevent others from copying the patent.

The best way to harmonize these provisions is to say that the Patent Act absolutely gives the assignee the right to practice the patent and integrate its technology into its own. It also has a default right to transfer the patent exclusion power, which is the power to prevent infringement by others. What it does not do, however, is create a right in the patentee to confer a market monopoly that was not created by the original patent grant. That is, it cannot be used to turn a simple boundary-exclusion right into a market-exclusion right.

Incidentally, this is precisely the rule that applies to productive assets generally. For example, ownership of a physical factory gives the owner the absolute right to exclude trespassers from entering. If that factory is sold to another firm, it will acquire the power to exclude trespassers. Nevertheless, transfer of the factory to a different owner is subject to the merger laws and can sometimes be unlawful if it creates a market monopoly or facilitates other noncompetitive outcomes. While the text of the Patent Act gives the patentee the power to sue infringers,[90] or people who violate the patent's boundaries, nothing confers the power to use transfers to create market monopolies.

Consistent with the Patent Act, a digital platform just as any other licensee should have broad power to acquire *non*-exclusive rights to acquired patents and other IP rights, but not the right to acquire exclusive rights if the effect is to create, enlarge, or strengthen a market monopoly. That enlargement does not flow from issuance of the patent by rather from its subsequent transfer to someone who is in a position to use it anticompetitively.

That leaves two questions: what about the smaller firm's objection that a non-exclusive right to a patent is worth much less than an exclusive right; second, should this rule apply in all cases?

---

89 35 U.S.C. § 261.

90 *See* 35 U.S.C. § 271.

On the first question, yes, limiting the platform's acquisition of a smaller firm to a non-exclusive right will reduce the value of the smaller firm's IP rights, and in the process very likely the acquisition value of the smaller firm itself. However, this value is not one that the acquired firm's owners are entitled to have. Indeed, if any merger threatens the creation of market power, the purchaser will be willing to pay a premium above the value of the acquired firm's productive assets that reflects the amount of market power that the merger creates. This is actually a well-known attribute of the social cost of monopoly. For example, if creation of a monopoly promises increased value of, say, $1,000, a prospective acquirer will be willing to spend any amount up to $1,000 to acquire it.[91] The same reasoning also applies to cartels. Selling an asset in such a way that the purchasing firm will now be able to form or enforce a cartel definitely increases value, but one principle of the antitrust laws is that firms are not entitled to the value that price-fixing creates.

It is also not the case that this is part of the "value" that the smaller firm has created. That value is the amount that its assets would be worth in a competitive market in which they are being put to full productive use. It is not the value of increased monopoly that results from the way that asset might potentially be combined with other assets.

The other question is when should the non-exclusive license rule apply. Not universally. Here, one important principle is that patents can be shared but ordinarily tactile products cannot be. For example, forcing Amazon to accept a "non-exclusive" right to the Whole Foods stores that it acquired would be unworkable and undoubtedly would have killed that transaction. Likewise, limiting acquisitions to non-exclusive rights in pharmaceuticals may not work. In that case the scope of the product may be very little more than the scope of the patent that covers it.

Here the ordinary rules of market definition may be all that is necessary. For example, suppose a larger firm has a patented product Alpha, which is highly valuable but perhaps its patent will expire in a few years. It then acquires a firm whose product, Beta, is a therapeutic substitute for Alpha, sufficiently close that physicians will prescribe them interchangeably. In such a case the conventional approach of placing Alpha and Beta into the same product market – perhaps making this a merger to monopoly – should provide a sufficient rationale. If it does not, then there is something wrong with the way we go about defining markets.

But that may be just another way of saying that the acquisitions of a pharmacy company is not necessarily aimed at its intellectual property right, but rather at the product[s] that the acquired firm is developing. That is what makes a remedy limiting acquisitions to a non-exclusive right much more promising when the principal target of the acquisition is intellectual property.

91 *See e.g.*, Richard A. Posner, *The Social Costs of Monopoly and Regulation*, 83 J. Pol. Econ. 807 (1975).

V. Conclusion

The future of competition policy involving digital platforms undoubtedly includes much more research and scholarship concerning how they work, what is good about them, and what are the competitive dangers that they pose. Pending that, there is little reason for antitrust policy to veer too far off the course it applies in other markets. This is not to say, of course, that this current course could not benefit from substantial correction, but only that most of the corrections should be more general and not limited to the digital economy.

Most importantly, we should not be selecting digital platforms for singular hostile treatment without good in return except loss of both competitive output and innovation. The previously referenced chain store episode in the United States presents a sobering reality, in which firms that were displaced by new innovations in distribution gained the upper hand politically and were able to do considerable damage in the name of antitrust law.

Proving Competition Violations under EU Law: Legal Approach and Economic Reasoning

FRÉDÉRIC JENNY*

ESSEC Business School, Paris

OECD Competition Committee

Abstract

This chapter analyzes the probatory mechanism in EU competition law resulting from the EU Commission decisions and the EU court practices. We review different aspects of this mechanism such as legal tests, treatment of direct and indirect evidence, allocation of the burden of proof, standard of proof, and evidentiary requirements and discuss how they relate to economic reasoning. We then focus on the use of different types of presumptions in EU competition law and consider whether they are justified from an economic standpoint. Finally, we discuss recent debates in the EU courts on the evidentiary requirements and the standards of proof with respect to antitrust and merger control. We analyze the extent to which the courts have hesitantly moved away from a formalistic approach to competition law enforcement and have shown some willingness to raise the bar with respect to the economic evidence required to establish a violation of competition law or to object to a merger.

---

* Professor of Economics at ESSEC Business School in Paris; Chairman of the OECD Competition Committee.

The goals of competition laws are not always explicit nor easy to reconstruct. Furthermore, competition law provisions are, in general, cast in such general terms that they leave a lot of room for interpretation by competition law enforcers and courts. As a result, similar provisions can be interpreted very differently from one jurisdiction to the next and a given set of provisions can be interpreted very differently across time in the same jurisdiction.

In order to assess the effectiveness, intensity, cost and predictability of the enforcement of competition law, one has to go beyond the letter of the law and consider the legal test which will be applied to establish a violation, the standard of proof which will have to be met to satisfy the legal test, the allocation of the burden of proof between the parties to the proceedings and the presumptions which may be used to simplify the analysis.

The effectiveness of the law will be a function of the adequacy of its goals (explicit or perceived) and the legal test; the intensity of the enforcement will be a function of the legal test and the standard of proof; the cost of enforcement will be a function of the allocation of the burden of proof among the parties and the use of valid presumptions to simplify the burden of proof; and the predictability of the enforcement will be a function of the consistency with which the legal test and the standard of proof are applied.

This chapter analyzes the probatory mechanism in EU competition law resulting from EU Commission decisions and EU court practices. We review different aspects of this mechanism and discuss how they relate to economic reasoning: legal tests, treatment of direct and indirect evidence, allocation of the burden of proof, standard of proof, and evidentiary requirements. We then focus on the use of different types of presumptions in EU competition law and consider what trade-offs they imply from an economic standpoint. Finally, we discuss recent debates in the EU courts on the evidentiary requirements and the standards of proof with respect to antitrust and merger control. We analyze the extent to which the courts have hesitantly moved away from a formalistic approach to competition law enforcement and have shown some willingness to raise the bar with respect to the economic evidence required to establish a violation of competition law or to object to a merger.

I. Legal Test

If the legal test does not fit the goals (explicit or assumed) of competition law, either because it is too strict or because it is not strict enough, the law will not be effective.

Two possible costs for society will be associated with this lack of effectiveness. One possible cost (associated with what economists call a type I error) is that some behaviors or transactions that the law meant to prohibit will be allowed (such a circumstance is, for example, at the heart of the criticism of the Chicago school approach by the Neo-Brandeisians in the US and their denunciation of the fact that competition authorities have used such a narrow legal merger test that they have not been able to stem the merger wave initiated by large digital platforms). The other possible cost (associated with what economists call a type II error) is that some behaviors or transactions that the law meant to allow will be prohibited (such a circumstance is at the heart of the criticism of the EU Commission decision blocking the Alstom Siemens merger[1] criticized by French minister Bruno Lemaire and German minister Peter Altmaier). In many cases controversies over the legal test used by competition law enforcers come from disagreements over the interpretation of the goals of competition law.

The competition statutes are very general.

Article 101 of the Treaty on the Functioning of the European Union (TFEU) prohibits "as incompatible with the internal market: all agreements between undertakings, decisions by associations of undertakings and concerted practices which may affect trade between Member States and which have as their object or effect the prevention, restriction or distortion of competition within the internal market."

Article 102 of the TFEU prohibits "any abuse by one or more undertakings of a dominant position within the internal market or in a substantial part of it shall be prohibited as incompatible with the internal market in so far as it may affect trade between Member States.

Such abuse may, in particular, consist of:

1. directly or indirectly imposing unfair purchase or selling prices or other unfair trading conditions;
2. limiting production, markets or technical development to the prejudice of consumers;
3. applying dissimilar conditions to equivalent transactions with other trading parties, thereby placing them at a competitive disadvantage;
4. making the conclusion of contracts subject to acceptance by the other parties of supplementary obligations which, by their nature or according to commercial usage, have no connection with the subject of such contracts".

There is not a unique legal test in EU competition law used by the courts to enforce these articles as Ibanez Colomo (2019)[2] has shown.

---

1 Commission Decision of June 2, 2019 Declaring a Concentration to Be Incompatible with the Internal Market and the Functioning of the EEA Agreement Case M.8677 (*Siemens/Alstom*), *see* Thomas Oster, *The EU Commission prohibits a railway merger due to very significant overlaps in the companies' activities in the fields of railway signalling and very high-speed trains and the risk of creating a dominant position (Siemens / Alstom)*, E-COMPETITIONS February 2019, art. No. 97918.

2 Pablo Ibáñez Colomo, *Legal tests in EU Competition Law: Taxonomy and Operation*, LSE LAW SCHOOL (May 27, 2019) https://papers.ssrn.com/sol3/papers.cfm?abstract_id=3394889.

Some practices are subject to a qualified prohibition in the sense that they are deemed unlawful without it being necessary to assess their effects. Examples with respect to Article 101 TFEU would be price or market sharing agreements between competitors and with respect to Article 102 TFEU would be predatory pricing. The prohibition of such practices, however, is qualified in the sense that the parties can bring forward evidence showing that, even though their practice is caught either by Article 101(1) or 102 TFEU, it fulfils the conditions laid down in Article 101(3) TFEU or has an "objective justification" (such as protecting or enhancing a public interest, defending the dominant company's commercial interests and/or generating efficiencies that would otherwise not be realised but for the conduct in question) for the practices examined under Article 102.

In extreme cases of practices deemed unlawful and those deemed lawful (such as, for example, quantity rebates by dominant firms) there are practices which are subject to a legality rule and will be found to violate Articles 101 or 102 TFEU, only if it is shown that not only have they been implemented, but that they have, or are likely to have, a negative impact on competition in the specific context in which they are implemented. An Article 101 example would include exclusive dealing arrangements and Article 102 would include quantity rebates or margin squeeze.

Finally there are practices for which the effect analysis does not, alone, suffice to establish liability. Those practices are closer to practices that are deemed lawful. In those cases, an enhanced effect analysis is necessary to establish their illegality. For example, the refusal to deal by a vertically integrated dominant player can be a violation of Article 102 only if it is established that it denied access to an input indispensable for non-integrated competitors to be able to compete with the dominant firm in a downstream market[3]. In the case of refusal to deal with respect to intellectual property rights, it must also be shown that the refusal to deal prevented the emergence of a new product for which there was a potential demand[4].

The existence of competition violations for which it is not necessary to assess the effects of the practices (object violations) is one of the characteristics of EU competition law and the source of controversy which we will address in more details in the following sections of this chapter.

The qualification of a practice as a violation by object has three consequences. First, it simplifies the burden of proof for the competition authority alleging such

---

3 Case C–7/97, Oscar Bronner GmbH & Co. KG v. Mediaprint Zeitungs- und Zeitschriftenverlag GmbH & Co. KG, Mediaprint Zeitungsvertriebsgesellschaft mbH & Co. KG and Mediaprint Anzeigengesellschaft mbH & Co. KG, ECLI:EU:C:1998:569, *see* European Court of Justice, *The EU Court of Justice holds that refusing access to a rival for a newspaper home delivery service does not amount to an abuse of a dominant position (Oscar Bronner)*, e-Competitions November 1998, art. No. 108303.

4 Joined Cases C–241 & C–242/91 P, Radio Telefis Eireann (RTE) and Independent Television Publications Ltd (ITP) v. Commission of the European Communities, EU:C:1995:98, (Magill), *see* European Court of Justice, *The EU Court of Justice upholds that the ownership of patents, trademarks and other intellectual property rights may constitute barriers to entry depending on their strength and duration without conferring themselves dominance (RTE / ITP)*, e-Competitions April 1995, art. No. 106483.

a violation since it does not have to prove that the practice had any effect on the market. Second, it shifts the burden of proof to the undertaking alleged to have violated Article 101. Third, it restricts the possibilities of defense by the undertaking alleged to have committed such a violation since the undertaking cannot argue that the practice had no anticompetitive effect on the market. However, the party alleged to have entered into a practice which violates Article 101 by object can argue that the practice should have been exempted under Article 101(3).

The controversy surrounding the presumption of violation by objects of Article 101 TFEU comes from the fact that, first, courts have not established a precise list of practices which would constitute violation by objects, second, that the courts have not provided consistent criteria to define what a violation by object could be, and, third, at least until the 2014 in the *Groupement des cartes bancaires (CB)* judgment,[5] the European courts allowed an extensive interpretation of the presumption of violation by object which gave the EU Commission (and national competition authorities) a considerable amount of discretion in deciding when a violation is a violation by object and, therefore, when the effect of the practice is irrelevant.

It is still not entirely clear whether and under which conditions a hardcore practice (such as price fixing or market sharing) can escape the qualification of violation by object and, conversely, under which conditions a non-hardcore practice can qualify as a violation by object. The main reason for this ambiguity is that the European courts (the European Court of Justice (ECJ) and the General Court) and the EU Commission have stated that to qualify as an object violation, the practice must exhibit a high potential of serious harm to competition on the basis of the nature of the restriction it implies or of experience and have also expressed the view that to make this assessment the context in which the agreement is applied and the behavior of the parties on the market should also be considered.

While this approach has allowed the concept of object violations to be extensively used by the Commission (and by EU national competition authorities), it has also blurred the lines between an object violation and an effect violation.

II. Direct and Indirect Evidence

The "new economic approach" to antitrust enforcement adopted by the Commission in the early 2000s (cf., for example, the Guidance Paper on Exclusionary Abuses of Dominance[6]), started from the (economic) premise

5 *See* Case C-67/13 P, Groupement des cartes bancaires (CB) v. European Commission, EU:C:2014:2204.

6 Commission Comm'n, Guidance on the Commission's enforcement priorities in applying Article 82 of the EC Treaty to abusive exclusionary conduct by dominant undertakings, https://eur-lex.europa.eu/LexUriServ/LexUriServ.do?uri=OJ:C:2009:045:0007:0020:EN:PDF, *see* Dominique Ferré & Karine Biancone, *Exclusionary practices : The European Commission publishes its "guidance" on the application of the EC Treaty*

that a given practice by a firm having market power could have anticompetitive effects in some contexts and be neutral or pro-competitive in other contexts. This new economic approach was therefore an attempt by the EU Commission to move toward a more generalized use of case-by-case analysis of the economic context in which the conducts of dominant firms being examined were implemented.

One of the consequences of such a move was to significantly increase the scope of potential cases for which the question of whether the Commission has met its "standard of proof" became an important issue. This is partly due to the fact that assessing a practice in the economic context in which it has been implemented requires the use of economic reasoning which is speculative and based on hypothesis. The task of the Commission to prove beyond any doubt in the mind of the court that a practice by a dominant firm is anticompetitive can thus be a daunting exercise. However, as we shall see, the Commission and the courts are able to bypass the difficulties associated with meeting the standard of proof to establish facts or the existence of an illegal practice by resorting to presumptions.

As the courts have mentioned, there are two possible approaches for proving a violation of competition law. First are the cases where the reasoning of the Commission is that the facts established cannot be explained other than by an anticompetitive behavior. Second are the cases where the violation is proven by the evidence adduced by the party claiming that there has been a violation.

An example of the first type of case would be where a firm holding a dominant position is accused of price predation because it sold at a price below some measure of its variable cost. In such a case, the reasoning of the Commission is that since no profit-maximizing undertaking would accept losses by selling at a price below its variable costs, the only possible explanation for such a behavior is that the undertaking is trying to eliminate existing competition or discourage potential competition.

In such cases, as stated by the General Court in its second *Intel* judgment of 2020,[7] "the EU Courts will find it necessary to annul the decision in question where those undertakings put forward arguments which cast the facts established by the Commission in a different light and which thus allow another plausible explanation of the facts to be substituted for the one adopted by the Commission in concluding that an infringement occurred. In such a case, it cannot be

---

rules against abuses of dominant positions (Art. 82) to exclusionary practices by dominant undertakings, CONCURRENCES No. 2-2009, art. No. 29593.

7 Case T–286/09 RENV, Intel Corp. Inc. v. European Commission, ECLI:EU:T:2022:19, at ¶ 166, *see* Wessel Geursen & Helen Gornall, *The EU General Court annuls a fine of EUR 1.06M against a semiconductor chip manufacturing company based on economic evidence (Intel)*, E-COMPETITIONS January 2022, art. No. 106033.

considered that the Commission has adduced proof of an infringement of competition law."[8]

The second type of case (where the violation is proven by evidence adduced by the party claiming that there has been a violation) can be divided into two sub-groups. In the first sub-group are cases where a violation is proven by direct evidence such as, for example, where the evidence produced to prove the existence of a cartel is the minutes of a meeting of the competitors agreeing to fix prices. In the second sub-group are cases where the violation is proven by indirect evidence (or by a combination of direct and indirect evidence).

The first sub-group is the group of cases with which the Commission and the courts feel most comfortable. However, as competition law becomes better known and gains prominence, economic agents become more aware of the fact that competition authorities will be looking first for direct evidence of competition violations and they become better at suppressing them.

As a result, circumstantial or indirect evidence is used to significant effect in most jurisdictions for all types of cases. For example, with respect to horizontal cases, unlike price fixing, pure price parallelism among competitors is not sufficient to qualify as a competition violation as it could result from the undertaking's independent profit maximization. However, additional circumstantial evidence can reveal that a price parallelism is, in fact, the result of a tacit agreement or of an explicit agreement for which direct proof is lacking. Such indirect evidence can come from economic reasoning. For example, if a series of parallel and simultaneous price increases occurs at a time of over-production or declining aggregate demand while the costs are stable or declining, it is unlikely to be the result of a competitive adjustment as, barring a collective agreement, each competitor has an incentive to reduce prices (rather than increasing them). Indirect evidence can also come from other circumstantial evidence (such as, the fact that the competitors met the day before each of the price increases).

Economic evidence used in horizontal cases can be either structural evidence (such as the fact that the market is highly concentrated, that there are high barriers to entry, that the opposite side of the market is unconcentrated, and/or that the product is homogeneous) or conduct evidence (such as, suspicious bidding patterns in public tenders, simultaneity in price increases, abnormally high profits, stable market shares, a history of competition law violations, and communication between the parties). Information exchanges, price signalling, freight equalization,

8 *See*, to that effect, Case 29 and 30/83, Compagnie Royale Asturienne Des Mines SA and Rheinzink v. European Commission, ECLI:EU:C:1984:130, at ¶ 16, *see* European Court of Justice, *The EU Court of Justice states that a change in the legal form and name of an undertaking does not create a new undertaking free of liability for the anti-competitive behaviour of its predecessor, when, two are identical (Compagnie Royale Asturienne des Mines / Rheinzink)*, E-COMPETITIONS March 1984, art. No. 107003, and Case C–89, C–104, C–114, C–116, C–117 & C–125 to C–129/85, Ahlström Osakeyhtiö v. European Commission, ECLI:EU:C:1993:120, at ¶¶ 126 and 127.

price protection and most favored nation policies or unnecessarily restrictive product standards are subsets of circumstantial evidence.

In order to facilitate the task of the Commission, the European courts (like courts in a number of foreign jurisdictions) accept that[9] the evidentiary elements produced should be examined in a holistic way, like pieces of a jig-saw puzzle.

It is not necessary for every item of evidence produced by the Commission to satisfy those criteria (i.e., precision and consistency to support the firm conviction that the alleged infringement took place) in relation to every aspect of the infringement. It is sufficient if the body of evidence relied on by that institution, viewed as a whole, meets that requirement, as is stated in the case-law concerning the implementation of Article 101 TFEU.[10] That principle also applies in cases concerning the implementation of Article 102 TFEU.[11]

III. Burden of Proof

The allocation of the burden of proof determines which party must put forward the facts and, where necessary, adduce the related evidence.

A distinction should be made between the legal burden of proof and the evidentiary burden of proof.

With regard to the legal burden of proof, under EU law, it is up to the party alleging an infringement (for example, the Commission) to prove that a given practice is contrary to Article 101(1). The ECJ stated in its *Aalborg* judgment:[12]

> 78. As the Council very recently stated in the fifth recital of Regulation (EC) No 1/2003 of 16 December 2002 on the implementation of the rules on competition laid down in Articles 81 and 82 of the Treaty (OJ 200 3 L 1, p. 1), it should be for the party or

9 *See* C–613/13 P, European Commission v. Keramag Keramische Werke, ECLI:EU:C:2017:49, at ¶ 52, *see* Etienne Thomas, *Fine: The European Court of Justice dismisses almost all the appeal brought against the judgments of the General Court of the European Union pronounced in the Bathroom fittings and fixtures markets cartel case and upholds two of them, considering that the General Court of the European Union erred in law in applying the 10% fines cap and in assessing the conclusive force of evidences in leniency applications (Aloys F. Dornbracht; Duravit; Hansa Metallwerke; Keramag Keramische Werke; Masco; Zucchetti Rubinetteria; Mamoli Robinetteria; Villeroy & Bosch AG; Villeroy & Bosch Austria; Roca Sanitario; Laufen Austria; Roca; Villeroy & Bosch Belgium; Villeroy & Bosch France)*, CONCURRENCES No. 2-2017, art. No. 83863, pp. 86–88.

10 Case T–385/06, Aalberts Industries NV and Others v European Commission, ECLI:EU:T:2011:114.

11 Case T–321/05, AstraZeneca v. European Commission, ECLI:EU:T:2010:266, at ¶ 477, *see* Jonas Koponen et al., *The EU General Court upholds "novel" approach to abuse of dominance in pivotal pharma appeal (AstraZeneca)*, E-COMPETITIONS July 2010, art. No. 41073.

12 Joined Cases C–204, C–205, C–211, C–213, C–217 & C–219/00 P, Aalborg Portland A/S v. Commission of the European Communities, ECLI:EU:C:2002:337, *see* European Court of Justice, *The EU Court of Justice upholds the judgment of the General Court in the cement cartel case and sets fines of €53.6 million (Aalborg Portland / Irish Cement / Ciments français / Italcementi / Buzzi Unicem / Cementir)*, E-COMPETITIONS January 2004, art. No. 93537.

> the authority alleging an infringement of the competition rules to prove the existence thereof and it should be for the undertaking or association of undertakings invoking the benefit of a defence against a finding of an infringement to demonstrate that the conditions for applying such defence are satisfied, so that the authority will then have to resort to other evidence.

Whereas these principles apply across the board, the ECJ stated in the previously mentioned *Aalborg* judgment that the allocation of the evidentiary burden of proof may be more complex. It stated:

> 79. Although according to those principles the legal burden of proof is borne either by the Commission or by the undertaking or association concerned, the factual evidence on which a party relies may be of such a kind as to require the other party to provide an explanation or justification, failing which it is permissible to conclude that the burden of proof has been discharged. The factual evidence on which a party relies may be of such a kind as to require the other party to provide an explanation or justification, failing which it is permissible to conclude that the burden of proof has been discharged.

The cost of enforcement is partly determined by the allocation of the burden of proof between the parties.

The allocation of the burden of proof is designed to minimize the cost of enforcement by ensuring that the party which has the burden of a proof is best placed to provide this proof, for example because it has a better access to the relevant information than the other parties or the competition authority. This is allegedly because firms are best placed to determine the existence and magnitude of the possible efficiency gains from an agreement or a merger transaction that the parties to this agreement or merger bear the burden of proof that their agreement should be exempted.

Recently in various jurisdictions there have been concerns about the apparent inability of competition authorities to block some mergers in dynamic sectors (primarily the pharmaceutical sector and digital sectors). Equally, there has been a concern about some mergers which do not meet the thresholds of merger control but might nevertheless raise competition concerns in those sectors. It is alleged, that such mergers between a very large pharmaceutical firm or a digital platform and start-ups could, under certain circumstances, lead to a decrease in competition even when the target has a very limited turnover in the jurisdiction because the acquiring firm may be tempted post-merger to either discontinue the activity or the acquired firm's research effort to shelter itself from competition or to decrease its own level of activity or R&D so as not to cannibalize the acquired firm's product or R&D efforts.

Alarmed by what they consider to be the inability of competition authorities to effectively establish that such mergers are anticompetitive and may reduce the rate of innovation, some authors have proposed lowering the threshold of scrutiny of mergers in those sectors and/or to reverse the legal and evidentiary burden of proof for the merger parties by creating a rebuttable presumption that such mergers are anticompetitive.[13] The parties to these mergers would have to prove that their mergers were not anticompetitive (or contributed to economic progress). Thus shifting the burden of proof can be a tactic used by public policy makers to overcome the difficulties raised by the exacting nature of the standard of proof.

IV. Standards of Proof and Evidentiary Requirement

The standard of proof determines the requirements which must be satisfied for facts to be regarded by the competition authority or the courts as proven.

Understanding the standard of proof applied by the court or competition authority to assess whether the legal test has been met is crucially important for the parties to formulate relevant arguments and to predict competition law enforcement outcomes. A high standard of proof may result, *ceteris paribus*, in fewer convictions and possibly a less deterrent system (if potential violators are more sensitive to the risk of being found guilty than to the severity of the sanction) but one which minimizes the costs of erroneously finding that a pro-competitive practice or transaction is anticompetitive (type I errors).

Having a clearly established standard of proof (and a consistent application of this) is also important to the legal predictability of the enforcement mechanism.

In common law systems, the standards of proof generally applied are: "beyond a reasonable doubt" (approaching 100% certainty for criminal matters) and "balance of probabilities" sometimes referred to as "preponderance of evidence" (met in civil cases if there is at least a 51% chance that the allegation is true). An intermediate standard of proof would be the "clear and convincing evidence" standard which is more demanding than the balance of probabilities but less exacting than the "beyond a reasonable doubt" standard.

In civil law systems such standards are generally ignored and the judges (or the competition authorities) discretionarily evaluate the evidence. In such systems the parties have to convince the judge of the existence of facts relevant to their argument and sufficiently convincing to satisfy their "intime conviction".

---

13 Tommaso Valletti, *How to Tame the Tech Giants: Reverse the Burden of Proof in Merger Reviews*, *ProMarket*, (Univ. of Chicago Booth Stigler Center, June 28, 2021), https://www.promarket.org/2021/06/28/tech-block-merger-review-enforcement-regulators/.

Gippini-Fournier (2010)[14] stated: "Inquiring about the applicable 'standard of proof' in EU law is an immediate reflex for lawyers from common law jurisdictions" but *that* "discussion of 'standards of proof' in EU competition cases runs the risk of reasoning from categories which lose much of their sense outside the common law." He further observed that in civil law jurisdictions the question: "how much evidence is required before a judge can conclude that a party has met its burden of proof does not typically receive an ex ante abstract answer in terms of probability."

With respect to Articles 101 and 102 TFEU, for example, the EU courts have repeatedly said that: "any doubt in the mind of the Court must operate to the advantage of the undertaking" to which the decision finding an infringement was addressed. The Court cannot therefore conclude that the Commission has established the infringement at issue to the requisite legal standard if it still entertains any doubts on that point, in particular in proceedings for annulment of a decision imposing a fine."[15] In order to discharge its burden of proof to the requisite legal standard, the Commission must produce "sufficiently precise and consistent evidence to support the firm conviction that the alleged infringement took place." As is obvious, none of those pronouncements tell us what the level of proof is that will convince the courts.

Finally Gippini-Fournier (2010) is of the view that the standard of proof defined with respect to the probability of finding a violation is, in any case, a poor predictor of the evidentiary requirements of the parties.

He makes the valid point that it is worth investigating the factors which: "play a role in the court's assessment of factual evidence and which determine where the standard is along the continuous sliding scale, which is the intime conviction." He suggests that three factors are important to understand the courts requirements: "First, the courts appear to distinguish between evidence of actions and evidence of their consequences. Second, the judge's prior views on economic 'normality' affect the assessment of the evidence. Third, an implicit analysis of 'error costs' may explain the differing degrees of scrutiny applied in different situations".

With respect to the distinction between the behavior by companies and the consequences of their behavior, the European courts seem to apply a higher level of exigency (a standard of proof similar to beyond a reasonable doubt) with respect to the factual assessment of companies' conduct than the issues of the

14 Eric Gippini-Fournier, *The Elusive Standard of Proof in EU Competition Cases*, 33 World Competition 187 (2010), https://papers.ssrn.com/sol3/papers.cfm?abstract_id=1433744.

15 *See*, for example, Case T–67, T–68, T–71 & T–78/00, JFE Engineering v. European Commission, ECLI:EU:T:2004:221, at ¶ 177, *see* General Court of the European Union, *The EU General Court reduces the fines on steel tube producers and clarifies the Commission's powers in the context of the geographical scope of infringement (JFE / Nippon / Sumitomo)*, e-Competitions July 2004, art. No. 93911. Case T–112/07, Hitachi v. European Commission, EU:T:2011:342, at ¶ 58, *see* Richard Burton, *The EU General Court partially annuls fines imposed on Japanese participants in gas-insulated switchgear cartel (Hitachi / Toshiba / Mitsubishi / Fuji)*, e-Competitions July 2011, art. No. 41081. Case T–286/09 RENV, Intel Corp., Inc. v. European Commission, ECLI:EU:T:2014:547, at ¶ 161.

causal relationship between the conduct and its consequences as well as whether the conduct amounts to an infringement of competition law (for which the courts seem to use a reasonable probability standard). Such a distinction in the standard of proof could be explained, both by a specific concern of the courts to respect the principles of personal responsibility and presumption of innocence and by the fact that the causal relationship between the conduct and its consequences and its qualification as a competition violation can usually be assessed only through inferences from imprecise and incomplete information.

With respect to the judge's prior view, the evidentiary requirements placed on the parties is a function of the level of scepticism of the judge which itself is determined by his or her concept of "normality" whatever the standard of proof used. As Lord Hoffmann explained in a well know appellate judgment:[16]

> 55. [....] some things are inherently more likely than others. [...] it would need more cogent evidence to satisfy one that the creature seen walking in Regent's Park was more likely than not to have been a lioness than to be satisfied to the same standard of probability that it was an Alsatian. In this basis, cogent evidence is generally required to satisfy a civil tribunal that a person has been fraudulent or behaved in some other reprehensible manner. But the question is always whether the tribunal thinks it more probable than not. This does not mean that the standard of proof is different.

Thus the judge's prior view as to what is to be expected will determine the evidentiary requirement on the parties. In some cases where judges have very strong views about normality, these views have been translated into legal presumptions (to be analyzed in the next section). This raises the question of how judges acquired their prior views which determines the level of evidentiary requirements for the parties. Having competition law judges who have some economic expertise means that their prior views will be better aligned with the economic reasoning.

Finally, with respect to the error costs, Gippini-Fournier suggests that: "[...] the Court's approach to evidence may reflect a conscious trade-off between the different rights and interests at stake, between the incentives and disincentives that a judgment may entail, for the parties to the instant case and for society as a whole. Many factors may come into play in this assessment of 'error costs': for example, the severity of the encroachment on individual rights or legitimate expectations; the possible 'chilling effect' on neutral, benign or even outright desirable conduct. This broad conception of 'error cost management' may be a singularly strong explanatory factor in the EU Courts' approach to the level of evidence required in competition cases."

---

16 *See* Case Secretary of State for the Home Department v. Rehman (AP) [2001] UKHL 47, [2000] 3 WLR 1240, at ¶ 55.

This could explain why the courts have a lesser threshold of exigency in merger analysis (where there is no absolute right to merge) than in antitrust (where the finding of a violation on the basis of little evidence may entail a breach of the legal principles of personal responsibility and presumption of innocence).

V. Rebuttable Presumptions

A presumption can be defined as the belief that something is true even though it has not been proven. The use of presumptions alleviates the burden of proof for a party by allowing the party to claim that a fact is established even if it is not proven and/or by shifting the burden of proof onto the other party.

Presumptions may come from the provisions of primary or secondary laws but they may also be created by the case law of the courts.

Three forms of presumptions are usually identified: procedural, evidentiary, and substantive.

With few exceptions, presumptions used in competition law are rebuttable and the law or jurisprudence may state the burden of proof on a party to rebut a presumption. Although the European courts have stated that it may be difficult to rebut a presumption (or that a presumption has never been successfully rebutted) this does not mean that the presumption is not a rebuttable presumption.

One exception to the principle that competition law presumptions are rebuttable can be found in the EU competition law Directive 2014/104 of 26 November 2014.[17] Article 9 of the Directive provides that, when an infringement has been found by a competition authority, it must be considered as: "irrefragably established for the purposes of an action for [reparation]." In the next section, we will discuss another example of non-rebuttable presumptions which comes from the recently adopted Digital Market Act (DMA).[18]

1. Procedural Presumptions

Procedural presumptions are an instrument to allocate the burden of bringing arguments and evidence, to structure the process and analysis, to make complex issues more administrable, and competition enforcement effective.[19]

17 Directive 2014/104 of the European Parliament and of the Council of Nov. 26, 2014, on certain rules governing actions for damages under national law for infringements of the competition law provisions of the Member States and of the European Union Text with EEA relevance 2014 O.J. (L 349).

18 Regulation 2022/1925 of the European Parliament and of the Council of Sept. 14, 2022 on contestable and fair markets in the digital sector and amending Directives 2019/1937 and 2020/1828 (Digital Markets Act) 2022 O.J. (L 265).

19 OECD Competition Committee, *Roundtable on Safe Harbours and Legal Presumptions in Competition Law – Note by the European Union*, (Dec. 5, 2017).

The best known example of a procedural presumption in European law is the presumption of innocence, which constitutes a general principle of EU law, laid down by Article 48(1) of the Charter of Fundamental Rights of the European Union.[20] In addition, according to ECJ case law, the principle of the presumption of innocence applies to procedures relating to infringements of the competition rules applicable to undertakings that may result in the imposition of fines or periodic penalty payments.[21]

As an application of the presumption of innocence, Article 2 Regulation 1/2003 states that: "In any national or Community proceedings for the application of Articles 81 and 82 of the Treaty, the burden of proving an infringement of Article 81(1) or of Article 82 of the Treaty shall rest on the party or the authority alleging the infringement. The undertaking or association of undertakings claiming the benefit of Article 81(3) of the Treaty shall bear the burden of proving that the conditions of that paragraph are fulfilled."

As mentioned by the EU Commission in its contribution to the OECD Competition Committee Roundtable on Presumptions and Safe Harbours:[22] "In several cases, the ECJ has ruled that the burden of proving a particular point does not rule out the possibility of burden-shifting: 'the factual evidence on which a party relies may be of such a kind as to require the other party to provide an explanation or justification, failing which it is permissible to conclude that the burden of proof has been discharged [...]."

The situation with respect to antitrust violations is different from that regarding merger control. With respect to merger control there is no presumption that the parties engaged in an anticompetitive merger and it is up to the Commission to make either a positive or a negative decision on the merger.

Other procedural presumptions in EU law pertain to the burden of responding. For example, when a party misses the deadline for responding, it is presumed that its silence means agreement. Along those lines, if a complainant does not reply to a pre-rejection letter, the complaint is presumed (deemed) withdrawn.

Another example can be found in Article 16 Regulation 773/2004 relating to the conduct of proceedings pursuant to Articles 81 and 82 TEU.[23] This Article allows the Commission to require undertakings: "which produce documents or statements pursuant to Regulation (EC) No 1/2003 to identify the documents

---

20 *See* Case C–89/11 P, E. ON Energie v. European Commission, ECLI:EU:C:2012:738, at ¶ 72 and the case-law cited, *see* Emanuela Matei, *The EU Court of Justice rejects an appeal by the German energy company for failing to substantiate the reversed burden of proof and the allegedly incorrect assessment of the fines imposed for breaching a seal during an EU dawn raid (E. ON)*, e-Competitions November 2012, art. No. 50125.

21 *See id.*, at ¶ 73 and the case-law cited.

22 *See* OECD Competition Committee, *supra* note 18.

23 Commission Regulation 773/2004 of Apr. 7, 2004 relating to the conduct of proceedings by the Commission pursuant to Articles 81 and 82 of the EC Treaty 2004 O.J. (L 123).

or parts of documents which they consider to contain business secrets or other confidential information belonging to them and to identify the undertakings with regard to which such documents are to be considered confidential." The Article provides that: "The Commission may set a time-limit within which the undertakings and associations of undertakings are to: (a) substantiate their claim for confidentiality with regard to each individual document or part of document, statement or part of statement; (b) provide the Commission with a non-confidential version of the documents or statements, in which the confidential passages are deleted; (c) provide a concise description of each piece of deleted information". Paragraph 4 of the Article states that: "If undertakings or associations of undertakings fail to comply with paragraphs 2 and 3, the Commission may assume that the documents or statements concerned do not contain confidential information."

Procedural presumptions pertaining to the burden of responding can also constrain the European Commission and be to the benefit of the parties. For example, Article 10(6) Regulation 139/2004 states that: "Where the Commission has not taken a decision in accordance with Article 6(1)(b), (c), 8(1), (2) or (3) within the time limits set in paragraphs 1 and 3 respectively, the concentration shall be deemed to have been declared compatible with the common market, without prejudice to Article 9."[24] Article 7 Regulation139/2004, regarding merger decisions, refers to "the presumption established in Article 10(6)."

2. Evidentiary Presumptions

The second type of presumption used in competition law is that of evidentiary presumption.

First, an evidentiary presumption is an inference drawn regarding an unknown fact based upon a known fact. Such an inference may be drawn from past experience (or economic reasoning) showing that, with a high probability, the unknown fact is observed when the known fact is established.

A frequently quoted example of an evidentiary presumption in EU law is the parental liability presumption where the courts and the Commission derive from the fact that a firm owns all of the shares of a subsidiary, that it exercises a decisive influence over this subsidiary, and that it has therefore parental liability.

As the ECJ stated in *Akzo Nobel*:[25] "it is sufficient for the Commission to prove that the subsidiary is wholly owned by the parent company in order to presume

---

24 *See* Cyril Ritter, *Presumptions in EU Competition Law*, (EC Directorate-General for Competition, 2017), https://papers.ssrn.com/sol3/papers.cfm?abstract_id=2999638.

25 Case C–97/08 P, Akzo Nobel NV v. Commission of the European Communities, ECLI:EU:C:2009:536, at ¶ 61, *see* Alexandre Lacresse, *Liability between parent company and subsidiary: The Court of Justice of the European Union excludes the benefit to a parent company of the limitation period expired vis-à-vis its subsidiaries (Akzo Nobel)*, CONCURRENCES No. 3-2017, art. No. 84581, p. 132.

that the parent exercises a decisive influence over the commercial policy of the subsidiary." In the *Stora* case,[26] the ECJ held that it was for the parent company (as the appellant) to rebut the presumption of an exertion of decisive influence by adducing sufficient evidence.

In *Akzo Nobel*, AG Kokott[27] explained why, in her opinion, the parental liability presumption is justified and not contrary to the presumption of innocence when she stated:

> 73. Where, in a group of undertakings, the parent company holds 100% of the shares in its subsidiary, the parent company is [...] in a position to exercise decisive influence over its subsidiary. In fact, it then has the sole right to appoint the members of the subsidiary's management bodies, and it is not unusual for there to be personal interconnections between the two companies. Moreover, it follows from the 100% shareholding that the interests of other shareholders cannot play any part either in strategic decisions or in the day-to-day business of the subsidiary. There is thus complete coincidence of interests between the parent company and its wholly-owned subsidiary. In those circumstances, the obvious conclusion is that the subsidiary does not determine its own market conduct independently, but in accordance with the wishes of its parent company.[28]
>
> 74. Recourse to a presumption rule such as that under discussion here does not lead to a reversal of the burden of proof that would be incompatible with the presumption of innocence. On the contrary, only the standard of proof which must be satisfied when attributing responsibility under antitrust law as between a parent company and its subsidiary is being laid down. Since the parent company's 100% shareholding in its subsidiary supports prima facie the conclusion that decisive influence is actually being exercised, it is for the parent company to rebut precisely that conclusion, adducing cogent evidence to the contrary; failing this, that conclusion is adequate to discharge the burden of proof. In other words, there is an interplay between the respective burdens of adducing evidence prior to consideration of the objective burden of proof.

---

26 Case C–286/98 P, Stora Kopparbergs Bergslags AB v. Commission of the European Communities, EU:C:2000:630, (*Stora*), at ¶¶ 38 and 39, *see* European Court of Justice, *The EU Court of Justice rejects the appeal brought by producers of carton board in a cartel case (Cartonboard cartel)*, E-COMPETITIONS November 2000, art. No. 93913.

27 Opinion Of AG Kokott, C–97/08 P, Akzo Nobel NV v. Commission of the European Communities, EU:C:2009:262, *see* Richard Burton, *The ECJ Advocate General Kokott renders opinion on parent liability (Akzo)*, E-COMPETITIONS April 2009, art. No. 42859.

28 *See* Opinion of AG Kokott, *supra* note 26.

A further development with respect to the presumption of parental liability came in 2014. On April 2, 2014, the Commission fined twenty-six legal entities for their participation in a cartel in the high-voltage power cable sector. Relying on the *Akzo Nobel* parental liability doctrine that a parent company holding all or almost all of a subsidiary's capital is presumed to have exercised a decisive influence over the conduct of the subsidiary, the Commission found Goldman Sachs jointly and severally liable with its indirect subsidiary Prysmian for violating Article 101(1) TFEU. This was because Goldman Sachs held all of the voting rights in Prysmian despite holding less than all of the capital. On appeal, the General Court endorsed the Commission's approach and the ECJ confirmed that the General Court had been right in deciding that Goldman Sachs was presumed to have exercised decisive influence over the conduct of the Prysmian subsidiary – not due to the level of its holdings in Prysmian's capital, but because Goldman Sachs controlled all of the voting rights associated with Prysmian's shares during the entire infringement period, even after its shareholding decreased to between 84.4% and 91.1%.

Another factual presumption is that cartels which affect an entire EU Member State affect trade between EU Member countries and therefore are potential violations of Article 101 TFEU. The ECJ confirmed the analysis of the Court of First Instance in *Lombard Club*[29] by stating:

> 38. [...] the ECJ has already held that the fact that a cartel relates only to the marketing of products in a single Member State is not sufficient to preclude the possibility that trade between Member States might be affected. A cartel extending over the whole of the territory of a Member State has, by its very nature, the effect of reinforcing the partitioning of markets on a national basis, thus impeding the economic interpenetration which the EC Treaty is designed to bring about (Asnef-Equifaxand Administración del Estado, paragraph 37 and the case-law there cited).
>
> 39. It follows that, contrary to the appellants' assertion, the Court of First Instance was right, in paragraph 181 of the judgment under appeal, to take as the starting point of its reasoning of the existence of a strong presumption that trade between Member States is affected, going on to say that '[t]hat presumption can only be rebutted if an analysis of the characteristics of the agreement and its economic context demonstrates the contrary.

Another factual presumption frequently used in EU competition law enforcement is the presumption of cartel participation for firms which have met with their

29 Joined Cases C–125, C–133, C–135 & C–137/07 P, Erste Group Bank AG, (formerly Erste Bank der österreichischen Sparkassen AG) v. Commission of the European Communities, ECLI:EU:C:2007:648, *see* Richard Burton, *The EU Court of Justice dismisses an appeal by four Austrian banks against a CFI judgment which upheld a Commission decision that fined €124.6 million eight banks for their participation in a series of illicit agreements (Lombard club cartel)*, E-COMPETITIONS September 2009, art. No. 41739.

competitors in circumstances where prices were discussed. According to this presumption – also referred to as the "presumption of causal connection" – an undertaking is guilty of cartel participation if it has participated in concerting arrangements and it has remained active on the market, subject to proof to the contrary, which it is for the undertaking to adduce.

As stated by the OECD Competition Committee Background note for the roundtable on Safe Harbours and Presumptions:[30] "This presumption is justified by the likelihood that the undertaking will take into account the information obtained from its competitors to determine its market conduct. Although, when first established, the presumption was considered to apply especially for concertation which had occurred over a long period and on a regular basis, it is now clear from the case law that the presumption applies even if the concerted action is the result of a contact between the participating undertakings on a single occasion."

Another commonly applied evidentiary presumption is that of continuous infringement. One of the difficulties which competition authorities may face when they investigate a long-term cartel is that its scope, form and membership may have evolved over time. In such a case the Commission would face a high evidentiary burden if it had to prove the existence of a series of distinct anti-competitive agreements and/or concerted practices, and the parties involved in each one. Furthermore, it could be that the statute of limitation would apply to the first few anticompetitive agreements. If a set of agreements or concerted practices could be presumed to constitute a single infringement, the statute of limitation would run from the end of the infringement for the whole set of agreements or concerted practices.

To overcome these problems and simplify its evidentiary requirement, in the *Polypropylene* case[31] the Commission invented the concept of "single and continuous infringement." For this case, the Commission found that fifteen petrochemical producers had set up a complex system of informal contacts, meetings, price-fixing and market-sharing arrangements all aimed at controlling the price of polypropylene in Europe between 1977 and 1982. Instead of treating each instance of consultation as a separate infringement, the Commission considered that they were interlinked by their common goal and, therefore, had to be regarded as a "single continuous infringement." The Commission stated in its decision:

> 80. From 1977 the producers of polypropylene supplying the EEC have been party to a whole complex of schemes, arrangements and measures decided in the framework of a system of regular meetings and continuous contact.

30 *See* OECD Competition Committee, *supra* note 18.

31 Commission Decision of Apr. 23, 1986 relating to a proceeding under Article 85 of the EEC Treaty Case IV/31.149 (*Polypropylene*) 1986 O.J. (L 230).

> The overall plan of the producers was to meet and reach agreement upon specific matters, including at various times:
>
> – the fixing of target prices;
>
> – the modalities of price initiatives;
>
> – the sharing of markets according to annual quota schemes or volume targets;
>
> – at times where no definitive quota was in operation, temporary measures to control or monitor sales volumes, the exchange of detailed information on their individual activities of a kind normally considered a business secret so as to facilitate coordination of their behaviour.
>
> By reason of the regular contacts in an institutionalized system of meetings the arrangements of the producers were constantly modified, varied or updated so as to take account of changing conditions and market reactions.
>
> 81. The Commission considers that the whole complex of schemes and arrangements decided in the context of a system of regular and institutionalized meetings constituted a single continuing 'agreement' within the meaning of Article 85(1).
>
> 82. In the detailed working out of the overall plan express agreement was reached in many areas (individual price initiatives and annual quota schemes). In some cases the producers may not have reached a consensus on a definitive scheme, such as quotas for 1981 and 1982. However their adoption of stopgap measures including exchange of information and the monitoring of actual monthly sales against achievements in some previous reference period not only involves an express agreement to set up and operate such measures but also indicates an implied agreement to maintain as far as possible the respective positions of the producers.

The Court of First Instance (now the General Court) upheld the findings of the Commission and endorsed the "single continuous infringement" by stating:[32]

> 297. As regards the question whether the Commission was entitled to find that there was a single infringement, described in Article 1 of the Decision as 'an agreement and concerted practice,' the Court points out that, in view of their identical purpose, the various

32 Case T–9/89, Huls AG v. Commission of the European Communities, ECLI:EU:T:1992:31.

> concerted practices followed and agreements concluded formed part of schemes of regular meetings, target-price fixing and quota fixing.
>
> 298. Those schemes were part of a series of efforts made by the undertakings in question, in pursuit of a single economic aim, namely to distort the normal movement of prices on the market in polypropylene. It would thus be artificial to split up such continuous conduct, characterized by a single purpose, by treating it as consisting of a number of separate infringements. The fact is that the applicant took part – over a period of years – in an integrated set of schemes constituting a single infringement, which progressively manifested itself in both unlawful agreements and unlawful concerted practices.
>
> 299. The Commission was also entitled to characterize that single infringement as 'an agreement and a concerted practice', since the infringement involved at one and the same time factual elements to be characterized as 'agreements' and factual elements to be characterized as 'concerted practices.' Given such a complex infringement, the dual characterization by the Commission in Article 1 of the Decision must be understood not as requiring, simultaneously and cumulatively, proof that each of those factual elements presents the constituent elements both of an agreement and of a concerted practice, but rather as referring to a complex whole comprising a number of factual elements some of which were characterized as agreements and others as concerted practices for the purposes of Article 85(1) of the EEC Treaty, which lays down no specific category for a complex infringement of this type.

But according to the case law, the presumption of a single continuous infringement requires that over and beyond their existence, the set of agreements or concerted practices be linked by two elements: an objective link (i.e., the existence of an overall objective), and a subjective link (i.e., the awareness as to the participation in a wider conspiracy). The Commission has at time interpreted these conditions in a rather loose way and the European Courts have intervened to strike down the decisions of the Commission.[33]

Another evidentiary presumption is the presumption that a firm holding a large market share has a dominant position in its market. In *Akzo*,[34] the ECJ confirmed the *Hoffmann-La Roche* judgment which had established that the fact that an

---

33 *Single Continuous Infringement*, Steptoe & Johnson LLP, https://www.steptoe.com/a/web/6045/88_-_Single_continuous_infringement.pdf.

34 *See* Akzo Nobel NV, *supra* note 24, established in Arnhem (Netherlands) v. Commission of the European Communities.

undertaking holds a large market share leads to the presumption that it holds a dominant position. In its judgment the EU Court of Justice stated:[35]

> 41. […] although the importance of the market shares may vary from one market to another the view may legitimately be taken that very large shares are in themselves, and save in exceptional circumstances, evidence of the existence of a dominant position.
>
> An undertaking which has a very large market share and holds it for some time, by means of the volume of production and the scale of the supply which it stands for – without those having much smaller market shares being able to meet rapidly the demand from those who would like to break away from the undertaking which has the largest market share – is by virtue of that share in a position of strength which makes it an unavoidable trading partner and which, already because of this secures for it, at the very least during relatively long periods, that freedom of action which is the special feature of a dominant position.

This presumption established by the court was confirmed in further judgments (for example in *Astra Zeneca*[36]).

There is a symmetrical negative presumption which is much less controversial. As the guidance on enforcement priorities states: "[…] dominance is not likely if the undertaking's market share is below 40%."

Kupcik (2021)[37] and numerous economists, have suggested that the presumption that firms with a large market share have a dominant position, is "highly questionable." They consider that the validity of the presumption, in other words the question of whether a firm's market is a sufficient indicator of its market power, is not established because a firm's market power depends on a combination of other elements besides its market share such as, the existence and the height of barriers to entry.

Besides finding the presumption invalid, Kupcik considers also that it is not effective. He notes that between 1992 and 2019, the Commission issued a total

---

35 Case 85/76, Hoffmann La Roche & Co v. European Commission, ECLI:EU:C:1979.36, *see* European Court of Justice, *The EU Court of Justice states that the Commission's erred in law in finding that a pharmaceutical company had abused its dominant position by concluding exclusive purchase agreements (Hoffman-La-Roche)*, e-Competitions February 1979, art. No. 105107.

36 In AstraZeneca AB and AstraZeneca plc v. European Commission, the court stated: "176 The Court has already clarified that, although the importance of the market shares may vary from one market to another, the possession, over a long period, of a very large market share constitutes in itself, save in exceptional circumstances, proof of the existence of a dominant position (Hoffmann La Roche & Co, at ¶ 41) and that market shares of more than 50% constitute very large market shares (Case Akzo v. European Commission, at ¶ 60)," *see* Emanuela Matei, *The EU Court of Justice entirely dismisses pharmaceutical company's appeal on abusive patent misuse (AstraZeneca)*, e-Competitions December 2012, art. No. 50294.

37 Jan Kupcik, *Akzo presumption of dominance: time to abandon*? Competition Forum No. 25 (2021), https://competition-forum.com/akzo-presumption-of-dominance-time-to-abandon/.

of 241 decisions concerning Article 102 TFEU or its predecessor (Article 82 TEU). Of these 16 decisions mention large market shares and in most of these, the Commission based its determination of dominance on other considerations such as regulatory constraints or characteristics of the distribution system, buying power on the part of the clients or barriers to entry. In fact there is only one decision, *IMS Health Interim Measure*,[38] in which the Commission based itself purely on the *Akzo* presumption.

Kupcik, also suggests that the European Commission may itself be doubtful of the validity of the presumption. In this regard, it should be noted, for example, that even in an early case like the *Hoffmann La Roche & Co*[39] the EU Commission considered a number of other factors besides the market share of the firm. Indeed as the court acknowledges: "36 The Commission is of the opinion that Roche has a dominant position on the seven markets (A, B2, B3, B6, C, E, H) and bases this view on the one hand, on the relationship between the applicant's market shares and those of its competitors and, on the other hand, on the existence of a number of factors which, if the market share is not in itself the determinative criterion, nevertheless secure Roche a marked ascendancy on the relevant markets."

Thus it is not clear that the Commission believed even in the early cases that market shares were sufficient to establish a presumption of dominance and it is likely that the formulation of the court went beyond what the Commission intended. Nevertheless, as long as it has not been officially repudiated by the ECJ, the presumption of dominance associated with large market share could be used by the ECJ.

The European courts have extended the concept of admissible evidentiary presumptions to cases where the unknown fact is not only the logical consequence of the established fact (such as in the preceding examples) but to cases where the unknown fact(s) can only be explained by the established fact.

This has been the case in parallel conduct of competitors. For example, in *Woodpulp*[40] the ECJ stated:

> 71. In determining the probative value of those different factors, it must be noted that parallel conduct cannot be regarded as furnishing proof of concertation unless concertation constitutes the only plausible explanation for such conduct. It is necessary to

---

38 Commission Decision of July 3. 2001 in Case D3/38.044 (*IMS Health*) (*Interim Measures*), at ¶ 57–62, *see* James Killick, *The EU Commission imposes interim measures on the world leader in data collection on pharmaceutical sales and prescriptions considering that its refusal to grant license constitutes an abuse of dominance (IMS Health)*, e-Competitions July 2001, art. No. 38052.

39 *See* Hoffmann La Roche & Co. AG, *supra* note 34, *see* European Court of Justice, *The EU Court of Justice states that the Commission's erred in law in finding that a pharmaceutical company had abused its dominant position by concluding exclusive purchase agreements (Hoffman-La Roche)*, e-Competitions February 1979, art. No. 105107.

40 Joined Cases C–89, C–104, C–114, C–116, C–117 & C–125 to C–129/85, Ahlström Osakeyhtiö v. Commission of the European Communities, EU:C:1993:120.

> bear in mind that, although Article 85 of the Treaty prohibits any form of collusion which distorts competition, it does not deprive economic operators of the right to adapt themselves intelligently to the existing and anticipated conduct of their competitors (see the judgment in *Suiker Unie*, cited above, paragraph 174).
>
> 72. Accordingly, it is necessary in this case to ascertain whether the parallel conduct alleged by the Commission cannot, taking account of the nature of the products, the size and the number of the undertakings and the volume of the market in question, be explained otherwise than by concertation.

Finally, different evidentiary presumptions were adopted in Directive 2014/104 (the Antitrust Damages Directive) with the explicit aim of facilitating civil actions for damages.

Paragraph 14 of Directive 2014/104 states: "Actions for damages for infringements of Union or national competition law typically require a complex factual and economic analysis. The evidence necessary to prove a claim for damages is often held exclusively by the opposing party or by third parties, and is not sufficiently known by, or accessible to, the claimant. In such circumstances, strict legal requirements for claimants to assert in detail all the facts of their case at the beginning of an action and to proffer precisely specified items of supporting evidence can unduly impede the effective exercise of the right to compensation guaranteed by the TFEU."

To partly alleviate this problem and on the basis of numerous economic studies showing the complexity of the plaintiff's task in civil damage cases and an Oxera study providing an estimate of cartel harms, Article 17(2) of Directive 2014/104 states: "It shall be presumed that cartel infringements cause harm. The infringer shall have the right to rebut that presumption" and thus reverses the burden of proof to the infringer.

Furthermore Article 14(2) of the same directive creates a rebuttable presumption in favor of indirect purchasers that the overcharge was passed on to these indirect purchasers under certain conditions. It states that:

[...] the indirect purchaser shall be deemed to have proven that a passing-on to that indirect purchaser occurred where that indirect purchaser has shown that:

1. the defendant has committed an infringement of competition law;
2. the infringement of competition law has resulted in an overcharge for the direct purchaser of the defendant; and
3. the indirect purchaser has purchased the goods or services that were the object of the infringement of competition law, or has purchased goods or services derived from or containing them.

This paragraph shall not apply where the defendant can demonstrate credibly to the satisfaction of the court that the overcharge was not, or was not entirely, passed on to the indirect purchase.

As mentioned by Hornkohl (2021):[41] "The wording 'cause' in Article 17(2) Damages Directive also ensures that the presumption includes the causal relationship between that harm and the cartel infringement, which is itself determined by Member State law subject to the principles of effectiveness and equivalence."

3. Legal or Substantive Presumptions

The third type of presumption used in competition law is legal presumption. Legal presumption uses a fact (or several facts), known or presumed, to draw a legal conclusion.

Among the legal presumptions some of the most important and controversial ones used in European competition law are the presumptions of "violation by objects."

It should be noted at the outset that for the characterization of "violation by objects" there is a combination of two presumptions: an evidentiary presumption and a legal presumption. Indeed, as AG Kokott suggested, violations by object are practices that: "can be regarded, by their very nature, as being injurious to the proper functioning of normal competition." These practices are presumed to have strong anticompetitive effects and, as a consequence, are legally presumed to be violations of competition law.

In its 2004 Communication on Article 81(3) TFEU,[42] the Commission explained that:

> 21. Restrictions of competition by object are those that by their very nature have the potential of restricting competition. These are restrictions which in light of the objectives pursued by the Community competition rules have such a high potential of negative effects on competition that it is unnecessary for the purposes of applying Article 81(1) to demonstrate any actual effects on the market. This presumption is based on the serious nature of the restriction and on experience showing that restrictions of competition by object are likely to produce negative effects on the market and to jeopardize the objectives pursued by the Community competition rules. Restrictions by object such as price fixing and market sharing reduce output

41 Lena Hornkohl, *The Presumption of Harm in EU Private Enforcement of Competition Law – Effectiveness vs Overcompensation*, 5 ECLIC 29–59 (2021) https://papers.ssrn.com/sol3/papers.cfm?abstract_id=3838588.

42 *Commission Communication "Notice – from the Guidelines on the application of Article 81(3) of the Treaty"*, 2004 O.J. (C 101) 97, *see* Marc van der Woude, *Guidelines: The European Commission adopts a communication concerning Article 81 § 3 EC*, Concurrences No. 1-2004, art. No. 1565, pp. 54–55.

> and raise prices, leading to a misallocation of resources, because goods and services demanded by customers are not produced. They also lead to a reduction in consumer welfare, because consumers have to pay higher prices for the goods and services in question.

But, in the next paragraph, discussing the factors to be considered in the assessment of a violation by object, the Commission explained that nevertheless elements specific to the case at hand could be considered. It stated:

> 22. The assessment of whether or not an agreement has as its object the restriction of competition is based on a number of factors. These factors include, *in particular, the content of the agreement and the objective aims pursued by it. It may also be necessary to consider the context in which it is (to be) applied and the actual conduct and behaviour of the parties on the market.* In other words, an examination of the facts underlying the agreement and the specific circumstances in which it operates may be required before it can be concluded whether a particular restriction constitutes a restriction of competition by object. The way in which an agreement is actually implemented may reveal a restriction by object even where the formal agreement does not contain an express provision to that effect. Evidence of subjective intent on the part of the parties to restrict competition is a relevant factor but not a necessary condition.

On the basis of this last paragraph, one would not expect that all violations by object derive from a general substantive presumption. Indeed what the Commission states is that the context in which the parties implement their agreement as well as the way in which they implement it, may be relevant to the determination of whether a practice is a violation by object. This means that a case-by-case approach can be necessary to establish the existence of an object violation when such a violation depends on the way in which the practice is implemented or on the context in which it is implemented (even if in these case-by-case analyzes the effects of the practice are not considered relevant).

The presumption that price-fixing, bid rigging, and market sharing are object violations of European competition law are the least problematic.

At a general level, in *Allianz*[43] the ECJ stated:

> 34. [...] where the anticompetitive object of the agreement is established it is not necessary to examine its effects on competition. Where, however, the analysis of the content of the agreement does not reveal a sufficient degree of harm to competition, the effects

43 Case C-32/11, Allianz Hungária Biztosító Zrt v. Gazdasági Versenyhivatal, ECLI:EU:C:2013:160, *see* Hans Vedder, *The EU Court of Justice rules on the dichotomy between anticompetitive object-effect with respect to bilateral arrangements between car dealers and insurance companies (Allianz)*, e-Competitions March 2013, art. N° 58656.

> of the agreement should then be considered and, for it to be caught by the prohibition, it is necessary to find that factors are present which show that competition has in fact been prevented, restricted or distorted to an appreciable extent.
>
> 35. The distinction between 'infringements by object' and 'infringements by effect' arises from the fact that certain forms of collusion between undertakings can be regarded, by their very nature, as being injurious to the proper functioning of normal competition.
>
> 36. In order to determine whether an agreement involves a restriction of competition 'by object', regard must be had to the content of its provisions, its objectives and the economic and legal context of which it forms a part. When determining that context, it is also appropriate to take into consideration the nature of the goods or services affected, as well as the real conditions of the functioning and structure of the market or markets in question.
>
> 37. In addition, although the parties' intention is not a necessary factor in determining whether an agreement is restrictive, there is nothing prohibiting the competition authorities, the national courts or the Courts of the European Union from taking that factor into account.
>
> 38. The Court has, moreover, already held that, in order for the agreement to be regarded as having an anticompetitive object, it is sufficient that it has the potential to have a negative impact on competition, that is to say, that it be capable in an individual case of resulting in the prevention, restriction or distortion of competition within the internal market. Whether and to what extent, in fact, such an effect results can only be of relevance for determining the amount of any fine and assessing any claim for damages.

This last paragraph clearly indicates that on a substantive level, the parties presumed to have engaged in a restriction by object have only two options: 1 either they argue that their practice could not have had the effect of restricting competition; or 2 that it should be exempted under Article 101(3).

Similarly, with respect to price-fixing agreements, the ECJ stated in *Groupement des Cartes bancaires* that:[44]

> 49. In that regard, it is apparent from the Court's case-law that certain types of coordination between undertakings reveal a sufficient degree of harm to competition that it may be found that there is no need

---

44 *See* Groupement des cartes bancaires (CB), *supra* note 5, *see* Matthew O'Regan, *The EU Court of Justice provides further clarity on when an agreement has the object of restricting competition (Groupement des Cartes Bancaires)*, E-COMPETITIONS September 2014, art. N° 69491.

to examine their effects (see, to that effect, judgments in *LTM*, 56/65, EU:C:1966:38, paragraphs 359 and 360; *BIDS*, paragraph 15, and *Allianz Hungária Biztosító and Others*, C-32/11, EU:C:2013:160, paragraph 34 and the case-law cited).

[...]

51. Consequently, it is established that certain collusive behaviour, such as that leading to horizontal price-fixing by cartels, may be considered so likely to have negative effects, in particular on the price, quantity or quality of the goods and services, that it may be considered redundant, for the purposes of applying Article 81(1) EC, to prove that they have actual effects on the market (see, to that effect, in particular, judgment in Clair, 123/83, EU:C:1985:33, paragraph 22). Experience shows that such behaviour leads to falls in production and price increases, resulting in poor allocation of resources to the detriment, in particular, of consumers.

Finally, with regard to market sharing, in *Toshiba*,[45] the ECJ stated:

27. The Court's case-law has also established that, in order to determine whether an agreement between undertakings reveals a sufficient degree of harm that it may be considered a 'restriction of competition by object' within the meaning of Article 101(1) TFEU, regard must be had to the content of its provisions, its objectives and the economic and legal context of which it forms part (judgment in *ING Pensii*, C-172/14, EU:C:2015:484, paragraph 33).

28. Thus, the Court has already held that market-sharing agreements constitute particularly serious breaches of the competition [...]. The Court has also held that agreements which aim to share markets have, in themselves, an object restrictive of competition and fall within a category of agreements expressly prohibited by Article 101(1) TFEU, and that such an object cannot be justified by an analysis of the economic context of the anticompetitive conduct concerned [...].

29. In respect of such agreements, the analysis of the economic and legal context of which the practice forms part may thus be limited to what is strictly necessary in order to establish the existence of a restriction of competition by object.

Besides horizontal market sharing, price-fixing or bid-rigging, there are a number of practices which are treated, at least when they are examined in the light of Article 102, as violations for which it is not necessary for the Commission to

45 Case C-373/14 P, Toshiba Corp. v. European Commission, EU:C:2016:26, *see* Alexandre Lacresse, *The EU Court of Justice affirms the need to clearly distinguish between restrictions by object and restrictions by effect (Toshiba)*, e-Competitions January 2016, art. No. 83699.

establish any effect. What is striking about these practices is that they tend to be treated differently when they are examined in light of Article 101 than in light of Article 102 or when they are possible results of a merger.

One of the major reasons for this difference in treatment is the fact that in 1983 the ECJ adopted, in *Michelin I*,[46] a wide ranging and somewhat imprecise interpretation of Article 102 which was reiterated in subsequent cases. This interpretation states that:

> 57. […] A finding that an undertaking has a dominant position […] simply means that, irrespective of the reasons for which it has such a dominant position, the undertaking concerned has a special responsibility not to allow its conduct to impair genuine undistorted competition on the common market.

Twenty-four years later, in 2007, in one of the Fiesole Colloquia organized by Claus-Dieter Ehlermann,[47] he raised the following provoking question: "does the concept of 'special responsibility' provide any real and useful guidance to the dominant company in order to identify which kinds of behaviour can be considered anticompetitive and which are merely 'normal competition' (whatever this expression may mean)?"

As Allendesalazar Corcho[48] observed:

> The answer is clearly no. The concept of 'special responsibility' neither helps to recognize when conduct will be considered abusive nor explains why it will be prohibited. […] The Commission, supported by the Community Courts, has repeatedly broadened the scope of the special responsibility with almost every new Article 82 decision, depriving this concept of any role it may have had in providing guidance as to when and why a specific unilateral practice should be considered anticompetitive. The concept of special responsibility has thus become a mere litany chanted by the Commission and the Courts to conclude that certain kinds of conduct that are ubiquitous in the market place will nonetheless be prohibited when practiced by dominant companies and will give rise to immense fines. In other words, in the traditional form-based approach to Article 82, the Commission and the Courts have relied on the doctrine of special responsibility to sanction

46 Case 322/81, NV Nederlandsche Banden Industrie Michelin v. Commission of the European Communities, ECLI:EU:C:1983:313, *see* European Court of Justice, *The EU Court of Justice implicitly confirms that price discrimination is an indicator of dominance (Michelin)*, E-COMPETITIONS November 1983, art. No. 106997.

47 Claus-Dieter Ehlermann was a former Director for Competition of the European Commission.

48 Rafael Allendesalazar Corcho, *Can We Finally Say Farewell to the 'Special Responsibility' of Dominant Companies?* in EUROPEAN COMPETITION ANNUAL 2007: A REFORMED APPROACH TO ARTICLE 82 EC (Ehlermann & Marquis, eds., 2008).

> perfectly sound commercial practices that are otherwise considered pro-competitive, without having to prove the anticompetitive effects of such practices.

This evolution is concerning, first, because as mentioned earlier, the distinction between object violations and effect violations does not exist with respect to Article 102 TFEU. However, the court has succeeded in creating a category of exclusionary practices by dominant firms which can be qualified as violations of Article 102 without the Commission having to examine their effect on competition.

A number of the potential exclusionary practices by a dominant firm requires some kind of contract or agreement between the firm holding the dominant position and its co-contractors (for example its retailers) and can thus also be examined under Article 101 TFEU. The question which then arises is whether there is any consistency in the approaches to the same practice depending on whether it is analyzed under Article 101 or Article 102 (or even in the context of merger control). The confusing reality is that there is very little coherence between the approaches followed for the same practice in these three different legal contexts.

For example, in *Delimitis*,[49] the ECJ examined whether exclusive beer supply agreements contravened Article 86 TEU. It stated:

> 10. Under the terms of beer supply agreements, the supplier generally affords the reseller certain economic and financial benefits, such as the grant of loans on favourable terms, the letting of premises for the operation of a public house and the provision of technical installations, furniture and other equipment necessary for its operation. In consideration for those benefits, the reseller normally undertakes, for a predetermined period, to obtain supplies of the products covered by the contract only from the supplier. That exclusive purchasing obligation is generally backed by a prohibition on selling competing products in the public house let by the supplier.
>
> 11. Such contracts entail for the supplier the advantage of guaranteed outlets, since, as a result of his exclusive purchasing obligation and the prohibition on competition, the reseller concentrates his sales efforts on the distribution of the contract goods. The supply agreements, moreover, lead to cooperation with the reseller, allowing the supplier to plan his sales over the duration of the agreement and to organize production and distribution effectively.

49 Case C–234/89, Stergios Delimitis v. Henninger Bräu AG, ECLI:EU:C:1991:91, *see* European Court of Justice, *The EU Court of Justice considers that a provision in an agreement between a brewery and a licensee of a public house whereby the licensee is required to purchase a minimin amount of beer each year is not restricting competition by its object (Delimitis)*, E-COMPETITIONS February 1991, art. No. 108455.

> 12. Beer supply agreements also have advantages for the reseller, inasmuch as they enable him to gain access under favourable conditions and with the guarantee of supplies to the beer distribution market. The reseller's and supplier's shared interest in promoting sales of the contract goods likewise secures for the reseller the benefit of the supplier's assistance in guaranteeing product quality and customer service.
>
> 13. If such agreements do not have the object of restricting competition within the meaning of Article 85(1), it is nevertheless necessary to ascertain whether they have the effect of preventing, restricting or distorting competition.

The ECJ went on to give the two conditions under which exclusive agreements could be considered to have exclusionary anticompetitive effects:

> 27. [...] a beer supply agreement is prohibited by Article 85(1) of the EEC Treaty, if two cumulative conditions are met. The first is that, having regard to the economic and legal context of the agreement at issue, it is difficult for competitors who could enter the market or increase their market share to gain access to the national market for the distribution of beer in premises for the sale and consumption of drinks. [...] The second condition is that the agreement in question must make a significant contribution to the sealing-off effect brought about by the totality of those agreements in their economic and legal context. The extent of the contribution made by the individual agreement depends on the position of the contracting parties in the relevant market and on the duration of the agreement.

As a contrast, in *Hoffmann-La Roche*[50] when assessing whether the exclusivity was a violation of Article 102, the ECJ stated:

> 89. An undertaking which is in a dominant position on a market and ties purchasers – even if it does so at their request – by an obligation or promise on their part to obtain all or most of their requirements exclusively from the said undertaking abuses its dominant position within the meaning of Article 86 of the Treaty, whether the obligation in question is stipulated without further qualification or whether it is undertaken in consideration of the grant of a rebate.
>
> 90. Obligations of this kind to obtain supplies exclusively from a particular undertaking, whether or not they are in consideration of rebates or of the granting of fidelity rebates intended to give the

50 *See* Hoffmann La Roche & Co. AG, *supra* note 34.

> purchaser an incentive to obtain his supplies exclusively from the undertaking in a dominant position, are incompatible with the objective of undistorted competition within the Common Market, because – unless there are exceptional circumstances which may make an agreement between undertakings in the context of Article 85 and in particular of paragraph (3) of that article, permissible – they are not based on an economic transaction which justifies this burden or benefit but are designed to deprive the purchaser of or restrict his possible choices of sources of supply and to deny other producers access to the market.

Similarly, in *Van den Bergh*,[51] the ECJ wrote:

> 160. The fact that an undertaking in a dominant position on a market ties de facto – even at their own request – 40% of outlets in the relevant market by an exclusivity clause which in reality creates outlet exclusivity constitutes an abuse of a dominant position within the meaning of Article 86 of the Treaty. The exclusivity clause has the effect of preventing the retailers concerned from selling other brands of ice cream (or of reducing the opportunity for them to do so), even though there is a demand for such brands, and of preventing competing manufacturers from gaining access to the relevant market. [...].

Thus when examining the question of exclusivity contracts under Article 102 TFEU, the fact that such contracts may benefit both the supplier and the distributors and that their shared interest in promoting sales of the product may guarantee product quality and customer service, which is crucial to understanding why these agreements are not violations by object under Article 101, is completely obliterated and the object of the exclusivity agreements is presumed to be exclusively the foreclosure of competitors (irrespective of its effects).

If one combines this presumption with the presumption that a market share of more than 50% suggests dominance and a market share of 40% or less does not indicate dominance, it is difficult to think why the exclusivity agreements of two firms, one with a market share of 60% and its competitor with a market share of 40% should be presumed to have radically different objects and thus should be treated differently from a competition law standpoint.

If we now turn to the practice of tying and bundling, similarly, there is a difference of treatment depending on whether the practice is considered under Article 102 TFEU or in the context of merger control.

---

51 Case T-65/98, Van den Bergh Foods Ltd v. Commission of the European Communities, ECLI:EU:T:2003:281, *see* Nicolas Petit, *The EU General Court rejects the application for annulment dismissing the argument that the reluctance of retailers to sell products of other ice-cream manufacturers could not be attributed to the exclusivity clause (Van den Bergh Foods/Commission)*, e-Competitions October 2003, art. N° 57069.

In Case C–3/37.792 (*Microsoft I*) decision,[52] the EU Commission decided that the four (formalistic) criteria to assess whether a tie is a violation of Article 102 were met. The General Court summarizing the decision stated:

> 854. [...] the Commission first observes that Microsoft has a dominant position on the client PC operating systems market (recital 799 to the contested decision).
>
> 855. Second, the Commission says that streaming media players and client PC operating systems are two separate products (recitals 800 to 825 to the contested decision).
>
> 856. Third, the Commission states that Microsoft does not give customers the choice of obtaining Windows without Windows Media Player (recitals 826 to 834 to the contested decision).
>
> 857. Fourth, the Commission claims that the tying of Windows Media Player forecloses competition in the media players market (recitals 835 to 954 to the contested decision). It observes, in particular, that in classical tying cases both it and the Community Courts 'considered the foreclosure effect for competing vendors to be demonstrated by the bundling of a separate product with the dominant product' (recital 841 to the contested decision). The Commission states, however, that in the present case there are good reasons not to assume without further analysis that tying Windows Media Player constitutes conduct which by its very nature is liable to foreclose competition (ibid.). The Commission considers, in essence, that 'tying [Windows Media Player] with the dominant Windows makes [Windows Media Player] the platform of choice for complementary content and applications which in turn [creates a risk of] foreclosing competition in the market for media players' (recital 842 to the contested decision). Furthermore, '[t]his has spillover effects on competition in related products such as media encoding and management software (often server-side), but also in client PC operating systems for which media players compatible with quality content are an important application' (ibid.).

The General Court then endorsed the reasoning of the Commission. However, neither in the Commission's decision nor in the judgment of the General Court was there any analysis of the effect of tying on competition.

The perspective of the Commission with regard to conglomerate mergers implies a quite different assessment of the costs and benefits of bundling and tying than the one followed in Article 102 cases.

---

52 Commission Decision of May 24, 2004 relating to a proceeding under Article 82 of the EC Treaty Case C–3/37.792 (*Microsoft*) 2004 O.J. (L 32), *see* Henri Piffaut et al., *The EU Commission adopts a decision in a case concerning the abuse of a dominant position by a leading US provider in the PC operating systems (Microsoft)*, E-COMPETITIONS March 2004, art. No. 38380.

The EC Non-Horizontal Guidelines[53] state:

> 92. Whereas it is acknowledged that conglomerate mergers in the majority of circumstances will not lead to any competition problems, in certain specific cases there may be harm to competition. In its assessment, the Commission will consider both the possible anti-competitive effects arising from conglomerate mergers and the possible pro-competitive effects stemming from efficiencies substantiated by the parties.
>
> 93. The main concern in the context of conglomerate mergers is that of foreclosure. The combination of products in related markets may confer on the merged entity the ability and incentive to leverage a strong market position from one market to another by means of tying or bundling or other exclusionary practices. Tying and bundling as such are common practices that often have no anti-competitive consequences. Companies engage in tying and bundling in order to provide their customers with better products or offerings in cost-effective ways. Nevertheless, in certain circumstances, these practices may lead to a reduction in actual or potential rivals' ability or incentive to compete. This may reduce the competitive pressure on the merged entity allowing it to increase prices.
>
> 94. In assessing the likelihood of such a scenario, the Commission examines, first, whether the merged firm would have the ability to foreclose its rivals, second, whether it would have the economic incentive to do so and, third, whether a foreclosure strategy would have a significant detrimental effect on competition, thus causing harm to consumers (3). In practice, these factors are often examined together as they are closely intertwined. [...]
>
> 114. The (unilateral) effect on competition needs to be assessed in light of countervailing factors such as the presence of countervailing buyer power (1) or the likelihood that entry would maintain effective competition in the upstream or downstream markets (2).
>
> 115. Further, the effect on competition needs to be assessed in light of the efficiencies substantiated by the merging parties (3).
>
> 116. Many of the efficiencies identified in the context of vertical mergers may, mutatis mutandis, also apply to conglomerate mergers involving complementary products.

Whereas in merger control analysis the possibility that the merging firms might tie or bundle their products or services after the merger gives rise to an analysis

53 *See Commission Guidelines on the Assessment of Non-Horizontal Mergers under the Council Regulation on the Control of Concentrations between Undertakings*, (2008 O.J. (C 265).

of the costs and the efficiency benefits of such a practice, such an analysis is usually ignored in the examination under Article 102 of the strategies of a dominant firm. The presumption is that bundling by a dominant firm is, barring exceptional circumstances, a violation of Article 102[54] without any need for the courts or the Commission to assess the effects of the practice.

It is interesting to note that the acknowledged failure of the remedy imposed by the Commission directly challenges the relevance of its analysis of the abuse. Indeed, the EU Commission imposed an obligation for Microsoft to offer a fully functioning version of Windows Client PC OS which does not incorporate Windows Media Player within ninety days of the notification of its decision while allowing Microsoft to retain the right to offer a bundle of the Windows Client PC OS and Windows Media Player. It appears that very few if any of these Operating Systems not incorporating a Windows Media Player were ever sold, which suggests that the buyers of Windows Client PC OSs did not want to have a choice and/or valued the efficiency benefits of the tying.

Finally, Ibanez Colomo (2019) gives examples of functionally similar practices which are treated differently with respect to presumptions. One of these examples is the comparison between the treatment of refusal to deal and margin squeeze.

A dominant firm can either flatly refuse to deal with a downstream competitor or impose conditions (margin squeeze) which are such that the downstream competitor will have no economic interest in accepting them. In this sense, the two practices are equivalent. But the legal standards that apply to each of them are different.

With respect to refusal to deal in *Bronner*,[55] the ECJ stated that to establish that a refusal to deal was a violation of Article 102, two conditions needed to be met: a condition related to the possibility of an exclusionary effect of the practice; and a condition related to the indispensability of the service provided by the dominant firm for its downstream competitor. The court stated that: "for the existence of an abuse within the meaning of that provision to be capable of being established in such circumstances, it would be necessary not only for that the refusal of the service comprised in home delivery to be likely to eliminate all competition in the daily newspaper market on the part of the person requesting the service and for such refusal to be incapable of being objectively justified, but also for the service in itself to be indispensable to carrying on that person's business, for lack of any actual or potential substitute for that home-delivery scheme."

---

54 The fact that, as the General Court stated "Community courts 'considered' the foreclosure effect for competing.

55 *See* Oscar Bronner GmbH & Co. KG, *supra* note 3, *see* European Court of Justice, *The EU Court of Justice holds that refusing access to a rival for a newspaper home delivery service does not amount to an abuse of a dominant position (Oscar Bronner)*, E-COMPETITIONS November 1998, art. N° 108303.

In contrast, the test for margin squeeze given in *TeliaSonera*[56] requires the fulfillment of only the first condition related to the possible exclusion of an equally efficient competitor. Indeed, in *TeliaSonera* the ECJ stated:

> 31. A margin squeeze, in view of the exclusionary effect which it may create for competitors who are at least as efficient as the dominant undertaking, in the absence of any objective justification, is in itself capable of constituting an abuse within the meaning of Article 102 TFEU (see, to that effect, Deutsche Telekom v Commission, paragraph 183).
>
> [...]
>
> 34. It must moreover be made clear that since the unfairness, within the meaning of Article 102 TFEU, of such a pricing practice is linked to the very existence of the margin squeeze and not to its precise spread, it is in no way necessary to establish that the wholesale prices for ADSL input services to operators or the retail prices for broadband connection services to end users are in themselves abusive on account of their excessive or predatory nature, as the case may be (Deutsche Telekom v Commission, paragraphs 167 and 183).
>
> [...]
>
> 64. It follows that, in order to establish whether such a practice is abusive, that practice must have an anticompetitive effect on the market, but the effect does not necessarily have to be concrete, and it is sufficient to demonstrate that there is an anticompetitive effect which may potentially exclude competitors who are at least as efficient as the dominant undertaking.

4. Rationales for the Use of Presumptions

The use of presumptions in competition law raises the obvious question of whether they are justified.

The EU contribution to the OECD competition committee discussion on Safe Harbour and Legal Presumptions[57] suggests three possible rationales for presumptions: experience, proof proximity and effectiveness.

56 Case C–52/09, Konkurrensverket v. TeliaSonera Sverige AB, ECLI:EU:C:2011:83, *see* Anne-Lise Sibony, *Margin squeeze: The Court of Justice rules that an abuse of a dominant position in the form of margin squeeze may be constituted even where intermediary services do not constitute an indispensable input for new entrants on the downstream market, provided potential exclusionary effect is established (Konkurrensverket/TeliaSonera)*, Concurrences N° 2-2011, art. No. 35666, pp. 108-110.

57 OECD Competition Committee, *Roundtable on Safe Harbours and Legal Presumptions in Competition Law – Note by the European Union*, (Nov. 30, 2017) DAF/COMP/WD(2017)64, https://one.oecd.org/document/DAF/COMP/WD(2017)64/en/pdf.

"Experience" is by far the most common source of presumption and, according to the EU, covers the following cases of presumptions:

Restrictions by object which according to the Article 101(3) are restrictions which in light of the objectives pursued by the Community competition rules have such a high potential of negative effects on competition that it is unnecessary for the purposes of applying Article [101(1)] to demonstrate any actual effects on the market. This presumption is based on the serious nature of the restriction and on experience showing that restrictions of competition by object are likely to produce negative effects on the market and to jeopardise the objectives pursued by the Community competition rules.

No "other plausible explanation." The Commission may infer the existence of illegal collusion from the parties' parallel behavior, when there is no other plausible explanation for such behavior. The presumption is based on prior experience of the economics of oligopolistic markets.

Predatory pricing. In *Akzo,*[58] the ECJ ruled that: "prices below average variable costs ... must be regarded as abusive ... since each sale generates a loss." This is interpreted as a presumption. In *Compagnie Maritime Belge*, AG Fennelly[59] explained that: "it is not usually rational to sell below average variable costs." In *France Télécom*, the ECJ held that selling below average variable cost: "is presumed to pursue no other economic objective save that of eliminating its competitors."

The second rationale for presumptions in EU law suggested by the EU contribution to the OECD debate is "proof proximity." The EU explains that: "It [...] makes sense to use a rebuttable presumption to cut the costs of adjudication by shifting the burden to the party which is more likely to have access to the evidence." This applies to the efficiency defense, for example, because the undertaking is much more likely than the authority to be able to access the relevant evidence.

The last rationale for using presumptions suggested by the EU Commission is "effectiveness." The EU explains that: "sometimes the law also uses presumptions because there is a policy interest in increasing the effectiveness of enforcement, or strengthening the claimant's position" (for example in cases of information asymmetry). As an example, in Directive 2014/104, the direct purchaser is presumed to have passed on the overcharge to the indirect purchaser.

The choice of words used by the Commission in its contribution to the OECD competition committee discussion on Safe Harbour and Legal Presumptions is important to note. The Commission does not say that restrictions by object are

---

58 Case C-62/86, Akzo Chemie BV v. Commission of the European Communities, ECLI:EU:C:1991:286, *see* European Court of Justice, *The EU Court of Justice states that an undertaking with a market share of 50 per cent could be considered dominant unless the undertaking proves the opposite (AKZO Chemie)*, E-COMPETITIONS July 1991, art. No. 107401.

59 *See* Opinion of AG Fennelly, Case C-395/96P, Compagnie Maritime Belge Transports v. European Commission, ECLI:EU:C:1998:518.

practices for which experience shows that they restrict economic welfare but practices: "likely to produce negative effects on the market and to jeopardise the objectives pursued by the Community competition rules." This distinction is important because the objectives pursued by the Community competition rules are multiple and, as Ariel Ezrachi[60] notes, have not always been clearly outlined. According to Ariel Ezrachi there are at least seven different goals of EU Competition law which are consumer well-being,[61] effective competition structure,[62] fairness,[63] efficiency and innovation, plurality and economic freedom,[64] and market integration.[65]

Thus a number of object violations used in EU competition law may be justified by experiences relating to goals other than welfare maximization (and may be unjustified from a purely economic standpoint).

Sibony (2012)[66] goes one step further in discussing the possible advantages and disadvantages of presumptions in competition laws.

---

60 Ariel Ezrachi, "Sponge", Journal of Antitrust Enforcement, 2017, 5, 49–75, September 2016.

61 Joined Cases T–213 & T–214/01, Österreichische Postsparkasse and Bank für Arbeit und Wirtschaft v. Commission, ECLI:EU:T:2006:151, "115. [T]he ultimate purpose of the rules that seek to ensure that competition is not distorted in the internal market is to increase the well-being of consumers. […] Competition law and competition policy[…] have an undeniable impact on the specific economic interests of final customers who purchase goods or Services." *See* Didier Ferrier, *Anticompetitive practices - Consumer: The CFI rules that a final customer may have a legitimate interest in making a complaint in order to seek a declaration that Articles 81 EC and 82 EC have been infringed (Österreichische Postsparkasse)*, Concurrences No. 3-2006, art. N° 27357.

62 Case C-8/08, T-Mobile Netherlands BV v. Raad van bestuur van de Nederlandse Mededingingsautoriteit, ECLI:EU:C:2009:343, "38 […] as the Advocate General pointed out at point 58 of her Opinion, Article 81 EC, like the other competition rules of the Treaty, is designed to protect not only the immediate interests of individual competitors or consumers but also to protect the structure of the market and thus competition as such." *See* João Rivas, *The EU Court of Justice clarifies the notion of concerted practice and holds that a single meeting amongst competitors where they exchanged sensitive information can be caught by EU antitrust rules (T-Mobile Netherlands)* e-Competitions June 2009, art. N° 35319.

63 Case C–52/09, Konkurrensverket v. TeliaSonera Sverige AB, ECLI:EU:C:2011:83, "34 It must moreover be made clear that since the unfairness, within the meaning of Article 102 TFEU, of such a pricing practice is linked to the very existence of the margin squeeze and not to its precise spread, it is in no way necessary to establish that the wholesale prices for ADSL input services to operators or the retail prices for broadband connection services to end users are in themselves abusive on account of their excessive or predatory nature, as the case may be (Deutsche Telekom v. Commission, at ¶¶ 167 and 183)."

64 *Id.* " 21 Article 102 TFEU is one of the competition rules referred to in Article 3(1)(b) TFEU which are necessary for the functioning of that internal market. 22 The function of those rules is precisely to prevent competition from being distorted to the detriment of the public interest, individual undertakings and consumers, thereby ensuring the well-being of the European Union (*see*, to that effect, Case C-94/00 Roquette Frères [2002] ECR I-9011, at ¶ 42)." *See* European Court of Justice, *The EU Court of Justice holds that national courts are required to verify that coercive measures adopted by the Commission for investigation purposes are not arbitrary or disproportionate (Roquette Frères / DGCCRFC)*, e-Competitions October 2002, art. No. 105214.

65 Commission Decision of Mar. 7, 2019 relating to a proceeding under Article 101 of the Treaty on the Functioning of the European Union and Article 53 of the EEA Agreement Case AT.40023 (*Cross border access to pay-TV*) 2019 O.J. (C 132), "(67) None the less, an agreement which might tend to restore the divisions between national markets is liable to frustrate the Treaty's objective of achieving the integration of those markets through the establishment of a single market. Thus, where a license agreement relating to a film protected by copyright is designed to prohibit or limit the cross-border provision of broadcasting services, it is deemed to have as its object the restriction of competition, unless other circumstances falling within its economic and legal context justify the finding that such an agreement is not liable to impair competition. *See* European Commission, *The EU Commission accepts remedies proposed by entertainment companies ending competition concerns in the pay-TV services market (Disney / NBC Universal / Sony Pictures / Warner Bros / Sky)*, e-Competitions March 2019, art. No. 89659.

66 Anne Lise Sibony, *Limits of Imports from Economics into Competition Law*, in The Global Limits of Competition Law 39–53 (Stanford University Press, I. Lianos & D. Sokol eds., 2012).

On the one hand, she argues that presumptions may serve as a vehicle for inserting economic logic into competition law.

Clearly, the presumption that cartels constitute an infringement of competition is an efficient response to the enforcement of competition policy and is in line with economic analysis. The use of such a presumption of illegality will minimize the production of type II errors (false acquittals).

Similarly, the fact that a firm selling below average variable cost is presumed to pursue no other objective save that of eliminating its competitors is to a certain extent in line with economic theory. However, there are qualifications which could usefully make the presumption more precise. Indeed, this presumption can be justified only in certain economic contexts in which the competing products are assumed to be undifferentiated and the competitors are assumed to have access to the same cost curves as the dominant firm. This is the main reason why in US law the additional condition for the presumption to apply is that it is shown that the firm has an ability to recoup (a condition which does not exist in European law).

Sibony gives as another example the presumption of legality of conglomerate mergers. In the *Tetra-Laval Sidel* merger judgment by the Court of First Instance,[67] the court referred directly to the economic literature to establish a presumption according to which conglomerate mergers are not anticompetitive and to define the (high) evidentiary burden which the Commission has to meet to establish that such a conglomerate merger is anticompetitive. The Court of First Instance states:

> 155. […] Since the effects of a conglomerate-type concentration are generally considered neutral or even beneficial to competition in the relevant markets, as recognized in the economic doctrine cited in the analysis attached to the written comments of the parties in this case, the anticompetitive effects of the conglomerate effect of such a concentration need to be carefully examined and confirmed by convincing evidence of the circumstances in which these effects are allegedly manifested. (*see* by analogy *Airtours v. Commission*, at 63)

On the other hand, Sibony (2012) argues, that presumptions: "may act as barriers to economic imports" and she mentions the presumption that consumer harm may be inferred from alteration of the structure of the market as an example of a presumption which stands in the way of a genuine fact-based analysis of consumer harm.

---

67 Case T–5 and Case T–80/02, Tetra Laval BV v. Commission, ECLI:EU:T:2002:265, *see* James Killick & Mark D. Powell, *The EU CFI overturns the EU Commission's decision to block a merger in the packaging equipment sector addressing the issues of conglomerate effects and leveraging (Tetra Laval / Sidel)*, E-COMPETITIONS October 2002, art. No. 37058.

Altogether, we are faced not only with the possibility that presumptions will contradict economic theory or observation but also with the possibility that they will prevent a more economic interpretation of competition law. This has implications not only for the substance of the interpretation of competition law but also for the rights of the parties.

Indeed, one of the issues frequently discussed is whether rebuttable presumptions can actually be rebutted. The European courts have rightly said that even if a presumption has not been rebutted in the past, it does not mean that it is not rebuttable. Other commentators have observed that the evidentiary burden on parties to rebut presumptions was largely unclear.

From this standpoint, there may be a difference between presumptions which are based on economic experience and presumptions which are based on elusive goals or values such as fairness, plurality, economic freedom, etc. Indeed, when a presumption is based on economic experience, there is usually a well-defined methodology (provided by economic analysis) available to rebut the presumption. With respect to presumptions based on more general values, it is often unclear how parties could argue that the practices could not have had the effect of undermining those values (for example could not have had the effect of being unfair or of altering effective competition structure).

VI. The Digital Sector: Non-Rebuttable Substantive Presumptions

An interesting example of the tendency to use presumptions to enhance the effectiveness of enforcement can be found in the digital sector. Competition authorities have been under double pressure. On the one hand, they have been perceived to be slow and ineffective when applying traditional antitrust tools to the digital sector. On the other hand, some have argued (mostly in the US) that the economic goal of competition law should not be the traditional maximization of consumer surplus but a more general goal of fighting economic power and exclusionary practices of very large platforms in order to protect pluralism and democracy.

Frustration with the ineffective use of the competition law instrument and the impression that that there was an asymmetry both in information and in resources between large platforms and competition authorities have pushed the European Commission to adopt an ex ante regulation, the DMA, which purports to complement the use of competition law.

It is important to note that the goal of this regulation is to address concerns regarding "fairness" and "contestability" with respect to large platforms designated as gatekeepers. Thus the scope of the DMA overlaps but is not identical to the scope of EU competition provisions applicable to the digital sector.

This regulation is based on two sets of presumptions: on the one hand, a presumption concerning which firms are "gatekeepers" and, on the other hand, a number of presumed undesirable practices, some of them outright illegal and others prohibited, subject to some further specifications. The presumption on which firms are gatekeepers is rebuttable but the presumption on the illegal nature of the undesirable practices detailed in Articles 5 and 6 of the Digital Market Act is non rebuttable.

The Digital Market Act defines the criteria which must be met to qualify a platform as a "gatekeeper." These criteria will be met if a company: 1 has a strong economic position, significant impact on the internal market and is active in multiple EU countries; 2 has a strong intermediation position, meaning that it links a large user base to a large number of businesses and 3 has (or is about to have) an entrenched and durable position in the market, meaning that it is stable over time if the company met the two criteria above in each of the last three financial years.

For the definition of gatekeepers, the DMA establishes a presumption based on three quantitative thresholds. First, the platform is presumed to have significant market power if it meets a turnover threshold of 6.5 billion euros per year in the EEA (European Economic Area) or 65 billion euros in market capitalization. Second, the platform is presumed to provide an "essential platform service that constitutes a major access point enabling business users to reach their end users" if the number of users of the platform reaches 45 million or more active end-users and 10,000 business users. Third, the platform is presumed to have "a strong and sustainable position in its business" if it meets the two preceding criteria in each of the last three financial years.

The presumption "of gatekeeping" is rebuttable. If an undertaking has presented "sufficiently substantiated arguments" and succeeded in manifestly calling into question the presumption derived from the quantitative thresholds, the Commission will have to analyze – through a "market investigation" – whether the evidence submitted shows that the core platform service concerned does not satisfy the qualitative criteria. However, the Commission can decide to designate as "gatekeeper" a provider of a core platform service that does not meet the quantitative thresholds but satisfies the above qualitative criteria. In that case it must first run a longer "market investigation."

Second, the Digital Market Act establishes a number of obligations and prohibitions for the platforms designated as gatekeepers. To a large extent the list of prohibited practices is informed by current or past antitrust cases which have been dealt with by the Commission. For example, Article 6(5) DMA prevents "gatekeepers" from treating "more favorably, in ranking and related indexing and crawling, services and products offered by the gatekeeper itself than similar services or products of a third party. The gatekeeper shall apply transparent, fair and non-discriminatory conditions to such ranking." This closely follows the theory of harm adopted by the Commission in *Google Shopping*.[68]

The Digital Market Act establishing an ex ante regulation of large platforms has been perceived by enforcers at the international level as a welcome development given the difficulties of competition law enforcement applied to the digital sector.

However, a word of caution is justified.

The digital sector is a sector for which competition authorities have relatively little experience. Furthermore, competition in the digital sector does not work in the same way as competition in non-digital sectors.

Competition among multisided platforms is different from competition among pipe-line firms;

- platforms are built around a technology which can then be used to provide a set of complementary services rather than being linked to a specific market, thus competition among platform is competition between conglomerates rather than competition between single line competitors;
- combinations of services offered by competing platforms are differentiated rather than homogeneous; -price competition does not play the same role in the digital sector as it does in other economic sectors since many services are provided "for free" by digital platforms;
- competition in the digital sector is mostly a Schumpeterian competition through innovation rather than a Stiglerian price competition;
- all competitors do not necessarily have the same business model which means that defining competition on the merits is more difficult than in most traditional sectors, because in vertical relations there are two types of competition issues with respect to digital platforms;
- competition between the platform and its complementors within the ecosystem and competition between the ecosystems which may be negatively related, etc.

Above all, the relationship between competition and innovation, which is always difficult to evaluate, is particularly complex in the digital sector.

Over the last five years, there has been a scramble among competition authorities to improve their understanding of competition in the digital sector. The OECD Competition Committee, for example, has devoted nearly thirty

---

68 Commission Decision of June 27, 2017 relating to a proceeding under Article 102 of the Treaty on the Functioning of the European Union and Article 54 of the EEA Agreement Case AT.39740 (*Google Search (Shopping)*) 2017 O.J. (C 9), *see* Thomas Höppner, *The EU Commission fines a search engine for market dominance by promoting its comparison shopping service (Google Shopping)*, E-COMPETITIONS June 2017, art. No. 96502.

panel discussions to various aspects of the digital sector. But the complexity of the issues means that we are far from a consensus view on how to deal with those issues as is evident in the differences between the various *Booking.com* decisions by European national competition authorities or as is shown by the controversy surrounding the *Facebook* decision of the Bundeskartellamt.

This means that not only are there few final judgments in antitrust cases but we also have a somewhat limited understanding of how economic competition works in the digital sector. This in turn means that presumptions in the digital sector can hardly be based on economic experience relating to competition law issues.

It should be mentioned however that the DMA's goals are only loosely related to economic competition. It is primarily aimed at protecting fairness and contestability which the DMA presents as complementary but different from the goals of competition law. Thus paragraphs 11 and 31 of the DMA state:

> (11) Articles 101 and 102 TFEU and the corresponding national competition rules concerning anticompetitive multilateral and unilateral conduct as well as merger control have as their objective the protection of undistorted competition on the market. This Regulation pursues an objective that is complementary to, but different from that of protecting undistorted competition on any given market, as defined in competition-law terms, which is to ensure that markets where gatekeepers are present are and remain contestable and fair, independently from the actual, potential or presumed effects of the conduct of a given gatekeeper covered by this Regulation on competition on a given market. This Regulation therefore aims to protect a different legal interest from that protected by those rules and it should apply without prejudice to their application.
>
> [...]
>
> (31) To safeguard the contestability and fairness of core platform services provided by gatekeepers, it is necessary to provide in a clear and unambiguous manner for a set of harmonised rules with regard to those services. Such rules are needed to address the risk of harmful effects of practices by gatekeepers, to the benefit of the business environment in the services concerned, of users and ultimately of society as a whole. The obligations correspond to those practices that are considered as undermining contestability or as being unfair, or both, when taking into account the features of the digital sector and which have a particularly negative direct

> impact on business users and end users. It should be possible for the obligations laid down by this Regulation to specifically take into account the nature of the core platform services provided. The obligations in this Regulation should not only ensure contestability and fairness with respect to core platform services listed in the designation decision, but also with respect to other digital products and services into which gatekeepers leverage their gateway position, which are often provided together with, or in support of, the core platform services.

This approach is, however, slightly contradicted by multiple statements from the EU Directorate-General Competition (DG COMP) officials arguing that one of the bases for the DMA is the experience acquired in competition enforcement activity dealing with large digital platforms and by the fact that most of the obligations imposed on gatekeepers can be precisely traced to past antitrust cases dealt with by the DG COMP as several authors have noted.[69]

In addition, the DMA and its list of prohibited practices seem to be justified both by a desire to overcome the lack of effectiveness of competition law in reining in their economic power and by proof-proximity considerations. Along those lines, some commentators have proposed *a reversal of* the burden of proof with respect to digital mergers initiated by the very large platforms.[70]

Time will tell whether the list of substantive obligations imposed by the DMA should be updated (such a possibility is provided for in the DMA) and whether there is a trade-off between these obligations and the effectiveness and intensity of dynamic Schumpeterian competition between digital platforms.

VII. The Current Decade: Has the Time Come for a More Economic Approach?

The second decade of this century has been rich in developments with respect to a number of the issues we have touched upon. This is, in particular, the case with respect to the criteria to determine an object violation, to the use of economic tests to assess exclusionary conduct, and to the standard of proof both for object violations and for mergers.

These developments point to a long-delayed clarification as to what could constitute a violation by object and, more generally, a reflection on the framework for presumptions in competition law, a growing attention by the courts to an

---

69 *See* for example, Fiona Scott Morton & Cristina Caffarra, *The European Commission Digital Markets Act: A translation*, CEPR (Jan. 5, 2021), https://cepr.org/voxeu/columns/european-commission-digital-markets-act-translation.

70 *See* also Valletti, *supra* note 12.

effects-based economic analysis of cases, and a more open and livelier, if slightly confused, discussion of the standards of proof in antitrust and mergers.

Two AGs, Kokott and Wahl, have played outsized, if opposite, roles in arguing respectively for and against a change of perspective on these issues and we shall refer to their opinions as well as to the cases in which they intervened. The courts have moved slowly, sometimes imperceptibly, rarely boldly, well aware both of the pressure to adapt their jurisprudence and of the difficulty of doing so without creating a legal uncertainty which would undermine the predictability of EU law.

A large part of the discussion on object violations stemmed from the confusion introduced by ECJ case *Allianz Hungária Biztosító*.[71] Indeed in this judgment, the ECJ stated:

> 36. In order to determine whether an agreement involves a restriction of competition 'by object', regard must be had to the content of its provisions, its objectives and the economic and legal context of which it forms a part [....]. When determining that context, it is also appropriate to take into consideration the nature of the goods or services affected, as well as the real conditions of the functioning and structure of the market or markets in question [....]." It thus suggested that it was necessary to look at the effects of the practice on the market to determine an infringement by object. This blurred the distinction between a violation by object and a violation by effect.

As AG Wahl stated one year later in his opinion in *CB v Commission*:[72]

> 46. It is clear that the case-law of the Court and of the General Court, while pointing out the distinction between the two types of restrictions envisaged by Article 81(1) EC, could, to a certain extent, be a source of differing interpretations and even of confusion. Certain rulings seem to have made it difficult to draw the necessary distinction between the examination of the anticompetitive object and the analysis of the effects on competition of agreements between undertakings.
>
> 47. In a number of cases, consideration of that context is similar to a genuine examination of the potential effects of the measures at issue
>
> [...]

71 *See* Allianz Hungária Biztosító Zrt, *supra* note 42.

72 Opinion of AG Wahl, Groupement des cartes bancaires (CB), *supra* note 5. *See* Michel Debroux, *Opinion: The Advocate General Niels Wahl reproaches to the General Court a too extensive conception of the notion of restriction of competition by object (Groupement des Cartes bancaires)*, CONCURRENCES No. 3-2014, art. No. 68065, pp. 87–88.

> 50. […] in *Allianz Hungária Biztosító and Others* […] it is difficult to distinguish how the examination of the context advocated by the Court, which consists in evaluating the risk of competition on the market in question being eliminated or seriously weakened, having regard, in particular, to 'the structure of that market, the existence of alternative distribution channels and their respective importance and the market power of the companies concerned', differs from the examination of possible anticompetitive effects.

AG Wahl first espoused the view of his predecessors that the category of object violations in EU competition law was useful for three reasons: it provides predictability and legal certainty for undertakings by enabling them to anticipate the legal consequences of some of their actions, it has a deterrent effect with respect to practices which are categorized as object violations and it furthers procedural economy since it allows the competition authorities to establish the violation without the need to assess the effects of the practice. However, AG Wahl pointed out that: "[…] such advantages materialise only if recourse to the concept of restriction by object is clearly defined, failing which this could encompass conduct whose harmful effects on competition are not clearly established."

AG Wahl then proceeded to (re)define what an object violation was and to define the standard of proof required to establish such a violation.

To understand the evolution proposed by AG Wahl with respect to object violation in his Opinion in *CB v Commission*, it is useful to go back to the discussion of the same issues in AG Kokott's opinion in *T-Mobile*.[73] Indeed, that case dealt with a similar issue: to what extent are the assessment of the specific market circumstances, the market conduct of the undertakings concerned and the effects of that conduct on competition required in order to presume an anticompetitive object.

AG Kokott, in her Opinion in *T-Mobile*[74] emphasized, as did AG Wahl in his Opinion in *CB v Commission*, the importance of clearly distinguishing violations by object from violations by effect.

Among other developments, AG Kokott indicated that:

> 43. The prohibition of a practice simply by reason of its anti-competitive object is justified by the fact that certain forms of collusion between undertakings can be regarded, by their very nature, as being injurious to the proper functioning of normal competition.

---

73 *See* T-Mobile Netherlands BV, *supra* note 60.

74 *See* Opinion of AG Kokott, T-Mobile Netherlands BV, *supra* note 60. *See* Richard Burton, *The EU Court of Justice Advocate General Kokott gives opinion on standard of proof with regard to anti-competitive concerted practices (T-Mobile Netherlands)*, e-Competitions February 2009, art. No. 43789.

And that to find a violation by object:

> 46. [...] it is sufficient that a concerted practice has the potential – on the basis of existing experience – to produce a negative impact on competition. In other words, the concerted practice must simply be capable in an individual case, that is, having regard to the specific legal and economic context, of resulting in the prevention, restriction or distortion of competition within the common market.

She had also opined that:

> 44. Certainly, the concept of a restricted practice having an anticompetitive object may not be subject to unduly broad interpretation, given the serious consequences which may befall an undertaking in the case of an infringement of Article 81(1) EC. However, nor may that concept be subject to unduly strict interpretation, if the primary law prohibition on 'infringement by object' is not to be erased through interpretation and, as a consequence, Article 81(1) EC deprived of an element of its practical effectiveness. From the wording itself of Article 81(1) EC, it follows that both concerted practices having an anticompetitive object and those with anticompetitive effects are prohibited.

These developments are interesting both because AG Kokott does not mention economic analysis as a tool to establish the potential of a practice to produce a negative impact on competition (she only refers to experience) and because she considers that the concept of violation by object should neither receive a broad nor a narrow interpretation.

If we now turn to AG Wahl's Opinion with respect to object violation in *CB v Commission*, he differs from AG Kokott's views, not on the necessity to clearly separate the two types of violations and to abstain from looking at the effects of the practice to qualify it as an object violation, but on the two points mentioned in the previous paragraph.

AG Wahl, first, discusses whether experience, taken as precedent, is a sufficient basis to qualify an object violation. He clearly expresses some reservations and feels that experience should be at least complemented by economic analysis for a qualification of object to be justified. More precisely he states:

> 142. [...] whilst experience can undoubtedly confirm the inherently anticompetitive character of certain types of cooperation in the case of patent and/or evident restrictions which, in all likelihood, have an impact on competition, I am not convinced that it is always possible to infer a strong argument from the Commission's decision-making practice. The fact that in the past the Commission did not

take the view that a certain kind of agreement was, by virtue of its very object, restrictive of competition cannot in itself prevent it from doing so in the future following an individual, detailed examination of the measures at issue.

Further, he states that economic analysis must be a crucial part of the analysis of violations by object:

> "55. […] In my view, it is only when experience based on economic analysis shows that a restriction is constantly prohibited that it seems reasonable to penalise it directly for the sake of procedural economy" and "79. […] 'Experience' must be understood to mean what can traditionally be seen to follow from economic analysis, as confirmed by the competition authorities and supported, if necessary, by case-law."

Second, with respect to the economic risks associated with an erroneous qualification of violation by object, AG Wahl takes a much more cautious approach than AG Kokott in advocating a high standard of proof.

He writes:

> 55. This formalist approach is thus conceivable only in the case of (i) conduct entailing an inherent risk of a particularly serious harmful effect or (ii) conduct in respect of which it can be concluded that the unfavourable effects on competition outweigh the pro-competitive effects. To hold otherwise would effectively deny that some actions of economic operators may produce beneficial externalities from the point of view of competition. In my view, it is only when experience based on economic analysis shows that a restriction is constantly prohibited that it seems reasonable to penalise it directly for the sake of procedural economy.
>
> 58. Because of these consequences, classification as an agreement which is restrictive by object must necessarily be circumscribed and ultimately apply only to an agreement which inherently presents a degree of harm. This concept should relate only to agreements which inherently, that is to say without the need to evaluate their actual or potential effects, have a degree of seriousness or harm such that their negative impact on competition seems highly likely. Notwithstanding the open nature of the list of conduct which can be regarded as restrictive by virtue of its object, I propose that a relatively cautious attitude should be maintained in determining a restriction of competition by object.

In *CB v Commission*, the ECJ followed its Advocate General on the cautious approach to violation by object when it stated:[75]

> 58. Secondly, in the light of that case-law, the General Court erred in finding, in paragraph 124 of the judgment under appeal, and then in paragraph 146 of that judgment, that the concept of restriction of competition by 'object' must not be interpreted 'restrictively'. The concept of restriction of competition 'by object' can be applied only to certain types of coordination between undertakings which reveal a sufficient degree of harm to competition that it may be found that there is no need to examine their effects, otherwise the Commission would be exempted from the obligation to prove the actual effects on the market of agreements which are in no way established to be, by their very nature, harmful to the proper functioning of normal competition.

The ECJ also faulted the General Court for not having explained: "in what respect that restriction of competition reveals a sufficient degree of harm in order to be characterised as a restriction 'by object' within the meaning of that provision."

Two years later, in 2016, AG Wahl was given the opportunity to continue arguing for a more economic approach in his opinion on *Intel*, a case where Intel Corporation, which was held to have a dominant position, had been found guilty of granting conditional rebates akin to exclusivity rebates to its customers with the possibility of foreclosing its competitors on the market for certain microchips.[76]

In its decision,[77] the Commission had argued that in the area of discounts, the finding of an exclusivity or a quasi-exclusivity rebate without objective justification granted by a dominant firm was sufficient to establish a violation of Article 82 TEU and that evidence of actual foreclosure was not necessary. The Commission added:

Although not indispensable for finding an infringement under Article 82 of the Treaty according to the case law, one possible way of showing whether Intel's rebates and payments were capable of causing or likely to cause anticompetitive foreclosure is to conduct an as efficient competitor analysis (section 4.2.3). On the basis of the results of this analysis and the qualitative and quantitative evidence (sections 4.2.4 and 4.2.5), and given the lack of objective justification

---

75 *See* Groupement des cartes bancaires (CB), *supra* note 5.

76 Opinion of AG Wahl, Case C–413/14 P, Intel Corp. v. European Commission, ECLI:EU:C:2016:788, *see* Bill Batchelor, *The EU Court of Justice AG Wahl delivers his opinion in a case regarding rebates and calls for a new approach to Article 102 (Intel)*, e-Competitions October 2016, art. No. 82101.

77 Commission Decision of May 13, 2009 relating to a proceeding under Article 82 of the EC Treaty and Article 54 of the EEA Agreement Case C–3/37.990 *(Intel)* 2009 O.J. (C 227), *see* Brice Allibert et al., *The EU Commission fines a US semiconductor chip manufacturer for abuse of a dominant position (Intel)*, e-Competitions May 2009, art. N° 35025.

and efficiencies (section 4.2.6), the Commission concludes that Intel's conditional rebates to Dell, HP, NEC and Lenovo, as well as Intel's conditional payments to MSH, were an abuse under Article 82 of the Treaty which deserve its particular attention.

This case gave AG Wahl the opportunity to reflect on the use of economics to assess violations of Article 102 in which there is no formal difference between object and effect violations but for which, as AG Wahl noted, the courts have historically treated some practices, such as conditional rebates, as object violation. It also gave him the opportunity to take a stand on the standard of proof for practices which have the capacity to foreclose and to call the attention of the court to the necessity to treat equivalent practices in the same way.

To fully appreciate AG Wahl's comments on the role of economics in Article 102 cases, it is useful to go back in time and recall AG Kokott's Opinion on *Post Denmark* which concerned the question of whether Post Denmark had abused its dominant position by implementing retroactive conditional rebates.[78]

AG Kokott started her Opinion with a rather strong (and somewhat provocative) pronouncement on the use of an economic tool in European competition law. She stated:

> 3. [...], the Court will have to clarify in this case whether, for the purposes of assessing the anticompetitiveness of rebate schemes from the point of view of Article 82 EC, it is legally necessary to carry out a price/cost analysis in which the commercial conduct of the dominant undertaking is compared with that of an equally efficient competitor (the 'as-efficient-competitor' (AEC) test).[...].
>
> 4. These questions are particularly important at a time when there are mounting calls for European competition law to adopt a more economic approach. It is my view that, in its replies, the signal effect of which is likely to extend well beyond the present case, the Court should not allow itself to be influenced so much by current thinking ('Zeitgeist') or ephemeral trends, but should have regard rather to the legal foundations on which the prohibition of abuse of a dominant position rests in EU law.

AG Kokott then explained that: "29. For the purposes of assessing the rebate scheme operated by a dominant undertaking from the point of view of Article 82 EC [...] what matters is whether the dominant undertaking grants rebates which are capable of producing on the relevant market an exclusionary effect which is not economically justified (that is to say, by the passing-on of a cost saving to customers)."

---

78 Opinion of AG Kokott, Case C–23/14, Post Danmark A/S v. Konkurrencerådet, ECLI:EU:C:2015:651, *see* Bill Batchelor, *The EU Court of Justice AG Kokott deals another blow to the economic assessment of rebates (Post Danmark II)*, e-Competitions May 2015, art. No. 75195.

Although she recognized that it was not inconceivable to use an "as efficient competitor" test to assess the exclusionary capacity of the rebate scheme, she warned against it in no uncertain terms stating:

> "65. such a reorientation of the case-law concerning Article 82 EC warrants some scepticism, on a number of grounds.
>
> 66. On the one hand, the added value of expensive economic analyses is not always apparent and can lead to the disproportionate use of the resources of the competition authorities and the courts, which are then unavailable for the purposes of effectively enforcing the competition rules in other areas. [...]
>
> 67. On the other hand, it is wrong to suppose that the issue of price-based exclusionary conduct can be managed simply and in such a way as to ensure legal certainty by applying some form of mathematical formula based on nothing more than the price and cost components of the businesses of the undertakings concerned. As I have already said, corporate data is not uncommonly open to different interpretations".

If we now turn to AG Wahl's opinion in *Intel*, while commenting on whether the General Court had been right to consider that the loyalty rebates granted by Intel were anticompetitive without looking at all the circumstances of the case, he emphasized the importance of the guidance provided by economic analysis in such cases by stating the following:

> 93. Experience and economic analysis do not unequivocally suggest that loyalty rebates are, as a rule, harmful or anticompetitive, even when offered by dominant undertakings.
>
> 94. contemporary economic literature commonly emphasises that the effects of exclusivity are context-dependent. [....]
>
> 95. Awareness of context-dependency may [...] help explain why the Court has, in its recent Article 102 TFEU case-law, highlighted the importance of considering all the circumstances.

In her conclusions in *Post Denmark*,[79] AG Kokott acknowledged that the EU courts had occasionally called for an "as efficient competitor" test in exclusionary cases to establish the capacity of a conditional rebate scheme to foreclose competition. She nevertheless justified her reticence to require such a test in the following words:

However, that case-law does not support the inference of an absolute requirement always to carry out an AEC (As Efficient Competitor) test for the purposes of

---

79 *See* Opinion of AG Kokott in Post Danmark A/S, *supra* note 76.

assessing price-based exclusionary conduct from the point of view of competition law. On the one hand, that case-law is specifically concerned with pricing practices by dominant undertakings, such as a low-pricing policy (loss leader pricing, for example) or margin squeezing through the reduction of the cost-price ratio, which are by their very nature closely related to the cost structure of the undertakings in question. On the other hand, the form of words chosen by the Court, 'among other things' (French: 'notamment'), makes it clear that it cannot always be assumed that an abuse of a dominant position exists only where the exclusionary effect is felt by undertakings which are as efficient as the dominant undertaking.

AG Wahl in his Opinion in *Intel*,[80] discussing the question of whether exclusivity rebates should be treated more harshly than loyalty rebates, had the opportunity to dissent implicitly from the view expressed by AG Kokott in *Post Denmark* and to say that different types of loyalty rebates should be treated similarly, thus addressing one criticism of the ECJ's jurisprudence to which we have alluded (that economically equivalent practices were occasionally treated differently). He wrote:

> 91. It is true, however, that the greatest competitive concern in relation to rebates is said to arise where the customers of a dominant undertaking must carry a percentage of its products and/or where the discount is conditional on the customer purchasing all (or a substantial part) of its requirements from it. That could be seen as an argument in favour of treating 'exclusivity rebates' more strictly. Yet, other types of rebates can have a similar distorting effect. This is so even where the scheme is not explicitly linked to exclusivity.
>
> 92. Indeed, as the case-law clearly illustrates, a mechanism that induces loyalty may take different forms. As was the case in *Hoffmann La Roche* and *Tomra*, the loyalty mechanism can be inherent in the requirement that the customer purchase all or most of its material requirements from the dominant undertaking. It can also take the form of individualised sales targets or bonuses, which are not necessarily tied to a particular proportion of requirements or sales.
>
> 93. Seen in that light, there is no objective reason why (exclusivity) rebates should receive a stricter treatment than (loyalty) rebates.

Finally, AG Wahl discussed the standard of proof to be applied to exclusionary abuses of dominance. In so doing, he clearly dissented from AG Kokott's assessment in *Post Denmark* that both over-inclusion and under-inclusion were to be avoided. His position that over-inclusion (i.e., the risk that pro-competitive

---

80 *See* Opinion of AG Wahl in Intel Corp., *supra* note 74.

practices by dominant firms might be found in violation of Article 102 TFEU) is a more concerning risk than under-inclusion is founded on his previously-mentioned economic view that "experience and economic analysis do not unequivocally suggest that loyalty rebates are, as a rule, harmful or anticompetitive, even when offered by dominant undertakings" and on the view that under-inclusion (i.e., failing to stop an anticompetitive practice) is less costly to society than over-inclusion (i.e., if one believes that markets correct themselves over time).

AG Wahl writes:

> 117. The aim of the assessment of capability is to ascertain whether, in all likelihood, the impugned conduct has an anticompetitive foreclosure effect. For that reason, likelihood must be considerably more than a mere possibility that certain behaviour may restrict competition. Contrariwise, the fact that an exclusionary effect appears more likely than not is simply not enough.
>
> [....]
>
> 120. To avoid over-inclusion, the assessment of capability as concerns presumptively unlawful behaviour must be understood as seeking to ascertain that, having regard to all circumstances, the behaviour in question does not just have ambivalent effects on the market or only produce ancillary restrictive effects necessary for the performance of something which is pro-competitive, but that its presumed restrictive effects are in fact confirmed. Absent such a confirmation, a fully-fledged analysis has to be performed.

The *Intel* judgment confirmed the previous jurisprudence, that Article 102 TFEU does not require dominant firm to behave in such a way that less efficient competitors should be protected against the rigor of competition and should remain on the market. It also confirmed that the "as efficient competitor" test could be used to assess conditional rebates and it stated, for the first time, that the presumption against exclusivity rebates under Article 102 is rebuttable and can be rebutted by economic evidence showing that the rebate scheme is incapable of foreclosing the market. The Commission must examine and discuss the evidence presented by the undertaking, if any, to that effect.

Finally, *Hutchinson 3G UK*, for which the judgment of the General Court[81] is still under review by the ECJ, allowed AG Kokott and the General Court to take a stand, for the first time, on the standard of proof to be applied in merger cases.

---

81 Case T-399/16, CK Telecoms UK Investments Ltd v. European Commission, ECLI:EU:T:2020:217, *see* Francisco Enrique González-Díaz et al., *The EU General Court raises the Commission's bar for mergers in concentrated markets (Telefónica UK / Hutchison 3G UK)*, E-COMPETITIONS May 2020, art. No. 108110.

In 2016, the Commission prohibited the proposed acquisition by Hutchison 3G UK (Three) of Telefónica UK (O2) which would have reduced the number of mobile network operators on the UK market from four to three and created a new leader in the retail market (with a share of more than 40%) and its various sub-segments, including, in particular, the key private post-paid segment.

The Commission developed three theories of harm, all of which were based on the existence of "non-coordinated" effects on an oligopolistic market. The first theory of harm related to the elimination of important competitive constraint on the retail market which would probably have led to an increase in prices for mobile telephony services in the United Kingdom and a restriction of choice for consumers. The second theory of harm related to the existence of non-coordinated effects on the retail market relating to network sharing which would be likely to have a negative influence on the quality of services for United Kingdom consumers and the third theory of harm related to the existence of non-coordinated effects arising from the elimination of important competitive constraints on the wholesale market.

The Commission blocked the merger following failed remedies negotiations.

The General Court annulled the decision in its entirety on the ground that the Commission had failed to meet the standard of proof concerning the demonstration of coordinated effects giving rise to a significant impediment to effective competition, for the purposes of Article 2(3) Regulation 139/2004. In particular, the General Court stated with regard to the evidentiary standard the Commission had to meet:

> 117. Since the second stage of the analysis which must be carried out by the Commission is the result of an assessment based on hypotheses, it cannot be required that proof be adduced that the scenarios and theories of harm underpinning that assessment will inevitably occur. However, those scenarios and theories of harm must appear sufficiently realistic and plausible, and cannot therefore solely be conceivable from a theoretical point of view, in the light of an analysis of all the relevant factors.
>
> 118. In the context of an analysis of a significant impediment to effective competition the existence of which is inferred from a body of evidence and indicia, and which is based on several theories of harm, the Commission is required to produce sufficient evidence to demonstrate with a strong probability the existence of significant impediments following the concentration. Thus, the standard of proof applicable in the present case is therefore stricter than that under which a significant impediment to effective competition is 'more likely than not', on the basis of a 'balance of probabilities', as the Commission maintains. By contrast, it is less strict than a

> standard of proof based on 'being beyond all reasonable doubt' (see, to that effect, Opinion of Advocate General Tizzano in Commission v Tetra Laval, C 12/03 P, EU:C:2004:318, points 72 to 77, and of Advocate General Jääskinen in France v Commission, C 559/12 P, EU:C:2013:766, points 34 and 35; see, a contrario, Opinion of Advocate General Kokott in Bertelsmann and Sony Corporation of America v Impala, C 413/06 P, EU:C:2007:790, points 209 to 211).

In her Opinion to the ECJ,[82] AG Kokott stated the following about the standard of proof that the Commission must meet in merger cases based on non-coordinated effects:

> 51. […] the case-law has clarified the criteria governing the judicial review of complex, including forward-looking, economic assessments by the Commission in the context of merger control. The Commission has a margin of discretion with regard to economic matters for the purposes of applying the substantive rules of Regulation No 139/2004, in particular Article 2. It follows that the review by the EU Courts of a Commission decision relating to concentrations is confined to ascertaining that the facts have been accurately stated and that there has been no manifest error of assessment. Accordingly, the EU Courts must not substitute their own economic assessment for that of the Commission for the purposes of applying those rules, even though that does not mean that the EU Courts must refrain from reviewing the Commission's interpretation of information of an economic nature. […]
>
> 56. (In the judgment of 10 July 2008, Bertelsmann and Sony Corporation of America v Impala) even though, (…) the Court did not expressly identify the relevant test for the standard of proof required as being the 'balance of probabilities' test, the fact remains that it required the Commission to provide evidence of the 'most likely' outcome or 'plausibility' of its prospective analysis, which consists of an examination of how, in the light of the various conceivable chains of cause and effect, the merger concerned could give rise to a significant impediment to effective competition. As both the Commission and the EFTA Surveillance Authority are fully entitled to argue, the requirement to demonstrate the 'most likely' outcome or plausibility of the Commission's prospective economic analysis seems to me to correspond precisely to the

---

82 Opinion of AG Kokott, Case C-376/20 P, European Commission v. CK Telecoms UK Investments Ltd (on appeal) *see supra* note 79), *see* Christopher J. Cook, *The EU Court of Justice AG Kokott advises the Court to uphold the Commission's appeal on the grounds that the General Court erroneously applied a stricter burden of proof for the SIEC test and erred in law by misinterpreting the concept of a SIEC (Telefónica UK / Hutchison 3G UK)*, e-Competitions October 2022, art. No. 109195.

> 'balance of probabilities' test, as described in my Opinion in that case and according to which the market development envisaged need not be 'very probable' or 'particularly likely' or established 'beyond reasonable doubt', in accordance with the particularly high standard applicable in criminal or quasi-criminal matters. [.....] In any event, only the standard of proof associated with the 'plausibility' or 'balance of probabilities' test seems to me to be compatible with the discretion enjoyed by the Commission in the context of its (forward-looking) complex economic analyses in relation to concentrations, which is why the scope of the judicial review is, in essence, limited to ascertaining whether there have been manifest errors of assessment (see point 51 above).

Finally, AG Kokott considers that, in view of the unitary nature of the concept of "significant impediment to effective competition," irrespective of the type of concentration concerned and the symmetry of the standard of proof, there is no justification for requiring a higher standard of proof in the case of concentrations giving rise to non-coordinated effects on oligopolistic markets than in the case of concentrations giving rise to "conglomerate" (groups of undertakings active in different areas) or "collective" (a number of undertakings which are legally independent of one another but which act, from an economic point of view, as a collective entity on the relevant market) type dominant positions.

One should note that both with respect to the scope of the review of merger control decisions in EU law and with respect to the standard of proof to be applied by the Commission this discussion is important but that unfortunately it is cast in terms which are somewhat confusing.

Indeed there are several sets of issues to be considered.

The first is related to the standard of review of merger decisions by the courts which is either a "manifest error of appreciation" or a "balance of probability" standard. Even if one recognizes that these low standards of review result from a consistent jurisprudence, this does not tell us much about what level of scrutiny the courts should exercise with respect to the Commission's merger decision when they assess whether it has met its standard of proof. Incidentally, the term "manifest," if one holds that the standard should be a manifest error of appreciation standard, is itself slightly ambiguous as it can describe errors which are easily visible or errors which are central to the Commission's reasoning as well as errors which are both easily visible and central to its reasoning.

Second, with respect to the Commission's assessment, two different questions can be asked about the standard of proof that it should use and, given that standard, what is the appropriate evidentiary requirement. As noted earlier, there may be a sliding scale of evidentiary requirements within a given standard of proof, depending on the complexity of the theory of harm employed. It may thus be that even if the standard of proof is low (a balance of probability) the Commission's evidentiary burden is high in assessing the plausible result of some mergers.

From that standpoint there may be a difference depending on whether the merger is likely to create a dominant position or whether it is likely to lead to a significant impediment of competition. The balance of probability may be more difficult to assess (and require further evidence) in the more complex theories of harm than when the merger reinforces a dominant position where the theory of harm essentially deals with the incentives and the abilities of the merging firms after their merger. For example, it may be more complex to anticipate how non-merging firms will react to the merged firms' decision in an oligopolistic setting and how this interaction will determine the intensity of competition than if the merged firms acquire a dominant position, in which case one can more easily ignore the reaction of their actual or potential competitors. Thus, the same standard of proof may give rise to two different levels of evidentiary burden on the merging firms.

VIII. Conclusion

Merger control is the only area of EU competition law where economic analysis plays a central role. Part of the reason why there is more acceptance of economic analysis is that few cases are reviewed by the EU courts. But, more fundamentally, merger control is different from antitrust in the sense that the EU Commission's merger decisions are decisions granting, refusing or conditioning an administrative authorization for the parties to merge.

Antitrust decisions, on the other hand, are decisions which assign liabilities and sanction, sometimes harshly, competition law violators. Competition law enforcement of Articles 101 and 102 TFEU is implemented without recourse to a detailed economic analysis of each case and relies frequently on the use of procedural, evidentiary, and substantive presumptions. The substantive presumptions used in EU law enforcement are to a large extent created by jurisprudence and secondary legislation and do not necessarily reflect the teachings of economic analysis. For a long time, the standard of proof in EU competition law enforcement was neither explicit nor even discussed which reflected the influence of a civil law approach in the EU legal system, relying on the "intime conviction" of the judge rather than on a probabilistic approach of standard of proof.

Around the turn of the century, the European Commission initiated a movement to bring a "more economic approach" to antitrust enforcement. However, until recently this move was defeated both by a resistance coming from the European courts where some of the judges or Advocate Generals were unconvinced of the usefulness of economic analysis to assess competition law violations and by the concerns of the Commission that the recourse to economic analysis would make antitrust enforcement more complex and take longer and that its decisions would become more fragile.

It is only within the last decade that we have witnessed major, although somewhat contradictory changes in EU antitrust enforcement. On the one hand, the courts, have started to move in the direction of being more explicit about the standards of proof to be used by the Commission in antitrust and merger cases, even if it remains true that within a standard of proof there may be different evidentiary levels to convince the judges of the existence of a violation. The assessment made by judges ultimately depends on the nature of the practices, the judges' subjective views of what is normal competition and the cost of the error risks associated with the decision. The courts have also started to be stricter about requiring the Commission to justify the basis on which it claims that some practices are violations by object. The courts have, finally, indicated how such presumptions could be rebutted and required the Commission to address the rebuttal when the parties choose to question the nature of the violation.

On the other hand, frustrated by the difficulties of applying economic analysis to the perceived abuse of power by large digital platforms, the EU Commission has embarked on a regulatory path which it sees as complementary to antitrust because it has the goals of fairness and contestability but which is related to antitrust since most of the prohibitions imposed on large platforms qualified as "gatekeepers" by the regulation were previously found to be anticompetitive abuse of dominance by platforms by the Commission.

These two developments may not be independent of each other and one could hypothesize that the growing economic scrutiny of the Commission's decisions by the courts in antitrust enforcement cases was perceived as a possible future complication that the Commission would have to face in digital cases for which its traditional antitrust apparatus was not ideally suited, hence the decision to move to a more regulatory approach which could be implemented more easily and at less cost and legal risk for the Commission.

There are two main elements revealed by the debate over the standards of proof, the use of presumptions and the recourse to object violations in European competition law.

The first element is a continued tussle around the goals of European competition law. Because the TFEU does not explicitly mention consumer welfare but presents competition law as an instrument to achieve the single market, some commentators (and judges as we have seen) have flatly rejected the relevance of economics in the interpretation of European competition law. For example Wils (2014),[83] writing about *Intel* stated:

The EU Treaties clearly specify the objective of the EU competition rules. Hence there is no room for the ECJ or the European Commission (or the

83 Wouter P.J. Wils, *The Judgment of the EU General Court in Intel and the So-Called "More Economic Approach" to Abuse of Dominance*, 37 World Competition 405–34 (2014) https://papers.ssrn.com/sol3/cf_dev/AbsByAuth.cfm?per_id=456087.

competition authorities and courts of the EU Member States, when applying EU competition law, or the Council, when exercising its legislative powers under Article 103 TFEU) to make a different choice. Indeed, it is clear from Protocol No 27 on the internal market and competition, annexed to the Treaty of Lisbon, that the objective of Article 102 TFEU (and of the other EU competition rules) is a system of undistorted competition, as part of the internal market established by the EU. [...] a system of undistorted competition as part of the internal market is the objective of Article 102 TFEU as determined by the EU Treaties. Whatever views this or that economist or other person or many or most of them may have as to what the objective of Article 102 TFEU should be is irrelevant, unless a debate were to be opened on changing the EU Treaties.

The holders of such a view seem to have lost ground recently as the EU courts have shown more willingness to challenge the EU Commission on the justification of its economic reasonings and some of its presumptions. If there is more acceptance of the fact that the protection of consumer welfare is at least one of the goals of competition law, the issue of the relative weight to be given to the different goals assigned to competition law in the EU remains controversial and some widely-used presumptions, which can be explained by the pursuit of the non-economic goals of competition law, can be unjustified or misleading from the standpoint of economic analysis.

The second element is the profound difference in judicial approach (at least in civil law countries), in the economic approach to law enforcement in general, and to competition law enforcement in particular. Whereas the judges start from the facts of the case and apply legal principles to those facts, economists start from the theory based on hypothesis and use the theory to decide what is/is not a violation of competition law. Whereas judges want to consider all the facts to make a judgment, economists focus only on the relevant facts (i.e., those suggested by economic theory) and disregard other facts. Whereas civil judges are concerned about the predictability of the law (and therefore can be reluctant to change their jurisprudence even in cases when they recognize that it is erroneous), economists are above all concerned about the short- and long-term economic social costs of decisions which are not aligned with economic reasoning. Whereas economic theory (validated by an econometric analysis of facts) provides the economists with a probabilistic assessment of the direction and strength of the relationship between two phenomena, civil judges are often wary of the validity of the underlying hypothesis (particularly when new theories are invoked). They are also often unconvinced that the correlations used by economists, even when they are backed by a theory of harm, are a sufficient basis to demonstrate causality and assign liabilities etc.... Distrusting economics, they tend to rely on alternative sources of inspirations such as their own normative view of competition or presumptions derived from other non-economic goals assigned to competition law.

The difficulties associated with the difference in perspective between judicial and the economic approaches to competition law can be, at least partly, overcome in competition law enforcement and the recourse to unjustified or misleading evidentiary or substantial "economic" presumptions by competition law judges can be limited, if on the one hand, judges better understand economics (which has been recognized by many commentators) but also if, on the other hand, economists better understand how the judicial mind functions (and therefore are more apt at addressing the concerns of civil judges in relevant ways), a need which has often been overlooked.

Could a Move to More Presumption-Based Legal Standards Be Justified for the Big-Tech Digital Markets on Error-Cost-Minimising Grounds?*

YANNIS KATSOULACOS**

Athens University of Economics and Business | Jiangxi University of Finance and Economics | CRESSE

Abstract

I present a methodology for defining different legal standards (LS) along the continuum of LS, depending on the number and type of screens assessed at different stages of the continuum; I then outline how the pertinent factors that could influence error minimisation interact to determine the optimal LS for different conduct types and markets; this shows that cost of decision error principles can be used to provide a useful and practical, yet rigorous, framework for analysing the choice of legal standards for specific categories of conduct in

---

* This article is based on my presentation at the Special Policy Session on Legal Standards for Digital Markets that took place in the annual CRESSE Conference (1–3 July 2022) and on the recently published article by Y Katsoulacos and D Ulph (n 8). I am grateful for comments by participants, and for helpful discussions on this subject over the years with Jacques Crémer, Eleanor Fox, Joe Harrington, Krisztan Katona, Pierre Regibeau, Thomas Ross and my co-authors of papers related to LS, Svetlana Avdasheva and Svetlana Golovanova and David Ulph. Of course, all errors, omissions or ambiguities are my own.

** Emeritus Professor, Department of Economic Science, Athens University of Economics and Business, Affiliated Chair Professor Jiangxi University of Finance and Economics (JUFE). Former Commissioner of the Hellenic Competition Commission. Founder and Chair of the Scientific Committee and Coordinator of the Annual Competition and Regulation European Summer School and Conference (<www.cresse.info>) Email: yanniskatsoulacos@gmail.com.

competition law enforcement. I then use this framework to examine whether more presumption-based LS can be justified for the Big-Tech digital platforms on error-minimising grounds and how this depends on whether the question is posed for developed or developing jurisdictions.

I argue that while the error-minimising framework cannot be used to support unambiguously a move to more presumption-based (rather than full effects-based or rule of reason) LS for specific conduct types in the case of the Big-Tech platforms, such a move is indeed more likely to be error-minimising than in traditional markets, when in the latter firms with significant market power and lacking contestability are involved. Also it is shown that such a move could be recommended for developing jurisdictions.

I. Introduction

The *legal standards* (LS) in antitrust enforcement are the *assessment procedures or decision rules* that provide the basis for how the assessment of potentially anticompetitive conduct must be undertaken. The appropriate choice of LS to decide whether there is liability or not has been hotly debated for many years. The debate has gained in intensity in recent years as a result of the concerns expressed by a significant number of academics and policy makers in many countries with the antitrust treatment of the major platforms.[1] Even in the US, an increasing number of commentators have been arguing that the current antitrust doctrines, rules and antitrust enforcement 'are too limited to protect competition adequately, making it needlessly difficult to stop anticompetitive conduct in digital markets' and growing market power.[2]

More specifically, it has been argued, for the US, that, 'as a result of unsound economic theories and unsupported empirical claims about the competition effects of certain practices....*antitrust rules* constructed by the courts reflect a systematically skewed error-cost balance:[3] they are too concerned to avoid

---

1 A number of references are provided below.

2 See the recent report by twelve of the most prominent competition economists and legal experts in US JB Baker and others, 'Joint Response to the House Judiciary Committee on the State of Antitrust Law and Implications for Protecting Competition in Digital Markets' (2020) CPI <www.competitionpolicyinternational.com/joint-response-to-the-house-judiciary-committee-on-the-state-of-antitrust-law-and-implications-for-protecting-competition-in-digital-markets> accessed 17 March 2023.

3 For a very systematic and extensive criticism of the view that the primary objective in antitrust enforcement is to limit false convictions rather than false acquittals, that has its origins in Frank H Easterbrook, 'The Limits of Antitrust' (1984) 63 Tex L Rev 1, see Herbert Hovenkamp, 'Antitrust Error Costs' (2021) CPI <www.competitionpolicyinternational.com/antitrust-error-costs> accessed 17 March 2023, that also contains many references to opposing views. AI Gavil and S Salop 'Probability, Presumptions and Evidentiary Burdens in Antitrust Analysis: Revitalizing the Rule of Reason for Exclusionary Conduct' (2020) 168 UPa J Int Econ L 2107 and JB Baker, 'Taking the Error Out of "Error Cost" Analysis: What's Wrong with Antitrust's Right' (2015) 80 ABAJ 1, 6 are also very critical. In another very useful contribution, Gavil and Salop point out that 'Many of the assumptions that guided this generation-long retrenchment of antitrust rules were mistaken, and advances in the law and in economic analysis have rendered them anachronistic. This is especially the case with respect to exclusionary conduct'.

chilling procompetitive conduct and the high cost of litigation, and too dismissive of the cost of *failing* to deter harmful conduct'. Also, that they have 'encouraged overly cautious enforcement policies and overly demanding proof requirements and have discouraged government enforcers and private plaintiffs from bringing meritorious exclusionary conduct cases'.[4]

It is argued that more presumption-based illegality LS would be suitable for the antitrust (ex post) assessment of potentially anti-competitive conduct by the major platforms, rather than full blown rule of reason.

As is evident from the chapter title, our objective here is to examine this issue. Our examination is based on the recent papers by Katsoulacos, Avdashava and Golovanova (2019) and Katsoulacos and Ulph (2023). Note first, however, that the move suggested by the question in the title, that is, a shift from effects-based to more presumption-based LS, can in principle be justified in two ways:

1. Legal standards can become more presumption-based *relative to full effects-based LS for proving welfare harm* (i.e. can rely less on the full examination of effect-related screens) by adopting a non-welfarist *substantive (liability) standard* (SS) e.g. by moving from the consumer welfare SS to a 'disadvantaging rivals' SS or a 'distorting the competitive process' SS.[5] I do not examine this here and will assume that the SS is that of consumer welfare, though, as will be mentioned below, this approach does not lack prominent supporters or

2. We can justify LS becoming more presumption based than full effects-based, while adopting a consumer welfare SS, if it can be shown that for a certain conduct type, under certain circumstances (e.g. in the high-tech digital markets), the presumption of welfare harm (and hence of illegality of the conduct) can be considered high enough so, without resorting to a full examination of all screens that are necessary in principle for showing welfare harm, we can decide that there is liability, given the

4 Baker and others (n 2) 4–5. This situation has 'been defended with reference to mistaken and unjustified assumptions – including erroneous claims that markets self-correct quickly, monopolies best promote innovation, firms with monopoly power can obtain only a single monopoly profit, vertical restraints...... almost invariably benefit competition even in oligopoly markets, courts and enforcers are manipulated by complaining competitors, and courts cannot tell whether exclusionary conduct harms competition or benefits it'. The authors go on to devote a distinct section on legal rules. See also discussion below of the work of other commentators.

5 The point is that, under the disadvantaging rivals SS, a liability decision can be reached once the exclusionary potential of a conduct is assessed; while with a welfarist SS, assessing the exclusionary potential does not allow us to reach a liability decision unless we can justify a very high presumption that exclusion leads to welfare harm (so no further examination needs to be undertaken). This has been examined in Y Katsoulacos, "On the Concepts of Legal Standards and Substantive Standards (and How the Latter Influences the Choice of the Former)" (2019) 7 JAE 3 365–85. Sometimes 'disadvantaging rivals' is lumped together with the 'distorting the competitive process' SS, though they should be distinguished – the former is stricter and may be used to protect competitors even at the expense of consumers, which is not true for the former. I am grateful to Eleanor Fox for this clarification. Using the concept of a continuum of LS (details below) the 'disadvantaging rivals' SS is relying on screen 2 on the continuum being satisfied while the 'distorting the competitive process' SS is relying on screen 3 being satisfied.

> discriminating quality of additional screens to distinguish without errors between harmful and benign cases. I examine this here using an error-minimising approach to the choice of assessment procedures or LS.

Thus, the discussion below concerns whether there is an error-minimising justification for a modification to the legal standards or to the screen tests applied when assessing *conduct types*[6] recognised as potentially abusive, in dominance cases which involve Big-Tech digital platforms. Our focus is on the choice of LS to be applied to general conduct types, which implies that we fully agree with Crémer, de Montjoye and Schweitzer[7] that 'competition law should not try to work with the error cost framework in a case-by-case basis'.

We show that for presumptively illegal conducts and even if the Easterbrook hypothesis (that the error-costs of false convictions exceed those of false acquittals) does hold at some intermediate stage, in which only a subset of the full range of screens that would be examined under a rule of reason have been assessed, it may be justifiable on error-minimisation grounds to continue and assess additional screens. Specifically, it may be justifiable to go beyond the assessment of the screen that just involves the identification of exclusion potential. On error-minimising grounds, this would be right if the decision error costs (DEC) having undertaken the assessment of additional screens that aim to identify consumer welfare harm and potential efficiencies, were lower than DEC of relying on just the finding regarding the exclusion potential. We show that this can be the case and hence the proposal for a more presumption-based LS cannot be established unambiguously. However, *adopting more presumption-based LS (based just on evidence of exclusion to reach liability decisions) is more likely to be error-minimising than in traditional markets,* when in the latter markets firms with significant market power and lacking contestability are involved. Of course, and even though below we focus just on comparing costs of errors of different LS, it should be remembered that the use of more presumption-based LS has the advantages of lower enforcement costs and faster decisions, considerations that have been very important in advocating the adoption of regulations such as the Digital Markets Act (DMA) in Europe.

---

6 Conduct types would include tying and bundling, exclusive contracts, predation, royalty rebates, refusal to deal, margin squeeze, etc.

7 J Crémer, Y-A de Montjoye and H Schweitzer, "*Competition Policy for the Digital Era: Report for the European Commission* (Luxemburg, Publications Office of the European Union 2019) <https://ec.europa.eu/competition/publications/reports/kd0419345enn.pdf> accessed 18 March 2023. An interesting extension of our analysis, beyond the scope of this chapter, would be to consider also the relative merits of adopting more traditional *ex ante* regulatory enforcement approaches in the Big Tech Digital Markets, like the Digital Markets Act (DMA) in Europe. A Witt in "The Digital Markets Act – Regulating the Wild West", Common Market Law Review (2023), in a very interesting discussion, considers the DMA as a move towards the use of *Per Se* legal standards in these markets. This is a novel way to describe DMA which we consider as reasonable given the nature of many DMA rules that are examined by Witt. However, we think that a more accurate description is to describe DMA as a hybrid regulation that combines both rules that prescribe what firms should not do (as in Per Se) and rules that prescribe what firms should do as in traditional ex ante ante regulation of natural monopolies. I would like to thank Ann Witt for an enlighting discussion on these issues.

II. The Continuum of Legal Standards

The analysis and the main results of the model presented below, are based on the recent article by Katsoulacos and Ulph.[8] This analysis, in turn, builds on a new methodology, that it revises and improves, as outlined below, for operationalising the application of the cost of decision errors approach to the choice of legal standards, for assessing different conduct types, in the enforcement of antitrust. The first version of the methodology was originally developed by Katsoulacos, Avdasheva and Golovanova[9] and has been applied for testing empirically the extent to which effects-based procedures characterise enforcement in a number of jurisdictions including the EU.[10] Some of the ideas underlying the approach are based on Katsoulacos and Ulph.[11] Important predecessors also include: Ehrilch and Posner[12,13] Easterbrook,[14] Breckner and Salop,[15] Hylton and Salinger[16] and Evans and Padilla.[17] Finally in the main section of the chapter we present the applications to the Big-Tech digital platforms and to developing jurisdictions.

The methodology originally presented in Katsoulacos, Avdasheva and Golovaneva,[18] makes use of an old idea, specifically, that there is a *continuum* of legal standards. The idea originated in the writings of legal scholars (Areeda, Hovenkamp and Kovacic, in particular) and judges (Judge Stevens), some time ago. It was present in the first edition of the '*Antitrust Law Treatise*' (as mentioned in Areeda and Hovenkamp).[19] The idea's articulation closest to our approach

---

8 Y Katsoulacos and D Ulph, 'Choosing Legal Rules or Standards in Antitrust Enforcement in Different Markets and Countries: a Proposal for Extending the Decision-Theoretic Approach' (2022) MDE 1 19 <https://onlinelibrary.wiley.com/doi/full/10.1002/mde.3787> accessed 17 March 2023.

9 Y Katsoulacos, S Avdasheva and S Golovaneva, 'A Methodology for Empirically Measuring the Extent of Economic Analysis and Evidence and for Identifying the Legal Standards in Competition Law Enforcement' in Nicolas Charbit and Sonia Ahmad (eds), *Frédéric Jenny Liber Amicorum: Standing Up for Convergence and Relevance in Antitrust*, Volume I (Concurrences 2019). https://www.concurrences.com/en/all-books/frederic-jenny-liber-amicorum

10 Y Katsoulacos and G Makri, 'The Role Of Economics and the Type of Legal Standards in Antitrust Enforcement by DGCOMP: An Empirical Investigation' (2021) 9 JAE 3 457–504; V Bageri and Y Katsoulaços, 'The Quality of Competition Law Institutions and Enforcement' (2020) 1(1) BRICS J Econ <https://brics-econ.arphahub.com/article/24155/list/9> accessed 17 March 2023.

11 Y Katsoulacos and D Ulph, 'Optimal Legal Standards for Competition Policy' (2009) 57 J Ind Econ 3 410–437.

12 I Ehrlich and RA Posner, 'An Economic Analysis of Legal Rulemaking' 3 (1974) JLS 1 257–286

13 RA Posner, 'An Economic Approach to Legal Procedure and Judicial Administration' (1973) 2 JLS 2 399, 400.

14 Easterbrook (n 3).

15 FC Beckner III and Steven C Salop, 'Decision Theory and Antitrust Rules' (1999) 67 Antitrust LJ 41.

16 KN Hylton and M Salinger, 'Tying Law and Policy: A Decision-Theoretic Approach' (2001) 69 Antitrust LJ 469.

17 D Evans and J Padilla, 'Designing Antitrust Rules for Assessing Unilateral Practices: A Neo-Chicago Approach' (2005) 72 U Chi L Rev 73.

18 Katsoulacos, Avdasheva and Golovaneva (n 9).

19 PE Areeda and Herbert Hovenkamp, *Antitrust Law: An Analysis of Antitrust Principles and their Application* (4th edn, Wolters Kluwer 2017). The first edition of the Treatise was by P Areeda and DF Turner.

is in Jones and Kovacic.[20] Other references include Gavil,[21] Kovacic[22] and Italianer.[23] The latter mentions that the US Supreme Court has explicitly recognised that 'the categories of analysis cannot be pigeonholed into terms like "per se" or "rule of reason'. No categorical line can be drawn between them, instead, what is required is a situational analysis, moving along what the Court referred to as 'a sliding scale'. It is worth mentioning here that the use of the idea of a continuum of LS also clarifies significantly the relationship between the notions of legal and substantive standards (see Katsoulacos).[24]

Our approach can be summarised in the following way. We define the continuum of LS as: a sequence of steps or stages, in each of which additional *screens* are examined, using further blocks or components of economic analysis, generating additional information, building on the information already gathered in previous steps. The question examined is: when is it best to add additional steps of economic analysis and hence move the LS from 'per se' closer to full effects-based? The objective of each of the steps of the information gathering and analysis process, is to examine whether certain *preconditions* or screens are satisfied that are considered necessary for demonstrating liability (welfare harm) – such as significant extant market power/ lack of contestability, potential for exclusion, potential for consumer harm and potential for efficiencies. Then, decision error-costs across steps or stages can be derived and compared in order to determine the optimal number of stages, that defines the error-minimising LS.

Given that in the literature a number of different terms are used, often very confusingly, in discussions of legal rules and the standard of proof, we should stress to avoid confusion that here, we use the term 'legal standard' to represent the 'quantity' of evidence, as measured by the necessary number and type of screens needed to be examined for proof of liability. It is also sometimes referred to in the literature as the *evidentiary standard of proof*. This is a very important dimension of the notion of the '*standard of proof*'.[25] However, the latter entails *also* the dimension of the '*level of certainty necessary for proof*', if, as assumed here, the objective is to minimise the cost of decision errors. Often authors refer to the standard of proof without clarifying which of the

---

20 A Jones. and W Kovacic, 'Identifying Anticompetitive Agreements in the US and the EU: Developing a Coherent Antitrust Analytical Framework' (2017) 62 Antitrust Bull 2 239–253.

21 AI Gavil, 'Burden of Proof in U.S. Antitrust Law' in *Issues in Competition Law and Policy*, vol 1 (ABA Section of Antitrust Law 2008) 125; AI Gavil, 'Moving Beyond Caricature and Characterization: The Modern Rule of Reason in Practice' (2012) 85 S Cal L Rev 733, 759.

22 W Kovacic, 'The Future Adaptation of the Per Se Rule of Illegality in US Antitrust Enforcement' (2021) 1 CBLR 34.

23 A Italianer 'Competitor Agreements under EU Competition Law' (40th Annual Conference on International Antitrust Law and Policy, Fordham Competition Law Institute New York, 2013).

24 Katsoulacos (n 5).

25 See for example *Merriam-Webster Dictionary of Law* (2016).

two dimensions they have in mind. We think it is best to distinguish between these two dimensions since to any given level of certainty necessary for proof there may be associated, depending on the case, different legal or evidentiary standards.[26] In Katsoulacos and Ulph[27] we discuss in more detail how the second dimension of the standard of proof can be incorporated in the analysis of LS and its influence on the choice of the optimal LS.[28] Finally, by the term "presumption" in this article we mean an assumption that a certain fact or condition is true/satisfied purely on the basis of establishing that another fact is true, and without any further investigation. Presumptions in this sense can be rebuttable or conclusive.[29]

III. Potential Investigation Stages, Screens and LS

A Competition Authority (CA) can assess whether a conduct violates competition law by undertaking one or more investigations, in each of which it successively examines a screen or precondition for identifying harm. Given that the ultimate objective (i.e. the SS) is to identify whether the conduct is harmful to consumer welfare, the CA could consider that this objective has been satisfied, depending on the type of conduct investigated, in a number of ways, differing in terms of whether some or all and which screens are examined. Specifically, *to reach a liability decision*, the CA's investigations can cover one or more of the following stages, each of which is associated with the examination of a specific screen or precondition:[30]

0. Conduct characterisation screen.
1. Market contextualisation and significant market power (SMP)/contestability screen.
2. Potential for significant exclusionary impact or enhanced ability to exercise market power screen.

---

26 For example to a high level of certainty (clear and convincing evidence or preponderance of the evidence) there may be associated different quantities of necessary evidence in different circumstances and for different conduct types, for proof of liability (depending, for example, on what economic theory directs us to presume with regard to what is the strength of the presumption of illegality associated with different quantities of evidence).

27 Katsoulacos and Ulph (n 8)

28 For example, when the necessary level of certainty is considered satisfied, additional evidence will not be examined in practice even though this evidence could reduce further the costs of decision errors. Our discussion has potential implications also for the *allocation of the 'burden of proof'*, though we do not delve much into this issue here.

29 See also Anne Sophie Chone-Grimaldi "Presumptions in competition law", Concurrences, 4, Nov. 2022 and F Jenny (in this book).

30 We note that in order to focus the analysis we omit the examination of exploitative conduct, which would have affected stage 2.

3. Potential consumer welfare loss, due to just anticompetitive effects, screen. This entails examination of effects on output, prices, quality,[31] variety and innovation.

4. Efficiencies assessment and balancing screen. While the burden of proof for screens 0 – 3 lies with the CA, the burden of proof for demonstrating the presence of efficiencies lies with the defendant, though the CA will have to assess the defendant's arguments and undertake the balancing between anti-competitive and efficiency effects.

1. A Typology of Legal Standards

Depending on the screens, i = 0, 1, ….4, examined, we can then distinguish the following legal standards:

(i) Strict per se LS (SPS LS): with this, the liability decision relies purely on the initial characterisation of the conduct (in stage 0) and on the presumption that this generates about its consumer welfare impact.

(ii) Modified per se LS (MPS LS): the liability decision then relies just on the information from stages 0 and 1 about the conduct and the presumption that this generates about its welfare impact.

(iii) Truncated effects-based I LS (TEB I LS): the liability decision relies on the information from stages 0, 1 and 2 about the conduct and the presumption that this generates about its welfare impact. The US 'quick look' LS can be considered as intermediate LS between MPS and TEB I, involving a quick look on the efficiency defence.[32]

(iv) Truncated effects-based II LS (TEB II LS): under this, a liability decision relies on the information from stages 0, 1, 2 and 3 about the conduct and the presumption that this generates about its final welfare impact.

(i) Full effects-based (or rule of reason) LS (FEB LS): under this, a liability decision relies on the information from all assessment stages 0–4 about the conduct and a balancing between anticompetitive and efficiency effects to determine the net effect on consumer welfare.

---

31 Thus for this screen no efficiencies are taken into account. Note that privacy would be an important dimension of quality when the role of data is part of the assessment. On the importance of this screen see Salop (n 82) and the discussion below on this and other relevant articles discussing cases where exclusion may not lead to consumer welfare harm even without taking into account efficiencies.

32 This ceased to be so popular after the Supreme Court decision in 1999 on *California Dental Ass'n v FTC* 526 U.S. 756 (1999) where it was noted that 'Where any anticompetitive effects of given restraints are far from intuitively obvious, the rule of reason demands a more thorough enquiry into the consequences of those restraints than the abbreviated analysis (of the FTC and) the Ninth Circuit performed in this case (769–781). An abbreviated or 'quick-look' analysis is appropriate when an observer with even a rudimentary understanding of economics could conclude that the arrangements in question have an anticompetitive effect on customers and markets. See, *National Collegiate Athletic Ass'n v Board of Regents of Univ of Okla* 468 U.S. 85 (1984). This case fails to present a situation in which the likelihood of anticompetitive effects is comparably obvious, for the CDA's advertising restrictions might plausibly be thought to have a net procompetitive effect or possibly no effect at all on competition'. I thank Eleanor Fox for pointing out this to me.

2. Determining the Error-Minimising Choice of LS for a Conduct Type

The question is: how many screens to investigate, i.e. which LS to choose in order to minimise costs of decision errors for any given conduct type?

Intuition, first formalised to the best of our knowledge by Katsoulacos and Ulph,[33] suggests that this depends on the strength of the presumption of illegality (or legality) in a given stage, for a conduct type, relative to the ability to discriminate whether conduct in a typical case of a specific conduct type is harmful or benign, that depends on the discriminating quality of information expected to be generated by the examination of the screen in the next investigative stage.

The first thing to determine is whether the conduct type is presumptively illegal (PI) or presumptively legal (PL). Also, it is very important to then examine whether there is a basis for the Easterbrook.[34] hypothesis. This has been severely criticised recently by many writers: Shapiro,[35] Hovenkamp and Scott Morton[36,37] the Stigler Committee Report[38] and Salop.[39] We can then finally determine the LS that minimises the DEC.

The following factors determine the the probability of and the size of false acquittals (FA), of false convictions (FC), and hence whether the Easterbrook hypothesis holds or not, and the size of DEC and how these are influenced when decisions are based less on presumption-based assessments and more on effects-based assessments: the probabilities γ, $\hat{\beta}$, p_H and p_B, $\hat{p}_H$ and $\hat{p}_B$, (shown in Diagram 1), with parameters H and B, where these are defined as follows:[40]

γ_i, $i = 1, \ldots, N$, is the probability that conducts for which precondition i is genuinely satisfied are genuinely harmful to consumer welfare, given that the first i – 1 steps have been undertaken and satisfied.

---

33 Katsoulacos and Ulph (n 11).

34 Easterbrook (n 3).

35 C Shapiro, 'Antitrust: What Went Wrong and How to Fix it' (2021) 35 Antitrust 3.

36 Hovenkamp (n 3).

37 Hovenkamp and Scott Morton, 'Framing the Chicago School of Antitrust Analysis' (2020) 168 UPa L Rev 1843 <https://papers.ssrn.com/sol3/papers.cfm?abstract_id=3481388> accessed 17 March 2023.

38 Chicago Booth School of Business, *Stigler Committee on Digital Platforms* (Final Report 2019) <www.chicagobooth.edu/research/stigler/news-and-media/committee-on-digital-platforms-final-report> accessed 17 March 2023.

39 Steven C Salop, 'Dominant Digital Platforms: Is Antitrust Up to the Task?' (2021) 130 Yale LJF <www.yalelawjournal.org/forum/dominant-digital-platforms> accessed 17 March 2023. See, however, also Geoffrey A Manne, 'Error Costs in Digital Markets' in *The Global Antitrust Institute Report on the Digital Economy 3* (11 November 2020) <https://papers.ssrn.com/sol3/papers.cfm?abstract_id=3733662> accessed 17 March 2023 for a dissenting view.

40 See for details Katsoulacos and Ulph (n 8), 13–14.

$\hat{\beta}_i < 1, i = 1, ... N$, is the probability that precondition i is genuinely satisfied in the total population of conducts of the type examined;

$\hat{p}_{H,i} < 1, i = 1, ..., N$, is the probability that having undertaken investigative step i, the precondition examined in step i is considered satisfied when indeed this is the case. Clearly, $(1 - \hat{p}_{H,i})$ is the probability that the precondition examined in step i is erroneously considered as not satisfied and hence the conduct is acquitted.

$\hat{p}_{B,i} < 1, i = 1, ..., N$ is the probability that having undertaken investigative step i, the precondition examined in step i is *not* considered satisfied when it is indeed not satisfied in fact. Clearly, $(1 - \hat{p}_{B,i})$ is the probability that the precondition examined in step i is erroneously considered as satisfied and hence there is conviction (if there is no further assessment after step i).

$p_{H,i} < 1, i = 1, ..., N - 1$[41] is the average fraction of the cases examined in which the conduct is identified as harmful when it is indeed harmful, having undertaken investigative step i. Clearly, $(1 - p_{H,i})$ is the average fraction of cases examined erroneously considered as benign (and acquitted) for which step i is satisfied and which reduce consumer welfare.

$p_{B,i} < 1, i = 1, ..., N$ is the average fraction of the cases examined in which the conduct is identified as benign when it is indeed benign, having undertaken investigative step i. Clearly, $(1 - p_{B,i})$ is the average fraction of cases examined erroneously considered as harmful (and banned, if there is no further assessment after step i) for which step i is satisfied but which increase consumer welfare.

H = average harm of conducts that are genuinely harmful.

B = average benefit from conducts that are genuinely benign.

Our approach to modelling the factors that determine DEC is exemplified by the decision tree in Diagram 1 (below and at the end of the paper in landscape format) which shows how these factors, the various probabilities (in parentheses in the Diagram) mentioned just above, determine the probability of FA – broken down into FA1 and FA2 – and of FC – broken down into FC1 and FC2. Diagram 1 focuses on the determination of DEC in a given investigative stage (i) in which screen/precondition i is assessed, with screen i been genuinely satisfied with probability $\hat{\beta}_i$ and not satisfied with probability $1 - \hat{\beta}_i$. The DEC are given by the sum of the error-costs: (FA1+FA2)*H + (FC1+FC2)*B.

---

41 Note that in our framework in makes sense to define this and the next probability for stage 1, ..., $N - 1$. In the last stage N, with all assessment steps completed, if the precondition in this stage, as all other preconditions, is considered satisfied the conduct is certainly harmful and convicted whilst if the precondition is not considered satisfied the conduct is certainly acquitted.

Diagram 1. The factors that determine DEC

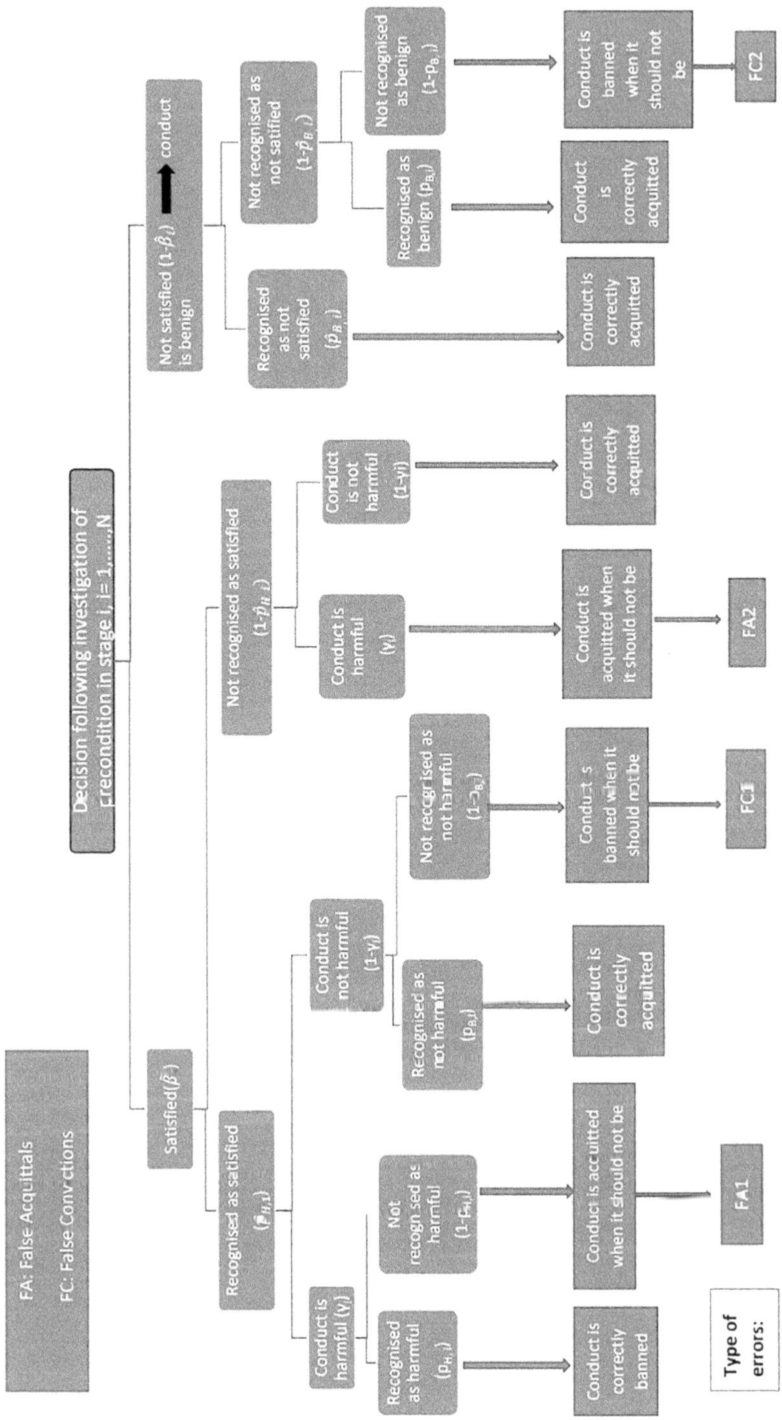

3. Comments on the Factors that Affect the Choice of LS

Parameters H, B, γ and $\hat{\beta}$ influence the strength of the presumption of illegality (or legality) of the conduct type. Parameters $\hat{p}_H$ and $\hat{p}_B$, p_H and p_B, influence, respectively, the ability to identify correctly whether the screen is satisfied or not and to discriminate whether the conduct in specific cases is harmful or benign, that is, the discriminating quality of the information expected to be generated by the examination of additional effects-related screens.

We can examine how these factors determine whether the conduct type investigated is Presumptively Illegal (PI) or Presumptively Legal (PL) and whether or not the Easterbrook hypothesis holds. Having carried out i investigative steps, $i = 0, ..., N = 4$, we can say that the conduct should be deemed PL or PI depending on whether average harm is, respectively:

$$\bar{h}_i = \gamma_i H - (1 - \gamma_i)B < 0 \qquad (1)$$

or,

$$\bar{h}_i = \gamma_i H - (1 - \gamma_i)B > 0 \qquad (2)$$

$\bar{h}_i$ being the expected harm (across all) of the conducts for which precondition i is satisfied. $\gamma_i H$ is expected harm from harmful conducts and $(1 - \gamma_i)B$ is expected benefit from benign conducts.[42] Decision error-costs of FA and FC are given, respectively by:

$$DEC\ FA_i = \hat{\beta}_i \hat{p}_{H,i} \gamma_i (1 - p_{H,i})H + \hat{\beta}_i (1 - \hat{p}_{H,i}) \gamma_i \mathrm{H} \quad (3)$$

$$DEC\ FC_i = \hat{\beta}_i \hat{p}_{H,i} (1 - \gamma_i)(1 - p_{B,i})B + (1 - \hat{\beta}_i)(1 - \hat{p}_{\mathrm{B},i})(1 - p_{B,i})B \quad (4)$$

According to the Easterbrook hypothesis, that has led to what Hovenkamp[43] calls an 'anti-enforcement bias in antitrust':

$$DEC\ FC_i > DEC\ FA_i \qquad (5)$$

But we see that this is likely to hold when:

- $\hat{\beta}_i$, is small (e.g. for stage 1, that the probability that firm genuinely has SMP is small);

---

42 I am aware, following discussions with Eleanor Fox, that the definition of the terms *presumptively illegal* (PI) or *presumptively legal* (PL) that we use here may not appear appropriate to lawyers, who may be associating the first with per se illegality (when the conduct is virtually always considered to be output reducing) and the second with all other cases in which the plaintiff must introduce evidence that the particular conduct is likely to have on balance anticompetitive effects to shift the burden of proof to the defendant. This (lawyers') approach makes good sense, when distinguishing whether a given conduct type is PL or PI relied just on information of the conduct's characteristics, in stage 1 above. But then, our (economists') approach would likely lead to exactly the same presumption. Since, in this case, with only this information, our approach would likely consider expected harm over all cases as negative for a conduct, which would therefore be characterised as PI. Once information concerning market contextualisation becomes available and is taken into account, however, if there is SMP and lack of contestability we are likely to recognise that in some cases the conduct will lead to output reduction but in some other cases it will not. It is then important to know what the *expected* outcome across all cases is (which may be positive or negative) in order to then examine and compare error costs depending on whether subsequent screens are examined.

43 Hovenkamp (n 3).

- $\hat{p}_{H,i}$ and $p_{H,i}$ are large, i.e. we can identify when harmful conduct is indeed harmful with a high degree of accuracy, while $\hat{p}_{B,i}$, $p_{B,i}$ are small, i.e. we cannot identify when benign conduct is indeed benign with a high degree of accuracy;
- γ_i is small, so the likelihood that the specific conduct type investigated is genuinely harmful (even by firms with SMP), is small;
- B is large relative to H.

Thus, the hypothesis relies on many assumptions and this explains why it has recently been the subject of severe criticism. According to Shapiro[44] "…Easterbrook argued that antitrust courts should err on the side of defendants, because "judicial errors that tolerate baleful practices are self-correcting, while erroneous condemnations are not". Like Bork, Easterbrook achieved his desired result based not on economic theory or empirical evidence, but by making strong and unjustified assumptions."

Hovenkamp,[45] criticises particularly the Easterbrook[46] assumption that the average welfare cost B from a false conviction is likely to be larger than the average welfare cost H from a false acquittal, but we see from the above that even if this were to be true (which may well not be in many cases, as noted by Hovenkamp), there is still no obvious reason to expect that $DEC\ FC_i > DEC\ FA_i$.

IV. The Case of the Big-Tech Platforms

We will now apply the above approach to the choice of legal standards for (a) the case of Big-Tech platforms[47] and (b) the case of developing countries (see also Bageri and Katsoulacos[48]).

Big-Tech platforms are generally characterised by extreme economies of scale and network externalities (creating very highly concentrated markets), the significant role of data (to which, there may be discriminatory access and lack of data portability), lack of interoperability, all of which act as a significant barrier to entry, often lack of multi-homing, and very significant economics of scope (that explain the emergence and growth of ecosystems and give incumbents a strong incumbency advantage). All of these may give dominant digital firms strong incentives to engage in anticompetitive behaviour (see e.g. Crémer, de Montjoye and Schweitzer).[49]

44 Shapiro (n 35).

45 Hovenkamp (n 3).

46 Easterbrook (n 3).

47 Based on Katsoulacos and Ulph (n 8).

48 V Bageri and Y Katsoulacos, 'Why Legal Standards in Antitrust Enforcement in Developing Jurisdictions Should Differ from Those in Mature Jurisdictions: a Decision-Theoretic Approach' (2022) 3 BRICS J Econ 2 63–76.

49 Crémer, de Montjoye and Schweitzer (n 7).

The above characteristics suggest that the Big-Tech platforms are likely to have significant and also not-fleeting market power, being non-contestable (in other words, $\hat{\beta}$ *is large*); the likelihood that, given their degree of dominance is high, the potentially abusive conduct types undertaken by them will be genuinely harmful (γ) is also large; and the value of H could well be higher than B, since their market power and financial strength implies that false acquittals will not be easily or quickly corrected by market forces, while the platforms are likely to have the means to find alternative ways to pursue falsely convicted conduct, and to persuade enforcers of their benign character. It follows that, these conducts should be characterised as presumptively illegal, that is, that (expression (2)) above holds.

The Stigler Center Report of the Committee for the Study of Digital Platforms[50] argues:

> While some markets may self-correct (making the cost of false acquittals small), the findings of this report suggest that rapid self- correction in markets dominated by large digital platforms is unlikely, and that harms to economic welfare from the exercise of market power in such markets are substantial. .... Moreover, while monopoly profits are a lure to competitors, incumbents can use those very profits to entrench themselves and protect their position. No matter how dynamic the technology, an entrant will not unseat a monopolist if the monopolist is permitted to buy the dynamic entrant for a share of monopoly profits. Both parties gain from such a transaction – and the public loses. The result is less entry than a more competitive environment would create. Less entry into digital markets means fewer choices for consumers, stunted development of alternative paths of innovation, higher prices, and lower quality. Self-correction is not a realistic expectation in this environment – indeed, the available evidence suggests it has not happened – and public policy should not rely exclusively on it.

Following on from the above, the Easterbrook hypothesis (expression (5)) is also not likely to hold and we can see this more formally using the model above. From expressions (3) and (4), expression (5) will not hold if:[51]

$$\frac{\gamma_i \mathrm{H}}{(1-\gamma_i)B} + \frac{\gamma_i \mathrm{H}}{B}\left(\frac{\hat{\beta}_i}{(1-\hat{\beta}_i)}\right) > (1-p_{B,i})\left[\left(\frac{1}{1-p_{H,i}}\right) + \left(\frac{1-\hat{p}_{B,i}}{1-\hat{p}_{H,i}}\right)\right] \quad (6)$$

Concerning the discriminating probabilities $\hat{p}_{H,i}$, $\hat{p}_{B,i}$ and $p_{H,i}$, $p_{B,i}$, (that determine the discriminating power in identifying correctly whether screen i holds, and, if

50 Chicago Booth School of Business (n 38).

51 And DEC of FA will be greater than DEC of FC. See for details Katsoulacos and Ulph (n 8).

it does, whether the conduct is harmful or benign), there are reasons for arguing that all these discriminating probabilities (and hence the discriminating power of our tests) will be lower, at least at present, in the digital sector in which platforms or ecosystems rather than traditional firms are the main actors. As noted by Jenny, in this sector:

> technology rather than the confines of economic markets provides the framework which determines the scope and type of activity of the platforms or the ecosystems, markets are multi-sided, competition is based on innovation, differentiation and quality rather than on price, cross-subsidization is rampant, and growth rather profit maximization may the principal concern of the platforms. As a result of the recent development of the digital sector and of its complexity, very little is known, at least by competition authorities, on how competition works between platforms and ecosystems and how innovation develops in this sector. What is clear is that most of the concepts and the instruments we use in competition law enforcement of non-digital sectors are of little use and little relevance when we deal with competition issues in the digital sector.[52]

The difficulty concerns both identifying correctly when there is genuinely exclusionary behaviour and when this does harm consumer welfare, but also identifying and balancing efficiency effects and so identifying correctly truly benign behaviour. Thus, our best guess about the relative value of the probabilities is that roughly:

$$p_{H,i} \approx p_{B,i} \text{ and } \hat{p}_{H,i} \approx \hat{p}_{B,i}$$

Then, using this assumption and rearranging terms in expression (6) we can re-write this inequality as follows:

$$(s_i - 1) + \frac{\gamma_i H}{B}\hat{w}_i + > 1 - p_{B,i} \qquad (6')$$

Where:

$$s_i = \frac{\gamma_i H}{(1-\gamma)B} > 1, \text{ since } \gamma_i H > (1-\gamma_i)B$$

(by the definition of presumptive illegality of a conduct), so s_i is the indicator measuring the strength of this presumption (for given $\hat{\beta}_i$), and

$$\hat{w}_i - \left(\frac{\hat{\beta}_i}{(1-\hat{\beta}_i)}\right)$$

is the extent of prevalence of precondition i, so, for example, $\hat{w}_2$ measures the extent to which a given conduct type among those examined under abuse of

52 See Frédéric Jenny, 'Competition law enforcement and regulation for digital ecosystems: Understanding the issues, facing the challenges and moving forward' (September 2021) 3 Concurrences 101662 38–62.

dominance has exclusionary effects when undertaken by genuinely dominant firms. $\hat{\beta}_i$ and so $\hat{w}_i$ falls with i, i.e. as additional investigative steps are undertaken.

Given what was mentioned just above, in the Big-Tech digital markets the values of γ_i and $\hat{\beta}_i$, and of (H/B) > 1, will tend to be higher and therefore s_i and $\hat{w}_i$ will also be higher. So the Left Hand Side (LHS) of (6'), which we may think of as measuring the strength of the presumption of illegality will be unambiguously higher in the Big-Tech digital platform markets. On the other hand, as also just mentioned above, $p_{B,i}$, $0 < p_{B,i} < 1$, will tend to be lower. Therefore 1- $p_{B,i}$ (on the RHS of (6'), which we may think of as the probability of false convictions given screen i is satisfied, will be higher in the Big-Tech digital platform markets relative to traditional (or pipeline markets).

So the Easterbrook hypothesis is more likely not to hold (i.e. ((6') to hold) in the Big-Tech digital markets than in traditional markets if the strength of the presumption of illegality in the former markets is higher than in the latter markets to an extent that compensates for the potential higher probability of false convictions, at least at present, in the former relative to the latter markets.

1. Enforcement Differences between US, EU and Other Countries

While the conclusions above seem to have indeed influenced enforcers in the EC/EU and many other countries, this has not been the case, at least until very recently, in the US. There have been a number of differences between the US, EU and other countries. To start with, the US tends to treat many more practices, even when undertaken by firms with significant market power, as *presumptively legal* (rather than illegal), that is, on average benign, than is the case in the EU, that would treat these practices when undertaken by dominant firms as *presumptively illegal*. Next and related to this, in the US, the dominant view has been for a long time that the primary objective in antitrust enforcement is to limit false convictions rather than false acquittals – a view that as we have noted has only started to be strongly criticised recently[53] – and a view that is not held in the EC. As an outcome of these views, in the US there has been a strong tendency to treat what are considered *presumptively legal* conducts using per se legality LS (or, quick look LS), an approach that leads to a high rate of acquittals and has been particularly criticised with respect to enforcement in the high-tech digital markets.

As the Stigler Committee Report[54] notes 'there have been few antitrust challenges to exclusionary conduct since the government's 1998 case against Microsoft, and courts have in several instances been hostile to such cases and have imposed

53 See in particular the detailed and very careful arguments of Baker and Hovenkamp (n 3) to which we have already referred above. See also Hovenkamp and Scott Morton (n 37) 19–20.

54 Chicago Booth School of Business (n 38).

daunting proof requirements on plaintiffs. Apparent under-enforcement is in part due to courts' reliance on so- called Chicago School assumptions that do not have a sound theoretical or empirical basis', Baker and others[55] mention that:

> Both the Federal Trade Commission and the Justice Department have at times abetted the judicial retrenchment in antitrust law, particularly as it applies to the conduct of high-tech platforms, by declining to challenge (or in some cases even investigate) nearly all of the large number of platform acquisitions of arguably nascent competitors, and declining to challenge platform conduct that has been the subject of enforcement actions by sophisticated competition agencies abroad. Without regard to the merits of any individual decision, this systematic pattern of enforcement avoidance suggests that until now, the agencies have been too cautious in their enforcement posture toward Internet platforms.

Another difference is that if, on the other hand, in the US a practice is considered *presumptively illegal,* then at least in the last two–three decades, there is a strong tendency to rely on extensive use of economic analysis and evidence in case-specific investigations, that is, to rely much more on the *rule of reason (or a full effects-based approach).*

This has not been the case in the EU, which has treated the practices considered *presumptively illegal* until recently by relying more on *object-based* or on intermediate LS rather than full *effect-based.* This is true both at the level of the EU Commission (EC) and that of Member States. The difference is thought to be particularly pronounced in abuse of dominance cases but also many vertical restraints.[56] As Gavil[57] notes, after the *Sylvania* decision[58] in the US 'the Court systematically went about the task of dismantling many of the per se rules…., and increasingly turned to modern economic theory to inform its interpretation and application of the Sherman Act'. See also Hovenkamp[59] for a thorough and very thoughtful review on the rule of reason LS. Neven[60], on the other hand, reviews the situation in the EU, identifying low levels of economic analysis, especially in abuse of dominance cases. Geradin and Petit[61]

---

55 Baker and others (n 2) 13, 64.

56 For an excellent overview of the application of economics in a century of antitrust enforcement in the US see WE Kovacic and C Shapiro, 'Antitrust Policy: a Century of Economic and Legal Thinking' (2000) 14 JEL 1 43–60 <https://www.aeaweb.org/articles?id=10.1257/jep.14.1.43> accessed 17 March 2023.

57 Gavil, 'Burden of Proof in U.S. Antitrust Law' (n 21).

58 Continental Television v. GTE *Sylvania*, 433 U.S. 36 (1977).

59 Herbert J Hovenkamp, 'The Rule of Reason' (2018) 70 UFla L Rev 81<https://papers.ssrn.com/sol3/papers.cfm?abstract_id=2885916> accessed 17 March 2023.

60 D Neven, 'Competition Economics and Antitrust in Europe' (2006) 21 Econ Policy 48 742–791.

61 D Geradin and N Petit, 'Judicial Review in EU Competition Law: a Quantitative and Qualitative Assessment' (2010) Tilburg Law School Research Paper 01/2011 <https://papers.ssrn.com/sol3/papers.cfm?abstract_id=1698342> accessed 17 March 2023.

note that under a presumption of illegality, the assessment of such cases in the EU has relied on 'old, formalistic legal appraisal standards, and (has shown) a reluctance to endorse a modern economic approach'.[62] However, Katsoulacos and Makri[63] show that there has been a systematic and *substantial move towards effects-based* in the Directorate-General Competition decisions in the last two decades. The difference with the US is still pronounced with respect to other jurisdictions.[64]

These differences in the treatment of presumptively illegal conduct seem to be due to two factors. The *strength* of the presumption of illegality and the weight placed on the cost of false acquittals that is higher in the EU, something which tends to favour a choice of more presumption-based LS rather than full effects-based. Another equally significant factor is that the substantive or liability standard has been more that of 'disadvantaging rivals' than 'consumer welfare' in the EU[65] and this naturally makes the choice of LS in the EU what we have called truncated effects-based LS that is based, in order to reach liability decisions, on just evidence of exclusion of (disadvantaging) rivals.[66] It is interesting that Khan[67] and Wu[68] as well as other Neo-Brandeisians have also been proposing the adoption of a non-welfarist substantive (liability) standard in the US.[69]

---

62 See also, J Gual and N Mas, 'Industry Characteristics and Anti-Competitive Behavior: Evidence from the European Commission's Decisions' (2011) 39 Rev Ind Organ 3 207–230; P Papandropoulos, 'The Implementation of an Effects-Based Approach under Article 82: Principles and Application' in *The Reform of EC Competition Law: New Challenges* (Kluwer Law International 2010) ch 14; Philip Marsden, 'Exclusionary Abuses and the Justice of "Competition on the Merits"' in I Kokkoris and I Lianos (eds), *The Reform of EC Competition Law: New Challenges* (Kluwer Law International 2010) ch 14; W Wils, 'The Judgment of the EU General Court in Intel and the so-called More Economic Approach to Abuse of Dominance' (2014) 37 World Competition 4 405–434; P Rey and JS Venit, 'An Effects-Based Approach to Article 102: A Response to Wouter Wils' (2015) 38 World Competition 1 3–29; Lucas Peeperkorn, 'Conditional pricing: Why the General Court is Wrong in Intel and What the Court of Justice Can Do to Rebalance the Assessment of Rebates' (2015) 1 Concurrences 70835 43–6. OECD, 'Ex Ante Regulation in Digital Markets–Background Note' (2021) DAF/COMP(2021)15 <https://one.oecd.org/document/DAF/COMP(2021)15/en/pdf> and for a recent extensive review P Ibanez Colomo'Beyond the "More Economic-Based Approach": A Legal Perspective on Article 102 TFEU Case Law' (2016) 53 CML Rev 3 709–39.

63 Katsoulacos and Makri (n 10).

64 See the empirical findings of Y Katsoulacos and others, 'Comparing the role of economics/effects-based in antitrust enforcement and its relation to the judicial review in the EC to other countries' (2021) 12 J ECL & Pract 2 122–42, covering France, Greece and Russia as well as the EC.

65 Interestingly, in addition to the authors mentioned below, Giulio Federico, Fiona Scott Morton and Carl Shapiro 'Antitrust and Innovation: Welcoming and Protecting Disruption' in Josh Lerner and Scott Stern (eds), *Innovation Policy and the Economy* (University of Chicago Press 2020), argue, in the context of assessing effects on innovation in favor of adopting the disadvantaging rivals' or 'distorting the competitive process' SS (see for distinction in introductory section above).

66 We already discussed the relationship between legal and substantive standards. See also Katsoulacos (n 5).

67 Lina Khan, 'The Ideological Roots of America's Market Power Problem' (2018) 127 Yale LJF <www.yalelawjournal.org/forum/the-ideological-roots-of-americas-market-power-problem> accessed 17 March 2023.

68 T Wu, 'After Consumer Welfare, Now What? The "Protection of Competition" Standard in Practice' (2018) CPI <www.competitionpolicyinternational.com/after-consumer-welfare-now-what-the-protection-of-competition-standard-in-practice-2/> accessed 17 March 2023.

69 See also F Lancieri and PM Sakowski "Competition in Digital Markets: a Review of Expert Reports"(2021), 149 – 150. For detailed criticisms of these views by strong adherents to the consumer welfare standard, see AD Melamed and N Petit, 'The Misguided Assault on the Consumer Welfare Standard in the Age of Platform Markets' (2019) 54 Rev Ind Organ 4 741–74 and Manne (n 38)

While the movement away from object-based LS identified in Katsoulacos and Makri[70] in the EC indicate that in the latter increased emphasis is placed on consumer harm. These developments suggest that enforcement procedures may be converging in recent years on the two sides of the Atlantic with respect to conducts treated as presumptively illegal.

2. A More Presumption-Based Approach for Big-Tech Platforms?

According to our conclusions above, in the case of the Big-Tech platforms many of the conduct types examined under abuse of dominance (or, monopolisation) should be treated as presumptively illegal. The strength of this presumption is higher for the digital sector than in traditional sectors and the Easterbrook hypothesis is less likely to hold in the former sector. This does *not,* however, necessarily or unambiguously imply that in this sector, on cost of error-minimisation grounds, we should adopt a more presumption-based LS in the enforcement of specific conduct types.[71] However, we show below that they do imply that *adopting more presumption-based LS are more likely to be error-minimising than in traditional markets.* We now discuss this.

To start with, we note, that a number of prominent commentators e.g. Crémer, de Montjoye and Schweitzer,[72] and Federico, Scott Morton and Shapiro,[73] have recently proposed that in the case of the Big-Tech digital platforms we should abandon a full effects-based approach and rely on the presumption created by the exclusion screen (though making this presumption rebuttable and assigning to the defendants the burden of proof for rebutting it). We focus our discussion on this specific proposal.

Federico, Scott Morton and Shapiro[74] argue, in the context of assessing effects on innovation:

> …the quantum of evidence required to conclude that a dominant firm's conduct has harmed innovation and thereby violated the antitrust laws is a critical element of competition policy. A more assertive antitrust regime will find antitrust violations in cases where the challenged conduct disrupts the competitive process by impeding the incentive or ability of rivals to innovate. This is justified because economists understand that when the incentives for a certain activity (such as investing in R&D) decline, profit maximizing firms

70 Katsoulacos and Makri (n 10).

71 As we should probably expect, given all the factors that influence the error-minimising choice.

72 Crémer, de Montjoye and Schweitzer (n 7).

73 Federico, Scott Morton and Shapiro (n 65).

74 ibid. Our emphasis.

> will predictably engage in less of that activity. Thus, if one has persuasive evidence of reduced incentives to develop new products, one can reliably conclude that innovation will be lessened. A more timid antitrust policy would require evidence showing that rivals actually reduced their R&D on particular projects as a result of the challenged conduct, and that this reduction harmed customers because certain specific products were not developed. *Proving those elements would be highly impossible in many dynamic markets. If the evidentiary burden of proof is set too high, antitrust enforcement will be ineffective in dynamic, innovation industries.*

Further:

> Exclusion of a disruptive entrant inherently harms the competitive process, even if that disruptive entrant is (currently) less efficient than the dominant firm. Indeed, that pattern tends to be the norm in industries subject to significant economies of scale (e.g. due to network effects and/or learning by doing). Disrupters that are less efficient at the outset than the established dominant firm can still pose a grave competitive threat to the incumbent, because they have countervailing characteristics that appeal to consumers, or their efficiencies will improve as they gain experience and scale. Regardless of an entrant's current level of efficiency, the competitive process requires they not to be squashed by conduct that does not constitute competition on merit, which can include conduct that would not make economic sense if not for its exclusionary impact on competitors.

Crémer, de Montjoye and Schweitzer express more clearly their preference for a more presumption-based approach for the Big-Tech platforms:

> ..... in the context of highly concentrated markets characterised by strong network effects and high barriers to entry (i.e. not easily corrected by markets themselves), one may want to *err on the side of disallowing potentially anti-competitive conducts, and impose on the incumbent the burden of proof for showing the pro-competitiveness of its conduct.* This may be true especially where dominant platforms try to expand into neighboring markets, thereby growing into digital ecosystems, which become ever more difficult for users to leave. In such cases, there may be, for example, a presumption in favour of a duty to ensure interoperability. Such a presumption may also be justified where dominant platforms control specific competitively relevant sets of user or aggregated data that competitors cannot reproduce.[75]

---

75 Crémer, de Montjoye and Schweitzer (n 7) 4, (authors' emphasis). See also F Lancieri and PM Sakowski (n 73) 149 – 150 for a summary of similar views advocated in other expert reposrt such as the Stigler Report. As Crémer et.al. notice, that "authorities balance error-costs in antitrust by modifying legal standards and presumptions and by inverting burdens of proof".

The argument by Federico, Scott Morton and Shapiro[76] outlined in the quotes above is in the same spirit, though they seem to frame their argument as a proposal to replace the consumer welfare substantive standard by the 'distorting the competitive process' or the 'disadvantaging rivals' substantive standard.[77] Both proposals lead to exactly the same result in this case, as we noted at the beginning: adopting this shift in SS is exactly the same as relying on LS that presume welfare harm without taking into account any efficiencies or even just on the basis of exclusionary evidence. We generally consider the proposal to reform enforcement by adopting a non-welfarist criterion for liability too far reaching and insufficiently justified at present and we would prefer, if a choice had to be made, to maintain the consumer welfare criterion and adopt more restricted (presumption-based) LS in certain cases (such as the one of the Big-Tech digitals examined here). So below, we consider whether such an approach is justified in cost of error-minimisation grounds using the model described above.

We show that for presumptively illegal conducts and even if the Easterbrook hypothesis does hold in some intermediate stage of the continuum of LS, it may be justifiable on error-minimisation grounds to undertake additional investigations. Specifically, it may be justifiable to go beyond stage 2 (that just involves the identification of exclusion potential). On error-minimising grounds, this would be right if the DEC having undertaken a stage 3 investigation (or an investigation of subsequent stages) were lower than DEC in stage 2. It is argued that this *can* be the case[78] and hence the proposal for more presumption-based LS cannot be established unambiguously.[79] However, *adopting more presumption-based LS (based just on evidence of exclusion to reach liability decisions) is indeed more likely to be error-minimising than in traditional markets* when in the latter markets firms with significant market power and lacking contestability are involved (so that H > B).

A detailed examination of expressions (3) and (4) in two subsequent investigative stages (i and i+1), can show the following:

First, concerning the DEC of FA, a necessary and sufficient condition for $DEC\ FA_{i+1} \leq DEC\ FA_i$ is that

$$\hat{p}_{H,i+1} p_{H,i+1} > \hat{p}_{H,i} p_{H,i}, \qquad (7)$$

i.e. that there is an increase in the 'overall' discriminatory power of the screens in identifying genuinely harmful conducts in stage i+1 relative to stage i. It is

76 Federico, Scott Morton and Shapiro (n 65).

77 Khan (n 67), generalises in this respect, arguing that the consumer surplus standard has crippled antitrust enforcement by prompting 'a shift away from per se rules and towards rule of reason analysis'.

78 Given the multitude and variety of factors involved this should have been expected.

79 On the other hand, more presumption-based standards in Abuse of Dominance (AoD) cases are more likely to be justifiable in developing jurisdictions on error minimisation grounds (see below).

generally reasonable to assume that the 'overall' discriminatory power of the economic analyses applied on identifying whether a screen is satisfied and, if it is, on identifying correctly whether it is harmful, i.e. $\hat{p}_H p_H$, is *increasing* with additional investigative steps.[80] However, it is more likely that this will not be the case for the digital platforms and ecosystems relative to the traditional markets. This is because $\hat{p}_H$ is likely to fall,[81]and the rise in p_H is more likely to be smaller (given the greater difficulties in correctly identifying consumer welfare loss in the absence of efficiencies in the digital cases), so the rise in p_H is less likely to be sufficient to compensate for the fall in $\hat{p}_H$ (therefore $\hat{p}_H p_H$ will fall). Having said that, it is also certainly the case, as indicated by many papers in the Industrial Organisation literature, that proving that the defendant is able and has incentives to exclude, i.e. that the screen of stage 2 is satisfied, does *not necessarily* imply consumer welfare harm, i.e. that the screen of stage 3 is satisfied – even, that is, before accounting for efficiencies (see Salop[82] and Chica, Chuck and Tamayo[83] and others), so a further investigation could be expected to improve our ability to discriminate correctly between cases where this is the case and where this is not the case. However, the many arguments discussed by Salop to prove this point were not meant to apply to digital platforms and the other references in the last footnote that are relevant to digital platforms provide good but only theoretical possibilities that exclusion may not lower welfare, rather than any clearly applicable tests for identifying when this would be the case empirically in specific cases.

So, the overall conclusion is that *when dealing with digital platforms and ecosystems there is a greater likelihood than in traditional markets that there will be an increase in the probability of FA by proceeding to investigative stage 3* (i.e. from stage 2 to stage 3).

---

80 See also Katsoulacos and Ulph (n 8). As we noted above while the assumption that p_H increases is uncontroversial, the assumption that $\hat{p}_H$ increases is not. However, we expect that generally the increase in the former will outweigh any fall in the latter (if there is a fall), in successive investigative stages, and so $\hat{p}_H p_H$ will increase.

81 $\hat{p}_H$ is the probability that having undertaken investigative step i, the precondition examined in step i is considered satisfied when indeed this is the case. Consider stages 2 and 3. In stage 3 the precondition is considered satisfied if our stage 3 tests suggest that consumer welfare will fall (in the absence of taking into account efficiencies) and that this is correct. In stage 2 the precondition is considered satisfied if our stage 2 tests suggest that we should expect exclusion and this is correct. In stage 2 the probability is likely to be higher (in stage 3, lower). A numerical example may be helpful. In a traditional market $\hat{p}_H = 0{,}8$ and $p_H = 0{,}5$ in stage 2 while in stage 3, $\hat{p}_H = 0{,}7$ and $p_H = 0{,}7$. So $\hat{p}_H p_H$ *increases* from 0,4 to 0,49 (the increase would be even greater if $\hat{p}_H$ increased). In a digital market, $\hat{p}_H = 0{,}5$ and $p_H = 0{,}6$ in stage 2, while $\hat{p}_H = 0{,}3$ and $p_H = 0{,}8$. So $\hat{p}_H p_H$ *decreases* from 0,3 to 0,24.

82 See S Salop, 'The Raising Rivals' Cost Foreclosure Paradigm, Conditional Pricing Practices, and the Flawed Incremental Price-Cost Test' (2017) 81 ABAJ 371–421. Salop discusses cases in which this has been recognised and led to acquittal in US. For a summary of the point see 391 (first paragraph).

83 C Chica, K Chuk and J Tamayo, (2021), 'Exclusive Dealing and Entry by Competing Two-Sided Platforms' (2021) Harvard Business School Working Paper 21-092 <www.hbs.edu/ris/Publication%20 Files/21-092_3905ed04-8a4c-4655-9f6b-b5242a0dbacf.pdf> accessed 17 March 2023; See also J Cong, Y Huang and W Zhou, 'Exclusive Dealing in Asymmetric Platform Competition' (2022) Working Paper <https://papers.ssrn.com/sol3/papers.cfm?abstract_id=4129788> accessed 17 March 2023; L Shao, 'Exclusive dealing in two-sided markets: For better or worse?' (Doctoral Dissertation, University of Texas 2016) <https://repositories.lib.utexas.edu/handle/2152/39434> accessed 17 March 2023.

Next, concerning the DEC of FC, it can be shown that a sufficient condition for $DEC\ FC_{i+1} \leq DEC\ FC_i$ is that there is significant *increase* in our ability to discriminate between harmful and benign conduct when the latter is genuinely benign (i. e a significant increase in p_B) as a result of the additional investigation. Also, for any given increase in $p_{B,}$[84] a reduction in the DEC of FC is more likely the greater the increase in γ, (i. e the probability that conduct is genuinely harmful) and the larger the fall in $\hat{\beta}$,[85] with the additional investigative steps. However, for DEC to fall we also require that the probability $\hat{p}_{B,i}$[86] increases or remains the same as additional screens are analysed (which is not guaranteed).

Now, the increase in p_B is likely to be smaller in digital markets and is also less likely that there will be an increase in $\hat{p}_B$. Both of these tend to make it more likely that the probability of FC will increase in digital relative to traditional markets. However, γ will rise more in the former which makes it less likely that the probability of FC will rise in the former rather than in the latter markets. Finally, $\hat{\beta}$ falls in subsequent investigative stages and this lowers the probability of FC, though the fall again is likely to be lower in the Big-Tech digital platforms.

Thus, the overall conclusion is that we cannot unambiguously say that when dealing with digital platforms and ecosystems there is a greater likelihood than in traditional markets that there will be an increase or a decrease in the probability of FC by proceeding to investigative stage 3 (i.e. from stage 2 to stage 3). While the change in the value of all (but one) parameters suggests that indeed it is more likely that there will be an increase, the increase in γ tends to decrease the probability of FC.

The results above concentrate on all the parameters that determine the *probability* of FA and FC neglecting H and B (since, comparing DEC of FA from one stage to another H cancels out and comparing the DEC of FC from one stage to another B cancels out); these must, however, be taken into account in order to determine the *costs* of these errors. Now, if the probabilities of both FA and of FC fall (increase) by the investigation of a further screen then DEC fall (increase) too irrespective of the size of H and B. But if one rises and the other falls, then:

(i) If the probability of FA rises and that of FC falls then total DEC will be more likely to fall exactly when B > H (as the Easterbrook hypothesis assumes), while if H > B, total DEC are more likely to rise).[87]

84 We assume that there is *some* increase, though the increase may be small and this is particularly relevant for the digital platforms, given what was mentioned above about these probabilities.

85 The probability that a precondition is genuinely satisfied in the total population of conducts of the type examined.

86 This is the probability that having undertaken investigative step i, the precondition examined in step i is *not* considered satisfied when indeed this is the case. Consider stages 2 and 3. In stage 3 the precondition is not considered satisfied if our stage 3 tests suggest that consumer welfare will rise (even in the absence of taking into account efficiencies) and this is correct. In stage 2 the precondition is not considered satisfied if our stage 2 tests suggest that we should not expect exclusion and this is correct.

87 See Katsoulacos and Ulph (n 8), s 4 for details of the results described here.

(ii) If the probability of FA falls and that of FC rises then total DEC will be more likely to fall when H > B (while if B > H, total DEC are more likely to rise).

Above we demonstrated that the probability of FA to rise in subsequent investigative steps is more likely for the Big-Tech digital platforms than for traditional sectors and that H > B is more likely to hold in the former than in the latter. The comparison for the probability of FC is not unambiguous. Thus, it is more likely (if the probability of FC does not also rise – of course, if both probabilities rise, DEC will rise) that case (i) above will apply in the case of the Big-Tech digital platforms. And it is more likely that case (ii), in which the probability of FA falls, will apply in traditional sectors. If the probability of FC also fall the DEC will certainly fall in such sectors. But even if the probability of FC rises (as in case (ii)), DEC will again fall in such (i.e. traditional) sectors when there is significant market power/lack of contestability which implies H > B (the first sub-case of case (ii)).

Thus, *we find that, overall, it is certainly more likely that presumption-based LS will be optimal in the Big-Tech digital platforms than in traditional sectors involving dominant firms for which H > B, i.e. when the harm from wrongly acquitting is greater than the harm from wrongly convicting.*

3. Enforcement Procedures in Developing Countries[88]

In this section we show, using the framework above that there is a reduced need to apply effects-based LS in developing rather than developed countries *for error-minimising reasons.* In developing countries[89] the ability of markets to self-correct will usually be much more limited than in developed economies, as entry barriers and other market failures will be much higher, and, also, the CA decisions are unlikely to have significant adverse incentive effects,[90] that is, H is more likely to be greater than B. Also the likelihood (γ) that the conduct undertaken by a dominant firm is genuinely harmful, which as we have seen is a very significant factor in determining whether conduct by dominant firms

88 For a fuller examination of this see Bageri and Katsoulacos (n 48).

89 Here we use the term 'developing countries' for convenience. Broadly speaking we have in mind jurisdictions that have developed the relevant laws and institutions and have been active in antitrust enforcement for at most the last 20 years. However, we *also* have in mind here countries that are 'developing' in the sense of their general economic, technological, political and socio-cultural conditions and characteristics. Details can be found in Bageri and Katsoulacos (n 10), including a description of a methodology developed for EBRD to construct a *composite indicator of 'development'* in the above sense by Yannis Katsoulacos and Frederic Jenny, using a number of indices available from various international organisations, specifically: World Bank, World Economic Forum, Organization for Economic Cooperation and Development, United Nations Conference on Trade and Development, International Monetary Fund, *European Bank for Reconstruction and Development* and the World Trade Organization.

90 Hovenkamp's (n 3), remark that: 'Firms are pretty good at inventing around legal rules' and that: 'Courts can also invent around their own previous ruling, construing them more broadly or narrowly as perspective changes' made in the context of developed jurisdictions, is even more likely to be true in developing countries where it is more common not to display full respect to legal rules.

is presumptively illegal, is likely to be much higher in developing countries.[91] Thus, in the latter, *the presumption is much more likely to be that of illegality and of false acquittals been more costly than false convictions.* To illustrate, consider a potentially anticompetitive conduct (such as predatory pricing or rebate schemes) that on their own would not limit entry into markets but which could do so (and will be used to do so) when other entry barriers or market failures are present. In this case, countries/jurisdictions with low/other entry barriers or market failures, might not even engage actively in enforcement against such practices, while in jurisdictions with many other entry barriers the value of enforcement will be very high. Further, in the former countries, if CAs do remain involved in enforcing competition law for such conducts, they should be using effects-based assessment, but (the administratively less costly) presumption-based assessment should be used in jurisdictions in which other barriers are relatively high (prevalence of contestability is low), since in the latter the presumption of illegality of these conducts – i.e. presumption that they create harm – is much higher[92] with the cost of false convictions more likely to be lower than the cost of false acquittals.

In short, the Easterbrook hypothesis is much less likely to hold in developing countries since all of the factors mentioned above under expression (5) are more likely not to be satisfied in those countries than in developed countries. We have already mentioned that H, B and γ and, $\hat{\beta}_i$, is also likely to be larger (e.g. for stage 1, the probability that the firm genuinely has SMP/market is non-contestable, is larger).

More importantly, the adoption of more presumption-based LS is more likely to be justified in developing countries on error-minimising grounds. That is, *DEC are less likely to fall by additional investigations beyond those in stages 1 or 2 or, if they fall, this fall will be much smaller and thus less likely to justify the additional administration cost.* Demonstrating, as we did above, that the strength of the presumption of illegality is higher, *ceteris paribus*, at any given stage of the investigative process in developing jurisdictions, is the first step towards showing that more presumption-based LS are more likely to be superior in such jurisdictions than in developed jurisdictions.

---

91 This is the reason that usually in developing countries the threshold market share for presuming dominance is much lower, for example in Brazil it is just 20%, in Egypt or Uzbekistan it is 25%, in Ukraine it is 35%.

92 See also EM Fox and M Gal, 'Drafting Competition Law for Developing Jurisdictions: learning from experience' (2014) NY University Law and Economics Working Paper 374–2014 <https://papers.ssrn.com/sol3/papers.cfm?abstract_id=2425329> accessed 17 March 2023 (see also The Economic Characteristics of Developing Jurisdictions (Edward Elgar 2015) ch 12, 296–35 for a closely related discussion concerning the need for enforcing competition law in developing countries. Their discussion reminds us that different jurisdictions are characterised by different degrees to which competition is workable in products and services markets, in the absence of CL enforcement. As we stressed in the introduction, the degree to which competition is workable, while it depends both on the anticompetitive conduct of firms, which enforcement seeks to eliminate, also, and perhaps primarily, depends on the more general conditions mentioned in footnote 80. Also see M Gal, 'The Ecology of Antitrust: Preconditions for Competition Law Enforcement in Developing Countries' (2004) NY University Law and Economics Working Paper 02-03 and Bageri and Katsoulacos (n 10).

The second step involves taking into account the improvement in discriminatory power when additional investigations are undertaken. Generally, the four probabilities that determine the ability to discriminate without errors between harmful and benign conducts, and how they change, essentially determine the improvement in the *discriminatory power of the assessment* after an extra screen is examined. There is a significant number of factors that tend to make the level and the increase in these probabilities, if additional assessments are made, much smaller in developing than in developed countries. These factors include limited experience, a 'short' case-law history on which to rely, often more limited skills and resources, and limited data in terms of availability and quality. This lack in the discriminatory power of the assessments is of course the most important factor for making LS closer to 'per se' than effects-based error-minimising choice in developing countries.

To be more precise, to determine how investigating an additional screen affects the DECs consider, as in the previous section, the probabilities of FA and FC. With regard to the former, the increase in the 'overall' discriminating probability $p_H \hat{p}_H$, is not likely to increase in developing countries as much as in developed jurisdictions, for the reasons just mentioned. Thus, given that an increase in this 'overall' probability is a necessary and sufficient condition for the probability of FA to fall, the probability of FA is more likely to rise by a further investigation in developing jurisdictions. Next, concerning the probability of FC, we noted above that a sufficient condition for this to fall is that there is a significant increase in our ability to discriminate between harmful and benign conduct when the latter is genuinely benign (i.e. there is a significant increase in p_B). Again, for the reasons above, this probability will not increase as much as in developed jurisdictions, which tends to make an increase in the probability of FC more likely in developing jurisdictions. While the change of all (but one) of the other factors influencing FC (see above) reinforces this conclusion, the increase in γ will be greater in developing jurisdictions tending to make an increase in the probability of FC less likely in developing jurisdictions. Thus there can be no unambiguous comparison of the change in the probability of FC when an additional screen is investigated between the two types of jurisdictions.

Nevertheless, the first of these results implies that it is *more likely* in developing jurisdictions that case (i) – from the previous section – will apply involving an increase in the probability of FA. Further, as we noted above, the difference between H and B will be higher in developing countries. Thus irrespective of whether the probability of FC rises or falls, there will be, in developing countries, an unambiguous increase in the likelihood that DEC rise relative to developed countries i.e. an unambiguous increase in the likelihood that more presumption-based LS will be optimal.

In short, *the examination of all the factors affecting the DEC of additional investigations implies quite strongly that there is a reduced need to apply effects-based LS in developing countries relative to developed countries for error-minimising reasons.*

V. Concluding remarks

The choice of LS in antitrust enforcement, to guide the assessment of potentially anticompetitive conduct, in order to decide whether there is liability or not, has been hotly debated for many years. The debate has gained in intensity in recent years as a result of the concerns expressed in many countries with the antitrust treatment of the major digital platforms. More specifically it has been argued that existing *antitrust rules* reflect a systematically skewed error-cost balance, being excessively concerned with falsely convicting procompetitive conduct and with the high cost of litigation, too dismissive of the cost of *failing* to deter harmful conduct. This has encouraged enforcement policies that are too cautious and overly demanding in terms of evidentiary standards that have led to too high a rate of acquittals in meritorious exclusionary conduct cases. This chapter argues that while the cost of error-minimising analysis cannot be used *unambiguously* to support a move to more presumption-based (rather than full effects-based or rule of reason) LS for specific conduct types in the case of the Big-Tech platforms, such a move is indeed *more likely* to be error-minimising than in traditional markets, when in the latter firms with significant market power and lacking contestability are involved. Also it is shown that such a move could be recommended for developing jurisdictions.

Competition Law Systems, Courts, and the Formulation of Presumptions

William E. Kovacic*
George Washington University Law School

Abstract

Courts often rely on presumptions to assess the legality of business conduct under competition law statutes. This chapter considers improvements in the processes by which courts formulate and reformulate presumptions. Courts decide cases one at a time and are not institutionally well suited, by recourse to their own institutional powers, to situate the resolution of individual cases within larger developments in learning in economics and law. The chapter suggests approaches that a competition law system can take to improve the capacity of courts to anchor presumptions in a sound understanding of empirical and theoretical learning in industrial organization economics.

---

* Global Competition Professor of Law and Policy, George Washington University Law School; Visiting Professor, Dickson Poon School of Law, King's College London. I am most grateful to Andrew Gavil and Alison Jones for may helpful discussions. Contact: wkovacic@law.gwu.edu.

I. Introduction

In many competition law systems, courts play a significant role in the formulation of rules that guide the analysis of business behavior.[1] In the United States, for example, the federal courts are the chief instrument for developing the operational criteria that determine the application of the Sherman Act's broad prohibitions on restraints of trade and monopolization.[2] Some legal systems define antitrust offenses more precisely. Article 102 of the Treaty on the Functioning of the European Union enumerates various behaviors that shall be considered abusive if carried out by a dominant enterprise.[3] Even with this greater level of specification, the interpretation of Article 102 has varied over time as the EU's courts have refined that methodology to be used in assessing the legality of challenged conduct.[4]

Presumptions about the actual or likely effects of business practices underpin the definition and application of competition law rules. Some presumptions are said to be conclusive, such as the per se condemnation of certain conduct under section 1 of the Sherman Act.[5] Others are generally rebuttable. In some instances, behavior is presumed to be legitimate unless the plaintiff shows that the behavior has actual or likely adverse competitive effects. In others, behavior is presumed to be illegal unless the defendant can show that offsetting benefits predominate. The formulation of presumptions for specific practices has changed over time – for example, for the treatment of vertical distribution practices in the United States – in light of new learning from the fields of economics and law.[6]

Modern debates about the treatment of large information services platforms focus heavily on the choice of presumptions to be applied to the behavior of these platforms.[7] The debate arises in two contexts: discussions about the enactment of statutes that establish new regulatory frameworks for the oversight of large platforms, and discussions about the refinement by courts of presumptions within the framework of existing laws. Some jurisdictions, such as the European Union (EU),

---

1 See generally Andrew I. Gavil et al., Antitrust Law in Perspective: Cases, Concepts and Problems in Competition Policy 72-81 (West Academic Publishing 4th ed. 2021); William E. Kovacic, *The Future Adaptation of the Per Se Rule of Illegality in U.S. Antitrust Law*, 33 Colum. Bus. L. Rev. (2021); Alison Jones & William E. Kovacic, *Identifying Anticompetitive Agreements in the United States and the European Union: Developing a Coherent Antitrust Analytical Framework*, 62 Antitrust Bull. 254 (2017).

2 See Kovacic, *supra* note 1, at 39.

3 See Gavil et al., *supra* note 1, at 75–76.

4 Richard Whish & David Bailey, Competition Law 180–223 (Oxford University Press 10th ed. 2021).

5 15 U.S.C. § 1.

6 See Gavil et al., *supra* note 1, at 925–1149. In all competition law cases involving concerted action, defendants have the opportunity to argue that their behavior is not properly classified as falling within the boundaries of the categorical prohibition or, in the case of Article 101(3) of the Treaty on the Functioning of the European Union, that the challenged conduct generates redeeming efficiency benefits that should save the conduct from condemnation. See Jones & Kovacic, supra note 1.

7 See Eleanor M. Fox, *Simple Rules for Antitrust*, in this book; Hervert Hovenkamp, *Making Antitrust Decisions About Digital Platforms*, in this book.

have created new regulatory commands that establish presumptions of illegality for specific forms of conduct undertaken by large information services platforms; others are contemplating similar legislative measures.[8]

How are courts to go about the task of devising the presumptions that govern the implementation of prohibition by dominant firms? In particular, how are courts to assemble the base of knowledge – from empirical and theoretical study – that should guide the establishment or refinement of presumptions? In many respects, courts have weak institutional tools to perform this task. A variety of institutional constraints limit their ability to situate individual disputes in a larger context that features ongoing change and increasing complexity in commerce. Courts decide cases one at a time based on the specific factual records before them. They do not perform their own studies of commercial conditions or the effects of existing legal rules. They do not convene proceedings, as legislatures or regulatory bodies do, to gather data and to obtain the views of expert analysts.

This chapter considers methods to improve the capacity of courts to anchor presumptions in a sound understanding of the competitive significance of business practices. It begins by setting out the processes that currently inform the efforts of courts to design presumptions, and it then discusses approaches that a competition law system can take to improve the ability of courts to make sound judgments about the structure and content of such presumptions. It seeks to improve and clarify the means by which courts are informed about ongoing learning in industrial organization economics.

This chapter highlights the possible contributions that competition agencies can make – for example, in conducting research, convening conferences and related proceedings, and issuing guidelines – to inform judicial decisions about the formulation of presumptions. The chapter also proposes ways in which academic institutions can participate in a periodic redetermination of the content of presumptions.

II. Judicial Formulation of Presumptions: Means for Discernment

Competition law jurisprudence has featured important adjustments over time to the presumptions that guide the analysis of business behavior. In general terms, the sensibility of presumptions depends on how well they resolve the tension between achieving accuracy in the diagnosis of specific conduct and attaining simplicity that facilitates understanding of the legal command and sound predictions about how the command will be applied. Reconciling this tension skillfully requires a continuing assessment of whether the empirical and theoretical assumptions that support the presumptions are valid.

---

8 For example, in April 2023, the government of the United Kingdom published the Digital Markets, Competition, and Consumers Bill, which would impose new obligations on certain digital platforms.

A key question for courts is how judges are to discern whether developments in theory and empirical study dictate alterations to the existing framework. This question focuses attention on the processes through which courts gather and absorb ideas and information about the competitive significance of various commercial practices. The discussion in this section reviews approaches courts have used to discern which form of presumptions should apply to business conduct.

1. Textualism

One basis for courts to set the content of presumptions consists of studying the texts of competition law statutes and discerning the meaning attributed to them at the time of their adoption.[9] This method has a checkered history in US antitrust experience. In *United States v. Trans-Missouri Freight Association* in 1897, the Supreme Court concluded that the price-setting arrangement of the defendant railroads was illegal because section 1 of the Sherman Act barred *every* contract in restraint of trade, without exception.[10] In 1911, in *Standard Oil Company of New Jersey v. United States*, the court retreated from its earlier literal reading of the statute and concluded that Section 1 prohibited only "unreasonable" trade restraints and leaving open the possibility that some restrictions might be banned because they were inherently unreasonable.[11]

2. Common Law Antecedents to Antitrust Statutes

On a number of occasions, the US Supreme Court has used common law principles developed before adoption of the Sherman Act in 1890 to guide the formulation of presumptions for concerted practices alleged to restrain trade. The court's formative decisions in the early history of the Sherman Act examined common law cases involving partnerships and sales of businesses in considering which agreements warranted condemnation under section 1. Lower court decisions made similar references to pre-Sherman Act common law cases. Perhaps the most notable example is William Howard Taft's Opinion for the US Court of Appeals for the Sixth Circuit in *United States v. Addyston Pipe & Steel Co.*[12] In a much-debated portrayal of common law jurisprudence, Taft cited common law decisions in deriving his distinction between naked and ancillary restraints.[13]

---

9 On the application of textualist analytical methods to the interpretation of the US antitrust statutes, see Daniel A. Crane, *Antitrust Antitextualism*, 96 Notre Dame L. Rev. 1205 (2021); Robert H. Lande, *A Traditionalist and Textualism Analysis of the Goals of Antitrust: Efficiency, Preventing Theft from Consumers, and Choice*, 81 Fordham L. Rev. 2349 (2013).

10 166 U.S. 290, 312–13 (1897).

11 221 U.S. 1, 60 (1911).

12 85 F. 271 (6th Cir. 1898).

13 *Id.* at 282–83.

Another source of common law guidance in framing presumptions in the US has been property law. In its analysis of distribution practices, the Supreme Court at times has premised rules of per se illegality on property law doctrines that disfavored restraints upon alienation. In 1911 in assessing the legality of resale price maintenance in *Dr. Miles Medical Co. v. John D. Park & Sons Co.*,[14] the court took note of the common law's hostility toward equitable servitudes on chattels. In ruling that RPM was illegal per se, the court said: "a general restraint upon alienation is ordinarily invalid," adding that such arrangements are "injurious to the public interest and void" when their purpose is to destroy competition by fixing prices.[15] Over a half-century later, in *United States v. Arnold, Schwinn & Co.*,[16] the court ruled that vertical territorial restrictions on distributors and retailers were illegal per se. As it had in *Dr. Miles*, the court invoked the common law's hostility toward restraints on alienation and said vertical contractual restrictions warranted condemnation "[o]nce the manufacturer had parted with title and risk."[17]

3. Experience from Earlier Antitrust Cases

A decision about how to frame presumptions requires a judicial assessment regarding how often observed conduct has harmful effects. US doctrine that applies a conclusive presumption of illegality mainly is confined to horizontal restraints (unless ancillary to a collaboration that enhances efficiency) and does not reach conduct with more ambiguous consequences, such as mergers and single-firm exclusionary behavior. The category of conduct subject to a conclusive presumption of illegality is adjustable and allows for the addition or subtraction of individual practices over time.

Many US judicial decisions refer to the role of experience in helping courts to discern whether conduct warrants the application of a categorical presumption of illegality.[18] The Supreme Court has indicated that the expansion of the category depends partly on the extent of "experience" that courts have had with a specific practice.[19] In speaking of experience, courts seem to have in mind several streams of knowledge. Two of these stand out. One is the learning that courts themselves have distilled from the resolution of past cases. Another form of experience is the accumulation of knowledge generated by empirical and theoretical scholarship that addresses the operation of markets and the competitive significance of various commercial practices within them.

---

14 20 U.S. 373 (1911), see Barbara Bruckmann, *The US Supreme Court holds it is per se illegal for a manufacturer to set minimum resale prices in agreements with independent resellers (Dr. Miles Medical / John D. Park & Sons)*, E-COMPETITIONS 1911, art. No. 52947,

15 *Id.* at 406–09.

16 388 U.S. 365 (1967).

17 *Id.* at 382.

18 See Kovacic, *supra* note 1, at 67–68.

19 Arizona v. Maricopa County Medical Society, 457 U.S. 332, 344 (1982). ("Once experience with a particular kind of restraint enables the Court to predict with confidence that the rule of reason will condemn it, it has applied a conclusive presumption that the restraint is unreasonable.").

There has been an evident trend in the United States since the mid-1970s for courts to rely more heavily upon experience in the form of modern learning about industrial organization economics to design presumptions. In *Continental T.V., Inc. v. GTE Sylvania Inc.*,[20] the court cautioned that conclusive presumptions of illegality for nonprice vertical restraints must be based on assessments of a practice's "demonstrable economic effect."[21]

Judicial decisions do not specify the quantum of experience needed to provide a confident basis for the creation of a conclusive presumption of illegality. To a large degree, the invocation of "experience" as a basis for inclusion or exclusion has an impressionistic quality. When relying upon this source of guidance, judicial tribunals tend to state, often without explanation, that the requisite level of experience with a practice has been attained or is lacking.[22] This is understandable. No well-developed metric tells courts when a critical mass of experience has formed to permit confident judgments about the classification of behavior as competitively dangerous. Courts vary widely in how completely they show their work by setting out the sources of information from which the court has discerned the lessons that experience teaches.

As suggested above, it is unsurprising that courts do not routinely provide a fully specified description of the foundations for adjusting a presumption (for example, converting a conclusive presumption of illegality to a rebuttable presumption, or adjusting the evidentiary burden that a plaintiff must bear to invoke a presumption of illegality). Legislative bodies can draw upon extensive hearings or studies prepared at their request by other public agencies to establish the basis for changes in the controlling legal framework, and they can convene proceedings that invite a wide range of observers to give their views about new legislation. By contrast, the obligation of courts is to resolve concrete disputes presented before them means that, unlike a legislator or a regulatory body, they take cases one at a time without the benefit of plenary proceedings to analyze developments in commerce, to examine broader policy issues, or to assess the efficacy of earlier judicial decisions.

Our awareness of how judges discern lessons from experience is incomplete, but we can identify some processes by which courts derive lessons from past experience. Several processes are described below:

Briefs filed by the parties and amici. Briefs provide an influential means for parties and friends of the court to assemble information about relevant experience and present this information to the court.[23] Sometimes this influence is evident from a published opinion whose arguments and authorities are directly traceable to

---

20 433 U.S. 33 (1977).

21 *Id.* at 58–59.

22 See Kovacic, *supra* note 1, at 68.

23 Stephen Calkins, *The Antitrust Conversation*, 68 Antitrust L. J. 625 (2001).

briefs submitted in the case. In other instances, the publicly available papers of jurists show how specific briefs helped shape the court's thinking about an issue.[24] Various collections of papers confirm that briefs in antitrust cases have played a formative role in making judges aware of developments – in commerce, in scholarship, and in the effect of previous judicial decisions – relevant to the resolution of the case at hand. One seemingly influential form of advocacy is the marshalling of theoretical arguments and empirical evidence that indicates that the assumptions that have guided the design of existing presumptions are infirm and require reexamination.

Pre- and post-appointment judicial background. A judge's understanding of accumulated experience, and her views about the utility of specific presumptions in antitrust law, may be determined partly by professional experience before appointment to the bench. For example, researchers have documented that Lewis Powell came to the Supreme Court in 1971 with deep skepticism about the existing framework of antitrust doctrine, which he regarded to be too interventionist.[25] One of his specific concerns was the breadth of existing per se prohibitions. The retrenchment of these rules became a focal point for his advocacy with colleagues inside the court and an important aim of his opinion-writing.[26] Other judicial appointees have been academics whose own research and teaching in the field equipped them with considerable understanding of current developments and informed their views about the appropriate future path for doctrine. In some cases, the perspectives these judges developed before coming to the bench made their way directly into their opinions about the scope of per se rules.[27]

In their time on the bench, judges in various ways acquire knowledge relevant to the resolution of antitrust cases. Judges on some courts may hear a number of antitrust cases, and these matters become part of the base of experience that a tribunal including these judges have acquired. Some judges, especially academics, continue to do research and publish papers on antitrust topics.[28] Some of this research deals with the design of presumptions.[29] Another form of post-appointment learning consists of courses approved by government administrative organizations that serve the judiciary and are conducted under the auspices of academic research centers.

Agency policy guidance. The efforts of courts to discern the lessons of experience has been influenced by the issuance of enforcement agency guidelines, notices, and speeches. Collectively, the use of these tools has sought to clarify the policy

---

24 Andrew I. Gavil, *Sylvania and the Process of Change in the Supreme Court*, ANTITRUST 8 (Fall 2002).

25 Camden Hutchinson, *Law and Economics Scholarship and Supreme Court Antitrust Jurisprudence, 1950–2010*, 21 LEWIS & CLARK L. REV. 145, 192–93 (2017).

26 See Gavil, *Process of Change*, supra note 24, at 9–10.

27 See Kovacic, *supra* note 1, at 70.

28 *Id.*

29 *Id.*

goals to be achieved, to specify the factors to be considered and the weight to be assigned to each, and to suggest the ordering of the analysis, The influence has been most pronounced in the field of merger control in the US, where judicial decisions frequently employ the methodology set out in agency guidelines.[30] Other competition agency guidelines have had exerted notably less influence in guiding judicial development of doctrine.[31]

Public agency adjudication. Although guidelines and other supplemental tools can be influential inputs in judicial decision making, the litigation of cases and the issuance of judicial decisions continue to supply the most important sources of policy development. A basic, sustaining level of litigation is necessary to give courts opportunities to upgrade doctrine as understanding about the competitive significance of individual practices evolves, and the state of the analytical art, as advanced in commentary and enforcement agency practice, improves.

Public agencies occupy a special position, through their choice of cases, to shape doctrine and provide courts with opportunities to adjust presumptions. This is evident in the general trend in modern US jurisprudence away from the heavy reliance on conclusive presumptions of illegality manifest in Supreme Court decisions from the early 1940s through the early 1970s.[32] In the earlier period, the court expressed concerns about judicial capacity and expertise to devise and apply rebuttable presumptions of illegality within an overall framework of the rule of reason.[33] In some systems, a competition agency might use its own process of administrative decision making to decide cases and bring to bear its full body of knowledge – derived not only from the resolution of cases but also from the use of its own data collection and research tools – upon the formulation of presumptions. The thoughtful use of the agency's own administrative machinery could be persuasive to reviewing courts in providing a confident basis for endorsing adjustments to existing presumptions.

An example of this dynamic appears in modern US jurisprudence that recognized the existing of the "quick look" as an intermediate form of analysis that stands between a conclusive presumption of illegality and the extensive collection and analysis of facts associated with the full rule of reason.[34] The Supreme Court's modern decisions have provided limited guidance about how the new conception of

---

30 See Gavil et al., *supra* note 1, at 738–870.

31 The US guidelines involving concerted action among competitors have had a relatively minor impact on judicial decision making. U.S. Dep't of Justice & Fed. Trade Comm'n, Antitrust Guidelines for Collaborations Among Competitors (2000), https://www.ftc.gov/sites/default/files/documents/public_events/joint-venture-hearings-antitrust-guidelines-collaboration-among-competitors/ftcdojguidelines-2.pdf. On the US competitor collaboration guidelines, see Robert A. Skitol, *Yes, the Competitor Collaboration Guidelines Are Ripe for Revision*, Antitrust 42 (Summer 2016); W. Stephen Smith et al., *Revising the Competitor Collaboration Guidelines: Three Easy Pieces*, Antitrust 47 (Summer 2016).

32 See Kovacic, *supra* note 1, at 71–74.

33 *Id.* at 41–49.

34 See Gavil et al., *supra* note 1, at 207–16.

the rule of reason should be applied, and how abbreviated variants should be structured. Lower court decisions and administrative rulings of the Federal Trade Commission (FTC) have sought to elaborate this alternative analytical architecture. A noteworthy example is *Polygram Holding, Inc. v. Federal Trade Commission*,[35] where the US Court of Appeals for the District of Columbia endorsed a truncated analysis framework employed by the FTC to assess restrictions that rival record labels had imposed upon each other in connection with the introduction of a commonly produced concert recording. In the Polygram framework, the plaintiff begins by demonstrating that that conduct is "inherently suspect" in its obvious tendency, based on a survey of its character and its similarity to other restraints found to present serious competitive dangers. The defendant then must come forward with plausible, legally cognizable justifications for the behavior. If the defendant provides such justification evidence, the plaintiff then must explain why the court may conclude, without further evidence, that anticompetitive effects are likely to predominate, or to provide evidence suggesting that such an outcome is likely. If the plaintiff meets this burden, the evidentiary burden shifts to the defendant to show that the restraint does not harm consumers or has net procompetitive virtues.

In a general way, *Polygram*'s burden-shifting approach resembles the framework that the same court used to decide the monopolization suit prosecuted by the Justice Department against Microsoft. In its *per curiam* Opinion in *United States v. Microsoft Corp.*,[36] the US Court of Appeals described the section two inquiry as having the following basic steps. The plaintiff first presents a theory of anticompetitive harm (which typically entails a demonstration that the defendant possesses substantial market power), and the defendant then offers justifications for its behavior. If the defendant presents sufficient justification evidence, the burden shifts to the plaintiff to rebut the justification evidence. If the parties have presented a mix of procompetitive and anticompetitive evidence, the court then balances the proof to determine liability.

III. Suggested Refinements in the Formulation of Presumptions

This section focuses on steps that government competition agencies can take to enhance the ability of courts to discern which presumptions are appropriate for specific forms of business behavior. The chief aims of the proposals set out here are to:

- Strengthen the informational foundations on which courts formulate presumptions;

35 416 F.3d 29 (D.C. Cir. 2005), see Don T. Hibner, *The US Court of Appeals for the DC Circuit upholds the finding of the FTC that the prohibition of discounts and advertising was inherently suspect as they would tend to raise prices and reduce output (PolyGram)*, e-Competitions July 2005, art. No. 67413.

36 253 F.3d. 34 (D.C. Cir. 2001) (*per curiam*).

- Increase the administrability of presumptions that entail more elaborate reasonableness inquiries as a way of avoiding pressure to avoid distortions that have resulted from the perception that categorical presumptions of illegality are the only means to enforcement antitrust laws effectively;
- Facilitate ongoing adaptation of presumptions; and
- Make the competition law system's operation criteria and the process of discernment more transparent.

1. Periodic Reassessment

Public antitrust agencies from time to time have convened events to examine developments in commerce and in academic learning that might dictate adjustments in antitrust law.[37] The agencies could apply their experience as convenors to conduct periodic assessments of the operation of presumptions. They could host proceedings in which academics, business officials, judges, policy makers, and practitioners analyze the existing presumptions and discuss possible adjustments. One could imagine that such proceedings might take place on a regular basis – perhaps every five years. As a recent example, the FTC in 2020 held a workshop on noncompete covenants in employment contracts as part of a larger set of deliberations on modern competition law and policy.[38]

An important aim of the periodic reassessment would be to take stock of ongoing advances in economic theory and learning about business practices.[39] This stock taking would help illuminate the impact of existing presumptions rules and help interpret the experience that courts invoke as a basis for adjusting the presumptions to be applied to different forms of conduct. Among other ingredients, this form of ex post evaluation could compare actual experience to the original assumptions that guided the formulation of the existing presumption. The public agencies could prepare reports that distill the results of the reassessment proceedings and thus provide accessible means for courts to consider future adaptations.

2. Research Agenda: Agencies and Academic Hubs

The public antitrust agencies routinely carry out research that explores the competitive significance of contemporary commercial developments and evaluates the effects of past programs. On their research agendas, the public

---

37 See Kovacic, *supra* note 1, at 76 77; William E. Kovacic, *The Federal Trade Commission as Convenor: Developing Regulatory Policy Norms without Litigation or Rulemaking*, 13 Colo. Tech. L. J. 17 (2015).

38 Fed. Trade Comm'n, Non-Competes in the Workplace: Examining Antitrust and Consumer Protection Issues (Dec. 2021), https://www.ftc.gov/news-events/events/2020/01/non-competes-workplace-examining-antitrust-consumer-protection-issues.

39 On the design of this and related forms of ex post assessment, see William E. Kovacic, *Using Ex Post Evaluation to Improve the Performance of Competition Policy Authorities*, 31 J. Corp. L. 503 (2006).

agencies could include topics relevant to the future elaboration of presumptions. The FTC is uniquely well positioned to lead antitrust agency research efforts by reason of its information-gathering authority under section 6(b) of the Federal Trade Commission Act[40] and its longstanding role in performing competition policy research and development.[41] Historically oriented research would supply valuable context for judges deciding whether to make adjustments in presumptions.

To design and execute a research program that informs adjustments in presumptions, competition agencies could form partnerships with academic research centers with expertise in business administration, industrial organization economics, and law.[42] The analytical and research capabilities of academic institutions can provide a valuable complement to the competition agency's own capabilities. Academic hubs also can serve as trusted convenors of events – acting on their own accord or in holding joint events with public bodies – that serve to improve the conceptual and empirical foundations for presumptions.

3. Litigation

The public antitrust agencies could work together to identify priorities for the development of cases that can serve to clarify and improve the analytical and empirical foundations for presumptions. A program of deeper interagency collaboration within and across jurisdictions could begin by mapping out the existing contours of doctrine and identifying areas in which the existing framework of presumptions might be strengthened. The collaboration described here might generate cases that the agencies, acting individually or in joint prosecutions, could pursue to advance doctrine. The agencies also could use *amicus* appearances in private litigation to provide courts with the context of experience that judges have deemed valuable in deciding how to formulate presumptions.

4. Rulemaking

Agencies with authority to promulgate trade regulation rules can use rulemaking to adjust presumptions. An agency with rulemaking authority could draw upon the reassessment proceedings and research programs suggested above, along with antitrust agency experience in law enforcement, to clarify the application of existing presumptions and adopt new analytical framework.

---

40 15 U.S.C. § 46 (2018).

41 Timothy J. Muris, Principles for a Successful Competition Agency, 72 U. Chi. L. Rev. 165, 176–77 (2005).

42 William E. Kovacic, *Academic Hubs and the Intellectual Infrastructure of Economic Regulation*, *in* The Contribution of the Postal and Delivery Services: Between E-Commerce and E-Substitution 1 (Pier Luigi Parcu, Timothy Brennan & Victor Glass eds., Springer 2018).

5. Policy Guidance

As noted above, antitrust agencies influence the development of doctrine in the courts by means other than litigation. The issuance of enforcement guidelines and related policy commentary is part of the conversation that agencies conduct with judges. Guidelines that offer a compelling intellectual vision based on a synthesis of theory and practice have supplied an influential way of translating enforcement experience into concepts that courts can use to interpret the antitrust laws.

IV. Conclusion

Courts deeply influence the performance of a competition policy system by shaping and interpreting presumptions that guide the evaluation of business conduct. To perform this function skillfully, courts should stand upon strong foundations in knowledge about the economic significance of business practices and about the suitability, in practice, of existing presumptions. Despite this formidable responsibility, courts have relatively weak institutional tools to establish the necessary predicates for the design and refinement of presumptions. Competition agencies, in cooperation with academic research centers, can take a number of steps to improve the basis on which the judiciary formulates presumptions and adapts them to changing circumstances over time.

Looking Beyond Courts for Competition Enforcement in Digital Platform Markets

HOWARD SHELANSKI*
Georgetown University

Abstract

This chapter examines the advantages and drawbacks of the adjudicative model of antitrust enforcement that has predominated in the United States. Ex-post, case-by-case enforcement of antitrust can avoid some costs of over-enforcement that results from over-broad ex-ante prohibitions. However, when courts erroneously find harmful conduct to be competitively benign, they can cause under-enforcement that endures because the precedent deters future plaintiffs from challenging the harmful conduct at issue. This chapter then draws on lessons from US Telecommunications regulation to discuss certain risks of ex-ante regulation but also why certain kinds of regulation might complement court-enforced antitrust to produce more comprehensive and effective competition policy for digital platforms.

---

* Professor of Law and Joseph and Madeline Sheehy Chair in Antitrust Law and Trade Regulation, Georgetown University; Partner, Davis Polk & Wardwell LLP.

This chapter will discuss reasons to both consider, and proceed selectively with, regulatory mechanisms for competition enforcement for digital platforms. It will draw on two sources of historical lessons: the US experience with competition enforcement through case-by-case adjudication in the courts, and the US experience with local telephone regulation under the Telecommunications Act of 1996. The first of these provides reasons why antitrust enforcement might warrant an administrative approach in some circumstances; the second provides lessons on the hazards that come with regulating networks during periods of dynamic technological change. The chapter will conclude with a discussion of regulatory mechanisms that might enable an integrated approach to competition policy that combines the traditional adjudicative approach with a complementary administrative approach.

I. Benefits and Limitations of Adjudicated Antitrust Enforcement in the US

The United States has little administrative tradition when it comes to antitrust enforcement. While the Federal Trade Commission (FTC) has promulgated competition rules on very rare occasions, and can choose to bring cases in the first instance before its own administrative law judge, enforcement of the American antitrust statutes usually takes place in federal court through complaints against a particular party's conduct. Courts determine liability in a specific case through fact-intensive trials against the backdrop of court-made antitrust doctrine. In other words, American antitrust enforcement is essentially a process of case-by-case common law adjudication. Despite the technical complexity of many antitrust cases, antitrust enforcement and policy in the United States has evolved primarily through precedent developed by generalist courts, and not through administrative processes adjudication and rulemaking by specialized agencies.[1]

To be sure, the Department of Justice (DOJ) and the FTC influence policy through the investigations they pursue and the consent decrees they reach with parties. The FTC itself adjudicates some cases, although it does so largely according to law developed in the federal courts, to which parties can appeal any FTC decision.[2] Academics and other commentators have also affected the evolution of antitrust in the United States, from supporting the rise of an economic efficiency paradigm for US competition policy to sparking a rethinking of that framework in contemporary debates. As the courts absorb such learning, antitrust doctrine evolves over time through incremental changes in case law,

1 *See* Douglas H. Ginsburg & Joshua D. Wright, *Antitrust Courts: Specialists Versus Generalists*, 36 Fordham Int'l L.J. 788, 789–90 (2013) (comparing "generalist courts" in the United States with the "more specialized model[s]" found in Portugal, France, Turkey, the United Kingdom, and India).

2 *See id.* ("[T]he twelve Circuit Courts of Appeals . . . review the decisions of the Federal Trade Commission.").

with the US Supreme Court periodically stepping in to clarify doctrine or resolve differences among the lower federal courts. Commentators often cite antitrust as a rare example of "federal common law" in the US system.[3]

Recently, there has been a growing call for US antitrust enforcers to make greater use of administrative mechanisms, most notably the promulgation of competition regulations. The FTC has set up a rule-making task force and recently proposed its first "unfair methods of competition" rules in decades: a broad, ex ante prohibition on employee non-compete agreements.[4] Calls for a more rule-oriented approach to competition enforcement in the US reflect two principal concerns. The first is that that case-by-case adjudication is inefficient, embeds poor precedent, and lags new knowledge about competitive effects of certain conduct (the FTC's non-compete rule seems responsive to this argument). The second is that certain kinds of competition problems lie beyond the reach of the current doctrinal toolbox and need regulation instead of, or in combination with, case-by-case enforcement in court (digital platforms are the main example here). We turn next to the first of these concerns.

1. Pros and Cons of Antitrust Adjudication

The adjudicatory model for antitrust enforcement has several key features, which in turn have both advantages and disadvantages that vary in degree depending on the expertise of the judge or the type of tribunal.

A. *Case-by-Case, Fact-Specific Approach*

Adjudication and the litigation process are well suited to resolving questions of liability that depend on case-specific facts. With the exception of very few kinds of conduct that the antitrust laws prohibit per se, courts review most competitive activities through a rule of reason, under which some conduct that is illegal in one set of circumstances might be allowable in another.[5] Liability depends not only on whether an allegedly illegal activity occurred but also on some weighing of the activity's likely effects on competition.[6] The more that liability is contingent on such case-specific facts related to competitive effects, the more difficult it is to determine liability in advance of the conduct's actual occurrence. Fact-intensity therefore has implications for using ex ante regulatory mechanisms for competition enforcement but also means that adjudication typically occurs

---

3 *See, e.g.*, Justin Hurwitz, *Administrative Antitrust*, 21 Geo. Mason L. Rev. 1191, 1217 (2014) ("[A]ntitrust is generally accepted as a form of federal common law.").

4 https://www.ftc.gov/news-events/news/press-releases/2023/01/ftc-proposes-rule-ban-noncompete-clauses-which-hurt-workers-harm-competition

5 E. Thomas Sullivan, et al., Antitrust Law, Policy, and Procedure: Cases, Materials, Problems at 192, Carolina Academic Press (8th Ed., 2019).

6 Id. at 193.

when conduct either is imminent or has already occurred, when facts about the effects of the conduct are, in principle, more readily assessed.[7] Such "ex post" mechanisms of enforcement can reduce over-enforcement when compared to approaches, like some forms of regulation, that prescribed in advance what actions are illegal.[8] However, whether reducing false positives is ultimately a virtue depends on the extent to which courts err in the other direction and under-enforce against harmful conduct or transactions.

B. *Slow, Usually Predictable Doctrinal Development*

A second attribute of the American adjudicatory process for antitrust is stability. While antitrust doctrine has occasionally changed abruptly, the common-law evolution of antitrust doctrine usually provides notice that a change is coming. As just one example, the Supreme Court's shift in *Leegin Creative Leather Products, Inc. v. PSKS, Inc.*,[9] from per se liability to a rule of reason for resale price maintenance likely caught few observers by surprise given related doctrinal changes that occurred over a number of years.[10]

However, antitrust adjudication's stability, like its suitability for fact-dependent situations, is potentially double-edged. Antitrust doctrine can be slow to adjust to changes in economic learning or changes in the underlying economy that alter the effects of a particular kind of business conduct. For example, nearly thirty years ago the Supreme Court in *Brooke Group v. Brown & Williamson Tobacco Corp.*,[11] required that plaintiffs claiming predatory pricing show not only prices below some measure of incremental cost, but also that the defendant could recoup its losses.[12] No plaintiff has prevailed in a predatory pricing case in a US federal court since. That outcome would not be of concern if the Supreme Court's test accurately captured the incidence of harmful price predation. Economic research demonstrates, however, that predatory conduct does occur and does not necessarily depend on either below-cost pricing or recoupment.[13] Predation is just one area in which court-made doctrine appears out of step with economic reality.

---

7 *See* Jeffrey J. Rachlinski, *Rulemaking Versus Adjudication: A Psychological Perspective*, 32 Fla. St. U. L. Rev. 529, 544 (2005) (noting that "adjudicative bodies act retrospectively and will thus always have injured victims or aggrieved parties before them").

8 *See* Ashutosh Bhagwat, *Modes of Regulatory Enforcement and the Problem of Administrative Discretion*, 50 Hastings L.J. 1275, 1325 (1999) (discussing problems of over-enforcement in connection with the ex ante enforcement authority of the FDA).

9 551 U.S. 877 (2007).

10 Id. at 888-893 (discussing evolution of precedent).

11 509 U.S. 209 (1993).

12 See Steven J. Cernak, The US Supreme Court establishes a test for proving the existence of predatory pricing (Brooke Group), E-COMPETITIONS June 1993, art. No. 98743.

13 *See, e.g.*, Aaron S. Edlin, *Stopping Above-Cost Predatory Pricing*, 111 Yale L.J. 941, 943 (2002) (arguing that although below-cost pricing and recoupment "may be sufficient to make out a predatory pricing case... they should not be necessary"); Patrick Bolton, et al., *Predatory Pricing: Strategic Theory and Legal Policy*, 88 Geo. L. J. 2239 (2000).

Exogenous mechanisms outside the courts and agencies could accelerate the common-law process of doctrinal development. For example, Congress could legislate changes to the scope, presumptions, and other parameters of antitrust law in ways that would immediately alter precedent and bind the courts going forward.[14] In practice, however, such intervention is rare, making significant lags in doctrine a reality of antitrust adjudication in the courts.

Some commentators have argued that the slow process of doctrinal change is a reason for courts to err in the direction of under-enforcement in antitrust cases. Judge Frank Easterbrook wrote in 1984 that, because markets change more quickly than doctrine, over-enforcement could create precedent that acts as long-term prohibition on conduct that is in fact pro-competitive or benign.[15] Conversely, Easterbrook argued that if courts erroneously allow anticompetitive activity to go unpunished, the harm will be shorter lived because markets more rapidly respond to and correct harmful inefficiencies than does case law.[16] There are two main problems with this argument. First, monopoly power can be durable and, once obtained, might not be corrected by market forces as easily as Easterbrook presumed. Second, doctrine might evolve more slowly to correct under-enforcement errors than it does to correct over-enforcement errors, which could lead to long-term harm through anticompetitive conduct that escapes scrutiny, as discussed next.

C. *The Market for Case Selection in the Courts*

In the United States, most adjudicative bodies do not select the cases that come before them. Courts have jurisdictional limitations that prevent them from hearing certain disputes and doctrines exist that allow courts to reject weak or poorly conceived complaints. However, those mechanisms aside, independent parties decide when and whether to pursue litigation to secure relief. One potential virtue of this separation between decision-making and case selection is that the market can drive the focus of judicial attention. Assuming the most widespread and most troublesome anticompetitive conduct will receive the greatest investment of litigation resources, that conduct will in turn receive the most adjudication and doctrinal development.

Unfortunately, the separation between adjudication and case selection will not necessarily lead to an efficient match between judicial attention and the most pressing antitrust violations. In practice, even conduct that is clearly prohibited can persist when offenders think detection is difficult; one only has to look at the consistently high number of civil and criminal price fixing cases that wind

14 *See* Hurwitz, supra note 3, at 1194–95 ("Congress can set other, non-economically efficient priorities that trump antitrust's normative goal. These policy choices are within the domain of Congress and its agencies.").

15 Frank H. Easterbrook, *Limits of Antitrust*, 63 Texas L. Rev. 1 (1984).

16 *Id.*

up in court, even though that conduct has clearly been illegal per se for nearly a century.[17] The most widespread anticompetitive conduct might therefore not be the conduct that most needs doctrinal development – it can be just the opposite, as the persistence of collusion demonstrates.[18] Bad acts persist even in the face of clear and correct legal precedent for liability. In such cases, however, plaintiffs will know they can go to court and get relief. The specific conduct, being clearly illegal, is in principle remedied. Moreover, if there is an error in the doctrine and it is overly restrictive, courts will have repeated opportunities to revise their precedents because plaintiffs are bringing cases given their favorable odds of winning. Defendants will have periodic opportunities to push back on doctrine they view as overly prohibitive. The imposition of liability therefore drives a market for evolution of precedent by creating incentives for plaintiffs to bring cases and opportunities for defendants to defend those cases and push for change in the law.

The ability, and therefore the incentive, to persist with some kind of conduct seems by definition even greater if courts have erroneously found the particular conduct not to violate the antitrust laws. If that conduct turns out in fact to be harmful, the courts would have made an error of under-enforcement. In the case of doctrine that embeds an under-enforcement error, however, the market for change in the case law might fail. When the prevailing doctrine provides low likelihood of relief through the courts, the doctrine deters the government or private plaintiffs from filing cases.[19] The market for judicial review of antitrust conduct will then work poorly because courts will not as regularly have cases before them that provide the opportunity to correct under-enforcement errors; once doctrine is settled, there may be no good mechanism outside of legislation or regulatory intervention to correct the under-enforcement error dynamically and within a reasonable timeframe. We return to this issue below.

D. *Generalists versus Industry Experts*

Who adjudicates antitrust cases can matter for substantive outcomes. In the US antitrust adjudication occurs almost entirely in generalist federal courts. That institutional choice might well make sense given the wide variety of conduct, industries, and factual circumstances that antitrust cases present. However, as specific industries come to pose particular challenges for antitrust enforcement, the case for more specialized enforcement decision-makers becomes stronger. Traditionally, where detailed, industry-specific knowledge is required to make

---

17 *See* Carl Shapiro, *Protecting Competition in the American Economy: Merger Control, Tech Titans, Labor Markets,* 33 J. Econ. Persp., 69 Summer 2019, at 72 (noting that the Department of Justice "has assessed roughly $10 billlion in criminal fines and penalties" in price-fixing charges).

18 *See* U.S. Dep't of Just, Antitrust Division Update, Spring 2019 (Mar. 26, 2019), https://www.justice.gov/atr/division-operations/division-update-spring-2019/cartels-beware (listing pending cartel investigations, including over ninety pending grand jury investigations).

19 *See supra*, (discussing predatory pricing).

sound competition policy decisions, Congress has assigned some degree of authority over those decisions to industry-specific regulatory agencies. Thus, the US Securities and Exchange Commission has authority over competitive conduct in key financial sectors.[20] The Federal Communications Commission (FCC) has parallel authority with the (DOJ) over telecommunications mergers and sole authority to establish terms for competitive entry into various telecommunications markets.[21] State regulators govern entry into hospital markets through certifications of public need.[22] The federal courts have increasingly safeguarded the domain of industry specific regulators over competition issues even when agency decisions might be in tension with antitrust law.[23]

As antitrust enforcement focuses on distinct challenges posed by a particular industry, whether digital platforms, pharmaceuticals, or something else, expert and specialized knowledge becomes even more essential to making good enforcement decisions. Under current law and enforcement frameworks, there is no systematic way to bring such specialization into the ultimate adjudication of antitrust cases in industries not already covered by specific, competition-related, regulatory statutes. The FTC and DOJ have divisions that specialize in various industrial sectors in which they have considerable expertise. Those divisions bring that expertise into their review of conduct and transactions, but neither the FTC nor the DOJ has ultimate adjudicative authority over the cases they choose to litigate. The DOJ must go to federal court to seek enforcement. The FTC can opt for an administrative enforcement mechanism with the Commission itself sitting in appellate review of initial adjudication by an administrative law judge. The Commission's decision is, however, subject to review by federal appellate courts, which have not hesitated to reverse the agency's decisions.[24] The result is that, even when agencies have brought specific industry expertise into antitrust enforcement, doctrinal application and resolution still proceeds through the common-law process of adjudication by generalist judges.

---

20 *See* Credit Suisse Sec. (USA) v. Billing, 551 U.S. 264, 283–84 (2007), see Stacey Chubbuck, *The US Supreme Court finds implied antitrust immunity in regulated securities industry related claims (Credit Suisse Securities / Billing)*, E-COMPETITIONS June 2007, art. No. 44418.

21 *See, e.g.*, 47 U.S.C. §§ 214, 310, 521(6), 532, 536 (2018) (outlining statutory requirements for the extension of telecommunication lines, license ownership, and cable channels for commercial use to maintain competition in cable communications).

22 *See e.g.*, N.Y. Pub. Health Law § 2801-A(3) (McKinney 2019) ("The public health and health planning council shall not approve a certificate of incorporation, articles of organization, or application for establishment unless it is satisfied . . . as to (a) the public need for the existence of the institution at the time and place and under the circumstances proposed.").

23 *See* Howard A. Shelanski, *The Case for Rebalancing Antitrust and Regulation*, 109 Mich. L. Rev. 683, 693–718 (2011) (discussing cases in which the U.S. Supreme Court has demonstrated that "[it] will interpret the substantive scope of antitrust liability narrowly in regulated settings even where Congress has expressly preserved the operation of antitrust law").

24 *See, e.g.*, California Dental Ass'n v. FTC, 526 U.S. 756, 759 (1999) (finding the FTC's level of analysis evaluating anticompetitive advertising restrictions to be insufficient); LabMD, Inc. v. FTC, 894 F. 3d 1221, 1224 (11th Cir. 2018) (vacating an FTC cease and desist order applied to a data-security program based on what the court considered an improper interpretation of section 5(a) of the FTCA); Rambus Inc. v. FTC, 522 F. 3d 456, 459 (D.C. Cir. 2008) (reversing an FTC finding of monopolization), see David S. Turetsky et al., *The US Court of Appeals for the DC Circuit overturns an FTC's ruling in the computer memory market for failing to prove unlawful monopolization (Rambus)*, E-COMPETITIONS April 2008, art. N° 37369.

E. *Tradeoffs Inherent in the Adjudicatory Approach to Antitrust*

As the foregoing discussion suggests, the ex post case-by-case approach, slow doctrinal evolution, and case selection mechanism of antitrust adjudication have potential advantages and disadvantages. The tradeoffs become particularly clear through the interaction of those three characteristics.

Adjudication can mitigate certain errors because proceeding case-by-case is less likely to produce false positives (over-enforcement errors) than are general rules that impose limits on business conduct in advance, regardless of specific circumstances. However, although broad ex ante specifications could prohibit beneficial or harmless conduct, narrow ex ante specifications could fail to prevent anticompetitive practices. As a decision-making process moves from strict ex ante prescription to pure case-by-case adjudication, particular facts and circumstances increasingly predominate over generic categorization of conduct.[25] In principle, the movement along that spectrum enables the decision-maker to avoid under- or over-inclusiveness of categorical rules.[26]

However, the extent to which an adjudicator actually succeeds in reducing enforcement errors in either direction depends on the doctrinal precedent through which it evaluates the case-specific evidence. Precedent will determine how a court allocates burdens, prioritizes facts, and weighs presumptions in evaluating the legality of conduct. If precedent provides mistaken guidance on those factors, case-specific adjudication might not do a better job than ex ante prohibitions in avoiding errors or bias toward either under- or over-enforcement – and it could do worse. For this reason, the evolutionary pace of doctrinal development through antitrust adjudication is very important. Where that evolution has been toward convergence with state-of-the-art analysis and evidence as to the effects of conduct, doctrinal stability is a virtue. Reasonable people disagree over the Supreme Court's movement from per se illegality to rule of reason treatment of vertical price restraints, as Justice Breyer's dissent in *Leegin* demonstrates.[27] The decision in that case nonetheless drew on a body of legal and economic analysis that, over decades, had continually narrowed the application of per se rules to vertical conduct and led logically (even if some might argue incorrectly) to the majority's conclusion.[28] Some commentators might therefore reasonably argue that *Leegin* is an

---

25 *See* Rachlinski, *supra* note 7, at 544 ("Adjudicative bodies act retrospectively and will thus always have injured victims or aggrieved parties before them.").

26 *See* Daniel T. Deacon, *Common Carrier Essentialism and the Emerging Common Law of Internet Regulation*, 67 Admin. L. Rev. 133, 136 (noting that reliance on ex post enforcement may lead to under-enforcement).

27 U.S. 877, 916 (2007) (Breyer, J., dissenting) ("How easily can courts identify instances in which the benefits are likely to outweigh potential harms? My own answer is, not very easily.").

28 551 U.S. at 900–02 (explaining how rulings in recent cases justify limiting the reach of a per se rule and promoting instead a rule of reason evaluation).

example of where the evolution of doctrine through adjudication worked well: stakeholders had notice and the doctrine moved in an internally consistent direction. While it is debatable whether the *per se* rule against restraints on intra-brand competition had in fact led to over-enforcement in the years before *Leegin*, there is evidence that it had done so in the past,[29] so that the doctrine plausibly moved in an error-reducing direction.

However, where doctrine gets on the wrong track, the application of precedent will perpetuate rather than reduce enforcement errors. In the case of predation, for example, there is a good argument that, in the light of current economic knowledge, the *Brooke Group* decision has led to under-enforcement.[30] The potential case-by-case advantages of adjudication are lost where judicial precedent renders important facts and circumstances irrelevant. In such cases, the relatively slow process of doctrinal correction through common law evolution is harmful to sound antitrust enforcement.

The discussion above shows that the error-reducing potential of a case-by-case, adjudicatory approach to antitrust enforcement depends heavily on the historical path of doctrinal development and on the precedent that courts apply to particular conduct. Similarly, whether case selection in an adjudicatory approach in fact directs judicial attention to the conduct that most warrants oversight depends on existing doctrine and precedent. The weaker the precedent for prohibiting conduct, the higher the burden – if it can be met at all – on plaintiffs challenging that conduct. If existing law under-enforces against an anticompetitive activity, then conduct causing significant harm is also conduct for which the courts impose high burdens of proof on plaintiffs. The deterrent effect of those burdens likely leads to fewer cases than the conduct's actual effects warrant.[31] Similarly, doctrine that too readily imposes liability could have the opposite effect: lower barriers for plaintiffs would lead to too many cases and more devotion of judicial resources than the conduct deserves – but in that case, the market for litigation is likely to create more opportunities for courts to correct doctrinal mistakes.[32] Like error-reduction, the distribution of antitrust cases brought for adjudication depends heavily on the state of the doctrine and on the ability of the common law process to correct course where necessary.

---

29 *See* United States v. Topco Assocs., 405 U.S. 596, 607–12 (1972) (holding that an association engaged in a per se violation of the Sherman Act even in the absence of price fixing and even though the district court determined as a factual matter that the activity at issue had fostered competition).

30 *See* Bolton et al., supra note 13, at 2242–49 ("To summarize, present judicial skepticism about predatory pricing assumes that predation is extremely rare, but sound empirical and experimental studies as well as modern economic theory, do not justify this assumption.").

31 *See, e.g.*, James Langenfeld & James Morsch, *Refining the Matsushita Standard and the Role Economics Can Play*, 38 Loy. U. Chi. L.J. 507, 512 (2007) (noting that heightening the burden at the pleading stage in horizontal antitrust conspiracy cases "would likely discourage potential meritorious cases").

32 *See* Mark Anderson & Max Huffman, *Iqbal, Twombly, and the Expected Cost of False Positive Error*, 20 Cornell J.L. & Pub. Pol'y 1, 4 (2010) (discussing the social costs of false positives where relaxed standards permit plaintiffs to proceed with non-meritorious claims).

The potential disadvantages of antitrust adjudication by generalist courts raise the question of whether a different approach might be preferable, specifically with regard to digital platforms. Digital platforms present relatively novel challenges, principally related to scale, network effects, scale of data intake to refine algorithms, and other factors well discussed in the literature and beyond the scope of this chapter. There is a tenuous fit between the current process and substance of US antitrust law with theories of harm related to digital platforms, complexity of the underlying technical issues, and interdependence of competition with adjacent policy goals related to privacy and content. This has led many commentators to argue that a more informed, comprehensive approach coordinated by an expert regulatory agency might foster more advantages than does the exclusive resort to traditional antitrust adjudication. It is therefore not surprising that several jurisdictions around the world have supplemented antitrust enforcement with a more regulatory framework for competition enforcement in digital platform markets. The European Commission has passed the Digital Markets Act, under which large platforms can be regulated.[33] Although the United States has not yet enacted any such legislation, both houses of Congress reached an advanced stage of debate over the American Innovation and Choice Online Act, which if enacted would regulate certain conduct by large digital platforms.[34]

Such legislation will require significant regulatory action to promulgate and apply implementing rules. Which raises an important question: what lessons can one draw from prior regulatory experience about the kinds of regulation that might be effective, and which kinds are counterproductive, in governing digital platform competition? Just as there are lessons in favor of an administrative process we can draw from the history of antitrust adjudication, there are historical lessons about the limits and challenges of regulation. To that end, this chapter will turn next to one historical case – that of local telephone service in the United States – for guidance on how to regulate digital platforms to increase competition.

II. The Telecommunications Act of 1996: Lessons for Digital Platform Regulation

Congress enacted The Telecommunications Act of 1996 both too late and too soon. The 1996 Act was overdue because, by the time Congress enacted the statute in February 1996, the need for a new regulatory charter for the structure of US telecommunications had been clear for some time. The Act was also premature, however, because its enactment came on the eve of unprecedented change in

33 REGULATION (EU) 2022/1925 OF THE EUROPEAN PARLIAMENT AND OF THE COUNCIL of 14 September 2022 on contestable and fair markets in the digital sector and amending Directives (EU) 2019/1937 and (EU) 2020/1828 (Digital Markets Act).

34 S. 2992, American Innovation and Choice Online Act 117th Cong., 2d sess. (2021–2022); S. 2710, Open App Markets Act 117th Cong., 2d sess. (2021–2022).

telecommunications markets. Current debates over digital platform therefore echo this perspective on the 1996 Act, with some commentators arguing that recognition of the need for regulation is coming too late, and others arguing that resort to enforcement beyond the current law and process is unwarranted and premature.[35]

Just over a decade prior to the passage of the 1996 Act, the telecommunications market in the US had undergone its first important change in decades because of a landmark divestiture agreement between AT&T and the US Department of Justice. Up until 1984, AT&T had been an integrated monopoly providing both local and long-distance telephone service to most American consumers. The separation of local calling from long-distance service resulting from the AT&T divestiture decree (the MFJ)[36] had the immediate objective of opening up the long-distance market to competition. The MFJ achieved this goal in part by imposing limits on the kinds of services that AT&T and the newly independent local operating companies could respectively provide. However, a dozen years later, although the MFJ opened long-distance markets to competition, it had become an impediment to broader industry evolution as new services and technologies began to emerge. Hundreds of petitions for waivers to the MFJ's line-of-business restrictions clogged the overseeing court's docket, and the MFJ did nothing to tackle the entrenched local exchange monopolies.

The 1996 Act directly addressed some unhelpful vestiges of the MFJ and instituted measures to introduce competition into the local exchange monopolies the MFJ had left in place. However, to the extent Congress intended the 1996 Act to be the foundation for future telecommunications policy, its focus on local telephone competition proved shortsighted. Within a short time, technological developments rapidly diminished the importance of local wireline service through dramatic changes that Congress did not – perhaps because it could not – anticipate. While there were certainly inklings of new technological directions by 1996, Congress did not foresee the speed with which wireline telephone service, the focus of US telecommunications policy up through and including the 1996 Act, would become less important for consumers and carriers alike, while a new class of information technologies would imminently become central to everyday life.

Within a few years of the 1996 Act's passage, two technologies just emerging on a mass consumer scale in the 1990s had become ubiquitous: wireless communications and internet access. By the end of 1995, as Congress was concluding its drafting of the 1996 Act, there were fewer than thirteen mobile phone subscriptions per one hundred Americans. Within just five years, that figure had nearly tripled and, less than a decade later, the number of cell phone subscriptions exceeded the number of potential subscribers as some people carried multiple

35 47 U.S.C. § 652 (1996).

36 United States v. AT&T, et al., 552 F. Supp. 131 (1982) (the "Modification of Final Judgment" or "MFJ").

devices.[37] Internet usage followed a similar pattern. In late 1996, a Pew Research Center Survey found that 22% of Americans reported having gone online from home, school or work, and still with only light internet usage: only 25% of those using the internet reported doing so every day.[38] By 2000, however, usage had grown to over 50% of American adults and had become far more varied, frequent, and intense.[39] Online access from that point only accelerated: according to FCC data, residential fixed internet connections grew from just 3 million in 2000 to 75 million in 2010.[40] With the rise of smartphones in the late 2000s, mobile wireless and internet access converged, marking the transformation from a world of fixed-location voice communications to a world of mobile, information-rich, multi-modal communications carried in a consumer's pocket.

Internet access, like wireless services, provided alternatives to traditional telephone service for individual communications, particularly as email and messaging applications became widely used. The significance of the internet, however, was much greater than merely providing a competitive communications platform. As broadband access and internet usage soared in the United States, the underlying telecommunications system became even more important as a gateway to essential information and as a facility for key aspects of everyday life rather than as a conduit for personal communications. Little in the Telecommunications Act of 1996 foresaw these developments and Congress had not designed the law to address the ensuing policy challenges. To name just a few of those challenges: incentivizing build-out of digital communications infrastructure; ensuring that networks remain open to new content, services, and users; avoiding monopoly bottlenecks at various levels in the provision of broadband services; and ensuring affordability and access for all consumers of essential communications technology.

The rapid growth of wireless communications and internet services in the wake of the 1996 Act quickly diminished the importance of local wireline competition as well as the distinction between local and long-distance service. This eroding importance of wirelines services to consumers was significant because the 1996 Act's core provisions aimed to facilitate competitive entry of new local providers by requiring incumbents to "unbundle" parts of their networks for use by rivals. Consumers' growing substitution of wireless service and digital communications for wireline telephone made entry into local wireline less attractive for new entrants and less important for economic or other policy objectives. Wireless

---

37 There are various sources and measures for data on wireless growth. These are World Bank figures that can be found at World Bank, Mobile Cellular Subscriptions (per 100 people) – United States (2019), https://data.worldbank.org/indicator/IT.CEL.SETS.P2?end=2019&locations=US&start=1960&view=chart.

38 Pew Research Center, News Attracts Most Internet Users (Dec. 16, 1996), https://www.pewresearch.org/politics/1996/12/16/online-use/.

39 John B. Horrigan, New Internet Users: What they Do Online, What They Don't, and Implications for the 'Net's Future 6 (2000), https://www.pewresearch.org/internet/2000/09/25/main-report-26/ (last visited Aug. 3, 2022).

40 FCC, Internet Access Services: Status as of June 30, 2010 (March 2011), https://www.fcc.gov/internet-access-services-reports.

competition and substitution therefore made the main objective of the 1996 Act less important and its mechanisms less effective.[41] Even as administrative proceedings and litigation over the 1996 Act's local competition provisions were in full swing, those provisions were serving little pro-competitive purpose within just a few years after Congress passed the statute.

This does not mean that the 1996 Act was without impact. Certain of its provisions did help to open the door for new kinds of networks, providers, and services to enter the telecommunications marketplace. Instead of its elaborate network unbundling rules, the provision's most important provisions were proving to be its preemption of state monopoly franchises for local telecommunications, its right-of-way provisions for infrastructure, and its requirement that rival telecommunications carriers exchange traffic to and from each other's subscribers. Those provisions allowed new competitive technologies to reach consumers without barriers from state law protections for incumbents or from adverse network effects resulting from incumbent refusals to exchange calls with rival carriers.[42]

The foregoing discussion suggests that the 1996 Act came along at just the wrong time. Congress enacted the law at a moment when imminent but unpredictable changes would quickly render the Act outdated. However, although the Act was costly and misdirected in its core goals, it still managed to do some good. In hindsight, one can draw a variety of lessons from the 1996 Act and the subsequent developments, lessons that push in somewhat different directions for future regulatory policy.

III. A Path Forward for Competition Rules for Digital Platforms

One on hand, the experience of the 1996 Act demonstrates that insufficient appreciation of emerging technological changes can lead to costly and counterproductive regulation.[43] It might not be possible to estimate the resources that went into regulatory battles and federal court litigation over implementation of the 1996 Act, but the figure is certainly enormous. One might take from this costly experience a presumption of caution and hesitation about regulating during a period of technological change and uncertainty, and in particular a presumption against heavy-handed rules that try to set the detailed terms and

41 For a discussion of the emerging substitution of wireless for wireline service and the diminution in importance of traditional telephone networks, see Howard A. Shelanski, *Adjusting Regulation to Competition: Toward a New Model for US Telecommunications Policy,* 24 Yale J. on Reg. 55, 69–75 (2007).

42 Howard A. Shelanski, *A Comment on Competition and Controversy in Local Telecommunications*, 50 Hastings L.J. 1617 (1999),https://repository.uchastings.edu/_law_journal///.

43 Jonathan E. Nuechterlein & Howard A. Shelanski, *Building on What Works: An Analysis of U.S. Broadband Policy*, 73 Fed. Comm. L.J. 219, 222 (2021).

conditions under which one set of actors must share their facilities with another set of putatively competing actors. However, a corollary is that when regulation diverts attention and resources to battles over obsolescent issues – even if that regulation was understandable when enacted – it can delay and make more difficult the resolution of new challenges created by the very innovations that replaced the regulated entities.

The lesson of the 1996 Act for digital platform regulation is therefore not so much that competition-oriented regulation in a technologically dynamic setting should never occur, but that it should be light-handed and nimble enough to address not just incumbent technologies, but to promote competition in the emerging technologies that replace them. In this regard, the history of telecommunications regulation is not without some helpful precedent for possible beneficial regulation of digital platforms. Indeed, not all of the positive developments in new communications networks and technologies that emerged in the decade after the Act would have happened as easily without certain provisions of the 1996 Act and other regulatory developments. Wireless communications would not have expanded as quickly and competitively without the requirement that all carriers must interconnect to exchange traffic, so that a customer of one network can call the customers of any other network. New infrastructure and technology would have emerged as quickly without regulatory requirements that rights of way for network facilities be shared. Online digital applications and underlying access networks would not have grown so rapidly without a common, non-proprietary protocol for connecting devices and sharing content and services across the internet. Therefore, although the 1996 Act's lesson of modesty about predicting the course of the telecommunications markets should influence digital platform regulation, so too should its lessons about the costs of regulatory lag in addressing new policy challenges and about the kinds of action that helped to open the door to new, competitive technologies.

Similarly, the history of antitrust enforcement through adjudication in the courts demonstrates that, while over-enforcement through overly prescriptive or prohibitive ex ante rules might be harmful, so too is under-enforcement through doctrine that erroneously permits harmful conduct to persist. The case-by-case approach can keep over-enforcement in check making liability turn on the facts of a specific course of challenged conduct; it works less well to check under-enforcement when doctrine deters challenges in the first place by making the factual requirements for liability overly stringent. Bad case law, like bad regulation, will divert effort and attention from addressing competition problems that warrant solution.

The current debate over competition regulation for digital platforms spans policy proposals that range from purely market-driven, unregulated approaches to full-scale public utility regulation of broadband networks, and includes just about everything in between. The combined lessons of the adjudicative approach to US antitrust enforcement and the public-utilities approach to telecommunications competition from the 1996 Act is that a combined, and complementary approach to digital platform regulation – one that rejects extreme reliance on either regulatory governance or ex post adjudication – might be well suited to the challenges of digital platforms. The specific directions this complementary, regulatory approach might take are beyond the scope of this chapter. Specific proposals and regulatory directions are the subject of recent studies by numerous commentators.[44] Many of those proposals center around supplementing antitrust enforcement in the courts with regulation that ensures access, interoperability, and interconnection sufficient to share network effects, reduce network barriers to entry, and ensure access to end-users for new applications and technologies. The purpose of this chapter is to provide some historical context for those proposals, and for why they represent worthwhile efforts given the lessons one can draw from the US experience with both the adjudicative model of antitrust enforcement and the public-utilities model of regulating telecommunications competition.

---

44 See, e.g., William P. Rogerson and Howard Shelanski, *Antitrust Enforcement, Regulation, and Digital Platforms*, 168 U. Pa. L. Rev. 1911 (2020).

PART II

Legal Standards in Brazil, China, Russia and South Africa

Appropriate Legal Standards in Competition Law: a South African Perspective

THEMBALETHU BUTHELEZI,*
JAMES HODGE** AND MPUMELELO TSHABALALA***
Competition Commission of South Africa
Competition Tribunal of South Africa

Abstract

The adoption of legal and liability standards of more mature jurisdictions has not necessarily served competition enforcement or the development agenda well in developing countries. As the case of South Africa shows, a full rule of reason analysis in abuse of dominance cases not only unduly raises the evidentiary burden but is complicated further by developing country factors such as asymmetric litigation resources and jurisdictional disputes. South Africa recently amended its Act to include a presumptive based standard for certain dominant firm conduct, alongside a lower liability standard where the complainants involve small and historically disadvantaged businesses. The amendments also granted decision-making powers in market inquiries with a lower liability threshold of demonstrating an 'adverse effect on competition' (AEC). This has resulted in more rapid and effective enforcement without necessarily compromising on the accuracy of legal decisions. The Constitutional Court (ConCourt) has given impetus to these changes

---

* Principal Economist in the Economic Research Bureau of the Competition Commission of South Africa.

** Chief Economist of the Competition Commission of South Africa.

*** Senior Case Manager at the Competition Tribunal of South Africa. The views expressed in this paper reflect the views of the authors in their personal capacity and do not represent the views of the organizations that they represent.

by softening the presumptive requirements where a human right is invoked or where conduct perpetuates exclusion from the economy. These changes promise to drive a more competitive and inclusive economy. The experience provides an interesting natural experiment that can offer insights for the current debate on appropriate legal standards for both developing countries and digital markets.

I. Introduction

The South African Competition Act No. 89 of 1998 (the Act) was predominately drafted based on the legislation and jurisprudence of more mature jurisdictions, such as the European Commission, the United States of America (US) and Canada. Whereas the purposes of the Act and merger control provisions uniquely included the public interest, the chapter on prohibited practices reflected both the legal tests and liability standards of those more mature jurisdictions. The legal standards included per se prohibitions for naked cartel conduct[1] and minimum resale price maintenance only, and a rule of reason approach for all other practices where the conduct could be justified by respondents by proving any off-setting technological, efficiency or pro-competitive effects. For prohibited practices, the requisite standard to prove liability under a rule of reason analysis was the consumer welfare standard established through the substantial prevention or lessening of competition (SPLC) test. The same SPLC test prevails in merger control for the competitive assessment, although a separate assessment of the merger's public interest effects is also required which is assessed by measuring the impact on specified public interest factors.[2]

The South African experience was that these legal[3] and liability[4] standards resulted in considerable delays and limited success for the Competition Commission of South Africa (Commission) in prosecuting prohibited practices, outside of cartel conduct. In a developing country context, prosecuting to meet the rule of reason legal test is complicated by: 1 the large inequity in litigation resources relative to respondents; 2 difficulties in securing evidence from multi-national organizations (MNOs) with a extra-territorial jurisdictional head office; and 3 a low standard and cost of appeal, along with a broad basis for review adopted. Coupling these practical difficulties with the courts' progressive raising

1 This included agreements amongst competitors to fix prices, divide markets or tender collusively. See South African Competition Act 1998 s 4(1)(b).

2 These included, prior to amendment, the effect of the merger on (a) a particular industrial sector or region, (b) employment, (c) the ability of small businesses, or firms controlled or owned by historically disadvantaged persons, to become competitive, and (d) the ability of national industries to compete in international markets. See Competition Act 1998 s12A(3).

3 The chapter uses the term legal standard to describe the legal onus required from per se prohibition through to full rule of reason.

4 The chapter uses the term liability standard to describe the economic test to establish liability, from the SPLC test through to AEC and an adverse effect on the welfare of a specific group as used in public interest provisions.

of the evidential burden required to establish contravention – arising in response to litigants' defences seeking a greater evidential burden (and, as we argue below, greater legal onus) – on the Commission to disprove alternative theories of causation on effects and to disprove the legitimacy of theoretical efficiencies. All these factors have led to considerable delays in the investigation and prosecution of prohibited practices, with cases typically taking five to eight years. Whilst there has been some success, many cases were dismissed for failure to meet the required standard for liability, typically failing to demonstrate compelling evidence on effects, complicated by the requirement to demonstrate a substantial causal relationship between conduct and effects. The courts current application of the legal test and liability standards is also out of step with the Act's purpose insofar as the evidentiary burden required to successfully meet SPLC test is near impossible to meet for complainants that are small and medium enterprises (SMEs) or firms owned or controlled by historically disadvantaged persons (HDPs). It also does not speak to the constitutional imperatives demanding access to essential services and transformation of the economy to redress historic exclusion.

The challenges faced prosecuting prohibited practices resulted in an amendment process that changed the legal standard for excessive pricing and introduced new provisions with a different legal test and liability standard in buyer power and price discrimination cases involving SMEs and HDPs. In multiple provisions, a new legal test is created by way of rebuttable presumption through the demonstration of a prima facie case, switching the evidentiary burden to the respondent. The amendments[5] also empowered the Commission to impose binding remedies in market inquiries, which have a different liability standard, namely the 'adverse effect on competition' (AEC), and a process permitting the legal standard that places more onus on respondents to disprove identified AECs or provide efficiency defences. The change in legal standards has enabled far more rapid prosecution of certain prohibited practices and securing of settlements without necessarily increasing Type I errors.[6] In recent years (possibly reflective of a correlation between rent seeking and economic hardship with the advent of the Covid-19 pandemic), there has been a marked increase in the use of interim relief applications by complainants, an application which makes use of the lower prima facie legal standard and which offers a speedy means to secure relief in the knowledge that the actual investigation and prosecution is likely to take much longer.

The amendments have occurred at a time where legal and liability standards for digital markets is the subject of much debate. Some have argued for a presumptive legal test which is based on certain conduct or acquisitions,

5 Competition Amendment Act No. 18 of 2018.

6 In a competition law context, a Type I error occurs where conduct that is not anti-competitive is incorrectly found in contravention of the Competition Act 1998.

rebuttable by the digital firm which bears the onus to show that the conduct or acquisition does not reduce competition and/or is outweighed by efficiency gains. The argument in favour of change to the legal test is often premised on the difficulty in assessing dynamic markets, the asymmetry in information and resources, and the strong network effects of digital markets making them prone to tip towards monopolisation. In a developing country context, the fact that digital markets are currently dominated by global tech firms exacerbates existing challenges in respect of asymmetry of resources and jurisdictional issues in securing information. Whilst the amendments to the Act did not specifically account for digital markets, the market inquiry provisions have in some respect opened a means to deal with conduct in these markets under a different legal and liability standard. In the South African context, a complainant against the conduct of Meta (Facebook/WhatsApp) was successfully able to secure interim relief preventing the complainant from being off boarded from the platform, under the prima facie case standard.

This chapter sets out the recent experience of a developing country that is adapting the legal and liability standards of more mature competition agencies and in doing so opening the door to more effective enforcement of prohibited practices. The chapter begins with a discussion of the legislative structure of the original prohibited practice provisions and the enforcement challenges under those legal and liability standards. This is followed by an outline of the core changes to the legal and liability standards under the amendment to the Act in 2019. The chapter then proceeds to discuss the enforcement experience under the new legal and liability standards in relation to both traditional abuse of dominance, public interest and digital markets. The chapter concludes with an assessment of whether different legal and liability standards are appropriate in a developing country context, including for digital markets.

II. Original Legal Standards and the Enforcement Record

Prior to the amendments to the Act, the central provisions prohibiting exclusionary practices were sections 8(c) and (d). These set out the instances where a firm will be considered to have abused its dominance by committing an 'exclusionary act'. An 'exclusionary act' was defined as 'an act that impedes or prevents a firm entering into, or expanding within, a market'.[7] This broad definition catches both pro-competitive and anti-competitive conduct.[8] The prohibiting sections also provide that in order to determine if the conduct was in fact an exclusionary abuse there is a need to balance the harmful effects

7 Competition Act 1998 s1(1)(x) prior to the amendments.

8 *Competition Commission v South African Airways* (2005) Competition Tribunal (18/CR/Mar01) at [108].

of the conduct against its pro-competitive gains. Textual interpretation of the Act's prohibitory sections provide that it is for the applicant alleging contravention (the *dominus litis*), namely the complainant or the Commission with the legal onus to establish that the anti-competitive effects of the conduct outweigh any justifications put forward by the dominant firm.[9] This meant that the legal and evidentiary onus, on the effects analysis or the full consideration of 'rule of reason', was primarily reliant on the evidence-gathering prowess of the complainant or the Commission and not on the dominant firm, which obviously was better placed to put forth evidence rebutting any argument brought forth by the Commission. This was the legal standard initially adopted.

Where section 8(c) was the catch-all provision, section 8(d) prohibited a number of specifi exclusionary acts. The following acts were prohibited, unless the firm concerned can show technological, efficiency or other pro-competitive gains which outweigh the anti-competitive effects of its act:[10]

(i) requiring or inducing a supplier or customer to not deal with a competitor;

(ii) refusing to supply scarce goods to a competitor when supplying those goods is economically feasible;

(iii) selling goods or services on condition that the buyer purchases separate goods or services unrelated to the object of a contract, or forcing a buyer to accept a condition unrelated to the object of a contract;

(iv) selling goods or services below their marginal or average variable cost; or

(v) buying-up a scarce supply of intermediate goods or resources required by a competitor.

At first glance, it would appear that once a dominant firm's conduct has been found to accord with the specific provisions outlined above, a presumption of anti-competitive effects arises and the onus shifts to the dominant firm to show technological, efficiency or other procompetitive gains justifying the conduct. Thus, the failure to provide a justification would establish a contravention whereas where justification exists, then the adjudicator would proceed to a weighing up exercise to establish if a contravention exists. However, in the *South African Airways* case the Competition Tribunal (Tribunal) held that the complainant or Commission must also provide evidence that the conduct had a significant

---

9 Philip Sutherland and Katherine Kemp, *Competition Law of South Africa* (LexisNexis 2010) 7-56. A complaint may be initiated by the Competition Commission or a third party. The Commission must then, following investigation, decide whether to refer the complaint to the Tribunal for adjudication. If the Commission decides that a third-party initiated complaint does not make out a contravention of the Act, the complainant may refer the complaint to the Tribunal for adjudication – effectively a private prosecution.

10 Competition Act 1998 s 8(d).

anti-competitive effect.[11] As explained by the Tribunal, the rationale for this interpretation is that:

> Without some notion of what the anticompetitive effect is it would be impossible to perform the weighing with the efficiency justification that both (c) and (d) require. In order to perform a weighing of the anticompetitive effect on the one side of the scale to the efficiency gain we need to have some notion of its quantitative effect.[12]

This interpretation was endorsed by the Competition Appeal Court (CAC) and it provides detail of the kinds of evidence required to demonstrate effects by way of evidence of actual competitive harm or by evidence that the exclusionary practice is substantially significant; that is the practice has the potential to foreclose the market to competition, in which case an anti-competitive effect can be inferred.[13] It is only once an anti-competitive effect has been proven that the onus then shifts to the dominant firm to provide evidence of efficiencies. Under this particular interpretation favoured by the courts, section 8(d), like section 8(c), requires the satisfaction of a full 'effects'[14] or rule of reason legal standard to determine exclusionary conduct.

However, encoded in the Act, are different consequences for contravention of these provisions. Contraventions of section 8(d) resulted in an administrative penalty of up to 10% of the firm's turnover for the previous financial year.[15] In contrast, a first time offence or contravention of section 8(c) did not carry an administrative penalty.[16] This posed a particular hurdle for the Commission in relation to the deterrence effect of any exclusionary (but not specifically named) conduct contravening section 8(c). This is because, once a firm was found to have contravened section 8(c), only *that firm* was deterred from replicating that conduct. If another dominant firm was to imitate the exclusionary strategy, after a complex investigation and protracted adjudication proceedings (possibly involving a number of appeals) the most likely remedy would be an order that the firm simply cease the impugned behaviour. As stated by Roberts, 'the construction of the... Act to specify certain conduct under 8(d) and provide a "catchall" effects-based test under 8(c), instead appears to have had a "catch-none" outcome'.[17]

---

11 *South African Airways* n 8 at [110]–[111], [132].

12 ibid at [110].

13 *South African Airways (Pty) Ltd v Comair Ltd* (2011) CAC: (92/CAC/MAR10) [2011] ZACAC 3; 2012 (1) SA 20 (CAC) (11 April 2011) at [112].

14 Roberts, Simon. "Effects-based Tests for Abuse of Dominance in Practice: The Case of South Africa." (2012) Centre for Competition Economics Working Paper 4/2012.

15 Competition Act 1998 s 59(1)(a).

16 ibid s 59(1)(b).

17 Roberts, Simon. "Effects-based Tests for Abuse of Dominance in Practice: The Case of South Africa." (2012) Centre for Competition Economics Working Paper 4/2012.

Another provision prohibiting exclusionary conduct was section 8(b). This provision stated that it is prohibited for a dominant firm to 'refuse to give a competitor access to an essential facility when it is economically feasible to do so'.[18] An essential facility is defined as an infrastructure or resource that cannot reasonably be duplicated, and without access to which competitors cannot reasonably provide goods or services to their customers. Contrary to the section 8(c) and 8 (d), anti-competitive effects are assumed under section 8(b) where it appears a dominant firm's conduct has been found to accord with the EU treatment of abuse of dominance, that is, 'prohibition without exemption'. However, the OECD remarks that the additional requirements to make a case under section 8(b) might make the provision less of a per se offense *in practice*.[19]

In terms of exploitative conduct, section 8(a) of the Act states that a dominant firm is prohibited from charging an excessive price to the detriment of consumers or customers.[20] In terms of the old section 1(ix) an 'excessive price' meant a price for a good or service which '(aa) bears no reasonable relation to the economic value of that good or service; and (bb) is higher than the value referred to in subparagraph (a)'.

Contrary to the US, one could read section 8(a) of the Act, in relation to excessive pricing, as making its contravention a 'per se' offense. On a reading of the legislation, one could say there is no 'rule of reason' defence available to a dominant firm found guilty of charging an excessive price to the detriment of consumers. However, consideration of the excessive pricing jurisprudence, shows that the full effects analysis with a large onus on the Commission is expected. Under section 8(a), prior to the amendments, the Commission referred six cases to the Tribunal for excessive pricing.[21] Of these, only two have been prosecuted before the Tribunal,[22] the remainder having either been settled before adjudication or await adjudication.

Before a firm can be found liable for excessive pricing under the Act, it must be found to be dominant.[23] The critical and most challenging aspect of

---

18 Competition Act 1998 s 8(b).

19 OECD, *Competition Law and Policy in South Africa* (2003) 27 <https://www.oecd.org/daf/competition/prosecutionandlawenforcement/2958714.pdf> accessed 2 April 2023

20 Competition Act 1998 s 8(a).

21 *Hazel Tau v GlaxcoSmith Kline*; *Harmony Gold v Mittal* (2004) Competition Tribunal: (13/CR/Feb04); *Competition Commission v Sasol Nitro* (2005) Competition Tribunal: (31/CR/May05) and (45/CR/May06), *Competition Commission South Africa v Foskor (Pty) Ltd* (2011) Competition Tribunal: (43/CR/Aug10); *Sasol Chemical Industries (Pty) Ltd v The Competition Commission* (2015) CAC: (131/CAC/Jun), see John Oxenham, 'The South African Competition Tribunal imposes fines for domestic excessive pricing of purified propylene and polypropylene (*Sasol*)' (2014) e-Competitions art No. 67452, *Competition Commission v SA Airlink* (pending) Competition Tribunal. (CR280Feb18); *Competition Commission v Afrimat* (2017) Competition Tribunal: (CR247Mar17).

22 Of these, it is only in respect of the *Sasol* case that a finding has been made. Although *Mittal* was heard in the CAC, it was referred back to the Tribunal for hearing, but was settled between the parties before the Tribunal heard the matter for the second time.

23 In the *Mittal* decision, the Tribunal considered that a firm must be '*super dominant*' before it would be found to have breached the excessive pricing provisions. This finding was criticized by the CAC, which noted (correctly) that there is no differentiation in the legislation between dominance and 'super-dominance'.

prosecuting such a case is obviously what constitutes an 'excessive price'. With reference to the stipulated definition of an excessive price, there exist practical challenges, namely, what constitutes 'economic value'? And how does one determine whether it bears a 'reasonable relation' to underlying costs?

The CAC's *Mittal* decision set out the four steps that must be considered to determine whether a price charged is 'excessive':[24]

a. firstly, the actual price must be determined;

b. secondly, the economic value of the good or service should be determined;

c. thirdly, a comparison must be done between the actual price and the economic value to determine whether there is a reasonable relationship between the two prices; and

d. finally, that the price charged must be shown to be detrimental to consumers.

One of the key contributions of the *Mittal* case was to set out a conceptual definition of 'economic value'. Crucially, the CAC held that the South African legislature must have meant that the 'economic value' is the notional price of the respective 'good' or 'service' under assumed conditions of 'long-run competitive equilibrium'.[25] Moreover, the CAC, in *Mittal*, held that economic value is a notional, objective, competitive market standard, and not one derived from the circumstances that may be peculiar to the specific dominant firm in question, such as a unique history of state support, subsidized finance, or a firm specific cost advantage.[26]

As indicated above, once a price has been determined to be higher than the economic value, it must then be determined whether the actual price charged is 'reasonably related' to the economic value. It is at this stage, being the test for 'reasonableness' that an enquiry into the circumstances peculiar to the dominant firm is to be taken into account.

Given the sections outlined above, it follows that from a South African competition law perspective, an 'excessive price' refers to a price that bears no reasonable relation to the economic value of the good or service provided; and is higher than the economic value of that good or service. The exact

---

24 *Mittal Steel South Africa Ltd, Macsteel International BV, Macsteel Holdings (Pty) Ltd v Harmony Gold Mining Company Ltd, Durban Roodepoort Deep Ltd* (2009) CAC: (70/CAC/Apr07), see Vitaly Pruzhansky and Mihael Raveggi, 'The South African Competition Appeal Court overturns an excessive pricing decision by the Competition Tribunal *(Mittal Steel)*' (2009) e-Competitions art. No. 38346. In this decision, the CAC acknowledged that this approach was not without its own difficulties, however, was meant to provide a framework for assessment.

25 ibid at [40].

26 ibid at [43].

definition of 'economic value'[27] and a 'reasonable relation'[28] between price and economic value is not defined in the Act itself. Case precedent indicates that the reasonableness assessment entails a value judgement.[29] In the reasonableness assessment, one should take a proper account of the origins of the firm's dominance, particularly the history of state support. One should also take into account the fact that the dominant position in the relevant market may not have been the result of any innovation or risk taking on the dominant firm's part. One should also take proper account of benefits flowing to the firm such as the subsidized loan, long term low rental or other special advantage. Such benefits may serve to reduce dominant firm's own long run average cost.[30]

As such, these concepts are left to the competition authorities' interpretation and are usually the centre of contentions in excessive pricing cases investigated by the Commission. This further indicates the difficulty of prosecuting conduct that, on the face of the Act's text should be considered per se prohibited conduct; but in practice, requires the meeting of a higher legal standard given the interpretative difficulties associated with the concepts as well as the evidentiary burden to be met by authorities.

III. Enforcement Record on Abuse of Dominance Cases

The former chair of the Tribunal once described prosecuting abuse of dominance offences as 'the most engaging and controversial area of competition law enforcement'.[31] In fact, it is said that in most jurisdictions, abuse of dominance complaints are notoriously challenging to prosecute successfully.[32]

South African competition authorities are not unique in their difficulties in prosecuting abuse of dominance cases. A total of 29 abuse of dominance cases had been considered by competition authorities and courts. These cases can be divided into two categories: 1 cases considered on the merits – this category includes cases prosecuted by the Commission and private litigants; and 2 cases resolved through settlement agreements. The table below gives a breakdown of these cases.

---

27 The definition of 'economic value' is given in case precedent. See ibid.

28 The acceptable 'reasonable relation' is given in case precedent. See Competition Appeal Court decision on the *Sasol* n 20.

29 See Competition Appeal Court decision ibid at [171].

30 ibid at [42].

31 D Lewis, *Thieves at the Dinner table – Enforcing the Competition Act* (2012).

32 J Oxenham and MJ Currie, 'South Africa Excessive Pricing – an Evaluation of the Sasol Chemical Industries Decision – a New Dawn, Or a Continuation of the Status Quo?' (2015) ABAJF.

Table 1: South Africa abuse of dominance, 1999–2022

Initiation	Case	Main alleged contravention	Status/finding
December 1999	*Competition Commission (CC) v SAFCOL, Yorkcor, CJ Rance* (Competition Tribunal Case no: 100/CR/Dec00)[33]	Price discrimination in timber	26/6/02 Tribunal dismissed application to confirm consent agreement reached between CC and SAFCOL, as it went to contractual provisions, without consent of the other parties
20 April 2000	*CC v Patensie Sitrus*[34] (Competition Tribunal Case no: 37/CR/Jun01)	Exclusive supply arrangement with packing and distribution company, contravening 8(d)(i) and 5(1).	4/8/02 Tribunal decision, upheld by CAC. Found articles of association of packing and marketing former co-op contravened 5(1) and 8(d)(i) in requiring customers/members not to deal with competitors; no penalty
13 October 2000	*CC v South African Airways*[35] (Competition Tribunal Case no: 18/CR/Mar01)	Inducing customer (travel agents) not to deal with competing airlines	28/7/05 Tribunal decision Found incentive scheme with travel agents contravened 8(d)(i); R45mn penalty
May-August 2002 complaints filed by 21 companies	*CC v Telkom* (Competition Tribunal[36] Case no: 11/CR/Feb04) – referral to the Tribunal 24 February 2014.	Excessive pricing, refusal to supply essential access facilities to independent VANS providers and inducement of customers no to deal with competitors.	Telkom challenged the Commission's referral at the Supreme Court. After 5 years of litigation at the SCA and on 27 November 2009, the SCA returned the matter back to Tribunal. On 7 August 2012, the Tribunal found Telkom guilty of refusal to give competitor access to essential facility and inducement. Penalty was imposed by the Tribunal.
19 September 2002 (CC non-ref 6/1/04)	*Harmony Gold v Mittal Steel SA* (Competition Tribunal[37] Case no: 13/CR/Feb04)	Excessive pricing of flat steel	27/3/07 Tribunal decision finding excessive pricing contravening 8(a) and penalty of R692mn 29/5/09 CAC overturned decision and remitted back to Tribunal to reconsider tests. Parties settled.

33 *Competition Commission (CC) v SAFCOL, Yorkcor, CJ Rance (2000)* Competition Tribunal: (100/CR/Dec00).

34 *CC v Patensie Sitrus (2001)* Competition Tribunal: (37/CR/Jun01).

35 *CC v South African Airways (2001)* Competition Tribunal: (18/CR/Mar01).

36 *CC v Telkom (2004)* Competition Tribunal: (11/CR/Feb04).

37 *Harmony Gold v Mittal Steel SA, (2002)* Competition Tribunal: (13/CR/Feb04).

Initiation	Case	Main alleged contravention	Status/finding
Sept 2002	*CC/Hazel Tau and others v GlaxoSmithKline & Boehringer Ingelheim* (Commission Case No. 2002 Sep226)[38]	Excessive pricing of antiretrovirals (ARVs)	Case non-referred by the Commission following agreement in Dec 2003 to license generic manufacturers
13 February 2003 (CC non-ref 13/5/03) 24/7/03 (CC non-ref 25/5/04)	*Mandla-Matla v Independent Newspapers*[39] (Competition Tribunal Case no: 48/CR/Jun04)	Exclusive arrangements with distributors contravening 8(d)(i) and 5(1); and refusal to supply distribution information contravening 8(c)	6/11/06 Tribunal decision, dismissed on all counts.
30 April 2003 complaint lodged (CC non-ref 12/11/03)	*Nationwide Poles v Sasol Oil*[40] (Competition Tribunal Case no: 72/CR/Dec03)	Price discrimination in creosote	31/3/05 Tribunal decision, found discount scheme was prohibited price discrimination 9(1). CAC decision – overturned.
1 October 2003	*CC, JTI v British American Tobacco South Africa*[41] (Competition Tribunal Case no; 55/CR/Jun05)	Arrangements with outlets for cigarette was exclusionary abuse under 8(d)(i) and/or 8(c), as well as under 5(1) referred by JTI.	25/06/09 Tribunal decision, dismissed on all counts Appeal to CAC lodged by JTI and then withdrawn
October 2003	*Nationwide Airlines, Comair v South African Airways*[42] (Competition Tribunal 80/CR/Sep06) – referral to the Tribunal in 2004.	South African Airways incentive schemes during the period 1 June 2001 – 31 March 2005 contravened 8(d)(i)	The Commission settled with South African Airways in 2006 without an admission and a penalty of R15mn. Comair and Nationwide Airlines objected and pursued a finding for the purposes of damages claims. 17 Feb 2010, the Tribunal Decision found contravened 8(d)(i), no penalty. Under appeal

38 *CC/Hazel Tau and others v GlaxoSmithKline & Boehringer Ingelheim* (Commission Case No. 2002Sep226).

39 *Mandla-Matla v Independent Newspapers (2004)* (Competition Tribunal: (48/CR/Jun04).

40 *Nationwide Poles v Sasol Oil (2003)* Competition Tribunal: (72/CR/Dec03).

41 *Competition Commission, JTI v British American Tobacco South Africa* (2005) Competition Tribunal; (55/CR/Jun05).

42 *Nationwide Airlines, Comair v South African Airways (2006)* Competition Tribunal: (80/CR/Sep06).

Initiation	Case	Main alleged contravention	Status/finding
3 November 2003 Nutriflo Aug04 Profert	*CC v Sasol Nitro*[43] (Competition Tribunal Case no: 31/CR/May05 and Competition Tribunal Case no: 45/CR/May06)	Excessive pricing, refusal to supply and price discrimination in ammonia and related fertilizer products	20/07/10 Tribunal confirmed settlement.
December 2003	*CC v Mittal Steel SA and others*[44] (Competition Tribunal Case no: 08/CR/Jan07)	Price discrimination in low carbon wire rod	Awaiting Tribunal hearing.
2 December 2004	*CC v Senwes*[45] (Competition Tribunal Case no: 110/CR/Dec06)	Pricing for grain storage excluding rival traders	3/02/09 Tribunal found exclusion in form of margin squeeze, contravening 8(c), upheld by CAC. SCA overturned on 1 June 2011.
25 November 2004	*CC v SAB*[46] (Competition Tribunal Case no: 134/CR/Dec07)	Inducement not to deal with a competitor; price discrimination	Tribunal dismissed 7/4/11, finding it did not have jurisdiction due to differences between complaint and Commission referral.
29 June 2005 and four further complaints consolidated	*CC v Telkom*[47] (Competition Tribunal Case No: 016865). (Referral to the Tribunal in Oct/Nov09) –	Excessive pricing and margin squeeze in pricing of broadband (leased lines)	On 18 July 2013, the Tribunal confirmed settlement between the Commission and Telkom on the complaints. Telkom agreed to pay an administrative penalty.
12 August 2005	*CC v Rooibos*[48] (Competition Tribunal Case no: 129/CR/Dec08)	Exclusive contracts with rooibos packers	November 2010 Tribunal confirmed settlement.
20 February 2007	*CC v Astral, Elite*[49] (Competition Tribunal Case no: 74/CR/Jun08)	Exclusive arrangements regarding poultry breeding stock and feed	On 12 November 2012, the Tribunal confirmed the settlement between Astral and the Commission. Astral admitted guilt of engaging in exclusionary conduct and an administrative penalty was imposed by the Tribunal.

43 *Competition Commission v Sasol Nitro* Competition Tribunal: (31/CR/May05) and Competition Tribunal: (45/CR/May06).

44 CC v Mittal Steel SA and others (2007) Competition Tribunal: (08/CR/Jan07).

45 Competition Commission v Senwes Ltd (2006) Competition Tribunal: (110/CR/Dec06).

46 Competition Commission v South African Breweries Limited (2007) Competition Tribunal: (134/CR/Dec07).

47 Competition Commission v Telkom SA SOC Ltd (2009) Competition Tribunal: (016865).

48 Competition Commission v Rooibos Ltd (2010) Competition Tribunal:(129/CR/Dec08).

49 Competition Commission v Astral Operations LTD, Elite Breeding Farms, and Ross Poultry Breeders (Pty) Ltd, (2011), Competition Tribunal:(74/CR/Jun08).

Initiation	Case	Main alleged contravention	Status/finding
August 2007	*CC v Sasol Polymers*[50] (Competition Tribunal Case no; CR042Aug10) – Referral to the Tribunal in August 2010.	Excessive pricing in the production and sale of purified propylene and polypropylene	The Tribunal on 5 June 2014 found Sasol guilty of charging domestic customers excessive prices for purified propylene and polypropylene, and penalty imposed. On 17 June 2015, the decision of the Tribunal was set aside by CAC.
December 2007	*CC v Foskor*[51] (Competition Tribunal Case no: 43/CR/Aug10).	Excessive pricing of phosphoric acid	28/02/11, Tribunal confirmed settlement.
Feb 2008	*CC vs Computicket* (Competition Tribunal Case no: CR008Apr10)[52]. The Commission consolidated the complaints between March 2008 and September 2009 and referred the matter to the Tribunal for prosecution on 30 April 2010.	Computicket's exclusionary terms in its contracts with providers resulted in inducement.	Contravened on 29 January 2019. Tribunal imposed penalty. CAC confirmed CT finding.
January 2009	*CC v Media24* (Competition Tribunal Case no: 013938 /CR154Oct11)[53] referral to the Tribunal on 31 October 2011.	Express predation and then in the alternative, the so called general exclusionary conduct.	Partial contravention confirmed by the Tribunal on 08 September 2015. The predation complaint was dismissed but found guilty of exclusionary conduct. On 19 March 2018, Media24's appeal to the CAC was successful and decision of the Tribunal set aside. On 3 July 2019, the Constitutional Court dismissed the Commission's appeal with costs.

50 Competition Commission v Sasol Chemical Industries Ltd and Safripol (Pty) Ltd, (2014) Competition Tribunal: (CR042Aug10).

51 Competition Commission v Foskor (Pty) Ltd, (2011) Competition Tribunal: (43/CR/Aug10).

52 Competition Commission v Computicket (Pty) Ltd, (2019) Competition Tribunal: (CR008Apr10).

53 Competition Commission v Media 24 (Pty) Limited, (2019), Competition Tribunal: (CR154Oct11).

Initiation	Case	Main alleged contravention	Status/finding
26 June 2012	*CC and Uniplate Group* (Competition Tribunal Case no: CR188Nov15)[54] – The Commission consolidated the initial complaint with that of 7 Feb 2013 and referral to the Tribunal was on 27 November 2015	Inducement – Uniplate strictly enforced its exclusive supply agreements and often threatened customers with litigation if they purchased or attempted to purchase their requirements from Uniplate's rivals.	Contravened 27 June 2019. Tribunal imposed penalty. CAC overruled Tribunal findings
March 2015	*CC v Afrimat, SA Block and Concrete, Concrete (Pty) Ltd; Clinker Supplies* (Competition Tribunal Case no: CR247Mar17)[55] – referral to the Tribunal in March 2017.	Excessive pricing of a main ingredient in clinker bricks – largely used in the construction of RDP houses	Awaiting Tribunal hearing.
13 June 2017 (On 6 December 2021, the Commissioner amended its complaint initiation to include Roche Basel and Roche SA)	*CC v Roche Holding AG* (Competition Tribunal Case no: CR176Feb22)[56] – referral to the Tribunal on 08 February 2022.	Excessive pricing of a breast cancer treatment drug, Trastuzumab.	Awaiting Tribunal hearing.
December 2018 (consolidated with complaints from Nov 2016 and March 2017)	*CC vs Airlink* (Competition Tribunal Case no: CR280Feb18)[57] – referral to the Tribunal on 12 February 2018	Excessive pricing for the provision of scheduled air passenger transport services.	Awaiting Tribunal hearing.

54 Competition Commission v Uniplate Group (Pty) Ltd (2019), Competition Tribunal: (CR188Nov15).

55 Competition Commission v Afrimat Ltd, SA Block and Concrete (Pty) Ltd, Concrete (Pty) Ltd and Clinker Supplies (Pty) Ltd, Competition Tribunal: (CR247Mar17).

56 Competition Commission v Roche Holding AG, Hoffman La Roche, Roche Products (Pty) Ltd, Competition Tribunal (CR176Feb22).

57 Competition Commission v SA Airlink (Pty) Ltd, Competition Tribunal: (CR280Feb18).

Initiation	Case	Main alleged contravention	Status/finding
March 2020	*CC v Babelegi Workwear* (Case no: CR003Apr20)[58] – referral to the Tribunal on 9 April 2020.	Excessive pricing in the sale of face masks (FFP1)	Tribunal found contravention on 1 June 2020. The CAC dismissed appeal by Babelegi on 18 November 2020 and penalty imposed by the Tribunal was set aside.
14 April 2020	*CC v Dis-Chem Pharmacies* (Competition Tribunal Case no: CR008Apr20)[59] – referral to the Tribunal on 23 April 2020.	Excessive pricing in the retail sale of face masks.	Contravened on 7 July 2020. Tribunal imposed penalty.
5 May 2020	*CC v Tsutsumani* (Competition Tribunal Case no: COVCR113Sep20)[60] – referral to the Tribunal in Sep 2020	Excessive pricing to the South African Police Services (*SAPS*), for the supply of bulk 3–ply surgical face masks ("*masks*").	Contravened on 28 April 2022. Tribunal imposed penalty.
20 November 2020	*CC v Meta, WhatsApp and Facebook ('the respondents')* (Competition Tribunal Case no: CR189Mar22)[61] – referral to the Tribunal in March 2022.	Exclusionary terms for access to the WhatsApp Business API.	The Tribunal granted the complainant, GovChat, an 'Interim-relief' order on 21 January 2021 in terms of which the respondents were interdicted from off boarding GovChat from their platform. The Commission investigated underlying conduct and referred a complaint to the Tribunal. Awaiting Tribunal hearing.

Source: Updated table from Thando Vilakazi, Sumayya Goga and Simon Roberts (Eds) (2020) "Opening the South African Economy: Barriers to entry and competition". Cape Town: HSRC Press (chapter 11).

As can be seen from the table above, and in the context of prevailing inequality and market concentration, it is worrying to observe that most of the cases considered were ultimately dismissed. The record for abuse of dominance prosecution shows that only eight cases were confirmed by both the Tribunal

58 Competition Commission v Babelegi Workwear and Industrial Supplies CC (2020), Competition Tribunal: (CR003Apr20).

59 Competition Commission v Dis-Chem Pharmacies Ltd (2020) Competition Tribunal: (CR008Apr20).

60 Competition Commission v Tsutsumani Business Entreprises CC, (2022), Competition Tribunal: (COVCR113Sep20).

61 Competition Commission v Meta Platforms Inc. Competition Tribunal: (CR189Mar22).

and CAC. All other cases were either dismissed by the Tribunal or the CAC for a variety of reasons. In terms of the duration of abuse of dominance cases, we calculate that the authorities can take up to five to eight years to prosecute them.

In recent years (possibly reflective of a correlation between rent seeking and economic hardship with the advent of the Covid-19 pandemic), there has been a marked increase in the use of interim relief applications by complainants, an application which makes use of the lower prima facie legal standard and which offers a speedy means to secure relief in the knowledge that the actual investigation and prosecution is likely to take much longer. As at November 2022, 43 interim relief applications have been considered by the Tribunal, 15 have been granted. The ratio of interim relief applications that were granted during various (inclusive) periods: were 9 out of 24, from 1999 to 2005;[62] 2 out of 5, from 2006 to 2010;[63] 0 out of 5, from 2011 to 2015; 1 out of 4, from 2016 to 2020;[64] and 4 out of 4, from 2020 to November 2022.[65]

Possible explanation for the dismissal of many of these early cases is because the affected parties, most of which were SMEs, have struggled to establish anti-competitive effects. In the *Normandien* matter, an application brought by a small sawmiller against alleged abuse of dominance practices by Komatiland Forest was unsuccessful and the Tribunal reasoned as follows:[66]

> Viewed in the best possible light, the applicant has depicted that a single player in a market may have been negatively affected (for example by having to pay a higher price). It does not follow necessarily that this translates into a substantial prevention or lessening of competition in the market as a whole. For such a finding to be reached,... it would have to be found that because of the negative effect on the applicant and the applicant's size/ relevance in the defined market, there has in fact been a substantial prevention or lessening of competition in the market as a whole. This has certainly not been shown and section 8(c) allegation is accordingly dismissed.

---

62 *DJ Mine v Chemserve* (1999) Competition Tribunal: (IR001Sep99) and (IR002Sep99); *SA Raisins v SAD* (1999) Competition Tribunal: (IR004Oct99); *South African Raisins (Pty) Ltd v SAD* (2000) Competition Tribunal: (IR014Dec99); *Cancum Trading No. 24 v Sev* (2000) Competition Tribunal: (IR015Dec99); *Jakobus JP Bezuidenhout v* (2000) Competition Tribunal: (IR025May00); *American Natural Soda Ash Corp v Botw* (2001) Competition Tribunal: (IR013Dec99); *Botswana Ash (Pty)* (2001) Competition Tribunal: (IR007Oct99).

63 *Nedschroef Johannesburg (Pty) Ltd and Te* (2006) Competition Tribunal: (IR070Oct05); *Directory Solutions cc and Trudon (Pty)* (2010) Competition Tribunal: (IR048Nov09).

64 *Vexall v Business Connexion* (2020) Competition Tribunal: (IR119Oct19).

65 *The Sekunjalo Group v Banks* (2023) Competition Tribunal: (IR153Dec21); *eMedia Investments v Multichoice and CC* (2022) Competition Tribunal: (IR194Mar22) was dismissed, but as discussed in this chapter, it was later granted on appeal *Emedia Investments Pty Ltd South Africa v Multichoice Pty Ltd* (2022) CAC: (201/CAC/JUN22); *Makarenge Electrical Industries v Allbro* (2022) Competition Tribunal: (IR095Oct21); *GovChat v Facebook and Whatsapp* (2021) Competition Tribunal: (IR165Nov20).

66 *Normandien Farms (Pty) Ltd v Komatiland Forests (Pty) Ltd* (2014) Competition Tribunal: (IR194Feb14).

This case provides an example of how for SMEs, the jurisprudence has contributed to them, as well as the investigative authority, facing a greater challenge in demonstrating that a SPLC has occurred. If such conduct against SMEs is pervasive then ultimately there is a greater harm to competition and the economy arising from the muted participation of such firms (which is contrary to the purpose of the Act).

The inability to prove anti-competitive effects is not the only challenge to successfully prosecuting abuse cases. Differences in the interpretation of the Act, as demonstrated by the excessive pricing cases, which evidence several adjudicative challenges with clarifying concepts such as 'reasonability' and 'economic value'. Similarly, in recent exclusionary conduct cases, the concept of margin squeeze was contested. Interestingly, margin squeeze was not directly included in the Act's wording or definitions but has found application in various cases before the courts, such as the *Senwes*[67] and *Telkom*[68] cases. While the concept of margin squeeze has been generally accepted as a form of exclusionary conduct under the exclusionary catch all provision, section 8(c); it remained uncertain how to establish an anti-competitive effect under this provision.[69]

In the *Telkom* case, the Tribunal clarified this by stating that in order to show harm for the purposes of section 8(d), it is not necessary to show that competitors have exited or have lost market share because of the harm. All that needs showing is that the conduct was likely to result in an SPLC, including impeding competition.[70] However, a different conclusion was reached in the later decided *Uniplate* matter.[71] Whilst this was not based on conduct falling under the scope of margin squeeze, the CAC found that the Commission's findings on the likely harm that could arise from the alleged conduct could not be sustained in relation to the evidence indicating the actual harm to competitors. This leaves a difficulty or lack of clarity on the actual standard required to establish anticompetitive effects particularly when there are both potential and actual effects for which the Commission has to account.

Some cases resolved through settlement have yielded positive results. Such outcomes are consistent with the socio-economic goals set in the Competition Act.[72] For example, in the settlement between the Competition Commission and Foskor, Foskor agreed to significantly reduce the price of phosphoric acid

67 *Competition Commission v Senwes Ltd* (2013) Competition Tribunal: (110/CR/Dec06).

68 *Competition Commission v Telkom SA Ltd* (2011) Competition Tribunal: (11/CR/Feb04), see Simon Roberts, Reena Das Nair, 'The Competition Tribunal of South Africa rules on exclusionary conduct in the telecommunications industry (*Telkom*)' (2012) e-Competitions art. N° 51091.

69 In *Senwes*, the Tribunal found that although customers of *Senwes* were induced to not deal with other silo traders (with no storage facilities), the anticompetitive effect was not established. *Senwes Ltd* n 67 at [139].

70 *Telkom SA Ltd* n 68 at [99].

71 *Competition Commission v Uniplate Group* (2020) CAC: (176/CAC/Jul19).

72 Nompucuko Nontombana, Itumeleng Lesofe, "A Review of Abuse of Dominance Provisions of the Competition Act – is it necessary?", (2016) 10th Annual Competition Law, Economics and Policy Conference.

and phosphate rock prices for the benefit of downstream markets that rely on these products as inputs. In another settlement, Sasol Chemical Industries agreed to divest and dispose of its granular and liquid fertilizer blending facilities. The purpose of this remedy was to open markets and provide smaller players with the opportunity to participate equitably in the fertiliser industry. Further, the Commission concluded a settlement agreement with ArcelorMittal SA Ltd (AMSA) in terms of which the latter agreed to pay a hefty penalty and introduce some changes in its pricing of flat steel products. However, these settlements, particularly for abuse of dominance cases have been too few and limited to significantly change the dynamics of the economy as intended.

Other factors also contribute to the challenges faced in abuse of dominance prosecution. These include:

a. the relative litigation resources and low cost of appeal along with the broad nature of such appeals. The CAC considers not only reviews on legal grounds but also a full appeal on the merits including findings of fact or economic interpretation by the Tribunal. This in essence provides litigants with a 'second bite at the cherry' to determine if the CAC sees the case differently, rather than limiting itself to a narrower question typically considered in review of whether the Tribunal misdirected itself or was clearly wrong on its findings;

b. information gathering against MNOs from home country – a recent example involves the Commission's excessive pricing investigation into breast cancer treatment by Switzerland based multinational healthcare company, Roche Holding AG (Roche AG), and its subsidiaries, F Hoffmann La Roche AG (Roche Basel) and Roche Products (Pty) Ltd (Roche SA). The Commission experienced significant challenges in gathering cost information required to conduct the excessive pricing assessment. Roche had declined to provide the Commission with its cost data (despite the Commission pursuing all available legal channels, including the diplomatic channels), allegedly on the basis that, that cost data sits in Switzerland.[73]

c. information asymmetry in general and 'signal jamming' behaviour, where respondents use economics and economic theory to conclude that the analysis relied on by the Commission is incomplete, but they do not rule out a particular reason nor do they provide contrasting economic evidence to allow for scrutiny before the Tribunal. 'Signal jamming' behaviour thrives where the courts place an undue burden on the Commission to effectively prove its entire case before shifting the burden to the dominant firm.

---

73 See <https://www.compcom.co.za/wp-content/uploads/2022/02/competition-commission-prosecutes-a-multinational-healthcare-company-roche-for-excessive-pricing-of-a-breast-cancer-treatment-drug.pdf> accessed 2 April 2023.

It is clear that while the Act may have been drafted with a particular socio-economic context in mind, the reality of abuse of dominance prosecution and jurisprudence has meant that a greater challenge is faced by authorities to meet the prevailing legal standard to these cases. Arguably the prevailing legal standard imposed by the courts has been overly burdensome relative to the intention of the legislature in respect of section 8(d), at least. Section 8(d) is drafted in a manner that suggests once the Commission establishes that a dominant firm is engaged in specific identified conduct then a presumption of negative effects, or a prima facie case, exists and the onus should shift to the dominant firm to demonstrate technological, efficiency or pro-competitive gains that outweigh such effects. By requiring the Commission to establish its entire case before the initial shift in onus has considerably raised the evidentiary burden. This in turn has opened the door to dominant firms resisting discovery of evidence and economic experts engaged in 'signal jamming' behaviour, which has made meeting the court's legal standard even more difficult. The implication of these challenges is glaringly obvious when one considers the enforcement record of the Commission as well as the limited impact competition policy and enforcement has to the goal of increasing participation of SMEs and HDPs in the South African economy (as evidenced by the growing concentration levels across the vast majority of sectors).

IV. Amendments to the Competition Act and the Legal and Liability Standards

The challenges faced in prosecution of prohibited practices resulted in an amendment process that changed the legal standard for excessive pricing and introduced new provisions with a different legal and liability standard in buyer power and price discrimination cases involving SMEs and HDPs. In 2016, the Commission identified as challenges to abuse of dominance enforcement, excessive pricing, predatory pricing and price discrimination. In excessive pricing cases challenges had arisen relating to the calculation of economic value. In terms of predatory pricing challenges arose regarding the definition of average variable costs and marginal costs (as evidenced in *Media24*[74]) and it was suggested that there be a move away from a strict definition in favour of average total costs and average avoidable costs. In terms of price discrimination, the challenge identified was the requirement of proof that transactions between different purchasers with different scale economies are equivalent.

In May 2017, in a background note issued by the Minister of Economic Development (now Department of Trade, Industry and Competition (DTIC)) regarding changes to the Act, seeking to address economic concentration, the

---

74 *Competition Commission v Media 24 Pty Ltd* (2016) Competition Tribunal: (CR154Oct11).

Minister stated: 'Despite its clear objectives, the current Competition Act is primarily concerned with anti-competitive effects arising from the conduct of market participants, as opposed to optimising the structure of the relevant contestable markets to achieve its purposes'. In terms of the priorities identified, the background note emphasized that section 8 of the Act is an important tool to address anti-competitive conduct in concentrated markets.[75] Challenges experienced by the authorities in prosecuting excessive pricing cases, predation and exclusionary conduct are also highlighted as being the underlying rationale to the proposed amendments. In particular, the allocation of evidentiary burdens between the Commission and the dominant firm are also raised as contributing to the challenges faced by authorities in abuse of dominance cases.

In December of that year the Background Note on the Competition Amendment Bill spoke to standards regarding excessive pricing,[76] predatory pricing,[77] price discrimination,[78] as well as buyer power,[79] and margin squeeze.[80]

After public comment, legislative endorsement, and executive approval, the final iteration of the update made to the tests was published in 2019. In abuse of dominance provisions, the amendments introduced the prima facie test for excessive pricing where, if established, the onus shifts to the respondent to prove why the price is reasonable. On SME/HDP inclusion, the amendments introduced a buyer power provision with an unfairness standard (not SPLC) and a prima facie case provision requiring respondent to show why it is not unfair. The amendments also adjusted the legal standard in price discrimination, from SPLC to 'impede effective participation' for SMEs/HDPs, with the prima facie element too. In market inquiries, outcomes are now binding, and the legal standard can

75 Explanatory memorandum to the amendments of the Competition Act 1998 14.

76 Regarding excessive pricing it was stated that 'Cases involving the abuse of dominance through charging excessive pricing have not to date been successfully prosecuted and this may continue to be the case unless the allocation of evidentiary burdens between the Commission and the dominant firm is addressed'. On this basis it was proposed that burden be placed on the dominant firm to show that its price is reasonable after a prima facie case against it has been established by the Commission. It was also proposed that there be a deletion in s 8(a) that an excessive price be shown to be to the 'detriment of consumers', since excessive pricing may also affect businesses that buy inputs from dominant firms.

77 Regarding predation, the Act is amended to accommodate a more general cost standard ('the firm's relevant cost benchmark') for determining whether a firm has engaged in predatory pricing. This amendment enables flexibility and the case-specific determination of the applicable and relevant cost benchmark to be applied in each case. This enables the competition authorities to determine which cost benchmark out of the possible range of options is best suited to the facts and circumstances of a particular case. The subsection also includes as possible benchmarks the practice of selling goods or services below their average avoidable cost or long run average incremental cost.

78 The Act also proposed that the ambit of s 9 be expanded to prohibit price discrimination by a dominant firm against its suppliers. In addition, it is proposed that the allocation of the burden of proof provisions be addressed so that the dominant firm must show that the action of price discrimination is not likely to have an effect of preventing or lessening competition.

79 The Act introduced buyer power provisions to protect suppliers to dominant firms from being required, through the abuse of dominance, to sell their goods or services at excessively low prices. This addresses the problem of monopsonies, namely when a customer enjoys significant buyer power over its suppliers.

80 Finally, in relation to margin squeeze, the amendments inserted to include the practice of engaging in a margin squeeze as a possible abuse of dominance.

be met with a showing of features or conduct having an 'adverse effect on competition' ie, impedes, restricts or distorts competition (not SPLC), with no offsetting efficiency or consumer welfare requirements.

The focus of the section below is to highlight the impact of the amendments in terms of the change in legal tests related to the excessive pricing, buyer power and price discrimination provisions, along with the liability standard for the latter two provisions and exclusionary conduct.

1. Excessive Pricing

In terms of substantive changes to the excessive pricing provisions, the amendments have outlined that the Act prohibits dominant firms from pricing excessively to the detriment of customers or consumers. An excessive price is determined with reference to whether the price concerned is higher than a competitive price, and whether such difference is unreasonable, considering all relevant factors.[81] The amendments also made a provision for the Minister of DTIC to publish regulations regarding the calculation and determination of excessive prices as an additional factor.

The excessive pricing prohibition in the Act provides that, if there is a prima facie case that a price charged by a dominant firm is excessive, the onus shifts to the respondent to prove that such is reasonable. Specifically, section 8(2) furthermore states that: 'If there is a prima facie case of abuse of dominance because the dominant firm charged an excessive price, the dominant firm must show that the price was reasonable.'

The excessive pricing provision did not previously articulate the factors that should be considered in assessing an excessive pricing claim, other than requiring a comparison of the price relative to the 'economic value' of the good or service in question. The amendments now require the price to be assessed relative to the notional 'competitive price' and provide parameters by reference to which this assessment may be carried out, for example the dominant firm's price-cost margin, internal rate of return, return on capital or profit history as well as other structural characteristics of the market. These parameters take into account various considerations raised in previous excessive pricing cases. This assists in providing some clarity in terms of the relevant factors which may be considered.

Viewed collectively, commentators have stated that these developments render it significantly easier to prosecute an excessive pricing complaint.[82]

81 Factors include respondent's price-cost margin, internal rate of return, return on capital invested or profit history; the respondent's prices for the goods or services in other markets; comparator firms prices and profits in competitive markets; duration of pricing; and the market characteristics.

82 H Ratshisusu and L Mncube, 'Addressing Excessive Pricing Concerns in Time of the COVID-19 Pandemic – a View from South Africa' (2020) 8 JAE 256–59.

2. Price Discrimination

The amendments to section 9 now incorporate three potential contraventions for dominant seller, namely;

a. where price discrimination is prohibited if it is likely to have the effect of substantially preventing or lessening competition (section 9(1)(a)(i)); or

b. where price discrimination is prohibited if it is likely to have the effect of impeding the ability of SMEs or HDP firms to participate effectively (section 9(1)(a)(ii));

c. where it is prohibited for a dominant firm to avoid selling, or refuse to sell, goods or services to a purchaser that is a SME or HDP firm in order to circumvent the operation of price discrimination in impacting SMEs or HDPs (section 9(1A)).

While in general, differential treatment of purchasers remains an infringement only if it 'substantially prevents or lessens competition', a lower legal standard is applied if the differential pricing is to SMEs or HDP firms. Such pricing will be an infringement if it impedes such firms' ability to 'participate effectively'.[83] Where there is evidence of an inability to participate effectively, differential pricing cannot be defended on the basis of differential quantities supplied to different buyers.

A plain reading of the updated section means that in the case of SMEs and HDPs the test required is not 'a substantial preventing or lessening of competition' test (which is expressly omitted in the subsection dealing with this class of firms, section 9(1)(a)(ii) of the Act). This means that a demonstration of an SPLC in the downstream market more generally is not required and as such, the inquiry does not require an assessment of the actual or likely effects on final consumers but rather the likely effect on firm(s) within the designated class of purchasers alone. Use of the word 'likely' from the legislated phrase, 'likely to have the effect', means the assessment can be a probabilistic one. As such, actual effects need not necessarily be demonstrated to establish a contravention when such effects are probable or likely given the conduct.

It is therefore not necessary to demonstrate that the ability of the entire designated class, as a whole, to participate effectively is likely impeded by the conduct, but only that the ability of members of the designated class to participate effectively is likely impeded. This may include a single complainant or a sub-category of firms within the designated class, such as SME or HDP firms only. This lower liability standard will hopefully correct for the challenges experienced by authorities in prosecuting price discrimination cases where the previous wording

83 Competition Act 1998 s 1(xxiii) defines 'Participate' as 'the ability of or opportunity for firms to sustain themselves in the market'.

of the Act (and in fact the standing jurisprudence) required the authorities to demonstrate actual effects such as the exit of a firm.[84]

The amendments have also introduced a reverse onus to show that the differential pricing does not impede effective participation if there is a 'prima facie' case.

The regulations[85] provide that firms owned or controlled by HDPs should only qualify for protection under the relevant section if they purchase less than 20% of the relevant goods or services supplied by the dominant seller. It appears that this provision seeks to filter out complaints by large firms owned or controlled by HDPs, focusing the section's scope on protecting smaller firms with limited negotiating power.

3. Buyer Power

The insertion of subsection 8(4) to the Act, expressly introduced buyer power provisions into the Act.[86] Of relevance to the consideration of buyer power within an abuse context is section 8(4)(a) and reads as follows:

> It is prohibited for a dominant firm in a sector designated by the Minister in terms of paragraph (d) to directly or indirectly, require from or impose on a supplier[,] that is a small and medium business or a firm that is controlled or owned by historically disadvantaged persons, unfair:
>
> I. Prices; or
>
> II. Other trading conditions.

The introduction of buyer provisions has meant that dominant firms in designated sectors[87] may not impose 'unfair' prices or trading terms on SMEs or HDP firms; and avoid or refuse to purchase from SME or HDP firms in order to circumvent the buyer power provisions (an 'anti-avoidance' provision).[88]

The underlying context to the introduction of this provision is centred around the possibility that there may be circumstances where buyers have bargaining power against SMEs and HDP firms which they may abuse by suppressing prices and transferring costs and/or risks onto SMEs and HDP firms. To this end, the existence and abuse of buyer power is likely to hinder the ability of, or opportunity for, SMEs and HDP firms to sustain themselves in the market. Given this context, buyer power is necessarily viewed as being more than just assessing monopsony

84 *Nationwide Poles cc v Sasol Oil (Pty)* (2005) CAC: (49/CAC/Apr05).

85 Price discrimination regulations, *Government Gazette* No. 43018 13 February 2020 <https://www.gov.za/sites/default/files/gcis_document/202002/43018gon168.pdf> accessed 2 April 2023.

86 S 5 of Competition Amendment Act n5

87 The provision only applies to sectors designated by the Minister by regulation.

88 Competition Act 1998 s 8(4)(b).

behaviour[89] but is rather an assessment that considers the impact of the relative bargaining power between firms on the public interest objectives of the Act. This means that the consideration of buyer power, whilst it is a public interest issue as outlined by section 8(4), is also an assessment of dynamic competition as the benefits of a thriving SME/HDP sector can offer greater choice for consumers and possibly lead to their growth and challenging of incumbents over time.

Regulators around the world are becoming more preoccupied with questions of 'fairness' on the part of such dominant firms. South Africa is one of the first to introduce specific rules and one can expect initial litigation to turn on the concept. In implementing the legal framework, the Commission in its guidelines has stated that in their assessment of contraventions of section 8(4), an inquiry under this provision is simply 'whether the prices and trading conditions imposed on suppliers in the designated class by a dominant firm are unfair or not'.[90] The focus of the inquiry is then limited to the treatment and welfare of suppliers in the designated class, and the application of a fairness principle to that treatment. The inquiry does not require an assessment of the effects on final consumers. For instance, it is not relevant whether an unfairly low price achieved through the exercise of buyer power is passed through to consumers or not. Further, the legislature does not make provision for any weighing up of the welfare of suppliers in the designated class against final consumers.

The newly introduced provision also introduces a reverse onus on dominant firms to prove that purchase prices or trading conditions are fair if a prima facie case of unfairness is established. Also, a reverse onus on dominant firms is also provided for to prove that it has not contravened the anti-avoidance provision.

4. Exclusionary Conduct

Whilst the general provision under section 8(c) – now section 8(1)(c) – did not change, the definition of what constitutes an exclusionary act did change. Whereas previously a prohibited exclusionary act constituted 'an act that impedes or prevents a firm from entering, or expanding within, a market', this was expanded to include 'entry into, participation in or expanding within a market'.[91] To participate in a market in turn is defined as 'the ability of or opportunity for firms to sustain themselves in the market'. The amendment therefore extends the notion of exclusion beyond simply preventing entry or expansion, but also acts that may undermine the ability of competitors to be sustainable.

89 This refers to the traditional consideration of monopsony behaviour premised on the consumer welfare standard – where the focus is on restricting supplier price and not passing on the lower price to consumers. In this instance harm is measured through the resulting restriction in output to the market.

90 Competition Commission of South Africa, "Buyer Power Enforcement Guidelines" (2020) para 2.2.1. <https://www.compcom.co.za/wp-content/uploads/2020/05/Buyer-Power-Guidelines.pdf> accessed 12 April 2023.

91 Competition Act 1998 (as amended) s 1(xiii).

V. Early Experience with Amended Legal Standards in Prohibited Practice and Market Inquiry Provisions

The amendments were signed into law on 13 February 2019, providing a few years of experience in how the change in legal and liability standard have impacted on the enforcement of abuse of dominance. A year after the amendments came into law, the global Covid-19 pandemic caused massive economic and social upheaval which diverted the priorities of the Commission to addressing the more immediate economic crisis. However, the economic crisis revealed its own unique types of market power abuse and therefore provided a suitable testing ground for the new amendments in terms of excessive pricing and abuse of buyer power. Once the immediate height of the pandemic was over, the Commission moved to use another of the amendments, namely the new market inquiry powers, to examine digital intermediation markets. This section examines that experience and whether the change in legal and liability standards affected the enforcement success and quality of decision making.

1. Excessive Pricing (Section 8(1))

Excessive pricing was the only pre-existing contravention of the Act which saw a revision in the legal onus under the amendments. This was due to the failure to successfully prosecute excessive pricing in the first twenty years of the Act, despite several fairly strong cases in respect of upstream super-dominant firms in the chemicals and steel industry. It was also due to the general concern that this type of abuse is likely to be more prominent in a highly concentrated economy and which would undermine the competitiveness of downstream industries and hence economic development.

As outlined above, the amendments brought in two changes in the construction of the relevant provisions. First, it introduced a clearer liability standard under section 8(3), namely that in determining if a price is excessive, one must establish that 'the price is higher than the competitive price and whether such difference is unreasonable'.[92] This is done in reference to a list of potentially relevant factors, which include any potential regulations made by the Minister.[93] In addition, the legal standard was altered to introduce a presumptive standard whereby under section 8(2) stipulates that if a prima facie case is established then 'the dominant firm must show that the price was reasonable'.[94]

The Covid-19 pandemic lead to South Africa declaring a National State of Disaster on 15 March 2020 and entering a hard lockdown of civilians on

92 ibid s 8(3).

93 ibid s 8(3)(f).

94 ibid s 8(2).

27 March 2020. The pandemic created a huge and immediate global spike in demand for personal protective equipment (PPE), including face masks, and sanitisers. At the same time, the move into lockdown caused panic-buying and stockpiling of PPE and food by consumers. This provided the perfect conditions for price gouging by opportunistic PPE suppliers and retailers. It was price-gouging, a particular species of excessive pricing, that would provide the first testing ground for the change in legal standard.

In anticipation of price gouging and stock-piling behaviour that may deprive poorer consumers of access to essential health products and food, the Minister made regulations on 19 March 2020 that set out relevant factors in determining a prima facie case of excessive pricing.[95] These were based on price-gouging laws in numerous US States and were simply whether the price increase 'does not correspond to or is equivalent to the increase in cost' or the price increase 'increases the net margin or mark-up … above the average margin or mark-up for that good or service in the three month period prior to 1 March 2020'.[96] Whilst the cases that were ultimately prosecuted first to establish the precedent did not rely on these regulations, as the conduct began prior to the promulgation of the regulations, the relevant factors still played an important role in the determination of a prima facie case because they were based on sound economic principles in respect of price gouging.

In the panic buying preceding the national lockdown and into the first month of lockdown, the Commission was inundated with complaints of price gouging on face masks, sanitiser and essential foodstuffs. The Commission sought to process the complaints quickly by requiring retailers or wholesalers to provide the current costs and prices of the product subject to the complaint, as well as for the three months prior to 1 March 2020 in line with the regulations. The Commission identified cases suitable to bring for prosecution which it could do so on an expedited basis due to other Ministerial regulations on Tribunal Rules for Covid-19 cases.[97] The first contested cases were against Babelegi Workwear (Babelegi) and Dis-Chem Pharmacies (Dis-Chem).

Babelegi was a wholesaler of workwear including FFP1 dust masks, which it sourced at R2.05 per mask prior to the pandemic and initially sold the masks at R2.53 or a 23% mark-up. Babelegi proceeded to increase the price of its stock of FFP1 masks to R500 per mask, or 987%, by 5 March, or a margin of 1120% given that the cost of the stock had not increased.[98] Dis-Chem is a leading

95 The Consumer and Customer Protection and National Disaster Management Regulations and Directions GN R350 GG 43116, 19 March 2020 (consumer protection regulations) <https://documentportal.george.gov.za/storage/level-one-covid-documents/December2020/xhWwpA8OGKPF2ZJIfnGZ.pdf> accessed 2 April 2023.

96 ibid para 4.

97 Government Notice No. R448 in *Government Gazette* No. 43205 of 3 April 2020 <https://www.gov.za/sites/default/files/gcis_document/202004/43205rg43205gon448.pdf> accessed 2 April 2023.

98 *Competition Commission v Babelegi Workwear Overall Manufacturers and Industrial Supplies CC* (2020) CT: (CR003Apr20) tables 1 and 2, 33 and 34 respectively.

national pharmacy chain, dispensing pharmaceuticals and retailing health and beauty products including PPE for consumers. Dis-Chem sold surgical masks through its chain and increased its 50 pack price by 261% during March 2020 and 5 pack by 43% without a corresponding increase in costs.[99] The *Babelegi* matter was heard on 24 April 2020 and the *Dis-Chem* matter on 4 May 2020, each within two weeks of the complaint referrals. The Tribunal found in favour of the Commission in both cases, which were subsequently appealed to the CAC. On the eve of the CAC hearing, Dis-Chem withdrew its appeal but Babelegi proceeded. The CAC dismissed the appeal, finding that the conduct contravened the excessive pricing provisions in the Act.

The change in legal onus required that the Commission needed to establish a dominance, and b that the price was excessive, to establish a prima facie case against Babelegi and Dis-Chem.

a. The Commission overcame the first hurdle by arguing that in the context of an economic demand shock of the size of the pandemic for face masks, market power may be conferred on even small resellers given the lack of alternatives in the market. The ability to impose price increases substantially in excess of costs was further evidence of the market power conferred by the pandemic.

b. The Commission overcame the second hurdle by arguing that the wholesale or retail mark-up in the period prior to the pandemic for these face masks represented the competitive price or margin of a reseller. This is because the mark-up is the effective price charged by the reseller to distribute the product to consumers. The Commission argued that the price increases unrelated to costs which substantially increased the mark-ups of both firms demonstrated that the price was higher than the competitive price.

The requirement to only establish dominance and excessiveness to establish a prima facie case was confirmed by the CAC in its *Babelegi* judgement (noting that on appeal Babelegi is the appellant and the Commission is the respondent):

> [58] Once dominance is established, the gateway is open for respondent to bring its case under s8(1). In the enquiry that follows, it must be established by respondent that the price charged was excessive. (See s 8(2)) In the present case, the evidence which is relevant to this enquiry is as the following: Appelant's price for the face masks prior to the commencement of the Covid 19 pandemic, was vastly lower than the prices that were charged during the complaint period. Secondly, there were a number of price hikes

99 *Competition Commission v Dis-Chem Pharmacies* (2020) Competition Tribunal: (CR008Apr20) at [7], see Michael-James Currie and John Oxenham, 'The South African Competition Tribunal publishes its written reasons to penalize a pharmaceutical chain for excessive pricing (*Dis-Chem*)' (2020) e-Competitions art. No. 95829.

> implemented by appellant over the complaint period subsequent to the onset of the pandemic which itself caused customers and consumers to pay significantly and increasingly more for their masks. The significant increases in the mark ups during the complaint period together with the absence of any price increases for the sales stock during the period is telling. Furthermore, as indicated earlier, appellant had an ability to price higher without any constraint imposed upon it by either its consumers or customers, not as a result of any new investment or commercial efficiency produced but simply because the onset of the pandemic created entirely different conditions for the market in which the appellant was located. Hence prima facie, the prices charged were excessive in terms of s8(2) of the Act. This conclusion shifts the evidential burden into the appellant's court.

Once the Commission had established a prima facie case in line with these two pre-conditions, then under section 8(2) the dominant firm is required to show that the price is reasonable. The reasonableness requirement is included under the liability standard outlined in section 8(3), namely that once the price is shown to be higher than the competitive price, the next determination is whether the difference is unreasonable. Under the legal standard introduced, this onus now rests with the dominant firm. However, section 8(3) is also relevant to the determination of excessiveness that the Commission is put to in establishing the prima facie case. This is set out by the CAC in the next paragraph of the judgement.

> [59] Section 8(3) of the Act now comes into play. It enjoins this Court to determine whether the price charged is unreasonable. Here the appellant must provide a justification for its price. The section is hardly drafted with the precision that should be demanded of national legislation. Section 8(3) covers both the s8(2) enquiry and the case that a defendant firm must produce to show that, notwithstanding the prima facie finding, the price it charged is reasonable. Both the determination of whether the price is excessive and the question of reasonableness are to be determined, inter alia, by the factors set out in s8(3). In the present case the price charged was manifestly far higher than the yardstick price, that is a price charged in a relatively competitive pre Covid 19 market.

In the *Babelegi* case the CAC made short work of the justification put forward by Babelegi in coming to its finding that there was a contravention.

> [60] Why then did the appellant contend that the price it charged was not unreasonable? As observed earlier, appellant did not seek to justify its decision to increase prices on the basis of a new

> competitive equilibrium. It produced no evidence to illustrate that its prices were conditioned by that of its competitors. The only plausible explanation proffered by the appellant was that it anticipated an increase in the price of acquiring further masks, once its existing stock had been exhausted.
>
> ...
>
> [62] The problem is that no evidence was produced to show that costs were expected to rise by an amount which was anywhere close to the 888% increase extracted during the complaint period. Hence, the evidence produced by appellant cannot sustain the argument that it based its price increases before, during and after the complaint period on clearly justifiable and anticipated price increases, which correlated with its own increases.
>
> ...
>
> [64] In summary, the evidence appellant adduced is unconvincing...
>
> [65] .... This is a manifestly inadequate explanation to rebut the prima facie case as required of appellant in terms of s8(2) of the Act.

In the *Dis-Chem* case the respondent also pursued the line of argument that the Tribunal should have regard to the anticipated higher prices that was being quoted by suppliers, and some actual higher procurement costs.[100] However, once more, when put to the onus of adducing evidence to support these contentions Dis-Chem was found wanting.

> [192] However, the factual evidence does not support any of these submissions.
>
> [193] Evidence of quotes Dis-Chem had received (but not actual orders placed) from several suppliers during March and April were put up in support of these higher anticipated costs. But these were quotes only, and in any event fall outside the Complaint Period. The RBB report does indicate that Dis-Chem's sales of its historically procured masks, which were locally produced, had largely run out by the end of March, and Dis-Chem proceeded to sell mainly imported masks, but again this was only in April
>
> [194] No quantification of increased procurement costs was handed up nor was any impact shown on Dis-Chem's cash flow or interest earnings.

100 *Dis-Chem Pharmacies* at [188].

The shift in onus for the respondent to explain why the prices are reasonable is the critical change in the legal standard that has aided the prosecution of these cases. The change in legal standard is likely to improve legal decision-making that allows the court to come to the correct decision, especially in a developing country context as is evident in these price gouging cases. This is because it places the onus with the party that has full access to all the information to adduce the evidence, rather than the party (the Commission) that can only seek to extract what information it can. The latter process is plagued by information asymmetries and 'signal jamming' conduct where respondents argue that the Commission has failed to discharge its onus because it has not exhausted all possible reasons for why the difference is reasonable. The new legal standard avoids Type I errors as the respondent is able to adduce the evidence where it is not in contravention, but it also avoids the Type II errors[101] where the respondent is in contravention but the Commission is simply unable to compile the evidence due to the information asymmetries.

The problem with the previous legal standard is self-evident in the recent referral against Hoffmann La Roche SA in a case of excessive pricing of a breast cancer drug Herceptin. The Referral Affidavit[102] sets out how Roche persistently refused to cooperate in providing the necessary evidence required by the Commission to make determination of excessiveness.

> 26. Throughout its investigation process, the Commission was frustrated by the persistent refusal of Roche to provide the Commission with relevant costing and financial information for the manufacture of Herceptin and Herclon, despite repeated requests by the Commission for such information, and exhaustive efforts taken by the Commission to obtain such information from Roche SA and Roche AG, since July 2017. In summary, Roche SA has, for its part, stated that the relevant information is not in its possession, and is owned and controlled by Roche AG, whilst Roche AG has simply refused to provide such information.
>
> 27. The Commission has exhausted all available legal channels, including diplomatic channels to obtain such information, but all these efforts have been in vain.

The referral affidavit proceeds to set out how it engaged in attempts to secure information over a three-year period[103] starting with a refusal to provide cost information in October 2017, followed by a response that the information was

101 In a competition law context, a Type II error occurs where conduct that is anti-competitive is incorrectly found not to be in contravention of the Act.

102 Non-confidential Founding Affidavit in *Competition Commission v Roche Holdings AG, F Hoffmann La Roche AG, Roche Products (Pty) Ltd* (CR176FEB22)

103 ibid at [28] and sub-paragraphs.

not in its possession but was in possession of Roche AG based in Switzerland after summons was issued. Following a request to Roche AG, there was a refusal to provide the information unless the information was requested through the Swiss Authorities using diplomatic channels. The Commission approached the Swiss Competition Authority which responded that it could not assist as there was no agreement between Switzerland and South Africa regarding cooperation on the application of competition laws. The Commission then pursued the diplomatic channels and the information request was served on the Federal Department of Justice and Police in Switzerland in February 2020 only to be told the same thing.

The Referral Affidavit concludes that despite the efforts to frustrate securing evidence, the benchmarks used are sufficient to make out a case of excessive price.

> 29. Roche's obstructive conduct has had the result that, in the absence of the costing and financial information it has sought from the respondents, the Commission has had to rely on various benchmarks to substantiate its case against the respondents, as set out in more detail below. The Commission contends that, despite Roche's attempts to frustrate the Commission" investigation, the benchmarks relied upon by the Commission are sufficient to make out a case of excessive pricing by Roche.

The challenges in securing information from multinational companies by developing country competition authorities is laid bare by the Hoffmann La Roche example. In the absence of a legal standard that permits a shift in onus, it is apparent that a proper legal assessment would be denied and hence a strong risk of a lack of enforcement and by implication Type II errors.

2. Abuse of Buyer Power (Section 8(4))

One of the provisions under abuse of dominance designed to provide a different legal and liability standard when dealing with SMEs and HDP firms, is the so-called 'buyer power' provision. As outlined above, this provision introduces a fairness standard for liability, ie, 'it is prohibited for a dominant firm … to … require from or impose unfair prices or trading conditions'.[104] The legal standard set out in section 8(4)(c) makes use of the prima facie case, which if established, shifts the onus to the dominant firm alleged to be in contravention 'to show that … the price or other trading condition is not unfair'. Furthermore, the Minister had issued regulations in respect of this provision as required under section 8(4)(d).[105] As regulations were included to provide more legal certainty

104 The Competition Act 1998 (as amended) s 8(4)(a).

105 *Government Gazette* n 85.

for new provisions, the regulations and subsequent guidelines issued by the Commission[106] have been an important tool in the enforcement of this provision in large part because they set out factors to be considered in establishing unfairness and hence a prima facie case. The regulations set out the following factors to determine unfair prices:[107]

(a) The prices paid to other suppliers of like goods or services, in particular those outside the designated class, and whether such prices are higher;

(b) the magnitude of any differences in prices to other suppliers of like goods or services;

(c) whether reductions in the existing purchasing price are directly or indirectly required from, or imposed on, the supplier;

(d) whether reductions to an existing purchasing price are retrospective, unilateral or unreasonable;

(e) whether costs are directly or indirectly imposed on or required from the supplier which reduce the net price received by the supplier; or

(f) whether the direct or undirect imposition or requirement of costs is retrospective, unilateral or unreasonable.

The Covid-19 pandemic also provided the first instances of enforcement under section 8(4) in the dairy industry which had been identified previously as a sector where such abuse was prevalent. In general, processors draw fresh milk from farmers in a small radius from the processing plant and frequently processors are geographically dispersed to draw from different farming communities. This provides the processors with buyer power given that dairy farmers do not have many immediate alternatives for the highly perishable product. There had previously been a processor cartel that fixed the farm gate price, and most processor contracts include a provision to adjust farm-gate prices in response to market conditions.

The announcement of the State of Disaster followed by the national lockdown to commence on 27 March 2020 resulted in stockpiling by consumers resulting in a shift in the dairy product sales profile towards long-life products. However, the food value chain did continue to operate to provide food for consumers. The other impact on businesses that did continue was the requirement for providing a higher level of hygiene including PPE for staff. A concern by the Commission during the pandemic was that inequitable bargaining power within the supply chain may result in those with buyer or market power shifting the burden of the pandemic onto their trading partners. The dairy industry was ripe for such a shift in burden and abuse of buyer power.

---

106 Buyer Power Enforcement Guidelines (12 May 2020) <https://www.compcom.co.za/guidelines> accessed 2 April 2023.

107 *Government Gazette* n 85 at 10.

On 30 March 2020 Dairy Producer A issued a communication to its supplying dairy farmers informing them of a 45c/litre levy effective from 1 April 2020 allegedly to cover its own costs of PPE and the potential shifts in the consumption bundle of dairy products. The Commission received a complaint the next day and on 1 April 2020 sent a letter to the CEO of the Dairy Processor. In essence, that letter set out why there was a prima facie case against the actions of Dairy Processor A, and requiring that the levy be immediately withdrawn lest the Commission prosecute for abuse of buyer power. Dairy Processor A subsequently sent a communication to its farmers on 3 April 2020 stating that the implementation of the levy would be postponed to 1 May 2020. Dairy Processor A subsequently consulted with its farmers and revised the potential premium to half the amount. However, ultimately not even the lower levy was imposed.

On 15 April 2020, Dairy Processor B issued a communication to its supplying dairy farmers stating that the winter premium which would ordinarily run through to August of each year would lapse on 1 May 2020 and not be paid for the rest of the period. Once more, the Commission received a complaint from the dairy farmers and issued a similar letter to Dairy Processor B indicating that there was a prima facie case of abuse of buyer power and that it should withdraw the previous communication or otherwise face prosecution. Once more the Dairy Processor withdrew the communication and continued to pay dairy farmers the winter premium.

The shift in onus, along with supporting regulations outlining the factors relevant to a determination of an unfair price, played an important role in securing this change in behaviour by the Dairy Processors without the need for litigation.

a. First, the change in legal standard required that the Commission needed to a establish dominance, and b establish likely unfairness, in order to establish a prima facie case against the Dairy Processors. The Commission overcame the first hurdle by reference to case precedent which generally found processors were dominant in their catchment areas, but also the unilateral ability to impose a levy or withdraw a premium was itself an indicator of dominance. The unilateral imposition of a levy or withdrawal of a winter premium constituted a unilateral reduction in a purchasing price which are factors cited by the regulations in determining if a price is unfair. Those regulations state in paragraph 4(d) that reductions to a purchase that is 'retrospective, unilateral or unreasonable' is a factor to determine unfairness.

b. Second, given the establishment of a prima facie case, the onus shifts to the Dairy Processors to demonstrate that the price is not unfair. As the Commission letter to each Dairy Processor indicated, the unilateral imposition is not in dispute which creates severe difficulties for their defence. In addition, the letter points out that the communications simply speculate as to the impact that may arise in terms of the supply and demand changes during the lockdown without actual evidence of any effect, which creates a second difficulty in their defence. The Commission followed up the initial letters to demand information on their costs and consumption bundles changes, as well as their profitability in order to drive home the point about the evidentiary burden they now bear. The implication that was not lost on their legal advisors was that the Commission could proceed to immediately refer the matter without having to gather any additional evidence, and that the Dairy Processors would then be under pressure to produce that evidence in answer to the referral affidavit.

c. The fact that both Dairy Processors retracted their communications to dairy farmers within days demonstrates that they were ultimately unable to discharge that evidential burden of showing that the levy or withdrawal of the winter premium was not unfair. This implies that the outcome itself, through the use of the new legal and liability standard, did not create a distorted legal outcome but rather a sound one. Furthermore, it created the sound legal outcome quickly and without unnecessary litigation, in so doing, preventing harm to dairy farmers from the abuse of buyer power.

d. In contrast, under the typical legal and liability standard the Commission would first have to establish the negative competitive effects on the farmers before accounting for any potential technological, efficiency or pro-competitive gains. Not only is the alternative legal standard far more burdensome on the Commission, but also would involve considerable delays in establishing the evidence from the complainants and respondent.

The example of the change in the legal and liability standard for buyer power demonstrates the value of a presumptive legal standard which shifts the burden to adduce evidence to the contrary on the respondent especially in a developing country context. This assists in reducing the regulatory resources required to address abusive conduct and overcomes the asymmetry of information often used by respondents to delay or frustrate investigations. The change in legal standard also permitted the matters to move more quickly to the referral stage, enabling a quicker prosecution of abuse of dominance cases that has been elusive for the Commission historically.

3. Market Inquiry (Section 43A–G) and digital markets

There has been considerable global debate as to whether the legal and liability standards need to be adjusted for digital markets, especially in relation to digital platforms which act as effective gatekeepers to consumers for business users on the platform. The call for a different legal standard is first premised on the entrenched super-dominant position of such platforms which means a presumptive harm from certain conduct is in fact more likely. The second premise is that the information asymmetries and complexity of these markets means it is appropriate to shift the onus to the platforms to demonstrate otherwise. The fact that the platforms have the ability to rebut the presumption ensures that there is a lower risk of Type I errors with this legal standard. On the liability standard, it is argued that the dynamic nature of these markets and the difficulty in predicting future outcomes, alongside the tendency to tip towards single-firm super dominance due to network effects, means a liability standard in favour of competition should be preferred. In other words, a requirement not to demonstrate that mergers or conduct have a SPLC but rather simply a likely AEC. As a result, the EC has pursued economic regulation of certain gatekeeper's conduct through the Digital Markets Act (DMA) as regulation provides that presumptive basis for remedial action.[108]

South Africa's amendments did not expressly consider the developments in digital markets. However, the amendment to strengthen the powers of the Commission in conducting market inquiries has opened the door to a potentially useful tool to tackle conduct in digital markets. Market inquiries were designed as a pro-competitive tool to tackle market features that have an adverse impact on competition. As a result, liability standard is lower than an SPLC, namely the 'adverse effect on competition' test which 'is established if any feature, or combination of features, of a market for goods or services impedes, restricts or distorts competition in that market'.[109] Such features may include the market structure and levels of concentration, the observed outcomes of the market, as well as single-firm and multi-firm conduct.[110] The liability standard of an adverse effect enables a broader set of issues to be brought into the ambit of an inquiry than simply those that result in an SPLC.

Once an AEC is identified, which includes express consideration of adverse effects on SMEs and HDPs,[111] then the Commission has a duty to remedy.[112] There is no explicit requirement to consider off-setting technological, efficiency or pro-competitive effects. However, it is in the remedial action where the strength of the AEC comes into play, insofar as 'the nature and extent of the adverse effect on competition' is one of the factors in determining reasonable and appropriate remedies.[113]

There are further beneficial aspects to a market inquiry in the context of digital markets and the current debates around legal standards and regulation. First,

108 Regulation 2022/1925 of the European Parliament and of the Council of 14 September 2022 on contestable and fair markets in the digital sector and amending Directives 2019/1937 and 2020/1828 (Digital Markets Act) 2022 O.J. (L 265).

109 The Competition Act 1998 (as amended) s 43A(2).

110 ibid s 43A(3) and sub-paragraphs.

111 ibid ss 43C(1) and (2).

112 ibid s 43D.

113 ibid s 43D(4) and sub-paragraphs.

as an inquiry, there are elements of the process which mimic that of establishing a rebuttable presumption and a shift in onus to the respondent. This is because an inquiry is not litigation and therefore can require submissions from respondents on substantiating the rationale for certain conduct or contractual provisions, and why such conduct does not have an AEC. Such evidence may still be used to determine an appropriate remedy as a lack of justification lowers the bar to removing the conduct through a remedy.[114] Second, an inquiry is into a market as a whole, which may be broadly construed, and not specific conduct unless expressly limited in the Terms of Reference, which enables the inquiry to explore the effect of different elements of the ecosystem on competition and seek a holistic set of remedial actions. Third, by incorporating all market participants into the ambit of powers to request or summons information, an inquiry is more easily able to test what is submitted with other market participants and identify contradictions in those submissions or contrasting evidence.

It is therefore unsurprising that the first market inquiry under the new amendments was into digital markets, specifically the *Online Intermediation Platforms Market Inquiry* (OIPMI) launched on 19 May 2021.[115] The scope of the inquiry included all major business to consumer (B2C) intermediation platforms including eCommerce marketplaces, online classifieds and price comparator services, software application stores and intermediated services such as accommodation, travel and food delivery.[116] The Terms of Reference for the inquiry set out the four areas of competition and public interest, namely: a market features that may hinder competition amongst the platforms themselves, b market features that may hinder competition amongst business users or undermine consumer choice, c market features that give rise to exploitative treatment of business users, and d) market features that may negatively impact on the participation of SMEs and/or HDP firms.

The OIPMI *Provisional Report* was released on 13 July 2022 for public and stakeholder comments before the finalisation of the inquiry.[117] The OIPMI *Provisional Summary Report* provides numerous examples of where intermediation platforms have been put to the onus of justifying specific conduct and providing the evidentiary basis for that justification. In many instances, the Provisional Report finds the evidentiary basis insufficient. A few illustrative examples highlight how the onus has been put on the respondents.

114 In determining a reasonable and practical remedial action, the legislation sets out factors which include ss 43D(4)(f) 'any other relevant factor arising from any information obtained by the Competition Commission during the market inquiry'.

115 See OIPMI, *Online Intermediation Platforms Market Inquiry* (2023) <https://www.compcom.co.za/wp-content/uploads/2023/02/OIPMI-Proposed-Regulations-and-Guidelines.pdf> accessed 2 April 2023.

116 See the terms of reference along with all other public information generated by the OIPMI <https://www.compcom.co.za/online-intermediation-platforms-market-inquiry/>> accessed 2 April 2023.

117 OIPMI, *Provisional Report* (2022) <https://www.compcom.co.za/online-intermediation-platforms-market-inquiry-provisional-report/> accessed 2 April 2023.

a. In the case of wide price parity clauses, in travel and accommodation platforms in particular, the inquiry made the following observations:[118]

> 59.3 The evidence from the removal of wide parity in Europe and even narrow parity in Germany shows that consumers continue to book on platforms and free-riding is not a material problem. The Inquiry invited Booking.com to provide any of its estimated impacts from this natural experiment but did not receive any evidence to the contrary. This was also the case with Amazon which removed parity in eCommerce in the EU and then later in the US.

b. In respect of price discrimination on food delivery, online classifieds and travel and accommodation platforms, the inquiry identified that whilst a rationale was put forward, no attempt was made to justify the rationale for the extent of difference.[119]

> 84.3 Third, even if the Inquiry were to accept the proposition that larger business users warrant a lower commission fee or listing fee because they bring more restaurants/listing/rooms to the platform (which is not accepted), there has been no evidence to justify the absolute extent of that difference, especially for food delivery and classifieds, rather than argument that some difference should exist. Given that another obvious explanation for the discrimination is simply the result of differences in bargaining power, and the ability to exploit SMEs/HDPs relative to larger business users, a critical assessment is required to distinguish between what may be value based and what may be bargaining power.

c. In some areas such as the failure to identify pay-for-position or pay-for-ranking boost as adverts, there was simply no rationale provided. The inquiry therefore could only infer the following:[120]

> 88. ...The reason for failing to label ads is obvious, namely that consumers may be less inclined to click on ads and may be put off platforms that serve too many ads if they are prominently labelled. This is the ad blindness that Google studiously researches to maximise its own paid search. As a result, by not labelling ads, platforms are able to serve more ads in the SERP and business users are willing to pay more for that advert, which maximises revenue from selling visibility.

From a developing country perspective, digital markets raise a host of additional competition-related and public interest issues insofar as the market features and global nature may exclude domestic platform competitors and domestic business users. Whilst some of the issues may be dealt with under the usual liability

118 OIPMI, *Provisional Summary Report* para 59.3.

119 ibid para 84.3.

120 ibid para 88.

standard of AEC, for instance in evaluating the effect of wide price party clauses by global firms, it remains necessary to adjust the liability standard to account for these other developmental objectives as set out in the Act. For instance, the Provisional Summary Report makes a provisional finding that global tax benefits provide a competitive advantage to global platforms competing with domestic ones.[121] At a business user level, the report makes a finding that within software application stores that features such as curation and promotion limit participation by South African app developers.[122] The report similarly devotes an entire section to the exclusion of HDPs from both platform and business user competition.[123]

What is evident from the first market inquiry into digital markets is that this may provide a potentially effective enforcement tool in digital markets as an alternative to regulation, such as the DMA, or wholesale reform of the competition law to accommodate new legal standards. A market inquiry may still need to determine the lower liability standard of an AEC, but its processes permit a different legal standard arising from a shift in the onus of respondents to provide a justification for their conduct. A lack of justification opens the door to remedial action that removes such conduct as there is no harm from doing so. Much like in the excessive pricing experience, when respondents are put to the onus then their submissions are frequently unconvincing or unsubstantiated. This suggests that this change in legal standards may enable more accurate legal decisions by avoiding Type II errors, whilst still protecting against Type I errors.

VI. Constitutional Developments

Recent ConCourt jurisprudence has added further impetus to the shift in legal and liability standards of the South African Competition Act. As a constitutional democracy, the ConCourt is the apex court (or final court of appeal) in South Africa. The 2019 amendments to the Act also clarified the confusion regarding whether appeals from the CAC had to be taken to the Supreme Court of Appeal (SCA) prior to being capable of appeal to the ConCourt. The amendments removed and modified sections referring to the SCA as a court to which appeals from the CAC may lie.[124] This was a meaningful legislative step in light of the opinion of certain commentators that SCA competition jurisprudence was increasingly restrictive in its interpretation of the Act, particularly relating to the initiation, investigation and prosecution of cases.[125]

121 ibid s 4.3.

122 ibid s 8.3.6.

123 ibid s 6.

124 See amendments made to the Competition Act 1998 ss 62 and 63.

125 See, for example, Heathrow Romeo Kariga 'Between a rock and a hard place? A closer look at the Competition Appeal Court' (Nelson Mandela Institute Conference on Competition Law, Economics and Policy in South Africa, 4 and 5 October 2011) <http://www.compcom.co.za/wp-content/uploads/2014/09/Between-a-rock-and-a-hard-place-PAPERfinal-Submitted-version.pdf> accessed 2 April 2023.

Despite removal of the SCA as an option for appeal, leave to appeal is not simply for the asking. In order to engage the jurisdiction of the ConCourt appellants need to pass the test on leave to appeal. What is most interesting are the varying jurisprudential grounds with which the ConCourt views competition enforcement as an area of law implicating the Bill of Rights – this is particularly fascinating given the nature of the South African Constitution's Bill of Rights[126] which provides for both vertical and horizontal application of rights, and which rights detail both negative and positive obligations upon the State. We provide brief overview of the ConCourt jurisprudence on the extent to which competition enforcement raises constitutional concerns, ultimately concluding that a constitutionally compliant interpretation lends itself to a generous interpretation of the Competition Act as a legislative instrument of redress, elevating competition enforcement to an area of social justice, further legitimising, what we argue for in this chapter, the reversal of legal presumptions and legal onuses in certain cases, and the lowering of legal standards.

Prior to the Constitution's seventeenth amendment of 2013,[127] leave to appeal was granted to appellants able to demonstrate that the merits of the matter concerned a constitutional matter[128] and it was in the interests of justice to decide the appeal. A constitutional matter was one which concerned the interpretation of any provision of the Bill of Rights or other provision of the Constitution. Early ConCourt cases that entertained competition appeals did so on the basis that the constitutional matter at stake was the constitutional pronouncement on the power and scope of the powers of competition authorities as public bodies (and consequently whether the authority had acted beyond their powers) – competition authority *vires* cases.[129]

---

126 The Constitution of the Republic of South Africa Act No. 108 of 1996 (The Constitution).

127 *Government Gazette* No. 36128 Vol. 572 published on 1 February 2013 <https://www.justice.gov.za/legislation/acts/const17th_2013gg36128no72.pdf> accessed 2 April 2023. The purpose of the amendment was, among others, to provide that the Constitutional Court is the highest court in all matters and further regulate the jurisdiction of the Constitutional Court and the Supreme Court of Appeal. A main feature of the seventeenth amendment was to provide that the ConCourt 'is the highest court of the Republic', a revision of the erstwhile 'highest court in all constitutional matters'.

128 The Constitution s 167(3), prior to amendment, and s 167(7) reads: '(3) The Constitutional Court – (a) is the highest court in all constitutional matters; (b) may decide only constitutional matters, and issues connected with decisions on constitutional matters; and (c) makes the final decision whether a matter is a constitutional matter or whether an issue is connected with a decision on a constitutional matter. … (7) A constitutional matter includes any issue involving the interpretation, protection or enforcement of the Constitution.'

129 *Competition Commission of South Africa v Senwes Ltd* (2012) CCT: (61/11) (handed down 12 April 2012); *Competition Commission v Yara South Africa (Pty) Ltd* CCT: (81/11) (handed down 26 June 2012), see John Oxenham, 'The Supreme Court of Appeal of South Africa establishes that complaints concerning a price cartel made by private persons may trigger a new course of action to be initiated by the Competition Commission and finds that the requirements for valid initiation and referral have been satisfied in the present case (*Yara*)' (2013) e-Competitions art. No. 60811; *Competition Commission v Loungefoam (Pty) Ltd* (2012) CCT: (90/11) (handed down 26 June 2012); *Competition Commission of South Africa v Pioneer Hi-Bred International Inc* CCT: (58/13) (handed down 18 December 2013), see Patrick Smith, 'The South African Constitutional Court sets aside a costs order decided by the Competition Appeal Court to overturn a merger prohibition decision (*Pioneer Hi-Bred International / Pannar Seeds*)' (2013) e-Competitions art. No. 62281; *SOS Support Public Broadcasting Coalition v South African Broadcasting Corporation (SOC) Ltd* (2018) CCT: (121/17) (handed down 28 September 2018).

In February 2019, the Constitutional Court in *HCI,*[130] which concerned questions of merger notifiability in circumstances of a change to a form of control; founded its jurisdiction on the basis of an arguable point of law of general public importance which the ConCourt ought to consider – the seventeenth-amendment introduced, additional basis upon which to found the jurisdiction of the ConCourt.[131] What was seen as the arguable points of law of general public import in this case related to the interpretation and application of the Act's merger control provisions; as well as, making *vires* pronouncements on the Commission's power to investigate and the Tribunal's power to issue a declarator in the circumstances.

The most interesting jurisprudential point about the debate on leave to appeal to the ConCourt is underscored in the *Media24*[132] case handed down in July 2019. The case demonstrates the extent to which there was a lack of unanimity about the kinds of fact patterns that elevate competition issues into constitutional (as amended) bases of appeal, regarding: (i) economic principles of competition enforcement; (ii) questions of transitional justice as found expression in the Constitution's equity clause; or (iii) pronouncements on matters of *vires*. *Media24* concerned predation in the newsprint market and produced four split opinions from the ten-member court. Six members of the court held that the application raised an arguable point of law of general public importance that it ought to consider, with the implication that certain dissenting judges felt that the jurisdiction of the court had not been invoked. On the reasoning employed to found constitutional court jurisdiction, three judges concurred with the first judgement, four judges with the second judgment, and three judges with the third.

The first judgment, per Goliath J, viewed it as an arguable point of law of general public importance that it ought to consider the question of whether 'pricing above average avoidable cost but below average total cost amounts to predation [which] requires the interpretation of the law relating to exclusionary acts and the consideration of which tests can be used to equitably establish predation'[133] – elevating a question of competition economics into one of constitutional import. The second judgment, per Cameron, Froneman and Khampepe JJ, criticised this approach stating that the question of what evidence should be considered to establish predation involves mixed questions of fact and law, which require evaluative assessments. As an appeal court, the ConCourt should only

130 *Competition Commission of South Africa v Hosken Consolidated Investments Ltd* (2019) CCT: (296/17) (1 February 2019).

131 The Constitution (post amendment) s 167(3)(b) now reads: 'The Constitutional Court may decide – (i) constitutional matters; and (ii) any other matter, if the Constitutional Court grants leave to appeal on the grounds that the matter raises an arguable point of law of general public importance which ought to be considered by that Court'.

132 *Competition Commission of South Africa v Media24 (Pty) Ltd* (2019) CCT: (90/18).

133 ibid at [34].

intervene in those 'rare instances where purely legal issues of interpretation arise'.[134] These judges opined that deference to expert bodies, being the Tribunal and the CAC, is required in relation to a question which invariably relies on the assessment of the relative merits of expert evidence. The third judgment, per Theron J, agreed that these facts did raise arguable point of law of general public importance but disagreed with the second judgment's finding that the question of the applicable economic test to be employed to establish a case on predation, was not a legal one. This is because, 'what renders an issue legal (and, in that context, potentially constitutional) as opposed to purely factual, is an enquiry into the social policy and normative content behind a rule', the question raised on predation required critical examination of the inarticulate premises of the policy and normative implications of various standards for predatory pricing, something Theron J views as a legal enquiry.[135]

The first judgment endorsed the Commission and Media24's argument that the Competition Act's transformative goals are a basis founding constitutional jurisdiction. The right to equality contained in the Constitution[136] enjoins organs of State to take legislative measures to advance equality and the protection of 'historically disadvantaged persons' through the Competition Act is one such legislative instrument. Further to this, consumer welfare and the protection of SMEs and HDPs from dominant firms' predatory practices serves to advance equality by aiming to interrupt how abuses of dominance perpetuate historical patterns of exclusion. The second judgment took issue with the alignment of competition policy with the right to equality, stating that the implication of this reasoning would be to make the interpretation and application of the entire Competition Act a constitutional matter for purposes of establishing ConCourt jurisdiction. In criticising the suggestion that the Competition Act had analogously gave expression of fundamental rights in the Constitution, the second judgement provided:

> [128] The Competition Act is not the legislation the Constitution mandated to give effect to the right to equality in the way that PAJA and the LRA are statutes specifically mandated by the Constitution in terms of, respectively, the rights to just administrative action and fair labour rights. The Competition Act is just legislation. It has no elite constitutional allure. All legislation must conform to the constitutional imperative of equality.

134 ibid at [134]–[135], 7.

135 ibid at [143]

136 The Constitution s 9 reads: '(1) Everyone is equal before the law and has the right to equal protection and benefit of the law. (2) Equality includes the full and equal enjoyment of all rights and freedoms. To promote the achievement of equality, legislative and other measures designed to protect or advance persons, or categories of persons, disadvantaged by unfair discrimination may be taken. (3) The state may not unfairly discriminate directly or indirectly against anyone on one or more grounds, including race, gender, sex, pregnancy, marital status, ethnic or social origin, colour, sexual orientation, age, disability, religion, conscience, belief, culture, language and birth.'

Finally, the parties argued that the earlier decided cases of *SOS* and *HCI*, wherein the pronouncement on the ambit of the Commission's investigatory powers was found to be an inherently constitutional issue, were bases upon which to establish constitutional jurisdiction, in this case. The second judgment criticises the sophistry with which the first judgement asserts that determination of the standards for the establishment of predation has impact on the ability of the Commission to gather evidence in the course of its investigation. Reasoning which the second judgment stated would be 'tantamount to saying, in other settings, that any ruling on excluding the admissibility of evidence in a criminal matter necessarily impacts on the powers of the South African Police Service to investigate crime'[137] – dismissing this proposition as it would serve to elevate every evidential matter into a constitutional one.

In the later decided 2021 *Mediclinic*[138] case, the Chief Justice's penned decision appears to speak back to the *Media24* second judgment reasoning, which distanced the Competition Act from considerations of equality; by setting out essential context regarding the imperative to transform the economy by addressing exclusion – as directed by the Constitution's own preamble and the very rationale for the Competition Act. In particular, Chief Justice Mogoeng provides:

> [3] It ought never to be acceptable for any of us, including the corporate citizens of this land, to indulge, talk less of over-indulge, in the unconscionable practice of seeking to record the highest profit margin possible by any means necessary, in wanton disregard for what that would do to the rest of humanity. Neither should the historic exclusion of some from meaningful participation, particularly in the mainstream economy, be normalised. For, this seems to be one of the most stubborn injustices of our past that require a more deliberate, intentional and systematic confrontation appropriately enabled by independent, incorruptible, efficient and effective law enforcement and justice-dispensing institutions.
>
> [4] Colonialism, neo-colonialism and apartheid orchestrated an institutionalised concentration of ownership and control of all things of consequence in our national economy along racial lines. Unsurprisingly, the commanding heights of the corporate sector are seemingly the exclusive terrain of our white compatriots. It is this indisputable reality and our shared commitment to ensuring that South Africa really does get to belong to all who live in it, that the constitutional imperatives, laid out in the Preamble, to improve the quality of life of all citizens and free the potential of each are realised, that the likes of the Competition Act had to and got to see the light of day.

---

137 *Media 24 Pty Ltd* n 74 at [132].

138 *Competition Commission of South Africa v Mediclinic Southern Africa (Pty) Ltd* (2021) CCT: (31/20) [2021] ZACC 35; 2022 (5) BCLR 532 (CC); 2022 (4) SA 323 (CC) (15 October 2021).

> [5] Sight must therefore never be lost of the central purpose for the enactment of [the Competition] Act and for the investigative and adjudicatory structures that it gave birth to. …
>
> …
>
> [7] Institutions created to breathe life into these critical provisions of the Act must therefore never allow what the [Competition] Act exists to undo and to do, to somehow elude them in their decision-making process. The equalisation and enhancement of opportunities to enter the mainstream economic space, to stay there and operate in an environment that permits the previously excluded as well as small and medium-sized enterprises to survive, succeed and compete freely or favourably must always be allowed to enjoy their pre-ordained and necessary pre-eminence. The legitimisation through legal sophistry or some right-sounding and yet effectively inhibitive jurisprudential innovations must be vigilantly guarded against and deliberately flushed out of our justice and economic system.

Mediclinic was a healthcare merger that still belied a lack of unanimity among the bench in respect of which competition appeals can be said to engage the ConCourt's jurisdiction. The eight-judge majority judgment founded jurisdiction on both bases where 'a matter is constitutional in character', and where 'the matter raises an arguable point of law of general public importance';[139] and the two-judge dissent would have dismissed the application on a failure to have made out a case on leave to appeal.

The majority went further than it had before by finding that a constitutional matter arose in this case given that the relevant market that impacts on a right protected by the Bill of Rights, in this instance the right to healthcare codified at section 27 of the Constitution.[140] As authority for doing so, the court emphasised that section 39(2) of the Constitution requires all courts, including those enforcing the Competition Act, to interpret legislation in a manner which promotes the spirit, purport and objects of the Bill of Rights, and noted that both the Tribunal and the CAC are 'institutions of the State', which places an obligation on them to aid in the realisation of the right of access to health services, or any other constitutionally protected rights. In particular, the Tribunal and CAC have an added responsibility to do so imposed on them by the preamble

139 ibid at [35].

140 The Constitution s 27: 'Health care, food, water and social security' reads:

'(1)(a) Everyone has the right to have access to health care services, including reproductive health care; …

(2) The state must take reasonable legislative and other measures, within its available resources, to achieve the progressive realisation of each of these rights.

(3) No one may be refused emergency medical treatment'.

to the Act and its purpose. The same obligation is also placed on the Commission, as an investigative authority tasked with giving effect to the Competition Act's provisions. The effect of this is that where constitutional rights are possibly infringed upon by the conduct of firms the effect of that conduct on broad consumer welfare is not the only concern. Taken together, we use this to argue that competition authorities act under constitutional mandate – 'the invocation of section 39(2) of the Constitution in interpreting legislation that implicates a right in the Bill of Rights, ought not to be viewed as an optional extra. It should rather be seen as a constitutional injunction'[141] – to take into account liability standards other than consumer welfare, namely the specific rights and welfare of individuals or groups as informed by the provisions of the Bill of Rights, must inform the substance of economic conclusions on liability. This is consistent with express public provisions in the Act where the liability standard is the welfare of the group (be it employees, SMEs or HDPs) and not consumers more broadly. If the welfare of that group is harmed by a merger or conduct, then liability is established in terms of the Act.

As a further basis to establish jurisdiction, the majority saw it as an arguable point of law for it to pronounce on when the CAC is entitled to interfere with the findings and remedies of the Tribunal. The ConCourt criticised the CAC for its complete revisiting of the factual evidence and economic reasoning in respect of market definition and the assessment of effects, (in line, we say, with its historic approach of adopting a broad review of Tribunal cases). The Commission argued that it was inappropriate for the CAC to effectively act as a court of first instance where its reasoning and interpretation of the facts could not be tested with factual or expert witnesses. The ConCourt concurred and its judgement set out the proper standard for overturning a decision on appeal, which should narrow the scope of appeal in future, stating in the case of *Mediclinic*:

> [83]...That the Competition Appeal Court saw the issues somewhat differently or holds the view that the Tribunal "erred", is not the test. The issue is whether the Tribunal, a specialist adjudicator which had embarked on a probabilistic investigation before it gave a predictive decision, misdirected itself or was clearly wrong in its key findings and did commit a material misdirection with regard to remedy. And the answer is NO!

The Theron J-penned dissent fundamentally differed with the majority on the issue of jurisdiction the logically consistent, and chosedly deferential, premise for this was to assert that it would be improper for the ConCourt to intervene in a finding of a lower court which the ConCourt itself was criticising for interfering with the court of first instance's assessment of the *facts*.

141 *Mediclinic Southern Africa (Pty) Ltd* n 138 at [9].

The *Mediclinic* majority dealt with the constitutional interpretation of the merger legislation, particularly, the interpretation of the SPLC test for mergers. It determined that the SPLC test needs to take account of the purpose of the Act; and, also sections 7 and 39(2) of the Constitution on the interpretative approach.[142] In general, the ConCourt took issue with a legal approach that effectively frustrated the realisation of the purpose of the Competition Act and the constitutional imperatives, by not dealing with dominance and competition problems, stating:

> [66] The Appeal Court's approach to the provision of private health care services in a sector so difficult to enter, to survive in and be accessed by the broader public seems to inadvertently but effectively undermine the section 27 constitutional imperative, the need to open up space and ease entry into this sector for new and previously excluded players. This approach effectively frustrates the need to tamper with regional, and by extension national, dominance and to enhance easy competition, which is the set objective of the Act.

More specifically, the ConCourt dealt with the interpretation of the SPLC liability standard where constitutionally protected rights are involved. It ruled that the infringement of constitutional rights is itself substantial even if the outcomes affect a small number of people or in a limited manner. In essence, this requires a constitutional interpretation of 'substantive' in the context of the SPLC test, whether in merger control or conduct case, which is lower than that typically considered in competition law. In this respect the ConCourt stated:

> [73] With that understanding, Mediclinic's predicted post-merger tariff hike, in this country of huge inequalities and in this distressed economy, would not have been understood and treated as insignificant or miniscule as the Appeal Court seems to have perceived it. To a wealthy South African, the percentage by which tariffs would go up after the merger is understandably negligible and inconsequential. But, not so to an average South African who is not even a member of any medical scheme, not that members of medical schemes necessarily find these high tariffs any easier to live with.

The implication of this *Mediclinic* judgment is substantial for enforcement going forward. First, it clarifies the need for a Constitutional interpretation to the Act, with a suitable adjustment in the liability standard where basic rights are implicated. Second, it seeks to impose a legal standard that enables the achievement of the Act's purposes, including addressing concentration and exclusion. Third, it restricts the appeal courts to a more limited and appropriate basis for overturning decisions of the Tribunal.

142 ibid at [53]–[55].

The frustration of achieving the purposes of the Act was part of a general observation made by the court in the judgement, taking aim effectively at a legal and liability standard institutionalised by the lower courts that inhibited, rather than promoted, economic inclusion. The previous *Media24* case had exposed the Constitutional Court to the full rule of reason approach adopted as the legal standard by the lower courts. The extent of evidence and complexity of the legal standard adopted led the Chief Justice to observe at the Commission's 2019 Annual Conference that competition law was artificially complex and impenetrable to the public. The *Mediclinic* judgement condemned what it termed 'inhibitive' legal standards that legitimised, in this case un-constitutional conduct, and inhibited its prosecution, stating in respect of the preamble and purpose provisions of the Act:[143] The Jafta and Khampepe-JJ penned majority in *Standard Bank*[144] provides jurisprudential underpinning for why a constitutional approach to legal standards must take into account the practical difficulties of enforcement:

> [128] It must further be underscored that the complaint and, by extension, the litigation procedure employed by the competition authorities, have been subjected to protracted legal challenges. Recognising this, the Competition Appeal Court in Senwes likened the acts of attempting to avoid and evade responsibility to the "Stalingrad" method of litigation. This was further echoed by the Supreme Court of Appeal in Woodlands Dairy, where it stated that "a veritable forest of interlocutory paper is generated in order to prevent cartel disputes from being determined on their merits". A legion of cases is not adjudicated on the merits due to these prolonged procedural challenges. The prolonged challenges are made possible due to the extensive resources often available to respondents in competition matters and the secretive, at times almost untraceable, nature of the prohibited practices that the Competition Act aims to regulate. These considerations challenge the notion that the Commission is an omnipotent state organ that enjoys unfettered powers and attacks defenceless and resource-constrained individuals. The courts have to be alive to the reality that the Commission is engrossed in complex legal and economic challenges against well-resourced, powerful entities.

As we hope to have explicated, these Constitutional debates regarding when competition enforcement disputes are significant enough to rise to the level constituting a constitutional matter or arguable point of law of general public importance is analogous to current global debates regarding the extent to which

143 ibid at [7].

144 *Competition Commission of South Africa v Standard Bank of South Africa Ltd; Competition Commission of South Africa v Standard Bank of South Africa Ltd; Competition Commission of South Africa v Waco Africa (Pty) Ltd* (2020) CCT: (158/18); CCT: (179/18); CT: (218/18) (handed down 20 February 2020).

competition rules should be infused with norms of public policy. The South African Constitution has bypassed the conceptual hurdles of *whether* competition rules should be suffused with public policy norms, and concerns itself, rather, with *how*. Debates about this have taken place under the banner of Constitutional jurisdiction and the South African case law provides examples of how interpretations of the Act's text pronouncing on *vires*; applicable economic tests and thresholds, protection of designated vulnerable groups, and the significance of the relevant applicable product market are areas of enforcement that can be infused with public policy concerns. The background to points of tension in the varying approaches does tend to hinge somewhat on questions of judicial activism or deference.

Two of the three judges on the CAC recently followed the ConCourt's injunction to evaluate anti-competitive conduct against the Act's purpose and the constitutional imperative for all law to be infused with the values of the Constitution. In the 2022 *eMedia/Multichoice* CAC decision,[145] eMedia's appeal was granted on the basis of reasoning which specifically contextualised the interim relief within the jurisprudential and transformative context of the Act.[146]

The CAC majority, per Victor J,[147] regarding the impetus to intervene, found that 'Despite the more recent approach to judicial deference the relevant Body must still apply the principles correctly to the facts. It did not do so in this case.'[148] This error was found to be inexcusable here because: 'Unless this transformative approach is applied even at an interim stage of proceedings, then the historical and insidious unequal distribution of wealth in South Africa will continue'.

The CAC found that the Tribunal erred in its failure to pay 'sufficient attention to the context and purpose of the Competition Act. Particularly when it is evident that there are high levels of economic concentration in this basic satellite platform which can easily result in economic exclusion. MultiChoice's market share in the markets defined in the founding affidavit (including in the premium and basic satellite markets) provide clear evidence of the excessive concentration of ownership which prevail in the broadcasting industry'.

The CAC found that while the Tribunal identified the correct competition principles, it erred in applying them to the facts in this case. It found that the Tribunal failed to take into account the purpose of the Act and that it failed to properly consider the extent of the prejudice and harm to eMedia. The CAC emphasised that 'competition jurisprudence requires an approach that looks

145 *Emedia Investments Pty Ltd* n 65.

146 ibid at [82]–[86].

147 Manoim J concurring.

148 *Emedia Investments Pty Ltd* n 65 at [97].

beyond the entitlement of a dominant firm to decide with whom they wish to do business and that the terms of their business dealings must be unfettered'.[149] In so doing, the CAC determined that the entrenched dominant position of MultiChoice, the satellite broadcast platform on which eMedia channels were contracted to, need not be preserved 'at the expense of [a] black-owned, medium-sized competitor'.[150]

The CAC applied its mind, and concluded that this was not a case requiring the kind of judicial deference to the Tribunal that Justice Mogoeng warned of in *Mediclinic* when interim relief by its nature requires adjudicators to summarily assess the facts for 'clear, non-speculative and uncontroversial facts have been presented by an applicant from which it could be reasonably and logically inferred, on a balance of probabilities, that the alleged irreparable harm would occur'.[151]

The context of an application for interim relief is that there is necessarily a presumptive approach, relief may be granted on the basis of a prima facie case. The CAC *eMedia* decision also recognises the importance of interim relief in rapidly changing markets. This resonates with the global debate about whether interim relief should more readily be granted in a digital market context because of the dynamic nature of the markets and the potential for long delays from appeals. The CAC decision incorporates this legal standard into the granting of interim relief, stating:

> [79] Central to our commercial era are companies trading in fast moving, dynamic and global markets. Competition law must be sufficiently agile to meet the needs of our fast paced economy when considering interim orders. If a too rigid approach is adopted by the competition authorities, the very interim relief may soon lose its relevance. Currently this is about a basic satellite platform, but with the rapid development of digital technology this may soon become dated hence the need to appreciate and understand the commercial exigencies and urgency when interim relief is sought. Delaying decisions until the main relief is decided may result in irreparable harm. For example, the relief in the main case may be appealed and this can take several years to reach the Constitutional Court. Meantime if there is irreparable harm it will continue unabated.

Considerations of constitution and context was followed by the thrust of the 2019 amendments to the Competition Act which introduced various definitions that ensured 'closer consistency with the transformative goals' of the Act.

149 ibid at [96].

150 ibid at [102].

151 ibid at [80].

Specifically, CAC considered the amendments' impact on understandings of 'exclusionary acts' – now defined in section 1(c) as an act that impedes or prevents a firm from entering into, participating in or expanding within a market. A further amendment in section 1(h) of the Act defined 'participate' as referring to the ability of or opportunity for firms to sustain themselves in the market. It is against these definitions that it argues for granting interim relief 'to preserve an existing situation and to temporarily safeguard a situation where interests are at risk'.[152]

Reading the implication of how an expanded definition of exclusionary conduct in line with constitutional injunctions for redress, a complainant need not provide evidence of irreparable harm but rather provide enough evidence to show that it has suffered sufficient harm to demonstrate an inability to sustain itself – the lower liability standard.

The CAC jurisprudence contained in *eMedia* means that as long as the complainant is able to provide clear and non-speculative evidence of possible anticompetitive effects, the consideration of this evidence should be in the context of the state of competition at least at a prima facie level.[153] This would include the level of concentration and dominance in the market of the firm whose conduct is the subject of the complaint, which impacts on any presumption that it will result in negative effects. This is observed in the CAC's consideration of the interim relief where it highlights that a dominant firm is acting in a manner that can cause irreparable harm to a smaller firm – which conduct that the Act seeks to guard against. Further without a proper explanation for the dominant firm's conduct, there should be a shift in probabilities in favour of the applicant.

VII. Conclusion

The historic push towards higher thresholds for legal liability, by requiring full rule of reason analysis, and a high evidentiary burden on the competition authorities to make out a complete case is the product of a debate that played out fifty years ago in the US. A US-led economic literature, the Chicago School, was sceptical that many of the anti-competitive concerns around restrictive conduct were justified as many may have pro-competitive benefits. This also spurred a legal practitioners view that Type I errors were more damaging than Type II errors, because in the US the market is more likely to correct a market distortion rather than a distortion created by the courts. This is in the context of a vast and innovative open US economy involving countless competitors and overall low concentration. However, in the era of digital markets, even the

152 ibid at [90].

153 ibid at [94].

vast US (and global) economy has come to be dominated by a few firms across various ecosystems. The shift in economic power has forced even the US to question the legal standards of the day, and whether they remain relevant to how it enforces antitrust. Legal and economic scholars are now questioning whether the market is even capable of correcting a digital market distortion, and hence questioning the prior preference for Type II errors over Type I errors.

The South African economy, and that of most developing economies, are a very far cry from the dynamic US economy. Much of South Africa's economy is highly concentrated across markets. In 2021 the Commission released a Concentration Tracker report entitled '*Measureming Concentration and Participation in the South African Economy: Levels and Trends*'[154] which used information from over 80 industry associations, regulators and government departments to depict the levels and trends in concentration of 178 'competition' markets across all sectors of the economy. Of the 144 sectors with sufficient data, the study found that 40.3% of these were highly concentrated with a presumptively dominant firm, and a further 29.2% were highly concentrated but without single firm dominance.[155] The US 'high tech dominance problem' is therefore a more common South African 'economic problem'. If the current legal standards are a concern for the US and Europe in digital markets, then they are equally a more widespread market concern for South Africa, and most likely many other developing countries.

This chapter has shown that these legal and liability standards borrowed from the more mature jurisdictions have not necessarily served competition law well in a developing country, particularly in relation to abuse of dominance. The high evidentiary burden to merely bring a case before requiring an answer, information asymmetries and jurisdictional disputes all served to considerably delay and often deny justice. A problem that mature jurisdictions are now facing with global big tech firms. South Africa recently amended its Act to change some of its legal standards for certain abuse of dominance provisions, alongside a change in liability standards where these involved SMEs and HDP firms. The experience of South Africa provides a useful natural experiment in the importance of legal standards by comparing the differences in enforcement pre and post the alteration of legal and liability standards.

The tentative lesson from South Africa in the immediate period following the amendments is that changes to legal standards can make a material difference to the speed of prosecution without necessarily compromising on the quality of the legal decisions. This is consistent with theory which suggests that more

154 Competition Commission, *Measuring Concentration and Participation in the South African Economy: Levels and Trends* (2021) <https://www.compcom.co.za/wp-content/uploads/2021/12/Concentration-Tracker-Main-Report-1.pdf> accessed 2 April 2023.

155 ibid figure 1, 7. The definition of highly concentrated is based on the US DOJ classification mapped onto concentration ratios.

presumption-based legal standards are not necessarily inferior from the point of view of a cost of error-minimization.[156] The important change in legal standard is a move towards the authority being able to create a rebuttable case at some early point which then requires a shift in onus to the respondents to justify their conduct and why it is not a contravention of the Act. In South Africa a prima facie case standard has been legislated for certain conduct only which means that the authority still needs to meet the various components required to create a rebuttable case before the shift in onus. Regulations on specific provisions setting out with more specificity the factors that may determine if a component is met have greatly assisted in clarifying when a prima facie case may be made. When the onus shifts and on what question are important parts of the design as it needs to be either where the information lies with the respondent, or alternatively where their conduct needs to be justified.

An important feature of the South African Competition Act is the separation of investigation and adjudication which may be necessary for robustness in the assessment of whether a prima facie case has been established, and whether the rebuttable assumption has been met by the respondent or not. Jurisdictions which lack this separation may face more difficulties in implementing such a legal standard.

A further tentative lesson from South Africa is that changes to liability standards may need to complement changes in legal standards in certain contexts. Whilst the South African changes for liability standards for SMEs and HDPs has been linked to public interest, these objectives are also rooted in a strong dynamic competition rationale. The objective is to prevent exclusion of SMEs and HDPs from participation in the economy where a dynamic ecosystem of SMEs and new entrants promotes competition in any market. Whilst their inclusion promotes long-term competition, their exclusion in the short term is difficult to prohibit on an SPLC test as their competitive significance may not be substantial at that point. This highlights the accepted problem with competition law, namely that it is more static in its assessment because the courts are poor at forecasting with any certainty the long-term dynamic effects. Unsurprisingly, this is precisely the problem identified with digital markets and therefore those too may warrant a change in liability standard for the same reason.

A final tentative lesson from South Africa is that the debate on legal and liability standards needs to be broadened to examine alternative enforcement toolkits. South Africa, along with a small number of other jurisdictions, has at its disposal a market inquiry provision in addition to the standard enforcement

156 Y Katsoulacos and D Ulph, 'Choosing Legal Rules or Standards in Antitrust Enforcement in Different Markets and Countries: a Proposal for Extending the Decision-Theoretic Approach' (2022) MDE 1–19 <https://onlinelibrary.wiley.com/doi/full/10.1002/mde.3787> accessed 2 April 2023.

of abuse of dominance. The market inquiry is unlike other elements of a competition law insofar as it aims to improve competition by addressing any features that have an AEC, and not just single-firm conduct by dominant firms. This widens the ambit of issues and actions that an authority may take to improve competition in a market, much like sector regulators trying to move markets from historic monopoly to competitive outcomes. In digital markets which have already tipped to a monopoly, market inquiries may be precisely what is needed to address the complex ecosystems that maintain that monopoly position.

There are lessons for South Africa too. The amendments to the legal standards are currently limited to excessive pricing and abuse of dominance against SMEs and HDPs. The Act already includes other named conduct under section 8(1)(d), such as predation or inducement, which remain under an unchanged legal standard. Whilst that may be appropriate for section 8(1)(c) capturing general exclusionary conduct, there is scope to introduce a more presumptive standard where precise conduct is identified. Arguably, the structure of section 8(1)(d) already involves a more presumptive standard where the onus shifts to the dominant firm after the conduct is established by the Commission and it is the courts that have inappropriately imposed the higher evidentiary burden on the Commission to establish the entirety of its case prior to this shift in onus. Whilst the court's reasoning was to permit the weighing up process that section 8(1)(d) envisages, providing for an initial shift in onus does not prevent such a weighing up.

An initial shift in onus can quickly establish whether there is any justification at all for the conduct, and if not, then a contravention is established. Similarly, if the justification generates trivial benefits that would clearly be outweighed by any effects, or could be achieved in a less restrictive manner, then a contravention may be established. It is only where the justifications are material and substantiated that a more quantitative weighing up may be required and then the onus may shift back to the Commission to establish the quantum of harm. Allowing for an initial shift in onus to the dominant firm would also curtail strategies such as limiting discovery of evidence or 'signal jamming' that lead to a much larger number of Type II errors and unnecessarily delay prosecution. The condemnation of the Constitutional Court of 'inhibitive jurisprudential innovations' that prevent achieving the purposes of the Act, including addressing dominance and exclusion, and the need to 'flush them out' may prompt this to be revisited by the courts. Absent that, further amendments are probably desirable. The lesson from doing so in other provisions is that this may greatly strengthen enforcement of abuse of dominance in South Africa, addressing the Type II error problem, without compromising of the quality of legal decisions and raising Type I errors.

The ConCourt has stressed the need for a constitutional interpretation of competition law, which has implications for the legal and liability standards where a constitutional right is possibly infringed upon by the conduct of firms. In such instances, the infringement of those rights is itself substantial even if it implicates only a few consumers or businesses, rather than a broader consumer welfare standard. In the South African context, this applies equally to exclusion from the economy of SMEs and HDPs. If that exclusion is a consequence of conduct or a merger, then the right to equity is infringed and that is itself must be considered alongside any consumer welfare standard. This is consistent with the application of express public provisions in the Act where the liability standard is the welfare of the group (be it employees, SMEs or HDPs) over and above consumers more broadly. If the welfare of that group is harmed by a merger or conduct, then liability is established in terms of the Act. The constitutional jurisprudence extends such a liability standard to all parts of the Act where rights or exclusion is implicated. This too is likely to promote a more competitive and inclusive economy.

Legal Standards in Competition Law Enforcement Against Digital Platforms in Russia

SVETLANA GOLOVANOVA*

SVETLANA AVDASHEVA**

National Research University Higher School of Economics (HSE University), Russia

Abstract

Large-scale Russian competition enforcement targets digital platforms among other large companies. Enforcement relies on general competition rules, but not on specific provisions on digital platforms. Specific amendments to the law "On protection of competition" were proposed as far back as 2017 but have not yet been adopted. Most decisions on the abuse of dominance by digital platforms are made using presumption-based legal standards. Since 2017–2018 the Russian competition authority, the Federal Antimonopoly Service (FAS Russia), uses the concept of digital companies as multi-sided platforms. For defining markets, FAS recognizes different groups of users that interact through the platform, but rarely develops a theory of harm to competition and consumers in specific case investigations based on network effects.

---

* Svetlana Golovanova is a professor of economics at the Department of Economic Theory and Econometrics, Nizhny Novgorod Campus HSE University, Russia. Extensive experience in economic expertise in antimonopoly investigations in Russia. svgolovanova@hse.ru.

** Svetlana Avdasheva is a professor of economics at the Department of Applied Economics, HSE University, Russia. Comparative competition enforcement is the main field of interest. avdash@hse.ru. The authors express deep gratitude to Yannis Katsoulacos for his fruitful comments and suggestions. Support from the Basic Research Program of the National Research University Higher School of Economics is gratefully acknowledged.

I. Introduction: Legal Standards in the Russian Competition Enforcement

In Russia, the first competition legislation entered into force in 1991.[1] A more recent law, on protection of competition, was adopted in 2006.[2] The recent version of the law widely adopted European competition rules. There are however important differences with EU competition legislation. First, the liability standard is non-welfarist. Second, distinguishing abuses of dominance between exclusionary and exploitative types (in other words, indirectly harming consumers by limiting competition and directly harming consumers or counterparty through excessive prices), law applies different system of sanctions and different legal standards. Specifically, if for the exclusionary abuses of dominance, a competition restriction effect should be proven, there is no need to do so if the abuse is exploitative. Being introduced in 2011,[3] over time this distinction affects competition enforcement more substantial.

Distinction between exclusionary and exploitative abuses, interact with the approach of Russian commercial courts which deal with the claims to annul the decisions of the Russian competition authority FAS. In the abuse of dominance cases, an important reason to claim for annulment is that competition authority did not prove competition restrictions effects. Over time, the Russian Supreme Court tends to push judges to be more sympathetic to the companies, to use contextual market analysis in competition cases, therefore, to apply higher legal standards in the cases of restrictions of competition. At the same time, decisions made with higher legal standards (therefore by developing and analyzing specific theory of harm, and especially on assessing the effects of the conduct) have higher chances of being overturned under judicial review. Russian commercial courts themselves rarely insist on higher legal standards (for instance, courts almost never ask to prove the effect of anticompetitive practice on consumer welfare) but when analyzing the conduct considered under higher legal standard (with specific theory of harm) impose burden of proof on competition authority completely.

As a result, when applying higher legal standards, the Russian competition authority increases the probability of annulment[4] for the decision. Together with other important factors, including motivation[5] and institutional structure

1 Law of the RSFSR of March 22, 1991 No. 948-I "On Competition and restriction of monopolistic activity in commodity markets".

2 Federal Law of July 26, 2006 No. 135-FZ "On Protection of Competition"

3 Federal Law of December 06, 2011 No. 401-FZ "On Amendments to the Federal Law 'On Protection of Competition"

4 Y. Katsoulacos et al., *Determinants of the (Slow) Development of Effect-Based Competition Enforcement: Testing the Impact of Judicial Review on the Choice of Legal Standards by Competition Authorities*, 21 J. Ind. Comp.& Trade 103–122 (2021).

5 S. Avdasheva et al., *The Impact of Performance Measurement on the Selection of Enforcement Targets by Competition Authorities: The Russian Experience in an International Context*, 42 Pub. Perf. & Man. Rev. 329–356 (2019).

of the competition authority[6]) this leads to two effects when analyzing a particular case. First, to apply the analysis anticipated by court, and do it better,[7] and second, to apply a presumption-based approach whenever it is possible, in order to avoid annulment. This has led to a tendency of increasing share of investigations opened on conducts which are illegal per se, or illegal because they are exploitative, relative to the share of exclusionary conducts.

In the network industries, for the operators of essential facilities (natural monopoly, according to Russian law), competition authorities use the presumption that direct harm imposed on counterparties limits competition in the adjacent market(s). In this group of cases, disadvantaging specific groups of customers, only this direct harm should be proven in order to make an infringement decision. We will show that the competition authority uses this approach in considering conducts of digital platforms also.

FAS Russia often imposes remedies requiring changes in the offending firm's conduct. In addition, FAS Russia actively uses precautions and warnings, which are specific procedures aimed at decreasing cost of investigation and reaching the decision. In cases of suspicious conduct FAS asks the company to stop the actions (behavior) in question. In case of compliance no further investigations or actions are undertaken. Since warnings and precautions do not include full-fledged investigations, their use also contributes to a presumption-based approach in competition enforcement.

Finally, FAS's enforcement actions are complemented by specific guidelines for competition enforcement in specific markets, elaborated in cooperation with and approved by the largest business associations. Guidelines or "principles of fair competition" in pharmaceuticals, auto-distribution, and retailing, specify the prohibitions of competition legislation as well as efficiency defense in the context of particular markets. Guidelines, as soft laws, normally clarify or make more precise presumptions on the (il)legality of particular actions of companies in markets.

In this chapter we analyze legislation related to digital platforms including but not limited to antitrust, and provide evidence on recent decisions on digital platforms in order to show how enforcement differs in these case from enforcement in regular cases, and which legal standards the Russian competition authority applies when deciding on presumably illegal conducts, and which evidence is used to support the decisions.

---

6 S. Avdasheva et al., *Optimal Institutional Structure of Competition Authorities under Reputation Maximization: a Model and Empirical Evidence from the Case of Russia*, 54 Rev. Ind. Organ. 251–282 (2019).

7 S. Avdasheva et al., *The Role of Judicial Review in Developing Evidentiary Standards: The Example of Market Analysis in Russian Competition Law Enforcement*, 58 Int. Rev. Law Econ. 101–114 (2019).

II. Competition Issues in the Legislation on Digital Platforms

There are no specific norms devoted to digital platforms and their anticompetitive conducts in the current version of Russian competition law. The recognition of the importance of competition issues regarding digital platforms resulted in certain legislative initiatives in 2017–2018. One of the triggering events for active discussions of specifics of multi-sided platform business models and related challenges to antitrust enforcement approaches was the VI BRICS International Competition Conference (Moscow, 2019),[8] devoted to the challenges BRICS competition authorities face due to the digitalization of the world economy. During that time a large number of publications devoted to platforms appeared on the FAS web site[9].

FAS announced the development of the amendments to the law "on protection of competition" devoted to digital markets, known as the Fifth Antimonopoly Package, in December 2017. In contrast to previous changes and amendments of competition law in Russia, the process of passing the bill[10] was very complicated. Influential groups of stakeholders, including IT business associations, and public authorities responsible for economic development and digitalization, strongly opposed the initial draft of the amendments which included the notion of network effect, pricing algorithms, abuse of dominance using big data, as well as the right of competition authority to impose remedies on non-discriminatory access to the data collected by digital platforms. Currently (January 2023) the draft has only passed the first-hearing stage.

In the current draft, amendments are limited. They include the definition of "network effect" and "digital platform." Definition of digital platform as intermediary in the transaction or matchmaking instrument narrows the scope of the new rules. For instance, the definition does not cover non-transaction platforms, based on search content. Amendments give to the competition authority the right to recognize a platform as dominant, in cases where the network effect is strong enough to provide unilateral impact on the market, and the share of the platform in the overall number of market transactions exceeds thirty-five percent. There are no specific provisions of abuse of dominance by digital platforms: they are subjects to the same requirements as for all other companies.

Along with introducing amendments to the law "on protection of competition", in February 2022 FAS Russia concluded an agreement with the largest Russian

---

8 *See* https://unctad.org/meeting/vi-brics-international-competition-conference.

9 *See, for example*, FAS news (06.09.2017): https://fas.gov.ru/news/23196 (in Russian); FAS news (23.10.2018): https://fas.gov.ru/news/26186.

10 Draft Law No. 160280-8 "On Amendments to the Federal Law 'On Protection of Competition"

IT companies (including Yandex, largest classifieds, marketplaces, as well as developers) and their business association on "principles of interaction in digital markets".[11] These principles remind one of the general statements of the European Digital Market Act,[12] including "reasonable openness" of platforms in terms of access to data and rules of ranking, avoidance of self-preferencing, allowing business users to conclude contracts independently, i.e., outside the platforms, clarity of rules and regulations, protection of users' rights, by timely and fair considerations of their requests.

Recently, digital platforms in Russia have also become subject to several legal requirements, aimed to protect domestic competitors vis-à-vis foreign companies or to control over the content available on the platform.

Among the first group, there is a requirement to pre-install Russian or Eurasian Union applications on every device (computer, tablet, smartphone, smart TV etc.) sold in Russia since 2021. The list of apps includes, among others: browsers, search, navigators, social networks, apps for online payments, and apps for public service provision and information. Before first use, consumers can choose the types of applications to be installed on the device automatically.

The second group of requirements cover the obligations of digital platforms to keep information on users and provide it to the Russian security agencies by request. During last few decades there have been several disputes with almost every large platform, including Google (YouTube), Telegram, and domestic Yandex, on the limits of privacy of platform users. Since 2022, enforcement on the issue has become harder. The right to control the content disseminated by digital platforms for security reasons is combined with the specific requirements of corporate nationality of platforms. For instance, recently in 2023, relatively large classifieds are obliged to operate under the ultimate control of Russian owners (based on controlling stake of shares). Being inspired by reasons which are far from pure economic arguments, these requirements inevitably affect the competitive landscape in the Russian markets.

Competition effects of the regime's use of personal data are still outside the scope of the legislation. The Russian equivalent of the European General Data Protection Regulation,[13] (law "on protection of personal data") was adopted in 2006 as a requirement covering the collection of personal data in relation to the provision of personal information on passport, ID etc. in response to public or corporate requests. Currently Russian competition law does not cover the use of personal data as an input in digital platform business.

11 *See* https://fas.gov.ru/p/protocols/1666.

12 *See* European Digital Market Act 2022.

13 *See* General Data Protection Regulation (DGPR) 2018.

To conclude, Russian competition rules on digital platforms have lagged behind in global perspectives. After a de-facto veto on radical amendments, elaborated in 2017, and later changes in 2022 the legislation does not distinguish competition issues concerning digital platforms from traditional markets. Rules similar to the EU Digital Market Act were introduced in the framework of soft law, an agreement on fair conducts between the competition authority and IT companies. None of the legal rules support more presumption-based, more effects-based enforcement, or specific analysis of the markets where digital platforms are present.

III. Overview of Cases Related to Digital Platforms in Russia, 2015–2022

Regardless of the absence of specific provisions on digital platforms in competition legislation, the competition authority may examine cases on their conducts differently, in comparison with the conducts of a traditional company. In the following section, we review the decisions that the Russian competition authority has made on digital platforms since 2015. The objective is to explain if FAS applies a different approach in these cases. We mean "different" mainly in relation to three aspects. First, does FAS recognize the multi-sided nature of platforms and the impact of network effects on the ability of platforms to influence users and markets. Second, does FAS analyze all sides of platforms, or all types of users, when considering their conduct? Third, how far does FAS go in the analysis of suspected illegal conducts: does FAS develop a particular theory of harm and test it, assess the impact of conduct on consumer welfare, or consider efficiency defense?

Below we consider the evolution of the approach to antitrust investigation of digital platform business practices in Russia. To do this we examine to what extent the screens that should be examined for identifying whether or not there is harm are assessed, using a methodology similar to that proposed by Katsoulacos et al. (2019),[14] for conducts other than exploitative, identifying case-specific analysis of the market(s) affected, potential for exclusion, theory of harm to (final) consumers, efficiency defense, together with the attempt to weigh the anticompetitive and pro-efficiency effects. However, we are able to do that only if the case is investigated as exclusionary abuse, i.e., conduct for which illegality arises because it limits competition. As we have mentioned, the Russian competition authority often decides on exploitative conducts. For this group of cases the aforementioned approach must be modified in order to be applicable.

---

14 Y. Katsoulacos et al., A Methodology for Empirically Measuring the Extent of Economic Analysis and Evidence and for Identifying the Legal Standards in Competition Law Enforcement, in Festschrift in Honour of Frédéric Jenny, Standing Up for Convergence and Relevance in Antitrust 131–150 (Nicolas Charbit and Sonia Ahmad eds., Concurrences 2019).

When analyzing market(s) affected, the most important issue is whether FAS Russia recognizes network effects, direct versus indirect (or same-side versus cross-side).[15] If network effects are not recognized, proper theory of harm is hardly possible to prove in a case. Table 1 contains a brief description of cases.

1. Visa and Mastercard (2011–2016)

The first reference to FAS's antitrust concerns relating to the business practices of international payment systems – Visa and MasterCard (which apply a platform business model) – dates to May–June of 2011. This occurred shortly after the European Commission issued its decision in a similar case against Visa. FAS's main antitrust concern was on the "excessive" interchange fees of international payment systems. Market definition was not given in the publication. FAS planned to test both abuse of dominance and anticompetitive agreement hypotheses. The potential total penalty size mentioned was $8.4–16.8 billion in RUR (approx. USD 0.3–0.6 billion). However, the concerns did not result in antitrust investigation. Instead, the Russian payment system MIR was introduced in order to induce better terms for users through competitive pressure.

The next case is dated September 2014 after Visa and MasterCard suspended services to several Russian banks due to authorization of international sanctions against them. FAS noted that it considered the practice of abuse of dominance in the form of refusal to sale and the only reason it hadn't opened a case against the companies was the "unwillingness to make things worse." Neither the particular market nor its multi-sidedness was mentioned at that time.

In 2015 the National Payment Card System (NPCS), controlled by the Central Bank of the Russian Federation was created. In April 2015 FAS made a statement about its readiness to take all necessary actions against NPCS in case it was involved in anticompetitive behavior. The concern expressed was that the company might achieve dominant position "on the corresponding market" and abuse it in the form of unfair (excessive) tariffs for its services. The market is not defined and was not named by FAS in the announcement.

In November 2016, again, a FAS announcement generated expectations of initiation of an antitrust case against Visa and MasterCard.[16] The alleged violation of Russian competition law by the companies was collusion between the payment systems and large Russian retailers that resulted in price

15 *See* Frédéric Jenny, *Competition law enforcement and regulation for digital ecosystems: Understanding the issues, facing the challenges and moving forward*, Concurrences No. 3-2021, art. No. 101662, pp. 38–62.

16 *See* https://fas.gov.ru/publications/444 (in Russian).

discrimination. Namely, acquiring fees (the fees merchants pay for card-acquiring services) were found to be 1% lower for large retailers compared to small businesses (1.5% versus 2.5%). It is worth mentioning that the announcement mentions the Visa reply that the size of the fee was aimed to balance the interests of different users of payment system services. There is no sign, however that FAS paid attention to this, when mentioning the platform nature of the business model. As of February 2023, no antitrust investigation against any payment system has been initiated by FAS.

2. Google (2015)

Market analysis. During the proceedings the company was found to have a dominant position (more than 58%) on the "market of pre-installed application stores localized for redistribution in Russia." According to FAS assessments Google's share in the number of pre-installed application stores was about 58% at that time. In fact, there were no mobile devices in Russia without pre-installed Google Play. FAS detected that binding Google Play with other Google Mobile Services (GMS) applications and restrictions for mobile phone producers regarding pre-installation of apps that competed with GMS apps on Android OS created obstacles for Google competitors to access the market. Thus, Google practice was aimed at limiting the ability for competing application stores to gain traction and therefore disadvantaging rivals. The company was found guilty of violating competition law.

The FAS decision and official public announcements did not mention the company's multi-sided business model as one could have expected taking into account a parallel investigation in European Union Case AT.39740 (*Google Search (Shopping)*).[17] In contrast to the European competition authority the Russian FAS did not link the company's single-homing strategy in the "market of pre-installed application stores for redistribution in Russia" to the profit derived by the company from advertising. As discussed below, interrelation with other markets was considered, while no mention was made regarding the monetization of Google Play.

Competition restriction effects. Theory of harm for the abuse of dominance was as follows. There is a package of applications (Google Mobile Services, GMS)[18] that includes among others Google Play app store – to be pre-installed. At the same time, Revenue Sharing Agreements (RSAs) between Google and Android device manufacturers makes refusal to pre-install competing apps a condition for receiving payments for Google. Therefore, bundling GMS with

17 Commission Decision of 27 June 2017, Case AT.39740 (*Google Search (Shopping)*), *see* Avantika Chowdhury, *The EU Commission fines a Big Tech company €2.42 billion for abusing its dominant position as a search engine by giving an illegal advantage to its comparison shopping service (Google Shopping)*, E-COMPETITIONS June 2017, art. No. 100820.

18 https://www.android.com/gms/?authuser=0&hl=ru_RU.

Android with additional premiums for non-installment of competing application (for instance, Yandex Search and Yandex Market apps) restricts competition.

The application of the concept of leveraging of market power can be seen when a dominant company uses its market power in some markets to restrict competition in a related market. Thus, FAS uses traditional rules for regular markets and "linear company" instruments of economic analysis.

Google submitted a claim to annul the infringement decision. After the negative decision of first instance in 2016, the Commercial Court, during the hearing in appellate instance, decided to request commitments with specific remedies. The remedies included refuse of the RSA conditional on strong anti-fragmentation requirements for the mobile devices which use Android OS to be sold in Russia, and also unbundling of the use of any apps from Google Play in automatic way. Technically, before first use consumer had to choose search application and app store to be used.[19]

3. Television Broadcasting (2016)

In 2016 FAS conducted a competition investigation on the "television broadcasting market" in Russia as a part of its regular monitoring work.

Market analysis. In the report[20] the product is defined as "terrestrial television, cable TV, satellite TV, and IPTV services." FAS compares prices of the services set by different television broadcasting companies (equipment cost and subscription fee). Calculation of market shares is made on the basis of the number of subscribers. Thus, a one-sided approach is applied by FAS, and no cross-side (indirect) network effects (particularly, the impact of subscription base on the demand for advertising) are mentioned. Despite the conclusion on the ability of some companies to influence market conditions in particular regions of Russia, as of February 2023 no further investigation against any broadcasting company has been officially initiated by FAS.

19 Yandex. Store as an alternative app store application, was closed by Yandex in 2020.

20 *See* https://fas.gov.ru/documents/562760 (in Russian).

Table 1. Overview of FAS enforcement actions related to platforms

Year	Target	Type of investigation	Market definition	Multi-sidedness* / network effects	Competition concerns	Decision	Theory of harm (to competition, to consumers)	Sources
2011–2019	Visa, Mastercard	Abuse of dominance	2011–2016: Market is not defined	1SA/no	Excessive pricing (transaction fees), price discrimination	No statement of objection	No: considered as exploitative abuses	FAS news[21]
2015	Google	Abuse of dominance	Market of pre-installed application stores	1SA/no	Exclusionary clauses	Infringement decision, then commitment decision with remedy	Theory of harm to competition in adjacent market(s)	Case No. 1-14-21/00-11-15[22]
2016	TV broadcasters	Abuse of dominance	Television broadcasting market	1SA/no	Excessive pricing	No statement of objection	No, considered as exploitative abuse	FAS market analysis report[23]
2017	Uber-Yandex	Merger (Joint Venture) clearance	Market for organization of information interaction between taxi drivers and passengers	2SM/no	Horizontal competition concerns	Conditional approval with behavioral remedies	Not applicable: not competition case	FAS news;[24] FAS market analysis report[25]

21 FAS news (13.05.2011): https://fas.gov.ru/publications/11374 (in Russian); FAS news (14.09.2014): https://fas.gov.ru/publications/4306 (in Russian); FAS news (03.04.2015): https://fas.gov.ru/publications/3236 (in Russian); FAS news (25.11.2016): https://fas.gov.ru/publications/444 (in Russian).

22 See https://br.fas.gov.ru/ca/upravlenie-regulirovaniya-svyazi-i-informatsionnyh-tehnologiy/ad-54066-15/ (in Russian), see Russian Competition Authority, *The Russian Competition Authority finds that a smartphone operating system developer abused its dominance on the market of pre-installed app stores (Google)*, e-Competitions September 2015, art. No. 75773.

23 *See* https://fas.gov.ru/documents/562760 (in Russian).

24 FAS news (24.11.2017): http://en.fas.gov.ru/press-center/news/detail.html?id=52562, *see* Russian Competition Authority, *The Russian Competition Authority clears the creation of a joint undertaking subject to remedies in the taxi market (Yandex / Uber)*, e-Competitions November 2017, art. No. 85567.

25 *See* https://fas.gov.ru/documents/678673.

Year	Target	Type of investigation	Market definition	Multi-sidedness* / network effects	Competition concerns	Decision	Theory of harm (to competition, to consumers)	Sources
2017	Microsoft	Abuse of dominance	Multilateral market of operating systems for stationary devices	2SM/no	Discriminatory treatment of apps developers by untimely access to new Windows versions	Warning with remedies, fulfilled	Not applicable: no full-fledged investigation	Case No. 1-00-168/00-11-16[26]
2019	Headhunter	Abuse of dominance	Market of services enabling informational cooperation between applicants, employers and personnel agencies in internet information and communications network	2SM/yes	Disadvantaging rival's app	Infringement decision with remedy	Yes, harm to competition	Case No. 11/01/10-9/2019[27]
2020	Booking.com	Abuse of dominance	Market for the provision of services by aggregators of information about accommodation facilities	2SM/no	Imposition of unfavorable conditions (price-parity clause)	Infringement decision, remedy, judicial review	Yes, harm to competition (equivalent to German case)	Case No. 11/01/10-41/2019[28]
2020	Apple	Abuse of dominance	Market for distribution of applications for mobile devices with iOS	2SM/yes	Disadvantaging rival's app by reducing functionality	Infringement decision with remedy		Case No. 11/01/10-24/2019[29]

26 *See* https://br.fas.gov.ru/ca/upravlenie-regulirovaniya-svyazi-i-informatsionnyh-tehnologiy/8e4961ce-3f9c-4b37-9f4b-b2804deeec88/.

27 *See* https://br.fas.gov.ru/ca/upravlenie-regulirovaniya-svyazi-i-informatsionnyh-tehnologiy/8e4961ce-3f9c-4b37-9f4b-b2804deeec88/.

28 *See* https://br.fas.gov.ru/ca/upravlenie-regulirovaniya-svyazi-i-informatsionnyh-tehnologiy/cdf15018-ef29-40e8-acbd-d39edc8aee39/?query=Booking.com, *see* Russian Competition Authority, *The Russian Competition Authority issues second warning to an online booking platform on termination of price parity clauses and restrictive conditions on hotels (Booking.com)*, e-Competitions September 2020, art. N° 97071.

29 *See* https://br.fas.gov.ru/ca/upravlenie-regulirovaniya-svyazi-i-informatsionnyh-tehnologiy/b70e9d96-8d39-46f5-9d7d-342da95b354b/, see Russian Competition Authority, *The Russian Competition Authority requires a Big Tech company to provide competitive conditions for mobile applications developers and to ensure that in-house apps do not take precedence over third-party apps (Apple)*, e-Competitions August 2020, art. N° 97065

Year	Target	Type of investigation	Market definition	Multi-sidedness* / network effects	Competition concerns	Decision	Theory of harm (to competition, to consumers)	Sources
2021	Google (You Tube)	Abuse of dominance	Market for collecting, storing, processing, providing, distributing, transmitting, viewing video content in the internet information and telecommunications network (video hosting services market)	1SA/no	Voluntary blocking of users' accounts	Infringement decision with remedy	No	Case No. 11/01/10-12/2021[30]
2022	Apple	Abuse of dominance	Market for distribution of applications for iOS operating system	2SM/yes	Exclusionary clauses	Warning with remedies, not fulfilled (2021) Infringement decision (2022), penalties, under judicial review	Yes, harm to competition	Warning No. МШ/72835/21[31] Case No. 11/01/10-30/2021[32]
2022	Yandex (RUS)	Abuse of dominance	Market of general search in the internet	IRM/no	Discrimination as preferential treatment of own services (using widgets)	Remedy (not fulfilled), statement of objection	Not applicable, no full-fledged investigation	Case No. 11/01/10-11/2021[33]

30 *See* https://br.fas.gov.ru/ca/upravlenie-regulirovaniya-svyazi-i-informatsionnyh-tehnologiy/030a28e3-c8d9-4129-b4ba-26c5013d9457/?query=google, see Russian Competition Authority, *The Russian Competition Authority initiates proceedings against a Big Tech company for abuse of a dominant position in the market for video hosting services (Google / Youtube)*, e-Competitions April 2021, art. N° 100385.

31 Russian Competition Authority, *The Russian Competition Authority issues a warning to a Big Tech company after receiving complaints that the company prohibits informing clients about the alternative payment methods in the App Store applications (Apple)*, e-Competitions August 2021, art. N° 103885.

32 *See* https://br.fas.gov.ru/ca/upravlenie-regulirovaniya-svyazi-i-informatsionnyh-tehnologiy/b9ebd434-8004-459a-b84e-92dc82683ce2/.

33 *See* https://br.fas.gov.ru/media/document_files/c026e2e4-0945-462f-a69d-fa5c9de473bc/Решение_в_отношении_ООО_Яндекс.pdf, *see* Russian Competition Authority, *The Russian Competition Authority initiates an investigation against a national search engine platform (Yandex)*, e-Competitions March 2021, art. N° 100192.

Year	Target	Type of investigation	Market definition	Multi-sidedness* / network effects	Competition concerns	Decision	Theory of harm (to competition, to consumers)	Sources
2022	Google	Abuse of dominance	Market for the distribution of applications through app stores for subscriber devices running the Android operating system	1SA/no	Self-preferencing and exclusionary clauses	Warning	Not applicable: no full-fledged investigation	FAS warning No. МШ/63572/22[34]

* 2SM – one "two-sided market" is identified by competition authority; 1SA – "one-sided approach" is applied; IRM – several "interrelated markets" are considered.

34 *See* https://br.fas.gov.ru/ca/upravlenie-regulirovaniya-svyazi-i-informatsionnyh-tehnologiy/b2f801e9-9562-4c63-9902-109a15a92b39/.

4. Uber v. Yandex (2017)

On November 24, 2017, FAS cleared the merger between Yandex Taxi and Uber, subject to conditions (conduct remedies).

Market analysis. Analyzing the market "for the organization of information interaction between taxi drivers and passengers"[35] the authority paid particular attention to the estimation of the potential market share of the merged company. FAS considered the market which included both aggregators and offline taxi order services.[36] The text of the FAS decision does not reflect, however, if the rate of substitution between the services was tested. In the report the volume of the market is measured by the number of rides (transactions) in natural and monetary terms. This is reasonable given that the market under consideration is an example of a transaction platform market. However, in the non-confidential version of FAS's decision on the merger case the word "platform" is never used, the role of relative prices and network effects was not assessed by FAS.

What is interesting is that there is a related document – the FAS official report[37] on the results of the analysis of the state of competition in the markets "for organization of information interaction between taxi drivers and passengers." The document dates from 2017 and it was posted to the authority's website in early 2019. The report classifies the market as a "two-sided platform which enables matching of demand for rides and supply of taxi services."

Conditional clearance of the merger contained remedies on multi-homing: "parties are obliged not to prevent taxi drivers and taxi companies from switching between different digital applications." Parties accepted the remedies without any discussions.

5. Microsoft (2017)

In 2017 Microsoft was found to have abused a dominant position in the "multilateral market of operating systems for stationary devices", to the benefit of its own software applications (with particular focus on antivirus software) and encouraging users to abandon third-party applications.

Market analysis. FAS stresses that an OS cannot function independently without hardware and, thus, has no value for the end user in the absence of a device on which the functionality of the operating system is implemented. Thus, the OS market was considered inextricably linked with the hardware device market. Based on the results of interviews with consumers, it was found that there is no substitution between laptops, stationary computers, tablets, or smartphones.

---

35 *See* http://en.fas.gov.ru/press-center/news/detail.html?id=52562.

36 *See* https://fas.gov.ru/documents/678673 (in Russian).

37 *See* the note 25.

Based on the above, it was concluded that stationary devices (computers and tablets) and mobile hardware devices (tablets and smartphones) form separate commodity markets. The number of stationary devices at which Microsoft and alternative operating systems were installed was used for measuring Microsoft's market share of the "multilateral market of operating systems for stationary devices." Microsoft was found to be a dominant company with a market share of 95.6%. Cross-side (indirect) network effects were not mentioned.

Competition restriction effects. FAS analyzed clauses of Microsoft's antimalware platform whitepaper[38] and Windows 10 antimalware API license and listing in the Microsoft Store agreement between Microsoft and the Russian developer of anti-virus software Kaspersky Lab. Kaspersky Lab's claims of self-preferencing by the OS producer were also inspected. FAS concluded that the absence of notifications about the removal, disabling (blocking) of Kaspersky Lab antivirus software and the activation of Microsoft's antivirus software – Windows Defender – without proper notification to the consumer, as well as the introduction of a complicated procedure for updating the installed Kaspersky Lab antivirus software compared to the procedures for updating Windows antivirus Defender software, created unequal treatment conditions for the applicant's antivirus software compared to the treatment of Microsoft Corporation antivirus software – Windows Defender. Non-price discrimination by a dominant company was the violation.

6. Headhunter (2019)

A claim of blocking of employers using third-party services by Headhunter resulted in an antitrust investigation against this automated personnel recruitment and selection service developer. An infringement is exclusion from the platform for those business users who apply searching and processing information programming tools on the platform page, therefore competing with matching services provided by Headhunter. Headhunter considers the application of independent programming tools as free-riding by business users.

Market analysis. In the investigation of Headhunter's business-practices, according to the results of interviews FAS argued on the non-substitutability of alternative ways of providing the "service to ensure information interaction between job seekers, employers and recruitment agencies", namely specialized internet services, print media and television media as only the first of these allowed the economic agents to communicate and transact directly. Thus, the market was defined as "the market of services enabling informational cooperation between applicants, employers and personnel agencies in the internet information and communications network."

---

38 The document is not available anymore. Mention of it can be found here: https://www.virusbulletin.com/uploads/pdf/conference_slides/2015/Batchelder-VB2015.pdf.

The agency considered different sides of the market, measuring its size by: (i) the number of CVs in the database since "the number of resumes attracts employers who are the main clients generating income by purchasing access to the CV database;" and (ii) by the number of employers using the service to search for employees. Thus, the market was determined to be multilateral and characterized by network effects, which were described but not quantitatively assessed. FAS concluded that Headhunter had a dominant position in the market (as part of a collective dominant position) based on the following:

- the aggregate share of LLC Headhunter, LLC Superjob and LLC RDV-Soft based on the number of CVs is 98% with individual market shares of the companies exceeding 15%;
- the aggregate share of LLC Headhunter, LLC Superjob and LLC RDV-Soft based on the number of employees is 91% with individual market shares of the companies exceeding 14%.

Competition restriction effects. Organizations (LLC Huntflow, LLC Stafori, LLC Smart Recruiting, etc.) that provide employers (recruitment agencies, applicants) the service of automated search for candidates (resumes, vacancies) in the databases of the above-mentioned platforms (rabota.ru, hh.ru, superjob.ru) were also considered as the platform's users. The automated search services (Amazing Hiring, Experium, Robot Vera, Huntflow, Potok, etc.) were paid and regulated by separate service agreements. Such services competed with the search engines offered by the platforms.

FAS analyzed the terms of the use of the web sides of LLC Headhunter" (hh.ru), LLC Superjob (superjob.ru) and LLC RDV-Soft (rabota.ru). Unconditional bans on the use of third-party automated search software when working with the web sites were revealed. The use of third-party software (Robot Vera) resulted in blocking the access of already registered hh.ru site users (employees). The software developer's account was terminated which made it impossible to get a unique API key necessary for the use of the software.

FAS concluded that Headhunter imposed entry barriers to the competing software. The company was found guilty of restriction of competition in the market for ensuring information interaction of applicants, employers and recruitment agencies on the internet information and telecommunications network, in the form of creating entry barriers.

7. Booking.com (2020)

In November 2019, FAS issued a warning to Booking.com to stop actions that could violate the antimonopoly law.[39] The company's requirements about the parity of prices and rooms with regard to third persons in agreements with Russian entities that render accommodation services was recognized as a business practice

---

39 *See* http://en.fas.gov.ru/press-center/news/detail.html?id=54555.

with "elements of abusing dominance." The company was recommended to exclude these requirements from agreements in order to avoid becoming the subject of an antitrust investigation. Since the company did not follow the recommendation, an antitrust case was opened. At that point dominance was simply assumed by FAS[40] as no market analysis had been undertaken yet.

Market analysis. In its market analysis FAS named the company a "platform" and "an aggregator of information about accommodation facilities." FAS interviewed representatives on both sides of the platform, namely providers and consumers of accommodation services, to assess the substitutability of accommodation aggregators' services. The list of potential substitutes was the following:

- provision of services for the dissemination of information about accommodation facilities and their booking directly on the websites of the accommodation facilities;
- provision of services for the dissemination of information about the accommodation and the reservation in search engines (Google, Yandex, Mail.ru, etc.);
- provision of services for the dissemination of information about accommodation facilities and their booking in meta-search systems (for example, Kayak, Trivago, RoomGuru, etc.);
- provision of services for the dissemination of information about accommodation facilities and their booking on websites (services) for placing ads for renting (selling) apartments, houses, rooms and other real estate objects (Avito, Yandex. Real estate, Cyan, etc.).

The alternatives were found to be different with regard to the list of services provided (search and comparison of hotels by availability; prices; customer reviews; booking and payment services; and marketing services etc.). According to the results of the "small but significant and non-transitory increase in price" (SSNIP) test 35% of accommodation facilities would stop using aggregators' services after a fee increase of 10%. FAS also used results of the Russian Public Opinion Research Center (VCIOM) Study, according to which 79% of respondents/travelers search for accommodation through various information aggregators on accommodation facilities, 48% also use specialized travel sites, 38% also search for hotels through search engines, and 37% use recommendations. None of the alternatives, however, provided clients with a full set of complementary services comparable to the one of Booking.com.

Based on the above FAS concluded there were no close substitutes for accommodation aggregators' services and defined the market as a "market for the provision of services by aggregators of information about accommodation facilities."

40 *See* https://br.fas.gov.ru/ca/upravlenie-regulirovaniya-svyazi-i-informatsionnyh-tehnologiy/ce12aabe-b261-4ce2-aa5a-d71d8a93cbe7/ (in Russian).

Cross-side (indirect) network effects were not discussed, however. Aggregators' market shares were calculated using the number of reservations made through the platforms which is in line with the logic of transaction markets. Booking.com was found to be dominant with a market share of about 80%.

Competition restriction effects, harm to consumers. FAS stated that the parity of prices requirements led to the following effects:

- restriction of price competition between aggregators and, thus, inability of new aggregators to offer better price conditions (smaller fee size) to attract consumers and enter the market;
- inability for hotels to differentiate prices and offer better prices to consumers;
- inability of hotels to develop different terms of providing services to "closed groups" of users;
- increased expenses of hotels for monitoring information on the internet to ensure parity of prices.

Based on the aforementioned, FAS concluded that Booking.com business practice led to a restriction of competition between aggregators and harm to users on both sides of the platform. The third parties room price parity in agreements with Russian accommodation services firms was found to be a violation of competition law in the form of imposing unfavorable contract terms.

Efficiency effects (arguments of the company). The company provided three arguments to justify application of the parity of prices and rooms:

- way to protect aggregators from free-riding;
- transformation of price competition between aggregators into quality competition;
- benefits of final consumers (on both sides) from better quality of the platform services and decrease of transaction costs and price uncertainty;
- The arguments were rejected by FAS with appealing to Germany experience (but not original empirical evidence from the Russian market).

8. Apple (2020)

According to the applicant (Russian application developer Kaspersky Lab.), Apple abused its dominant position in the market offering mobile devices running its iOS operating system, forcing Kaspersky to significantly degrade the functionality of its mobile parental control application Kaspersky Safe Kids in order to promote its own similar (competing) application Screen Time.

Market analysis. FAS named App Store a platform for hosting applications. Thus, the service provided by Apple was considered to be services for hosting applications on its own platform. To define the market FAS found substitution between:

- distribution of applications for stationary devices (running on various operating systems, including Windows, MacOS29, Linux30, etc. or for a specific operating system);
- distribution of applications for mobile devices running a specific mobile operating system (iOS, Android, Windows Mobile, etc.).

According to the results from interviewing application developers (quantitative results of the analysis are published in the decision on another case against Apple in 2022[41]):

- most developers will not abandon the development of applications for mobile devices, because it is unprofitable and will lead to the loss of a huge user base;
- many developers develop applications for both iOS and Android at the same time, and most of them have separate teams of specialists, because these OS are significantly different;
- developers are not ready to abandon the development of applications for one mobile OS in favor of any other, because this will lead to the loss of users and income;
- a very small proportion of developers believe that an alternative to the App Store for distributing content (subscriptions, etc.) are televisions, game consoles, web versions of applications, etc.;
- most developers consider the App Store to be the only way to distribute apps and content for iOS;
- all developers believe that the App Store has no alternatives for distributing iOS apps;
- many developers have indicated that developing iOS apps without using the App Store to distribute them would be unprofitable and would not allow entry into the mobile app market.

According to the results from interviewing application users:

- 80% of iOS device users and 71% of Android device users are not ready to give up their device and switch to a device with a different operating system in case of an increase in the average monthly time and effort spent on searching and installing applications by 10%.

41 *See* the case Apple (2022) below.

– while 78% of iOS device users and 80% of Android device users are not ready to abandon their device and switch to a device with a different operating system in case of a 10% increase in their average monthly spending on the purchase of applications, subscription fees and/or additional functions.

So, user behavior on both sides of the platform was investigated. The product boundaries of the market studied were defined as the market for the distribution of applications for mobile devices with iOS operating system. Multi-sidedness of the market and network effects were explicitly mentioned. Given the market definition Apple was found to be dominant with a market share of 100%.

Competition restriction effects. FAS analyzed Apple's developer documentation for their parental controls app[42] in its entirety. It was revealed that since June 3, 2019, Apple had established (i) a ban on the use of configuration profiles in B2C applications, (ii) the possibility of using mobile device management (MDM) technology only with Apple's written permission exclusively for B2B applications and, as an exception, only B2C parental control applications, and, (iii) a ban for MDM applications to sell, use or disclose any data to third parties for any purpose.

The above actions by Apple have actually led to a ban on developers of parental control applications (Russian Kaspersky, an applicant in particular) using analytics tools, since such an application would either not use the configuration profile and therefore becoming unattractive to the consumer (functionally useless, uncompetitive with Screen Time), or would use a configuration profile, but only containing MDM payload, and thus would fall under the ban on the use of analytics tools. Such tools are critically important for the development of applications, and their absence can negatively affect the subsequent functioning and, as a result, the further competitiveness of the application.

At the same time, Apple continued to use analytics tools to develop, support and improve its own applications, including Screen Time. FAS concluded that such actions by Apple were aimed to create a competitive advantage for Screen Time and restrict competition of developers of mobile parental control applications for iOS. The theory of harm therefore was self-preferencing. FAS made an infringement decision with a penalty of about 12 million USD together with remedy prohibiting self-preferencing.

9. Google (YouTube) (2021)

In 2021 FAS initiated an antitrust investigation against Google based on the concerns that the user agreement of the video hosting YouTube resulted in the abuse of dominance on the market for collecting, storing, processing, providing,

---

42 *See* https://developer.apple.com/documentation/familycontrols.

distributing, transmitting, viewing video content in the internet information and telecommunications network (video hosting services market) harming consumers (users) and limiting competition in the adjacent digital advertising market.

Market analysis. Data on the traffic (the volume of data transmitted from/to video hosting services) was used to measure the size of the market to prove the dominant position of the company. No analysis of network effects or ways of content monetization were investigated. Thus, only one side of the platform was analyzed. Digital advertising markets where the presumed competition restrictions took place, and the effects of conduct on competition in digital advertising were not examined in the decisions. Arguments by the company on incorrect definition of the market were rejected.

Competition restriction effects, harm to consumers. The user agreement stated the ability of the video hosting platform to block/delete any account/content on the service arbitrarily and without warning, as well as the inability to export/move content from blocked/deleted accounts to new service accounts and/or to external sources (other video hosting services). FAS found that the actions could harm the interests of economic entities in the content distribution market restricting their ability to get profits from advertising. Corresponding evidence on the harm to particular users was provided. FAS concluded that Google violated competition law in the form of abuse of dominance. The approach that harm to the group of consumers (users) implies restrictions of competition in adjacent markets is often used by Russian FAS. In many investigations of essential facilities operators in network industries (natural monopolies, according to the wording of Russian legislation) competition authorities use the same line of reasoning. Disadvantageous conditions of access to essential facilities are considered as anticompetitive per se, without developing and testing a specific theory of harm in adjacent market(s).

10. Apple (2022)

Particular clauses in the App Store Review Guidelines[43] and Developer Product License Agreement[44] were found to be formulated in a way that restricted the ability of application developers to inform and motivate consumers to use alternative payment methods to in-app purchases. The case is inspired by worldwide lawsuits of Spotify to Apple (and all the similar cases) The corresponding warning sent to the company was ignored, so FAS initiated an antitrust investigation.

Market analysis Within the analysis the App Store was named "a platform", network effects were described without quantifying. It is worth mentioning that deciding on the market definition the agency stressed the impossibility of using SSNIP test in its traditional way given that a large share of applications was

43 https://developer.apple.com/app-store/review/guidelines/.

44 https://www.imperial.ac.uk/media/imperial-college/staff/web-guide/public/Apple-Developer-Agreement.pdf.

distributed for free. Thus, for the purposes of product substitution assessment FAS formulated questions without mentioning the price. The following results became the basis for delineation of the market:

- 80% of developers will not abandon the development of applications for mobile devices as this would lead to the loss of a huge user base;
- 93% of developers develop applications for both iOS and Android, and 76% of them have separate teams of specialists, because these OS are significantly different;
- 86% of developers are not ready to abandon the development of applications for one mobile OS in favor of any other, because this would lead to the loss of users and income;
- 97% of developers consider the App Store to be the only way to distribute iOS apps;
- 73% of developers consider the App Store to be the only way to distribute apps and content for iOS;
- 72% of developers indicated that developing iOS apps without using the App Store for its distribution would be unprofitable and would not allow entry into the mobile app market.

Users on the other side of the platform (app buyers) were not interviewed. However, it was mentioned that switching between App Store and an alternative app store would mean buying a device with a different OS.

Based on this the market was defined as "the market for distribution of applications for iOS operating system." FAS found Apple dominant on the market with a market share of 100%.

Competition restriction effects. On the basis of analysis of the App Store Review Guidelines and Developer Product Licensing Agreement clauses and communications between Apple and app developers FAS confirmed the ability of the company to unilaterally influence market conditions and restrict competition in the adjacent markets (apps for iOS). FAS concluded that the clauses restricted the ability of software developers to inform their customers about the ways of purchasing their products alternatively to App Store.

Remedies were implemented to stop actions that restricted competition in the market for distribution of applications for iOS operating systems. The agency required the company to remove clauses that allowed it to decline a request for (or to stop) distribution of an application through App Store "by any reason even if it suits requirements of the company." The company was also ordered not to give priority to applications developed by Apple in comparison with third-party applications and to ensure that developers of applications could distribute them in the App Store without losing important functionality.

11. Yandex (2022)

An antitrust investigation against Yandex was initiated in 2021 based on concerns of self-preferencing by manipulating search results through the use of various interactive elements in the search results, including so-called “sorcerers”, which are algorithm that forms an interactive information block in the search results (an image, on which a user can click to get the necessary information without going directly to the Yandex service website (Yandex group). The case is similar to the *Google Shopping* case in Europe[45]

Market analysis. FAS concluded that Yandex had a dominant position in the general search market (as part of a collective dominant position with Google) based on the analysis of traffic. FAS also appealed to the EC decision in *Google Shopping* to support its market definition and the conclusion on the dominance position. The dominance in the general search was named as a key factor for leveraging of market power to related Yandex services markets.

Competition restriction effects. FAS found that Yandex sorcerers were located in priority places in the search results (top positions on the first page after advertising). Thus, information about Yandex services attracted consumer attention and traffic, increasing the attendance of Yandex services to the detriment of applicants. This was considered by FAS as a discriminatory condition for promotion of the company’s services.

All parties in the *Yandex* case, including FAS and the group of complainants, signed a settlement agreement, which was approved by the Moscow Arbitration Court. The IT company complied with the requirements of the antimonopoly service and eliminated all discrimination factors mentioned by the applicants.

12. Google (2022)

In 2022 FAS established that according to Google’s Developer Program Policy[46] the sale of digital goods and services in applications distributed on Google Play was only allowed through its payment system. So, antitrust concerns were similar to the ones in the case against Apple (2022). Stating that Google dominated in “the market for the distribution of applications through app stores for subscriber devices running the Android operating system” FAS considered these “unfavorable terms of the contract.” FAS warned the company and ordered it to eliminate discriminatory conditions and to allow application developers to use alternative payment methods. The company was given one month to change the Developer

45 Commission decision of 27 June 2017 relating to a proceeding under Article 102 of the Treaty on the Functioning of the European Union and Article 54 of the EEA Agreement (Case AT.39740 – Google Search (Shopping)). A. Buttà, *Google Search (Shopping): an Overview of the European Commission's Antitrust Case*, 5 Antitrust & Pub. Pol. (2018), http://a-p-p-review.com/issue/view/811/showToc.

46 *See* https://support.google.com/googleplay/android-developer/answer/12867690?hl=en.

Program Policy to avoid the opening of an antitrust case. FAS Russia reports that Google complied with the remedy.[47]

IV. Concluding Remarks

The overview of cases above illustrates that FAS undertakes enforcement actions toward digital platforms despite the absence of specific norms related to this business model in competition law.

Until 2017 enforcement actions against digital platforms does not imply proper analysis of the markets. We observe no signs that FAS uses relevant economic tools and models for the analysis of competition in platform markets when it is appropriate. It applies a traditional one-sided approach in investigating platform markets instead, focusing on one side of a platform and ignoring the role of cross-side network effects and relative prices. Thus, the very first investigative step, which is product market definition, is often incorrect and does not allow for an explanation of restrictions of competition and theory of harm to consumers.

Between 2017 and 2018 FAS demonstrated recognition of a principal difference between platform markets and traditional one-sided markets. Violators are named "platforms", network effects are sometimes identified.

In recent cases the authority mentions that traditional instruments of economic analysis for the purposes of competition law enforcement are not applicable in cases of platforms and tries to modify them. Also, FAS undertakes efforts aimed at adopting tools of economic analysis for the purposes of competition law enforcement:

- in the Apple cases given the impossibility of applying an SSNIP test FAS develops an approach to adopt SSNDQ (small but significant non-transitory decrease in quality) test.[48]
- in the absence of any specific norm related to anticompetitive conducts of gatekeepers[49] FAS considers different sides of a platform as related (adjacent) markets and applies the concept of leverage of market power by a dominant company to related markets in a similar way to the essential facilities concept.
- where appropriate, FAS appeals to the enforcement practice of mature jurisdictions (*Google* and *Booking.com* cases).

---

47 *See* https://fas.gov.ru/news/32126 (in Russian).

48 E. Pontual Ribeiro & S. Golovanova. *A Unified Presentation of Competition Analysis in Two-Sided Markets*, 34 J. Econ. Surv. 548–571 (2020). The test was for the first time applied in *Google Android* case, Commission Decision of July 18, 2018 relating to a proceeding under Article 102 of the Treaty on the Functioning of the European Union and Article 54 of the EEA Agreement Case AT.40099 (*Google Android*) 2018 O.J. (C 402).

49 Gatekeepers as defined by Digital Market Act are digital platforms that provide an important gateway between business users and consumers – whose position can grant them the power to act as a private rule maker, and thus creating a bottleneck in the digital economy.

While defining relevant markets using the concepts of platforms and network effects, FAS does not take multi-sidedness or cross-side network effects into account when assessing the impact on competition in particular cases. Usually investigations do not provide case-specific empirical evidence on the effects of restrictions of competition. Large parts of conducts are considered in terms of exploitative abuses. In many cases there is no fully-fledged economic analysis because the competition authority applied warnings and precautions, or refers to the guidelines on fair competition in the sector. Development of a theory of harm is observed in very few cases. We may conclude that enforcement against digital platforms in Russia does not utilize an effects-based approach more often than in decisions against companies in traditional markets.

To sum up, we may conclude that Russian FAS understands specific features of digital platforms as targets for competition enforcement. This understanding does not result in developing new rules specific to platforms. Instead, the Russian competition authority uses a similar approach to enforcement used with any other large company that may influence adjacent markets due to control on an essential facility. Expected to be finally adopted, the latest version of the Fifth Antimonopoly Package does not contain revolutionary rules. Traditionally, FAS actively applies "soft law" in the form of guidelines and agreements, and remedies in the form of warnings and precautions. Neither of these procedures require an effects-based approach. Therefore, enforcement against digital platforms remains mostly presumption based.

China's Antitrust Regulation of the Digital Economy: Recent Developments and an Evaluation

PING LIN AND CLARE G. YE*

Shandong University

Abstract

China has made substantial progress establishing a modern antitrust system in the fourteen years since its Anti-Monopoly Law (AML) took effect in 2008. This chapter introduces China's AML and the recent developments regarding antitrust in the digital economy. We review China's Antitrust Guidelines for the Platform Economy, the main amendments to its AML, and its Draft Guidelines for Platform Responsibilities, all published during the past two years.[1] *We also provide an extensive review*

* Ping Lin, School of Economics, Shandong University, email: plin@sdu.edu.cn. Clare G. Ye, School of Law, Shandong University, email: gaofenye@sdu.edu.cn. The authors acknowledge financial support by the Natural Science Foundation of China (Major Program 72192842).

1 On February 7, 2021, China unveiled its ANTITRUST GUIDELINES FOR THE PLATFORM ECONOMY [HEREINAFTER THE "PLATFORM GUIDELINES"]. *See* 国务院反垄断委员会关于平台经济领域的反垄断指南 (samr.gov.cn), https://gkml.samr.gov.cn/nsjg/fldj/202102/t20210207_325967.html. This event signaled that China is ready to curb anti-competitive conduct of internet platforms under its AML. In October of the same year, China issued two draft guidelines regarding regulation of platforms, or public consultation: the Guidelines on Classification of Internet Platforms, which classify platforms according to the nature of businesses they perform and their sizes, and the Guidelines for Business Responsibilities of Internet Platforms (here within Draft Responsibility Guidelines). The Draft Responsibility Guidelines specify various "duties" or "responsibilities" of the so-called super-large platforms. See the Notice for the Public Consultation on the Draft Guidelines for Business Responsibilities of Internet Platforms 市场监管总局关于《关于平台经济领域的反垄断指南（征求意见稿）》公开征求意见的公告 (samr.gov.cn), https://www.samr.gov.cn/hd/zjdc/202011/t20201109_323234.html. In June 2022, China promulgated its 2007 AML which, among other things, incorporates features of and new business practices that have emerged in the digital economy and that may hurt competition.

of the landmark exclusive dealing case of Alibaba,[2] paying particular attention to the economic reasoning behind the decision. While being proactive in establishing a structured antitrust system for its digital economy, China's next big challenge is to support its newly established framework with more solid economic analysis.

I. Introduction

On August 30, 2007, China enacted its Anti-Monopoly Law (AML), which came into on August 1, 2008. Since then, China has become the world's second largest economy and the third largest antitrust jurisdiction. Over the past few years, China has made significant progresses in enforcing its AML in all areas the law covers, including monopoly agreements, abuse of dominant position, mergers, and administrative monopolies. Since late 2020 there have been rapid and drastic changes in China's antitrust policy, as marked by the promulgation of relevant guidelines on its digital economy, investigations of its tech giant firms with historic fines, and amendment to its AML which explicitly incorporates elements of digital economy.

Three major recent developments have formed the Chinese system of antitrust and its digital economy: 1 promulgation of the Antitrust Guidelines on the Platform Economy in February, 2021, which were considered to be first set of such guidelines in the world; 2 the issuing for public consultation of the Draft Guidelines for Platform Classification and the Draft Guidelines for Platform Responsibilities in October, 2022, which resemble the EU gatekeeper system and may be officially published soon; and 3 the amendment of the AML in June, 2022. With these developments, China signals to the markets and the rest of the world that it is ready to curb anti-competitive conduct in the digital era.

We first briefly introduce the content of China's AML, including its central provisions, enforcement, and unique features. We then review the above-mentioned main developments and provide a detailed case study of the antitrust prosecution against the Chinese tech giant Alibaba Group in 2021. An evaluation of China's newly established antitrust system for its digital economy is attempted, focusing on the economic principles and reasoning behind its digital economy.

II. Overview of China's Anti-Monopoly Law

On August 30, 2007, China enacted its AML, which came into effect on August 1, 2008. Since then, China has become the world's second-largest economy and third-largest antitrust jurisdiction. This section briefly introduces China's AML before the amendment in 2022.[3]

---

2 See *Alibaba* Decision – SAMR Administrative Penalty Decision (2021) No. 28 http://download.caixin.com/upload/P020210410314261904015.pdf.

3 H. Ju & P. Lin, *China's Anti-Monopoly Law and the Role of Economics in its Enforcement*, 6 Ru. J. E. 19 (2020) contains detailed review of China's AML and the use of economics in its enforcement since 2008.

1. Major Provisions

China's anti-monopoly law aims to prevent and restrain monopolistic conduct, protect fair competition, improve economic efficiency, safeguard the interests of consumers and social interests, and ensure healthy socialist market economy development. The AML covers four principal areas: monopoly agreements, abuse of market dominance, anti-competitive mergers, and administrative monopoly. The last area, administrative monopoly, represents a unique feature of China's competition law.

Article 13 AML prohibits undertaking(s) from making price fixing, output restriction, market sharing, production or technology restriction, boycotts, and any other horizontal monopoly agreements, determined by the enforcement agencies.

In Article 16, the AML bans undertaking(s) from abusing its (their) market dominant position to restrict market competition. Six kinds of abusive conduct are particularly prohibited. They are unfair pricing, below cost pricing, dealing refusals, exclusive or designated dealing, discriminatory dealing, and imposition of unreasonable transaction terms.

The AML requires mergers and acquisitions to undertake competition clearance through a general regime before completion. Article 20 AML refers the undertakings' mergers to the following situations: 1 the merger of the undertakings, 2 the acquisition of other undertakings' holding through asset or share purchase, 3 contract acquisition or any other means of control of other undertakings, including the ability to exercise decisive influence on other undertakings. Article 31 AML refers to a possible national security review when mergers involve foreign parties.

Besides monopoly agreements, abuse of market dominance merger control, China's AML also prohibits public authorities (including government agencies, organizations empowered by law, and public affair administration) from abusing their administrative power to restrict or eliminate competition. Such government conduct is referred to as "administrative monopolies."

2. Enforcement

Prior to 2018, there were three authorities that enforced AML in China: the Price Supervision and Antimonopoly Bureau of the National Development and Reform Commission (NDRC), the Antimonopoly and Unfair Competition Enforcement Bureau of the-then State Administration for Industry and Commerce (SAIC), and the Antimonopoly Bureau of the Ministry of Commerce (MOFCOM). The NDRC was responsible for prosecuting cartel pricing and price related abuse of a dominant position (such as predatory pricing, unfair pricing, and price discrimination). The SAIC enforced AML on non-price-related abuse of a dominant position and monopoly agreement involving non-price coordination. MOFCOM focused on merger control. The AML also set up China's Anti-Monopoly Commission, which promulgates guidelines, coordinates enforcement activities, and reports directly to the State Council.

In 2018, the three enforcement agencies were combined to form the Anti-Monopoly Bureau of the State Administration for Market Regulation (SAMR), the sole AML enforcement agency in China since then. In January 2019, SAMR granted provincial regulatory authority partial autonomy in prosecuting monopoly agreements and dominant position abuse. Before that time, a local authority could only start investigating a suspicious case after obtaining authorization from the AML enforcers at national level. The unified AML enforcement agency was replaced by the National Anti-Monopoly Bureau (AMB), which was established in late 2021 with increased manpower and internal revamp, whereby three new divisions (Competition Policy Co-ordination Division, Anti-Monopoly Enforcement Division I, and Anti-Monopoly Enforcement Division II) have been set up. Ms. Gan Lin (vice minister of SAMR) was appointed as head of the new AMB in China.

Under the AML, private parties who fall victim to direct or indirect anti-competitive practices are granted the right to sue. Both stand-alone and follow-on cases are allowed.[4] The Intellectual Property Division of the Chinese courts is responsible for handling private antitrust litigation.[5]

3. Administrative Monopolies and Fair Competition Review

As mentioned above, a special feature of China's AML is its target on administrative monopoly. Administrative monopoly refers to government bodies or organizations abusing their executive power to hinder market competition. The AML classifies and prohibits six types of administrative monopolies: 1 designated transactions, 2 commercial obstruction, 3 discrimination on bidders, 4 exclusive clauses against non-local undertakings or investors, 5 abuse of public authority to facilitate monopolistic conduct, and 6 anti-competitive provisions. Both the AML agency and the courts can investigate alleged administrative monopoly cases.

A landmark development of China's legal system to combat administrative monopoly is establishing the Fair Competition Review (FCR) system. In 2016, China set up the FCR system whereby government agencies' policy proposals and existing regulations must be reviewed to identify anti-competitive regulations. The State Council issued two documents: Opinions on Establishing a Fair Competition Review System in the Market System[6] and Implementation Rules for the Fair Competition Review System (Interim Regulation). Under the FCR system, any existing or new laws, regulations, and policies introduced by any

---

4 According to the judicial interpretation by the People's Supreme Court of China, *Application of Laws to Anti-Monopoly Private Actions (Judicial Interpretatio*n), (May 8, 2012).

5 The People's Supreme Court of China designated its IP divisions this responsibility as courts in China generally have not developed expertise in complex economic analysis yet.

6 The Opinions state that "establishing a Fair Competition Review System and preventing any improper intervention by the governments help secure resources allocation, thus strengthen the rule of the market, the price system, and competition to maximize return and efficiency." State Order No. 34, 2016, http://www.gov.cn/zhengce/content/2016-06/14/content_5082066.htm.

government or organization below the State Council level must undergo a competition review conducted by the policy-making body and/or a third party. The criteria for assessing the competition impacts of a regulation or policy cover four aspects: market entry and exit, free flow of factors of production across regions, impacts on the costs of undertakings, and impacts on the behaviors of undertakings. A more detailed list of "18 don'ts" is specified. Regulations/policies that violate any of the "18 don'ts" must be modified and relevant anti-competitive provisions removed.

III. Amendment to China's 2007 Anti-Monopoly Law

1. Background

Even though the AML plays a vital role in safeguarding fair competition, improving economic efficiency, and protecting the general public's interests, the authority encountered issues such as rigidity on relevant provisions and insufficient penalties for certain monopoly behaviors, during the enforcements of the AML.[7] Moreover, new challenges unique to the digital economy started to concern the authority, such as whether/how to regulate firms' usage of data and algorithms.

In January 2020, SAMR published a draft amendment and sought public opinion. The Standing Committee of the National People's Congress approved the amendment in October 2021 and enacted it in June 2022. The new AML, which officially came into effect on August 1, 2022, expanded the overall scope of its application, and significantly increased the legal liabilities for anti-competitive behavior. Six implementing rules and regulations related to the AML have been updated and concluded in subsequent months. The following sections briefly review key aspects of this amendment.

2. Greater Considerations toward Monopoly Agreement

Article 18 of the amended AML prohibits undertakings from forming agreements on price-fixing and resale price maintenance with a third party. The amendment adds that undertakings can defend their price-fixing and minimum resale price agreements if they are able to prove that those agreements do not restrain or exclude market competition. The amendment also states that price agreements with a third party are allowed if there is evidence that such agreements meet the anti-monopoly enforcement institutes' standards and conditions. Those changes provide SAMR with more flexibility with regard to the investigation of monopoly agreements. Article 19 prohibits undertakings from forming monopoly agreements or facilitating the formation of other parties' monopoly agreements.

---

7 *See* the statement by the deputy head of SAMR in 2021, http://www.npc.gov.cn/npc/c30834/202206/d5eb7f283661462bb8af84e5929f62e7.shtml.

3. More Sophisticated Merger Regulation

Article 26 requires the undertakings to report to the State Council once the merger notification threshold has been exceeded. The amendment adds that the undertakings must report to the agency if there is evidence indicating anti-competitive results of the planned merger. This change encourages voluntary notification by the undertakings, as intended mergers could be subject to scrutiny from SAMR even if they do not reach the notification thresholds specified in the AML.

Article 32 allows SAMR to suspend a merger review under the following circumstances: 1 the undertakings failed to provide relevant documents or proofs as required, 2 the emergence of new facts that hinders the investigation without further examinations, 3 the undertakings made a suspension request, or there is a need to re-evaluate the market concentration conditions. SAMR can review mergers with more time and flexibility with this amendment.

4. More Comprehensive Regime of Administrative Monopoly Control

Article 40 bans administrative parties and organizations with public-affair management functions from abusing their executive power and forming agreements with undertakings to deter entry and hinder competition.

Article 43 bans administrative parties from discriminating or restricting non-local undertakings' local investment and development. The amendment adds that the administration is also prohibited from forcing non-local undertakings to invest in local markets or establish local branches. The revised Article 44 prohibits administrations from forcing undertakings to engage in monopoly conduct directly or indirectly. Overall, the amendment included more anti-competitive scenarios with respect to administrative monopoly.

5. Tougher Penalties

The amendment increased penalties for various contraventions of the AML. Moreover, individuals are now liable and subject to fines for anti-competitive conduct. For example, Article 56 states that a fine of up to 3 million Chinese RMB[8] will be imposed on undertakings that have formed monopoly agreements but have not yet executed them. Before the amendment, such a fine was only up to 0.5 million Chinese RMB. Also, according to Article 56, individuals who organize, facilitate, or were responsible for forming the monopoly agreements can be fined up to 1 million Chinese RMB. By increasing the level of penalty and the scope to individual level, the amendment further disincentivized monopolistic conduct.

---

8 One US dollar is currently worth about 6.6 Chinese RMB.

6. Focus on the Digital Economy

In 2021, the digital economy in China accounted for more than 38.6% of China's GDP.[9] Nonetheless, before the amendment, the 2007 AML barely considered any factors related to the digital economy. The amendment showed the efforts made by China to improve its antitrust system in the era of the digital economy, as many other developed economies have been doing.

Article 9 prohibits undertakings from exploiting data, algorithms, technologies, capital advantages, and platform institutions to conduct monopolistic behaviors. Article 22 bans undertakings with dominant market positions from exploiting data, algorithms, technology, and platform institutions to abuse their dominant positions. All those terminologies mentioned are unique to the digital economy and, as believed, could significantly affect the market if not appropriately regulated.

Such provisions were also added to (Article 22) governing the abuse of market dominance, further signaling the concern that abuse of market dominance in the digital economy may be particularly prevalent.

Article 16 of the AML defines monopoly agreement as "any decision, agreement or other forms of collusion that restrain or exclude competition." According to the Anti-Monopoly Guidelines on Platform Economy (Articles 6 and 7), undertakings are subject to antitrust investigation for monopoly agreement if they coordinate price or conduct, restrict dealings, and exclude market competition through data, algorithms, or platform institutions. These provisions are sensible as economists have found experimental evidence that firms are able to sustain collusion through algorithms alone.[10] The inclusion of data and algorithms as means for monopoly agreement reflects that the Chinese Government has been aware of the potential anti-competitive conduct made possible by new technology and are acting accordingly.

Another important addition to the AML is its consideration of privacy. There are growing concerns from consumers about the protection of their data and privacy in China. Though sometimes useful for firms to provide better products, consumer information collected by firms can also potentially harm consumers through data-based price discrimination or leak of sensitive personal information.[11] Protection of personal and commercial information is also a concern under Article 49 AML.

---

9 *See* China Academy of Information and Communications Technology, *White Paper on Digital Economy Development in China* (2021) (in Chinese), http://www.caict.ac.cn/kxyj/qwfb/bps/202104/P020210424737615413306.pdf.

10 E. Calvano et al., *Artificial Intelligence, Algorithmic Pricing, and Collusion* 110 Am. Econ. Rev. 3267–297 (Oct. 2020).

11 Y. Chen, *Improving Market Performance in the Digital Economy*, 62 China Econ. Rev. (Aug. 2020).

IV. China's Antitrust Guidelines for the Digital Economy

For a significant amount of time, competition authorities in China took a "prudent and tolerant" attitude towards the digital economy. On the one hand, academia had not provided much clear-cut insight on regulating the new digital economy. On the other hand, the authority had little resources and experience in applying competition law to deal with challenges from the complicated digital economy.

According to a white paper[12] issued by the Chinese Academy of Information and Communications Technology, China's digital economy was estimated to be worth USD 7.1 trillion in 2021, ranking second in the world. A number of homegroup internet companies, such as Baidu, Alibaba, Tencent, and Jingdong, among others, have emerged as giant platforms despite not having international status during the past ten to fifteen years.

As the digital economy develops rapidly, it has been believed that the internet sector had entered the "youth stage" from its "infant stage". What was considered as the "inclusive and tolerant" approach to regulation is no longer suitable.[13] Perhaps in parallel to or even influenced by the "antitrust movement" developing globally during the past five years, the media, scholars, and lawmakers in China started to discuss strengthening the regulation of its digital economy.

The calls for tightened regulation fall not only in antitrust, but also in other areas such as anti-unfair competition, consumer protection, and broad regulation of e-commerce. As the demand to regulate antitrust conduct in the digital economy rose, China started to act. On December 24, 2020, the Anti-Monopoly Bureau of SAMR initiated an investigation into Alibaba, a tech giant that owns two of the largest e-commerce platforms in China, because of its "either/or" clauses in the provision with its merchants. This case marks China's effort and determination to tackle anti-competitive conduct in the two-sided platform market. In February 2021, the State Council published the Platform Guidelines. In November of the same year, the SAMR published the Draft Guidelines for Platform Responsibilities and sought public opinion. On December 16, 2021, SAMR set up the Competition Policy and Big Data Centre with the aim to research antitrust in the platform economy.[14] Because of the active and high-profile legislative activities, 2021 marks the first year of Chinese AML's proactive role in the digital economy.[15]

---

12 *See* Xinhua, *China's Digital Economy Hits $7.1t: White Paper*, China Daily, July 30, 2022, http://www.chinadaily.com.cn/a/202207/30/WS62e4ef9ca310fd2b29e6f520.html#:~:text=Digital%20economy%20is%20a%20key,20.9%20percent%20to%2039.8%20percent.

13 *See, e.g., Strengthen Antitrust Regulation to Create a Benign Interaction Between Competition and Innovation*, Guangming Daily, Jan. 31, 2021, https://news.gmw.cn/2021-01/31/content_34586213.htm.

14 State Administration for Market Regulation (SAMR), *Competition Policy and Big Data Centre Affiliated with the State Administration for Market Regulation is Officially Established*, (2021), https://www.samr.gov.cn/xw/mtjj/202112/t20211220_338237.html.

15 X. Wang & Y. Gao, *China's Antimonopoly Law Enforcement in the Digital Economy*, 67 Antitrust Bull. 562–578 (2022).

1. China's Antitrust Guidelines for the Platform Economy 2021

On February 7, 2021, SAMR promulgated the Platform Guidelines with immediate effect.[16] The Platform Guidelines "aim to prevent and curb monopolistic conducts in the platform economy, create a fair and competitive market on online platforms and to safeguard consumer interests and public interests (Article 1)."

To a large extent, the Platform Guidelines are a restatement of China's AML, regarding its digital economy. It is extensive, covering all fields of anti-competitive conduct, including horizontal, vertical, hub-and-spoke agreements, various types of abuse of market dominance, as well concentration of undertakings. The Platform Guidelines clarify that a monopoly agreement is identified when different operators behave in a coordinated way due to the use of data, algorithms, and other tools that allow them to synchronize their activity. The guidelines contain a number of provisions identifying what is considered as anti-competitive behavior and the practices that must not be adopted by platforms operators, such as squeezing other operators out of the market, sharing sensitive consumer data, adopting the "either/or" contract or "choose one from two" practice whereby a seller cannot operate on different platforms and must choose one single platform, or using big data to manipulate the market to their own advantage (for example, drafting the profile of a user, based on their online behavior, with the aim of setting different prices).[17]

Under the category of abuse of market dominance, the Platform Guidelines contain a number of specific provisions regarding new forms of abusive conduct: exclusive dealing (including "either/or" conduct, refusal to deal, and big-data-based differential treatments (including price discrimination) – all may constitute abuse of market dominance under the AML.

In particular, Article 15 of the Platform Guidelines states that exclusive dealing can be achieved through a written or verbal agreement, or through the setting of actual restrictions or obstacles through platform rules, data, algorithms, technical means, etc. This stipulation shows that the real concern is the impact on competition rather than the forms of conduct. It is noteworthy that the Platform Guidelines

---

16 *See*, 国务院反垄断委员会关于平台经济领域的反垄断指南 (samr.gov.cn), https://gkml.samr.gov.cn/nsjg/fldj/202102/t20210207_325967.html. The final version of the Guidelines does not substantially differ from the initial draft unveiled by the SAMR at the end of November 2020. The short time needed to finalize the Guidelines reveals the urgency felt by China to regulate its fast-growing digital economy to prevent and stop monopolistic behaviors and promote the sustainable and healthy development of online commerce and the Notice for theThe Guidelines for Business Responsibilities of Internet Platforms 市场监管总局关于《关于平台经济领域的反垄断指南（征求意见稿）》公开征求意见的公告 (samr.gov.cn), https://www.samr.gov.cn/hd/zjdc/202011/t20201109_323234.html.

17 For a detailed review of the Platform Guidelines, see, W. Huang et al., Antitrust Guidelines for the Platform Economy in the Era of Enhanced Antitrust Scrutiny, CPI (Mar. 2021), https://www.competitionpolicyinternational.com/wp-content/uploads/2021/03/10-Antitrust-Guidelines-for-the-Platform-Economy-in-the-Era-of-Enhanced-Antitrust-Scrutiny-By-Wei-Huang-Wendy-Zhou-Xiumin-Ruan-Xi-Zhang.pdf.

also divide exclusive dealing into two sub-categories: one where the arrangement is to be implemented by means of punitive measures and the other, by positive incentive measures, and suggest different regulatory approaches toward them. Specifically, exclusive dealing implemented by punitive measures will directly harm market competition and consumer interests, and thus shall generally be banned. For exclusive dealing arrangements based on incentive measures, the Platform Guidelines state these may have certain positive effects on the interests of the undertakings operating on the platform, consumer interests, and overall social welfare. However, such practice may also be found to be restrictive dealing if there is evidence showing that it materially eliminates or restricts market competition.[18]

Regarding refusal to deal, Article 14 of the Platform Guidelines specifies factors to be considered in deciding on whether a platform function or access constitutes an essential facility and what justifications are "valid." It is worth noting that a valid reason might be that "the counterparties have expressly refused to or actually failed to comply with fair, reasonable and non-discriminatory platform rules." This indicates that Chinese antitrust rule-makers accept the globally popular fair, reasonable, and non-discriminatory (FRAND) rule in IPR licensing and apply it to antitrust in the digital economy without much hesitation. The above justification was used in a well-known refusal to deal court ruling which was selected as one of the ten most influential cases of internet judiciary in China by the Supreme People's Court.[19]

Article 17 of the Platform Guidelines sets out that "undertakings in platform economy with market dominance may, without justification, abuse their market dominance to apply differentiated treatment to counterparties with the same transaction conditions, thereby excluding or restricting market competition." One of the factors to be considered in assessing whether an undertaking has engaged in discriminatory treatment is "by using big data and algorithms, applying differentiated transaction prices or other transaction conditions according to the payment capacity, consumer preference, user habits, and etc. of the counterparties." Thus, the Platform Guidelines specifically address the hot issue of price discrimination on the part of large platforms which have huge competitive advantages thanks to their capability for gathering and processing personal user data, with the help of AI and algorithms.

The Platform Guidelines also contain provisions regarding mergers and acquisitions in the digital economy. In particular, Article 20 stipulates that when evaluating the competition effects of mergers that involve platforms, the agency

18 This distinction is considered to be one of the main breakthroughs made by the PLATFORM GUIDELINES (*id.*). We will provide an evaluation of this after we review the *Alibaba* "either/or" case later in this chapter.

19 The case was Shenzhen WeiRMBma Software Development Co., Ltd. v. Tencent Technology (Shenzhen) Co., Ltd. and Shenzhen Tencent Computer System Co., Ltd., (2017) for alleged abuse of market dominance. The intermediate court ruled that since the plaintiff had breached the Operation Specifications and Service Agreement agreed by both parties, it is proper for Tencent to suspend the account of the plaintiff according to the Operation Specifications and Service Agreement. See, Shenzhen Weiyuanma Software Development Co., Ltd. v. Tencent Technology (Shenzhen) Co., Ltd. China Intellectual Property (http://chinaipmagazine.com/).

"may need to consider both sides or multi-sides of the platform, as well other types of businesses of undertakings, and need to value the direct and indirect networks effects that may be present." In addition, the Platform Guidelines also refer to acquisitions of start-ups by platforms and state that potential effects on innovation will be considered in merger review, echoing the widely discussed "killer acquisitions." In the provisions regarding merger remedies, the following means of structural and behavioral remedies are explicitly listed, reflecting the distinctive features of the digital economy: 1 Divesture of tangible assets and intangible assets such as intellectual property rights, technology, and data, 2 Opening internet access, data or platform, licensing key technology, ceasing exclusive agreements, modifying platform rules or algorithms, commitment or interoperability or not to lowering the level of interoperability (Article 21).

As explained by the State Council Anti-Monopoly Commission of the during a press interview released on February 7, 2021,[20]monopolistic behaviors in the platform economy have their own characteristics. For instance: 1 the behavior is more concealed, and the use of tools, such as data and algorithms, among others, may help operators to quickly exchange sensitive information making it more difficult to discover and determine monopoly agreements, 2 it is easier to reach hub-and-spoke agreements, made possible by using algorithms or other technical tools, to assume the role of market organizer and coordinate the activities of other operators on the platform, as well as to determine or interfere in the price-setting mechanism, and 3 platform operators may impose trading conditions, in terms of price and quantities, on merchants within the platform compared to those of other platforms, thus restricting competition among different platforms.

The promotion of the Platform Guidelines is a clear signal that China is ready to regulate "monopolistic conduct" in its platform/digital economy. It is worth noting that the Platform Guidelines were published during the four-month investigation of the landmark case of Alibaba's exclusive dealing conduct in the market for online retailing platform services. We will review the *Alibaba* case in detail below.

2. China's Gatekeeper Regulation: Stricter Regulations on the Way?

Another important development is the publication of two sets of draft guidelines which resemble the EU's gatekeeper system, albeit still yet to be formally published. In particular, in October 2021, China issued two draft guidelines regarding the antitrust regulation of platforms, or public consultation. The first set of guidelines is entitled the Guidelines on Classification of Internet Platforms, which classify platforms into six categories according to the nature of businesses they perform and their sizes. Specifically, the Draft Classification Guidelines

20 *See* https://gkml.samr.gov.cn/nsjg/xwxcs/202102/t20210207_325971.html; see Yajie Gao & Wei Han, *The Chinese State Administration for Market Regulation publishes anti-monopoly guidelines on platform economy*, E-COMPETITIONS February 2021, art. No. 99227.

define super large platforms as those having more than 50 million users, a wide range of business types, and a market value of more than 100 billion RMB (approx. $16 billion), a description that would apply to tech giants such as Alibaba Group, Tencent Holdings and Meituan.

The second set of guidelines, The Guidelines for Business Responsibilities of Internet Platforms (here within Draft Responsibility Guidelines), specifies various "duties" or "responsibilities" of the so-called super-large platforms.[21] These listed duties are very specific and range from antitrust to consumer protection, as well privacy protection. The key for the second set of guidelines is that platforms must bear extra duties if they are larger sized, an approach similar to the gatekeeper classification of the recent EU regulation.[22] The responsibilities outlined by the SAMR relate to issues for which some big tech companies have already been criticized recently as part of a wide-ranging crackdown by Chinese regulators. It said that super large platforms should abide by the principles of fairness when offering services and should open their services up to other platform operators. They should not obtain data without user consent and should be transparent when using big data to recommend products.

Article 1 of the Draft Responsibility Guidelines provides that: 1 without valid reasons, super-platforms shall not utilize the unpublicized data generated or provided by the undertakings or their customers when using the platform services, and 2 shall not require users to use services of other related platforms as a condition for visiting, registering, logging-in or accessing platform services.

Article 2 specifies that super-platforms adhere to a fair and non-discriminatory principle. In providing products or services, they must treat themselves (or related undertakings) and undertakings using the platform equally and shall not engage in self-preferencing. Article 3 provides that super-platforms shall promote interoperability between services and those provided by other platforms. Unless justified with valid reasons, a super-platform shall provide convenience to other undertakings or users in obtaining its services.

Article 9 provides that super-platforms shall utilize their advantages in data, funds, personnel, users and technologies to increase investments in innovation, enhance technological capability, target core innovation, and help SMEs to innovate, thereby invigorating the innovative capacity of the platform.

---

21 See The Notice for the Public Consultation on the Draft Guidelines for Business Responsibilities of Internet Platforms 关于对《互联网平台分类分级指南（征求意见稿）》《互联网平台落实主体责任指南（征求意见稿）》公开征求意见的公告 (samr.gov.cn), https://www.samr.gov.cn/hd/zjdc/202110/t20211027_336137.html.

22 In December 2020, the European Commission published its much-anticipated draft Digital Markets Act (DMA) which imposes a suite of regulatory obligations on digital platforms who meet the requirements of "gatekeeper" for one or more pre-defined services. A company will be considered a gatekeeper for one or more core platform services if it: (1) operates a core platform service which serves as an important gateway for business users to reach end users; (2) has a significant impact on the internal market; and (3) enjoys an entrenched and durable position in its operations or it is foreseeable that it will enjoy such a position in the near future. The DMA was enacted in September, 2022. See https://competition-policy.ec.europa.eu/dma_en.

The Draft Responsibility Guidelines also contain provisions regarding such non-antitrust matters as data security, risk management, platform governance, etc.

Two major points are worth discussing in relation to the two sets of Draft Guidelines. First, while there have been discussions and concerns regarding the various problems that giant tech platforms have been raising in China as well as in other digital economies, the challenge is how to "embed public values in platforms" and how to hold them accountable. Regarding this, the two sets of draft guidelines are designed to fulfill main social objectives. For instance, the Draft Responsibilities Guidelines states that:

> Internet platforms shall maintain national interest and societal public interests, safeguard the health, livelihood and property of the people, adhere to the principles of voluntary, equal, fair, and credibility, obey the laws, regulations, commercial ethics, public order and virtue customs, enhance openness and creativity, participate in market competition in a fair manner, sincerely fulfill the legal obligations, actively assume their obligations, and accept monitoring by the public.

Second, within the scope of antitrust provisions under the two sets of draft guidelines, some potential trade-offs or even inconsistencies are yet to be further considered in terms of the responsibilities set for super-large platforms. For example, banning self-preferences unconditionally may have adverse impact on innovation (Article 2 versus Article 9). Also, requiring interoperability (Article 3) without limit may also affect the degree of product differentiation and multi-homing, as economic theory might suggest. How to balance different goals set out in the Responsibility Guidelines and evaluating the underlying trade-offs seem to deserve further and careful consideration.

We believe that these two sets of draft guidelines, if promulgated as they are now, will have profound impact on China's anti-monopoly regulation and on the developments of the platform economy. The Chinese Government should caution on how to move forward. More importantly, these two sets of draft guidelines have adopted the presumption that "being large means anti-competitive" which is inconsistent with the rule of reason approach (or an effects-based approach) that traditionally antitrust adopts towards conduct of dominant firms. While the draft guidelines are not meant to tackle competition issues solely, the antitrust provisions should at least not be at odd with the current approach of the AML system which after all is the main competition law of China. From the perspective of the "error-cost" minimization approach introduced by Easterbrook (1984), new antitrust rules should balance the social costs of the "false positives" against that of the "false negatives."[23] As they are currently, the draft guidelines seem likely to lead to significant false positive regulatory errors, because of the "structural approach" they seem to have adopted.

---

23 Frank H. Easterbrook, *The Limits of Antitrust*, 63 Tex. L. Rev. 1–40 (1984).

Secondly, after the antitrust crackdown of big tech firms, such as Alibaba, Meituan, and others (see the next section on the case of *Alibaba*). The market seems to have cooled down substantially, for the fear of even further antitrust probes and fines for problematic business practices that may be deemed to be anti-competitive in the digital economy. China's policymakers may have come now to the belief that the powers generated by these recent antitrust developments have proved to be much bigger and stronger than previously expected. In fact, at its nationwide annual meeting in January 2022, the Head of SAMR, Ms. Gan Lin stressed the need to better manage the market expectation and pay attention to macroeconomic stability. That can be a sign of adjustment in the speed and strength of AML enforcement, shortly after the drastic developments in 2021 which saw the closing the landmark case of *Alibaba* and historic fine, promulgation of China's Platform Guidelines, and the amendment of the AML which incorporates substantial provisions towards monopolistic behavior in the digital economy to its 14 years old competition law.

V. Alibaba's "Either/Or" Case (2021)

1. Background

On December 24, 2020, SAMR initiated an investigation on Alibaba, one of the largest tech giants in China, for its "either- or" provision with its merchants. Alibaba owns two of China's largest e-commerce platforms, Tmall and TaoBao. The "either/or" clauses prevent Alibaba's contracted merchant from selling on other rival platforms. In April 2021, SAMR punished Alibaba for its "either/or" clauses, which abused Alibaba's dominant market position. This case, which will be studied in detail in the next section, marks a turning point in China's antitrust interventions in the platform economy in the swift shift from a very tolerant and cautious approach towards a more proactive and stringent one.[24]

Alibaba introduced "either/or" clauses with its largest merchants either contractually or verbally in 2015. Under the "either/or" clause, merchants wishing to sell their products or services on Alibaba's online retail platform are prohibited from selling on or even engaging with Alibaba's rival platforms. To provide incentives, Alibaba rewarded the merchants who stuck to "either/or" with user traffic support and punished those who did not through such means as disqualification for sale promotion, less search visibility, and reduced resource support, etc.[25] There had been complaints and reports from the affected merchants and from other platforms since 2015. However, the antitrust authority did not take consequential action until December 24, 2020, when the SAMR started an investigation into the controversial "either/or" clause.

---

24 Y. Xiao, *China's Antitrust Probe into the Platform Economy–A Comment on the Alibaba Decision*, 71 GRUR INT. 432–38 (May 2022).

25 *See Alibaba* Decision *supra* note 2, see Alexandr Svetlicinii, *The Chinese State Administration for Market Regulation fines an online market platform $2.8 billion for abusing its dominant position (Alibaba)*, E-COMPETITIONS March 2021, art. No. 100212.

Less than four months later, SAMR found that Alibaba abused its dominant position in the online retail platform services market with the "either/or" conduct and levied a fine of 18.228 billion RMB (approx. $2.8 billion). The penalty imposed, equivalent to % of the company's 2019 turnovers in China, is the heftiest ever for a contravention of the AML and is three times higher than the second-biggest fine given to Qualcomm in 2015.[26]

2. SAMR's Administrative Decision

A. *Relevant Market Definition*

The SAMR in its decision defined the relevant antitrust market of this case as online retail platform service market within China's territory.

The Decision states that online retail platform services include the provision of virtual marketplace, transaction facilitation, and information hub. The SAMR regards each online retail platform as a two-sided market, with two groups of users, namely the merchants and the buyers on the two sides of a such platform. The SAMR applied economic principles to its reasoning as well: it acknowledges that one of the prominent features of a two-sided market is the indirect/cross-side network effect. The indirect network effect says that the utility (or value) one group of users gain by participating in the two-sided market depends on the number of users from the other group. In the case of Alibaba, SAMR states, there is a positive "cross-side network effect": merchants would benefit more if more buyers were on the platform, and vice versa.

Applying the demand substitution test, as set up in the Guidelines for Defining Antitrust Relevant Markets, promulgated by the Anti-Monopoly Commission of the State Council in 2008, SAMR found that the retail services provided by the traditional brick-and-mortar stores, were not a close substitute for the online retail platform service. It performed such a test through a comprehensive analysis concerning both the demand and the supply side. In terms of demand, the two services differ in terms of service location, time frame, cost, buyer-matching efficiency, and marketing feedback for the merchants. The buyers also find different product scopes, convenience levels, and match efficiencies from the two services. On the supply side, the two services have different profit modes: online platforms profit from commissions and advertisement fees, while offline service usually earns turnover from commercial rent.

Next, SAMR's relevant market definition analysis involved whether the online platform market can be sectioned. It found that the services provided by the platform belong to one market, independent of the merchant groups, sale methods, and product types. As the last step to define the relevant market,

26 S. Colino, *The Case against Alibaba in China and its Wider Policy Repercussions*, 10 J. Antitrust Enforc. 217–29 (Mar. 2022).

SAMR defined China as the relevant geographical market. The reason is that there is barely any foreign substitute for the Chinese platform due to substantial startup costs. On the demand side, users seldom use overseas platform services due to indirect network effects, language barriers, after-sale services, and switching costs.

B. *Determination of Market Dominance*

To establish Alibaba's dominant market position, SAMR took several factors into account, in line with the provisions of the AML, including market share, market concentration, ability to influence the market, financial and technological strengths and resources, and entry barriers. SAMR pointed out that Alibaba's market share ranged from the highest of 86.07% to the lowest of 71.17% between 2015 and 2019. The HHI indexes in the relevant market in those five years were 7408, 6008, 6375, 5925, and 5350, respectively, whereas the CR4 were 99.68, 99.46, 98.92, 98.66, and 98.45. Both indexes indicate an extremely high level of market concentration, the decision noted. In addition, SAMR also noted that Alibaba had control over service prices, buyer traffic, and sale channels. Those advantages, together with its affluent financial and technological resources, locked in Alibaba's users at both sides of the platform and made entry rather difficult due to the indirect network effect. Based on all those facts, the SAMR established Alibaba's dominant market position in the relevant market of China's online retail platform services.

3. Identify Abuse

Alibaba was accused of abuse of its dominant market position by restricting its merchants from selling or participating in promotional activities on competing platforms. SAMR first noted that to incentivize such exclusive obligation, Alibaba took a "carrot-and-stick" approach, where the "obedient" merchants would be rewarded with more tech support or more buyer traffic, and the merchants who did not follow such obligation would be punished with downgrade in search results, cancellation of certain rights, and exclusion from promotional exercises. To make this reward–punishment mechanism work, Alibaba monitored its merchants using its big data and advanced algorithms.

The decision states that during the investigation Alibaba claimed: 1 that the contracts signed were voluntary on the part of the suppliers and that specific investments were included as consideration as incentive measure, there having valid reasons, and 2 it implemented the restrictions only to those suppliers that did not obey the contractual terms, with the purpose of protecting the specific investments necessary for the transactions.

SAMR rejected the above explanations of Alibaba. The decision states that: 1 most of the "either/or" contracts were not signed voluntarily by the suppliers, 2 some of the suppliers who kept to the contract terms did not get the "considerations" or discount from Alibaba. SAMR further argues that "the exclusionary contract" was not indispensable for protecting the "specific investments"; the investments made by the platform during its routine operations were necessary for its own operations, rather than made for the benefits of the merchants who use the platform. SAMR supports its above claims with evidence obtained from Alibaba's internal documents including email and chat records, business plans and summaries of subdivisions, as well as contractual agreements signed with some merchants, interviews with Alibaba staff, and so on.

SAMR found that Alibaba's practice restrained and excluded competition, harming both merchant and consumer interests, hindered the efficiency of resource allocation, and curbed innovation. By preventing its merchants from engaging with other platforms, Alibaba restricted the user supply to rival platforms. Moreover, fewer merchants make the rival platform less attractive to the buyers due to the indirect network effect. Alibaba's tight grab on its merchants also prevented potential entrants from entering the market. The "either/or" conduct also damaged the merchants' autonomy on platform choices, SAMR argued. Also, the punishment induced by Alibaba for merchants' failure to cooperate harmed the merchants.

SAMR concludes that "Alibaba Group restricted its users to contract with other competing platforms or participating in promotional activities organized by other platforms, led to a 'lock-in' effect, so as to weaken the competitive pressure it faced, thus unreasonably maintained and entrenched its market position. Such conduct betrayed the idea of open, inclusive, and sharing for platform development, SAMR continues, and excluded and restricted competition in the relevant market, harmed the interests of the platform suppliers and consumers, weakened the innovation motive and development rigor, and curbed the orderly, creative, and health development of the digital economy."

In supporting its claims, SAMR laid out detailed arguments for the above-mentioned aspects respectively, as presented below.

A. *Restricting and Excluding Competition in the Online-Retailing Services Market*

First, regarding restriction and exclusion of competition in the online-retailing services market, SAMR referred to the conceptions of cross-market network effect, arguing that Alibaba's "either/or" contract had the effect of reducing the number of consumers of other competing platforms by decreasing the number of suppliers who would have also used those platforms.

Moreover, SAMR argued that the Alibaba "either/or" contract had also prevented potential competition. Its reasoning is that due to the network and scale effect of the platform economy, potential competitors would need to have certain levels of merchants who would collaborate with them before they could profitably enter the market. Alibaba's contract raised the difficulties of potential platform service providers to reach suppliers as many of those have been locked in with Alibaba's platform under its contract, thereby raising the entry barriers and restricting the potential competition in the relevant market.

B. *Harmed the Interests of the Platform Merchants*

SAMR reasoned that Alibaba's conduct had directly restricted the business autonomy of the platform merchants, reduced the intra-brand competition with respect to the products and services to be sold on the platform, and harmed the interests of those merchants.

Regarding business autonomy, SAMR argued that as different platforms service different groups of consumers so merchants normally prefer multi-homing to raise efficiency, obtaining multiple distribution channels to reach a wider range of consumers, to realize greater sales. Alibaba's "either/or" conduct deprived the merchants of the right to choose collaborating platforms, thereby restricting their managerial autonomy.

Secondly, the "either/or" requirement had disrupted the operation stability of the merchants who had to cancel their planned transactions with other platforms, resulting in promotional and inventory losses for those merchants. Such unfair requirements directly harmed the interests of the merchants, including the foregone sales from other platforms.

Lastly, SAMR claimed, merchants selling the same brands would benefit from intra-brand competition via different platforms, especially during promotional periods when platforms would use subsidies to attract merchants. The "either/or" conduct therefore restricted the range of platforms a merchant could choose from, thereby reducing intra-brand competition.

C. *Hindering Efficient Allocation of Resources and Restricting Development of the Platform Economy*

Thirdly, SAMR's decision specifically argued that Alibaba's "either/or" contract "had curbed the efficiency allocation of resources, hindered the rigors of market entities, and restricted innovation and development of the platform economy." Here, SAMR focused on the effects of Alibaba's contract on platform users' ways of selling their products or services. In particular, it argued that because of the restrictions the "either/or" contract imposed on them, platform users' decisions with respect to which platforms to choose to sell their products or services had been unduly restricted. This adversely affected free flow of production factors among different platforms and, consequently, lowered the matching efficiency between supply and demand, thereby decreasing the distribution efficiency of economy activities.

Furthermore, the "ether/or" contract also hindered the range of product differentiation on the part of the platform users who had been affected by the contract, by preventing them from distributing their products in other platforms that would compete with Alibaba. These foregone business collaboration opportunities had restricted the innovation activities of these business firms.

Lastly, SAMR stated that Alibaba's "either/or" contract had decreased the innovation incentive of other competing platforms (actual or potential), by maintaining and enriching its competitive advantages via unfair method of competition. This has hindered the innovative and healthy development of the platform economy which depends on fair competition and technological progress.

D. *Restricting "the Interests of the Consumers"*

The fourth SAMR argument centers on the effects of Alibaba's "either/or" contract on the "interests of the consumers." Specifically, the decision states that Alibaba's conduct had restricted consumers' rights to free choice and fair trade, by limiting the range of brands and commodities available in online retailing platforms, and by forcing consumers to passively accept the offers available on a given platform. In the long-term, SAMR continued, that "either/or" contractual arrangements would potentially cause harm to aggregate social welfare. This is so, SAMR claims, because Alibaba's conduct had restricted market competition, reduced platform operational efficiencies, and hindered business innovation. It had also prevented new entrants to the market and hence reduced the level and intensity of competition. The harms caused would be passed on to final consumers, resulting not only in current losses to consumers but also in reduction of consumers' "expected interests as well as aggregate social welfare." It is worth noting that the decision made reference to the concept of "aggregate social welfare" in this part of the argument, which seems to echo the wording in the Platform Guidelines.[27] We will return to this important point below.

4. Understanding SAMR's Economic Reasoning

The SAMR *Alibaba* decision was a turning pointing in China's antitrust on digital platforms. Below are some reflections about SAMR's reasoning in its decision, particularly from the perspective of economics.

A. *Treating Two Sides of the Platform as a Single Relevant Market*

First, in defining the relevant markets, SAMR specifically pointed out the two-sided market feature of online retail platform services by referring to "the cross-side

27 *See* Platform Guidelines (Article 15) specifically refers to the notions of consumer welfare and "aggregate social welfare" when stating the possible competition effects of restrictive dealing (which includes exclusive dealing).

network effect." As is now known, whether one side of a platform alone constitutes a relevant market or whether it needs to be considered together with other sides of the platform, lies at the core of antitrust market definition in digital economy. Such a task is extremely challenging and there is no accepted economic theory about how this can be done.[28] However, SAMR's decision has considered this issue. It is not clear whether SAMR's market definition was informed and influenced by the classic case Ohio v. American Express Co., the United States Supreme Court considers credit card service networks as a two-sided transaction platform and consequently defines the two sides of the platform as one antitrust relevant market, namely one that combines the card companies' merchant-related services and shopper-related services.[29] But the reasoning, which we see as very solid and convincing, seems very consistent with that in that case. The willingness of SAMR to take on the challenge of defining relevant markets in the digital economy and to incorporate experiences from developed jurisdictions ought to be applauded.

B. *Silence on Declining Market Shares of Alibaba and Counterfactual Perspective*

Second, in its determination of Alibaba's market dominance, SAMR provided some data on market shares as well as HHI of the market. In particular, SAMR stated that Alibaba's annual online retailing market shares since 2015 when it first introduced the "either/or" clause were 86.07% to 71.17%. Specifically, SAMR claimed that among the top ten online retailers in China, Alibaba's market shares in terms of income were 86.07%, 75.77%, 78.51%, 75.44%, and 71.17%, respectively. In terms of transaction volumes of all online retailers in China during this period, Alibaba's market shares were 76.21%, 69.96%, 63.58%, 61.70%, and 61.83%, respectively. While way above the 50% threshold specified in the AML as presumption of possession of market dominance, these data showed a clear trend of decline from 2015. SAMR did not elaborate on how they understood the observed time trend of the market share data in its decision. It simply stated the statistics without any discussion.

Noting that the accused's "either/or" conduct was occurring during this time period, one may tend to infer from Alibaba's declining market share data that its conduct may not have been effective as competing platform market shares were increasing. However, if one appealed to the notion of counterfactual, Alibaba's observed declining market share does not necessarily contradict that its "either/or" conduct was anti-competitive. Logically, under the counterfactual, Alibaba's market share could have been declining faster than the observed time trends.

---

28 *See* for example, OECD, Rethinking Antitrust Tools for Multi-Sided Platforms 42 (2018), https://www.oecd.org/competition/rethinking-antitrust-tools-for-multi-sided-platforms.htm.

29 Ohio v. American Express Co., 138 S. Ct. 2274 (2018), see Natalie Hayes & Carrie C. Mahan, *The US Supreme Court rejects Government antitrust challenge against anti-steering provisions of a credit-card network company (American Express)*, e-Competitions June 2018, art. N° 88732.

In that case, the "either/or" conduct had indeed slowed down the decline of Alibaba's market share. Alternatively, the "either/or" contract had slowed down the growth of the competing online retail platforms, and restricted competition in the relevant market. SAMR could have provided some discussion of Alibaba's observed declining market shares, by referring to the notion of counterfactual. That way, the decision would have been more solid in terms of the economic analysis.

C. *Competition Effects in Complementary Markets?*

Third, in its evaluation, it is clear that SAMR was concerned not only about competition in the relevant market of online retailing services, namely competition among platforms (actual or potential), but also the effects of Alibaba's "either/or" contract on competition among platform users. This concern about competition effects of a dominant firm's conduct in the complementary market, more precisely competition in one side of the dominant firm's platform, seems to need further clarification and justification.

Strictly speaking, platform merchants are users of online retail platform services, and their interests thus belong to the category of "consumer welfare" in antitrust analysis. It seems debatable as to whether competition among the merchants who are group users of online platform retail services ought to be a concern in this particular case. While these merchants' welfare must be considered in evaluating the effects of Alibaba's conduct on competition among platforms who serve them, as the effect on one-side of the market, an evaluation of competition among these merchants themselves seems to be a different matter; after all, what is the relevant market for performing such a competition test and who are the consumers? SAMR did not discuss these issues in its decision.

D. *Other Reflections*

The *Alibaba* decision marked a clear turning point in antitrust enforcement in China's online platform economy with the shift from a very tolerant and cautious approach toward a more proactive and stringent one. Since the decision in 2021, some scholars have written on the *Alibaba* decision, including Marco Colino (2022),[30] Wang and Gao (2022),[31] and Xiao (2022).[32] Among other things, these authors noted the extremely short time-period (less than four months) it took the SAMR to complete this abuse of dominance investigation and to reach a historic administrative fine during the thirteen years' enforcement of China's Anti-Monopoly Law. Such a speedy enforcement action indeed is rare in comparison with other landmark

30 *See* Colino, *supra* note 26.

31 *See* Wang & Gao, *supra* note 15.

32 *See* Xiao, *supra* note 24.

abuse of dominance cases of large platforms. Interestingly, Marco Colino (2022) states that "SAMR ought to continue to target anti-competitive practices in the sector regardless of the perpetrator, without hints of favoritism or protectionism (p. 229)," hinting that China's quick decision on Alibaba may stem from the motive or the need to signal to the rest of the world that China's Anti-Monopoly Law does not target foreign firms only.

We are unsure that this is the main motive behind SAMR's speedy decision in the *Alibaba* case. But the fact that the unusually quick decision in *Alibaba* has caused many to speculate on the real motives of the enforcer is indeed not ideal. More fundamentally, this may be related to the fact that China's Anti-Monopoly Law has been perceived by many to have been tasked with multiple objectives, including protecting competition and the pursuit of industrial policy. Once a law is seen to have been tasked with several and possibly conflicting objectives, it is challenging for the enforcer to inform the market about its true intention in a given case. In particular, theoretically, the motive and intention of an antitrust agency is private information and hence difficult to verify, leaving the public only to infer the true intention based on specific features of a given decision.

It may be noteworthy that although no formal antitrust investigations had been conducted until late 2020 when SAMR's investigation started, competition regulators had laid the groundwork for the probe into Alibaba's abusive conduct over several years. Specifically, since 2015, regulators have held dialogues with individual undertakings, symposiums, and industry guidance meetings to understand the market and to propose non-mandatory compliance requirements to platform companies to address their problematic unfair competition behavior. At the administrative guidance symposium on online business activities joined by about twenty online platform companies in November 2019, SAMR stated that "choose one from two" and other kinds of exclusive dealing arrangements were clearly prohibited by the AML. Put differently, the competition agency had been preparing for the investigation of Alibaba's "either/or" conduct way before the official investigation in late 2020 and its administrative decision less than four months later in April 2021.[33]

VI. An Evaluation of China's Antitrust System for its Digital Economy

In less than two years, from late 2020 and June 2022, China established a structured antitrust system toward its digital economy based on its 2007 AML and fourteen years' enforcement experiences since. It achieved remarkable outcome by drafting and promulgating detailed guidelines with swift and powerful enforcement actions towards its homegrown giant internet companies, in response

33 *Id.*

to the domestical demand for curbing "monopolistic conduct" in its rapidly developing digital economy. Based on the reviews in the previous sections, we offer here an evaluation on China's achievement. We focus on the following aspects: 1 the speedy development, 2 influences by international debates and discussions surrounding antitrust reforms/improvements in digital economy, 3 the economic foundation of the new system, and 4 total welfare standard or consumer standard?

1. Speedy Developments

On February 7, 2021, China's State Council Antimonopoly Commission promulgated the world's first antitrust guidelines on the platform economy, the Platform Guidelines which took less than seventy days to complete after the end of the consultation period. While previous antitrust guidelines usually took years to be officially promulgated, the Platform Guidelines set the record for taking the shortest time. This demonstrates China's determination to intensify antitrust scrutiny on the platform economy (Huang et al. 2021).[34] The Platform Guidelines clarify the antitrust rules for the platform economy, taking thorough account of the unique features of the digital economy, with the aim of providing detailed guidance for AML enforcement in China. This came from the Government's realization in late 2020 that its rapidly developing digital economy might well be entering a stage of "monopoly" and hence swift action was needed.

In terms of enforcement, it took SAMR less than four months to investigate and decide on the case of abuse of dominance by Alibaba, along with other less publicized enforcement actions against other giant platforms (e.g., in the area of mergers). While one may note that some prior work had been carried out regarding Alibaba's conduct before the official investigation in late 2020, as mentioned earlier, reaching a decision on an alleged abuse case following "the rule of reason approach" in less than four months appears extraordinary swift by any standard. In future, it is of crucial importance that SAMR be given an ample amount of time to perform its duties, particularly for abuse of dominance cases in the digital economy. Time is also a resource for antitrust enforcement. A sufficient amount of time is needed to reach a balanced decision. This is especially so in the case of China whose AML system is only fifteen years' old. From the perspective of the economics of information, antitrust reasoning in a given case is credible only if seen to be so by the market.

We believe that, because of its complexity, and the effect-oriented approach as informed by industrial economics, antitrust regulation is better seen as a "dialogue" between the enforcer and the market. By upholding the legal and economic principles behind the law, the regulator informs the market participants what conduct ought to be prohibited and in what cases, whereas market

---

34 *See* Huang et al., *supra* note 17.

participants at large react to enforcement, particularly landmark cases, by adjusting their conduct, including scaling up or down their future investments in response to perceived risks. China seems to have started to recognize the importance of this two-way relationship between antitrust regulation and market.

2. Informed by World-Wide Debate Surrounding Antitrust in Digital Economy

Over the past few years, academic and policy research in China on antitrust in the digital economy has been ongoing. Discussions and debates on the challenges antitrust faces have informed and influenced Chinese scholars, law enforcers and policymakers. Views and insights from policy reports by reputable international institutions and research teams were taken into account when new guidelines were designed and the AML amended.[35]

Indeed, the newly published Platform Guidelines, as well as the amendments to China's AML both refer to some basic concepts in antitrust economics of digital economy with specific mentioning of such concepts as network effect, two-sided market, user lock-in, algorithm, switching costs, and specific investments in business relationships, data-driven acquisitions, etc. The Platform Guidelines also provide that when defining relevant markets in the digital economy, all sides of a multi-market platform can be reviewed as one single relevant market, if cross-side demand interdependence is substantial. As reviewed above, in the *Alibaba* case, SAMR indeed applied this approach, and correctly in the authors' view.

For each given type of conduct, specific economic concepts are also provided. For example, the Platform Guidelines specifically list "protecting specific investments" as one possible "valid reasons" for justifying "exclusive dealing." This is a clear recognition of the economic principles that industrial economics provides for understanding the competition effects of exclusive dealing. While widely accepted in antitrust economics, the concept of specific investment is relatively new to China's AML regime. Explicit reference to the concept and the role of specific investments officially in the Platform Guidelines is another demonstration of SAMR's learning and accepting of modern antitrust economic reasoning in its rule-setting. All the above certainly ought be applauded.[36]

---

35 Including the influential "the Crémer Report", "the Furman Report", and the "Stigler Report", see, respectively, J. Crémer et al., Competition Policy for the Digital Era (2019), https://ec.europa.eu/competition/publications/reports/kd0419345enn.pdf; J. Furman et al., Unlocking Digital Competition: Report of the Digital Competition Expert Panel (2019), https://assets.publishing.service.gov.uk/government/uploads/system/uploads/attachment_data/file/785547/unlocking_digital_competition_furman_review_web.pdf; and Stigler Center for the Study of the Economy and State, Stigler Committee for Digital Platforms: Final Report (2019), https://www.chicagobooth.edu/-/media/research/stigler/pdfs/digital-platforms---committee-report---stigler-center.pdf.

36 *See* Interim Provisions on Prohibiting Abuse of Dominant Market Positions (Article 17) (《禁止滥用市场支配地位行为暂行规定》), promulgated by SAMR on June 26, 2019, provided a list of valid reasons for exclusive dealing, including the necessity to satisfy product safety requirements, to protect intellectual property rights, and to protect transaction-specific investments, etc. The Interim Provisions aim to provide more guidance to the public as to how SAMR would go about investigating possible cases of abuse of dominant market positions under the AML, particularly on what it would consider as "valid reasons" under the relevant provisions.

3. More Economics is Needed to Support the Details in Regulation and Enforcement

Nonetheless, there are certain places in the new legislation and enforcement where further clarifications and even re-considerations are needed.

Taking the amended AML as a point of demonstration, specifically stating "algorithms" in general competition law (in provisions on collusion and abuse of dominance) seems unnecessary. After all, algorithms are just a type of technology, albeit new and complex. In future, technological progress will certainly continue to lead to even more advanced technologies that might help facilitate collusion or sustain abusive behavior. Contents of a general competition law ought to be "technology-neutral" (so to speak) and need not match too closely with industrial specifics at a given point of time. In addition, to define "algorithm" legally may not be an easy task in given enforcement cases.

Certain places in China's new antitrust system also seem to call for further economic reasoning. For instance, what is the standard when determining the legality of exclusive dealing such as "either/or" conduct? How should one go about evaluating the competition effects of exclusive dealing in a given case? The Platform Guidelines provide some guidance but may have raised some new questions.

The Platform Guidelines do attempt to provide structured reasoning for evaluating exclusive dealing. In particular, the guidelines distinguish two situations: one where exclusive dealing is implemented via punitive measures and the other, via rewards (subsidies, discounts, and user traffic support). The Platform Guidelines state that the first type of exclusive dealing can "normally be decided as" breach of the AML, whereas positive-incentive based exclusive dealing "may have positive impacts on platform users, consumer interests and aggregate social welfare, and may be decided as anti-competitive if there is evidence of restricting and excluding market competition" (Article 15). As specified, the Platform Guidelines seem to hold that punishment-based "either/or" contracts are normally illegal seems to echo views of some legal scholars in China that "forced 'either/or'" conduct should be prohibited.[37]

It is not clear that the competition effect of an "either/or" contract should be determined based on whether it is voluntary between the parties or "forced" by one party on another. If one takes the perspective of the economics behind exclusive dealing, whether exclusive dealing conduct is anti-competitive or not crucially depends on whether specific investments are a key element for establishing and maintaining an efficient relationship between the two parties, and whether or not free riding problems are prevalent in the absence of an exclusive dealing arrangement. If specific investments are crucial and free riding on the

37 See, e.g., Wang (2021) in which the author (a very prominent and influential antitrust scholar in China) argued that coercive "either/or" conduct is anticompetitive and hence should be banned under the AML.

part of competitors is prevalent, there will exist incentives for the two parties concerned to find ways to protect the specific investments. However, the means to achieve protection of specific investments may not be unique. In fact, a contract phrased in terms of a punishment can be equally viewed as one with a reward arrangement. It is not clear how one can distinguish between the two but in substance it is the same arrangement.[38] In this sense, the distinction made in the Platform Guidelines, which had been regarded as one of the bright points of the guidelines (Huang et al. 2021), deserves further consideration.[39]

Likewise, the Draft Responsibilities Guidelines are silent on such important issues such as how does banning self-preferencing potentially affect competition and innovation, and how to achieve the best trade-off between short-term competition and long-run competition. These issues are fundamental and need to be further addressed as well.

4. Consumer Welfare Standard or Total Welfare Standard?

The Platform Guidelines (Article 15) refer to the concept of "aggregate social welfare" (社会整体福利), a rare use of this concept in antitrust since China's AML in 2008. This in itself is something remarkable, because it has never been made clear by either the enforcement agency or courts in China whether the AML adopts consumer welfare standards (as per competition law in the US and EU) or total welfare standards (as in some countries e.g., Canada). Rather, it appears that the issue of welfare standards has not been taken as a core issue in China's antitrust legislation during the fourteen years of AML enforcement. Nor has it received due attention from academia. While a few studies have stressed its crucial role in antitrust and China's seemingly lack of it so far (*see* e.g., Lin and Zhao 2012),[40] China is yet to officially declare the welfare standards its AML uses and intended to use when it came into effect in 2007. The usage of "aggregate social welfare" in the 2021 Platform Guidelines, whether intended or not, is of historical significance one may argue. The inclusion of social welfare rather than consumer welfare in the Platform Guideline is consistent with the argument that China's AML when drafted in 2007 implicitly had total welfare as its welfare standard, as argued by (Lin 2012), for instance.

---

38 For instance, suppose that party A offers the following contract with party B: you will be paid $x if you choose not to deal with other platforms, or nothing otherwise. This may be regarded as a "penalty-based" contract in that B will be punished via a reduction in support/payment if it chooses to deal with A's competing platforms. Equally, the above contract could be framed or structured as B is paid nothing if it (continues to/chooses to) deal with some of A's competing platforms, but will be rewarded $x if it instead chooses to deal with A exclusively. For a rational party, the above two statements are clearly equivalent, but framed differently. The framing effect can be described as a cognitive bias wherein an individual's choice from a set of options is influenced more by the presentation than the substance of the pertinent information (see, A. Tversky & D. Kahneman, *The Framing of Decisions and the Psychology of Choice*, 211 SCIENCE 453–58 (1981)). For a discussion of application of behavioral economics to antitrust, see, G. De Moncuit, *Relevance and shortcomings of behavioural economics in antitrust deterrence*, 11 J.E.C.L. & PRACT. 228–237 (2020).

39 *See* Huang et al., *supra* note 17.

40 P. Lin & J. Zhao, *Merger Control Policy under China's Anti-Monopoly Law*, 41 REV. INDUST. ORGAN. 109–132 (2012).

However, there are differences between the administrative decisions in the *Alibaba* "either/or" case and another landmark "either/or" case against China's online food delivery giant Meituan, which ended six months later on October 8, 2021. As shown in the SAMR Meituan decision, the effects on consumer welfare were analyzed, and no mention was made of "aggregate social welfare."[41] It is not clear why these two decisions by SAMR have not used the same description in terms of welfare standards.

In sum, China needs to pay particular attention to the issue of welfare standard in future AML enforcement, and clearly and formally specify its standard, whether in the digital economy or not. Only when this critical step is made, can China's antitrust system be said to enter into a matured stage.

VII. Concluding Remarks

Through the recent developments in China's Anti-Monopoly Law system subsequent to 2020, China has established an antitrust regulation framework for its digital economy, as reflected in a series of legislation, new guidelines, and landmark cases against its giant tech firms. The new competition rules and case rulings are informed by global discussions and debates on how to best meet the challenges the digital economy places on antitrust. With these developments, China signals to the markets and the rest of the world that it is ready to curb anti-competitive conduct in the digital era.

Taken together, China's newly established antitrust regulatory system, as reflected in its Platform Guidelines and relevant provisions of the amended AML, and in SAMR's ruling in the *Alibaba* exclusive dealing case, is well-structured, and largely in line with economic understanding of competition in a digital economy that economists have to offer so far. It is indeed remarkable for a young antitrust jurisdiction, the second largest economy in the world, to have achieved this within fifteen years.

However, two main challenges remain ahead for China which are: 1 to support this system with more solid economic reasoning, and 2 to best balance protection of competition with the other social goals of the newly promulgated rules which are also important for China's governance of its rapidly developing digital economy.

41 On Oct. 8, 2021, SAMR imposed a $534 million fine on Meituan for abusing its dominant market share in food delivery to force restaurants into exclusivity arrangements. It's similar to the violation and penalty levied against which was fined $2.8 billion.

Conduct Analysis in Digital Cases: a Review of the Brazilian Antitrust Authority Decisions

CAMILA C. PIRES-ALVES,
LUIZ CARLOS DELORME PRADO, EDUARDO P. RIBEIRO
AND DIANDRA C. DE OLIVEIRA VIEIRA DA ROCHA*
GDEC Research Group**
Institute of Economics – Federal University of Rio de Janeiro (IE-UFRJ)

---

* Camila C. Pires-Alves Associate Professor at the Institute of Economics of the Federal University of Rio de Janeiro (IE-UFRJ). She coordinates the Research Group in Law, Economics, and Competition (GDEC/IE-UFRJ) as well as the Graduate Program in Economics (IE-UFRJ). Email: camila.alves@ie.ufrj.br; Luiz Carlos Delorme Prado is Associate Professor of Economics at the Institute of Economics, Federal University of Rio de Janeiro (UFRJ) and director coordinator of the PPED – Graduate Program of Public Policy of Federal University of Rio de Janeiro. Member of the Research Group on Law, Economics and Competition of the Institute of Economics, UFRJ. Former Commissioner at CADE. Email: lcdprado@gmail.com; Eduardo P. Ribeiro is Professor of Economics at the Institute of Economics of the Federal University of Rio de Janeiro (UFRJ) and is a co-coordinator in the Competition Law and Economics Research Group (GDEC) at UFRJ. Email: eribeiro@ie.ufrj.br; Diandra C. de Oliveira Vieira da Rocha is PhD Candidate in Economics at the Federal University of Rio de Janeiro (UFRJ) and researcher at GDEC. Email: diandra.rocha@ppge.ie.ufrj.br.

** We thank Y. Katsoulacos for comments and discussions and S. Golovanova for extensive ideas exchanges on legal standards without implicating them for any errors. Disclaimers: (i) L.C.D. Prado and E. Pontual Ribeiro acted as commissioners at CADE Tribunal when some of the cases cited in the chapter were decided; (ii) the authors have not been retained by any party in the cases in Table 1. This chapter is an independent research work and the conclusions and statements should not be taken as the official position of the institutions with which we are associated. Pontual Ribeiro acknowledges the partial financial support from CNPq. Corresponding author: Eduardo Pontual Ribeiro eribeiro@ie.ufrj.br.

Abstract

This chapter explores the legal standard used by CADE, the Brazilian antitrust authority, in digital platform abuse of dominance or vertical restraints cases. The analysis of digital cases has used the same legal framework as in non-digital cases. The analysis contrasts the decision-making process in non-merger digital cases using a legal standard classification. The relatively short case experience does reveal some patterns. In unilateral abuse of dominance cases, such as the Google shopping case, the majority report stands with an efficiency presumption, stemming from the innovation characteristics of the platforms (amplified by the Easterbrook hypothesis of harm from unwarranted antitrust intervention). On vertical restraints, such as exclusive dealings and MFN clauses, in a truncated rule of reason, these are presumed to be illegal. The decision often rests on the presumption of harm from the exclusion of rivals. Digital platform competition characteristics such as network effects and the potential for market tipping contributed to the harm presumption.

I. Introduction

Digital technologies and digital markets have been evolving fast in emerging countries as they are in developed countries in the last twenty years, and there is a growing debate as how the antitrust authorities should address the challenges of analyzing and enforcing competition policy in digital markets especially for the large technology companies (Big-Tech).[1]

The characteristics of these companies, such as innovation and dynamic competition, their cost structure, (cross) network effects, single/multi-homing, zero-price platform services and the use of algorithms may have led to new competition effects such as winner takes-most dynamics, tipping, and the resurgence of conglomerate effects and leveraging practices (see e.g., World Bank 2021[2]).

Many reports and reviews by different authorities and organizations, have highlighted the interest in these markets in recent years.[3] A recent report by the Word Bank[4] has pointed out that developing countries have a more reactive approach for antitrust enforcement in these markets, compared to industrialized countries.

---

1 Usually associated with Alphabet (Google), Amazon, Apple, and Facebook, as well as Microsoft and others.

2 World Bank, Antitrust and Digital Platforms: An Analysis of Global Patterns and Approaches by Competition Authorities, (Equitable Growth, Finance and Institutions Insight, 2021), https://documents.worldbank.org/en/publication/documents-reports/documentdetail/893381632736476155/antitrust-and-digital-platforms-an-analysis-of-global-patterns-and-approaches-by-competition-authorities.

3 One meta-analysis of these reports may be seen in F. Lancieri & P. Sakowski, *Competition in Digital Markets: A Review of Expert Reports*, 26 *Stan. J.L. Bus. & Fin.* 65 (2021).

4 *See* World Bank, Antitrust and Digital Platforms Report, *supra* note 2.

One should expect an expansion in competition policy enforcement with an increase in abuse of dominance/conduct cases on these expanding markets. Complaints should arise as these digital platforms, often fast-growing companies, dislodge competitors. The growth in the number of abuse of dominance cases and non-horizontal agreements brings to the fore the perennial question of what legal standards the authority should apply when analyzing conduct by digital platforms.

There is extensive literature on the legal standards applied in competition law practice for agreements and dominance conduct across different jurisdictions. One strand of the literature discusses whether the (US) per se and rule of reason[5] standards should be applied, based on a cost-benefit analysis of type I (false convictions) and type II (false acquittals) errors. As explained by Hovenkamp (2022)[6] the so-called Easterbrook hypothesis claims, mistakenly in his view, that false convictions in antitrust are more costly to welfare than false acquittals. This has led to enforcement in the US being biased towards treating too many potentially abusive practices as presumptively legal and in too many cases being acquitted.

Another strand of the literature, that has also focused on error-costs, moves beyond the polar "per-se"/"rule of reason" debate and focuses on the optimality of presumptions when analyzing antitrust non-merger cases. As is often associated with Judge Stevens in US competition law,[7] one can consider a continuum of standards between the polar cases of rule of reason and per se, depending on the stage at which the presumptions are made on the effects of a given conduct. Central to the legal standards continuum analysis is the screen information content that could be used by competition authorities in the many steps of the analysis (to prove harm/to verify efficiencies) along the continuum.[8]

In this chapter we provide a retrospective study of recent decisions of Brazilian Competition Authority (CADE), in cases of unilateral abuse of dominance – or economic power in the Brazilian legal analysis – on digital platforms. The review aims to clarify what the legal standards practice of the authority has been in digital platforms.

A list of digital platform cases, at CADE (and other BRICS countries) up to 2020 is presented in Golovanova and Ribeiro (2022)[9] who examine issues of relevant markets and network effects analysis. We expand this review of digital platforms to consider more recent cases (up to 2023), while focusing on a more

---

5 In European competition law partly associated with object-based and effects-based standards

6 Herbert J. Hovenkamp, *Antitrust Error Costs* 24 Univ. Pa. J. Bus. L. 293 (2022).

7 S.W. Waller, *Justice Stevens and the Rule of Reason*, 62 SMU L. Rev. 693–724 (2009).

8 See for example, Y. Katsoulacos, *Could a Move to More Presumption-Based Legal Standards Be Justified, for the Big-Tech Digital Markets, on Error- Cost-Minimizing Grounds?* (*forthcoming* 2023), and references therein, where the ideas are discussed at length.

9 S. Golovanova & E. Pontual Ribeiro, *Multisided Platform Analysis and Competition Law Enforcement Practice in BRICS Countries*, 18 J. Comp. L. & Econ. 730–769 (2022).

complete examination of abuse of dominance and agreements cases, whether convicted or not. For comparison, as far as the case list is concerned see Pereira Neto et al. (2022).[10] We provide a different perspective on the cases, as we read and review them in the context of legal standard analysis.

Digital platforms and digital competition may bring new challenges from either innovation-based competition, competition characteristics and monetization practices that can influence the legal standard in such cases. These challenges may reduce the screening power of steps in the analysis and justify a more extensive role of presumptions for different conducts.[11]

The legal standard as seen by the decisions in non-merger cases at CADE vary from a close to per se illegality in classical cartels/horizontal agreements, towards a rule of reason in other abuse of dominance and vertical cases. In the latter standard, the authority recognizes that efficiencies should be investigated to evaluate potential consumer harm,[12] though this recognition may not be translated into efficiencies been rigorously taken into account.

The legal standard in conduct cases in Brazil has been reviewed in Golovanova and Ribeiro (2022)[13] based on convicted cases using the Katsoulacos et al. (2019)[14] scale of stages in the continuum.[15] The authors conclude that the legal standard falls short of the full rule of reason; closer to per se in horizontal agreements (classical cartels) and to a truncated rule of reason standard for vertical agreements. The analysis here uses a legal standard classification that may differ from what the competition authority sees itself doing. The chapter does not seek to evaluate what the appropriate or optimal legal standard should be in digital cases, as we leave this for later research.

The chapter is organized as follows: the next section follows the introduction and clarifies the legal standard as has been applied by CADE in non-merger antitrust cases. The following section discusses the digital markets' case analysis, and the final section offers concluding comments.

---

10 C.M.S. Pereira Neto et al., *Competition Law Enforcement in Digital Markets: The Brazilian Perspective on Unilateral Conducts*, 67 Antitrust Bull. 622–641 (2022).

11 *See* Katsoulacos, *supra* note 8.

12 OECD, Peer Reviews of Competition Law and Policy: Brazil 2019 § 4.1 (Paris, OECD 2019), https://www.oecd.org/competition/oecd-peer-reviews-of-competition-law-and-policy-brazil-2019.htm#:~:text=This%20review%20finds%20that%20Brazil's,reviews%20in%202005%20and%202010.

13 S. Golovanova & E. Pontual Ribeiro, *Testing the Convergence of Legal Standards in BRICS Countries*, CRESSE Conference (2022), https://www.cresse.info/wp-content/uploads/2021/10/2021_ps9_pa1_Golovanova.pdf.

14 Y. Katsoulacos et al., *A Methodology for Empirically Measuring the Extent of Economic Analysis and Evidence and for Identifying the Legal Standards in Competition Law Enforcement,in* Festschrift in Honour of Frédéric Jenny, Standing Up for Convergence and Relevance in Antitrust (Nicolas Charbit and Sonia Ahmad eds., Concurrences 2019). *See also*, Katsoulacos, *supra* note 8.

15 Where a cumulative level of economic analysis moves the legal standard under the following classification: strict per se, modified per se, truncated effects-based i, truncated effects-based ii and full effects-based (or rule of reason).

II. The Brazilian Legal Standard in Antitrust Cases: an Overview

The Brazilian Competition Law (Law No. 12.529/2011) in Article 36 it notes that business conducts that aim to or may generate adverse competitive effects are a violation of the "economic order"[16] if they: (i) limit or hinder in any way free enterprise or free competition; (ii) lead to dominance of a relevant market; (iii) unjustifiably increase profits; or (iv) generate an abuse of market power. The wording is very similar to that of the previous competition law of 1994, that ushered in the modern competition policy in the country.

From this wording, it appears that a conduct would be unlawful if it harms competition itself (i) and is characterized by an *abuse* of market power. Interestingly, when handling mergers, the legal standard is such that a merger should not be cleared if it causes the elimination of competition in a significant part of the relevant market (Article 88 Law No. 12.529/2011, para. 5). At the same time, mergers may be cleared under the situation that efficiencies are passed on to consumers (Article 88 Law No. 12.529/2011, para. 6). This has led to the understanding that consumer welfare harm is the ultimate criterion for finding illegality.

Article 36 includes, inter alia, horizontal agreements and coordinated practices, types of vertical restrictions and exclusionary practices. This is a sharp contrast with other jurisdictions, such as Europe, where separate articles in competition law deal with agreements and with abuse of dominance cases.

The law does not require the effects of these conducts to be measured nor must that intent be proven. At the same time the law states that a dominant position by a firm, when obtained from more efficient activities in the natural competition process does not constitute an infringement.

The article goes on to define what a dominant position is: when a firm or a group of firms have more than 20% in the relevant market *or* when the firm or group of firms have the power to unilaterally or coordinately alter market conditions.[17]

Article 36 uses the terms "aims/goals/object/constitute" (*tem por objeto*) and also "may generate effects" (*possam produzir efeitos*). This would suggest the use of a per se legal standard while leaving open the possibility of a rule of reason analysis, broadly speaking. The legal standard should abide by the law dictum that effects may be potential and that no intent would be required for illegality.

---

16 "Economic order" is a construct in the Brazilian 1988 Constitution, that should guide economic activities (public or private) under the principles of free enterprise, free competition, social role of property, consumer protection and economic power abuse repression (Law No. 12.529/2011 art. 1).

17 The code states that the threshold may be altered for specific industries, but up to 2022 CADE has not issued any official statement of such change.

It should be noted that a rule of reason is indeed recognized by the law which suggests taking into account efficiencies and balancing pro- and anti-competitive effects.[18] And CADE does sometimes mention what the rule of reason would involve, but then, as will become clear from the examination of the cases below, there are too many missing elements of analysis, that would have to be undertaken (or use of presumptions) if indeed the rule of reason was followed.

It is interesting to note that the discussion of "per se" vs "rule of reason" legal standard was subject to strong debate in the early years of the revised competition law. CADE is no stranger to presumptions in its analysis in non-horizontal agreements abuse of dominance cases. In the extensively discussed SKF minimum retail price maintenance practice case,[19] Commissioner Verissimo noted that: (i) in the US tradition of rule of reason, it is well known that there is a continuum between per se and rule of reason, with significant role of presumptions for efficient and effective antitrust practice (see details in Waller 2009,[20] cited in the Opinion); (ii) contextualization of the practice may safely point to a presumption of illegality by rendering basically impossible that a practice may have pro-competitive effects that compensate highly likely anticompetitive effects.

In his view, "per se" and "rule of reason" are extremes of a continuum of additional evidence-gathering that is required to reach a conviction by the deciding judge, with presumptions used to "fill the gaps" in the absence of direct evidence or measurement of either harm or efficiencies. The presumptions would be constructed from very high probability of certain outcomes, gathered from previous cases or established economic analysis relating to the case or international experience. However, in a presumption-based decision such as an illegal per se, the authority does not close the door for possible efficiencies arguments by parties. Yet, CADE would not feel required to empirically demonstrate (potential) harm.

The detailed empirical analysis of convicted conduct cases by Golovanova and Pontual Ribeiro (2022)[21] confirms the view that a rule of reason is rarely observed. Generally, the analysis in horizontal agreements reaches the market dominance stage. Assessment of unilateral conducts as abuse of dominance conducts, usually alludes to economic theory arguments of potential harm to consumers and recognizes that efficiencies may be present (but do not attempt to prove that this harm is likely with a significant probability). Vertical restraints usually present an analysis beyond market dominance, proving harm to competition but not necessarily efficiencies analysis.

18 The 2016 official document "Compliance Guide" states that the following steps should be followed: (i) proving that the conduct existed; (ii) showing if the firm or group of firms has/have a dominant position; (iii) evaluating (potential) anticompetitive effects from the conduct, considering market structure; and (iv) the evaluation of pro-competitive efficiencies mainly as benefits to consumers.

19 *See* Procon/SP v SKF Brasil Ltda, No. 08012.001271/2001-44 Jan. 2013 (Port.).

20 *See* Waller, *supra* note 7.

21 *See* Golovanova & Pontual Ribeiro, *supra* note 9. The analysis applied the legal standard index proposed in Katsoulacos et al., *supra* note 14 ranging from a pure per se (only the conduct is proven to convict the case) to a full rule of reason.

The arguments for a "truncated rule of reason", or for the use of presumptions when analyzing cases is often couched in terms of practicalities, that may be understood as a cost-benefit analysis from the perspective of enforcement. A full rule of reason standard could strain the authority's limited resources and hinder an effective competition policy. On the other hand, a per se analysis, while possible under the competition law and used for classic cartels, is sometimes described as insufficient and that it should be complemented with additional analysis in the continuum of legal standards.[22]

We now turn to the actual practice in digital platform cases in Brazil in the next section.

III. Case Review of Digital Platform Conduct Cases

As mentioned in the introduction, we review abuse of dominance and agreements cases involving digital platforms. The case list builds upon the survey by CADE's Department of Economic Studies (DEE)–CADE Digital Platform Markets Report (2021).[23] This includes 10 cases that had a decision (convicted, and cease and desist agreement ((TCC) for its acronym in Portuguese) or dismissed) by the time of the report. We are also including cases that have been dismissed in the administrative inquiry stage without going further into administrative proceedings. We include three additional cases, based on a search of decisions by the authority for 2022 and early 2023, after the DEE–CADE report was published. The list is presented in Table 1 below.

Table 1: Digital Platform Conduct Cases Reviewed

Item	Case No.	Plaintiffs and Defendants	Nickname	Start Year	End Year	Final Decision
1	08012.010483/2011-94	*E-Commerce Media Group Informação e Tecnologia Ltda v Google Inc. e Google Brasil Internet Ltda*	*E-Media v. Google*[24] (Google Shopping)	2011	2019	Case dismissed

22 *See* the notes in Fernandes, V.O. Direito da Concorrência das Plataformas Digitais. São Paulo Thomson 2022, ch. 2.3. and, in English, the discussion as early as 2013 Damien Geradin & Caio Mario da Silva Pereira Neto, *A Symposium on Vertical Restraints*, with important discussion by Paulo Azevedo et al., CPI (July 29, 2013), https://www.competitionpolicyinternational.com/assets/Uploads/CPI-Spring-2013-Geradin-Silva.pdf.

23 Department of Economic Studies (DEE)/CADE Mercado de Plataformas Digitais 2021 (Port.), https://cdn.cade.gov.br/Portal/centrais-de-conteudo/publicacoes/estudos-economicos/cadernos-do-cade/plataformas-digitais.pdf.

24 *See* E-Commerce Media Group Informação e Tecnologia Ltda v Google Inc. e Google Brasil Internet Ltda, No. 08012.010483/2011-94 Oct. 2013 (Braz.).

Item	Case No.	Plaintiffs and Defendants	Nickname	Start Year	End Year	Final Decision
2	08700.005694/2013-19	*CADE "ex officio" v. Google Inc. e Google Brasil Internet Ltda*	*Bing/CADE v. Google*[25] (Google AdWords)	2013	2019	Case dismissed
3	08700.009082/2013-03	*E-Commerce Media Group Informação e Tecnologia Ltda v. Google Inc. e Google Brasil Internet Ltda*	*Buscapé v. Google*[26] (Google Scrapping)	2013	2019	Case dismissed
4	08700.003132/2014-11	*CADE"exofficio" v. Universal Music Brasil Ltda*	*CADE v. Universal Music*[27] (Universal Streaming)	2014	2016	Case dismissed
5	08700.006964/2015-71	*Diretório C. dos Estudantes Honestino Guimarães e Uber do Brasil Tecnologia Ltda v. Assoc. Boa Vista de Táxi – Ponto 1813; Sindicato dos Perm. de Taxi et al.*	*Uber v. Taxi Associations*[28] (Uber Sham)	2015	2018	Case dismissed
6	°08700.010960/2015-97	*Comissão de Defesa do Consumidor da Câmara dos Deputados v. Uber do Brasil Tecnologia Ltda*	*Consumer Protection Commission v. Uber*[29] (Uber Consumer)	2015	2017	Case dismissed

25 *See* Cade "exofficio" v. Booking.com Brasil Serviços de Reserva de Hoteis Ltda et al., No. 08700.006295/2017-07 which discusses broad and narrow MFN clauses.

26 *See* E-Commerce Media Group Informação e Tecnologia Ltda v. Google Inc. e Google Brasil Internet Ltda, No. 08700.009082/2013-03 Oct. 13, 2013 (Braz.).

27 *See* CADE "exofficio" v. Universal Music Brasil Ltda, No. 08700.003132/2014-11 Nov. 18, 2014 (Braz.).

28 *See* Diretório C. dos Estudantes Honestino Guimarães e Uber do Brasil Tecnologia Ltda v. Assoc. Boa Vista de Táxi – Ponto 1813; Sindicato dos Perm. de Taxi et al., No. 08700.006964/2015-71 Aug. 7, 2015 (Braz.).

29 *See* Comissão de Defesa do Consumidor da Câmara dos Deputados v. Uber do Brasil Tecnologia Ltda, No. 08700.010960/2015-97 Nov. 2105 (Braz.).

Item	Case No.	Plaintiffs and Defendants	Nickname	Start Year	End Year	Final Decision
7	08700.004530/2015-36	*Associação Boa Vista de Táxi – Ponto 1813* *v.* *Uber do Brasil Tecnologia Ltda*	*Taxi Drivers v. Uber*[30] (Uber Unfair)	2015	2015	Case dismissed
8	08700.006295/2017-07	*Cade "ex officio"* *v.* *Booking.com Brasil Serviços de Reserva de Hoteis Ltda et al.*	*Booking, Expedia, Decolar OTA*[31]	2016	2018	TCC
9	08700.008318/2016-29	*MPSP e Daniel Braga Frederico* *v.* *Uber do Brasil Tecn. Ltda*	*AMAA v. Uber*[32]	2016	2018	Case dismissed
10	08700.006067/2018-18	*SEPRAC – Ministério da Economia* *v.* *Prefeitura do Rio de Janeiro, Pref. de São Paulo e Pref. de Manaus*	*Finance Ministry v. City of Rio and Sao Paulo*[33]	2018	2019	Case dismissed
11	08700.004588/2020-47	*Rappi Brasil Intermediação de Negócios Ltda; ABRASEL* *v.* *IFood.com Agência de Restaurantes Online S. A.*	*Rappi v. IFood*[34]	2020	2023	TCC

30 *See* Associação Boa Vista de Táxi – Ponto 1813 v. Uber do Brasil Tecnologia Ltda, No. 08700.004530/2015-36 May 13, 2010 (Braz.).

31 *See* CadeEx Of. v. Booking.com Brasil Serviços de Reserva de Hoteis Ltda et al., No. 08700.006295/2017-07 July 27, 2016 (Braz.).

32 *See* MPSP e Daniel Braga Frederico v. Uber do Brasil Tecn. Ltda, No. 08700.008318/2016-29.

33 *See* SEPRAC – Ministério da Economia v. Prefeitura do Rio de Janeiro, Pref. de São Paulo e Pref. de Manaus, No. 08700.006067/2018-18 Oct. 18, 2018 (Braz.).

34 *See* Rappi Brasil Intermediação de Negócios Ltda; ABRASEL v. IFood.com Agência de Restaurantes Online S.A., No. 08700.004588/2020-47 Sept. 25, 2020 (Braz.).

Item	Case No.	Plaintiffs and Defendants	Nickname	Start Year	End Year	Final Decision
12	08700.006611/2021-19	*Total Pass Participações Ltda ("Total Pass") e Ynegócios Soluções Tecnológicas Ltda. ("Yooou p").* *v.* *GPBR ParticipaçõesLtda*	*Total Pass v. Gympass*[35] (Gympass)	2020	2022	TCC
13	08700.003211/ 2016-94	*Yelp, Inc.* *v.* *Representadas: Google Inc. e Google Brasil Internet Ltda*	*Google v. Yelp*[36]	2016	2022	Case dismissed

Source: Authors' case review. TCC – cease and desist agreement.

We note many cases involving Uber, a taxi-hailing platform and lead provider of these services in Brazil, and four cases with Google as defendant. Most of the Google cases were opened in the span of a couple of years (2011–2013) and the Uber cases started in the first years of operation of the platform (2015–2016). The cases took several years to close, from eight (*Google Shopping*) to two (*AMAA v. Uber*). More recent cases (*GymPass* and *IFood*) dealt with exclusive agreements and Most Favored Nation (MFN).[37] Most of the cases were closed, as the competition authority concluded no competition harm was found, and three were settled with a cease and desist agreement.

Regarding digital markets, it could be argued that CADE has been at the forefront of BRICS countries in incorporating digital and platform antitrust analysis concepts over time, such as cross-network effects and two-sided markets.[38] It has also led the working group on digital platforms and published at least three reports on the issue.[39]

---

35 *See* Total Pass Participações Ltda ("Total Pass") e Ynegócios Soluções Tecnológicas Ltda.("Yoooup") v. GPBR Participações Ltda, No. 08700.006611/2021-19 Feb. 3, 2022 (Braz.).

36 *See* Yelp, Inc. v. Representadas: Google Inc. e Google Brasil Internet Ltda, No. 08700.003211/ 2016-94 Sept. 19, 2018 (Braz.).

37 The Online Travel Agencies case Cade Ex Of. v. Booking.com Brasil Serviços de Reserva de Hoteis Ltda et al., discuss broad and narrow MFN clauses.

38 *See* Katsoulacos, *supra* note 8.

39 *See* Alexandre Barreto et al., BRICS AUTHORITIES DIGITAL MARKET REPORT (2019), https://www.competitionpolicyinternational.com/wp-content/uploads/2019/12/CPI-Barreto-Morita-Park.pdf, the already mentioned DEE–CADE Digital Platform reports and Lancieri & Sakowski, *Concorrência em mercados digitais: uma revisão dos relatórios especializados* (DEE–CADE, Working Paper No. 5, 2020). An English summary has been published in Lancieri & Sakowski, *supra* note 3. An update of the of the BRICS report has been discussed for release later this year (2023) and was discussed at the BRICS+ Digital Competition Forum (Nov. 24–25, 2022), https://cyberbrics.info/wp-content/uploads/2022/12/BRICS-Digital-Competition-Forum.pdf.

We will revisit the cases summarized or listed in the DEE–CADE report shortly, focusing on the decision-making process under the legal standard applied in the different cases.

The taxonomy used to understand the legal standard used follows the legal standard methodology of Katsoulacos et al. (2019) and Katsoulacos (2023).[40] This analysis differs from CADE's view of the legal standard in two ways. First, the taxonomy emphasizes the use of economic screens to gather evidence on dominance, anticompetitive effects, consumer harm and efficiencies balancing. Second, an additional step, as seen in Table 2 is introduced, namely, an analysis of the potential consumer welfare loss. In Brazilian competition law theory, the consumer harm effect from anticompetitive practices is proven under potential effects, or presumptions, under specific case characteristics, with consumer harm screens often presented as efficiency arguments (e.g., a least efficient entrant analysis in exclusive dealings cases). For international comparison we differentiate the steps for a full rule of reason analysis. In either classification, a move to a rule of reason analysis would entail moving beyond the per se analysis that may not even measure market concentration.

In other words, the additional step in the analysis takes into account that while one may associate the anticompetitive effect of a reduction in competition in (step 3) with consumer welfare loss as prices could increase, and quality decrease in (step 4), even before considering efficiencies, economic theory may suggest this is not a one-to-one relation.[41] The classification does not evaluate whether the merit of the analysis may be correct or incorrect, given case information and economic analysis.

Table 2: Legal Standard Classification on Digital Platform Conduct Cases

Step	Description	Classification up to that step
1	Proving that the business practice existed	Per se
2	Whether the firm (in unilateral conduct) has a dominant position: relevant market definition; market shares calculation and other market characteristics description	Modified per se
3	Showing that the conduct has exclusionary effect or enhances market power	Truncated rule of reason I
4	Showing harmful (potential) effects that the business practice has on consumer welfare through price increases, quantity or quality decreases and a reduction of incentives to innovate	Truncated rule of reason II
5	Pro-competitive efficiencies assessed and balancing	Full rule of reason

Note: Prepared by the authors, Katsoulacos et al. (2019) and Katsoulacos (2023).

40 See Katsoulacos et al., *supra* note 14 and Katsoulacos, *supra* note 8.

41 We thank Yannis Katsoulacos for the reminderon this point. *See* Katsoulacos, *supra* note 8 (*forthcoming* 2023) and the associated discussion.

As a clarification on the analysis, we consider only the discussion on the final decision, whether this is the last General Superintendence (SG) report or the Tribunal leading commissioner report. These may have a more limited analysis than what is discussed in the case, if CADE concludes that the business practice could not be identified or had no possibility of creating harm. If there is no material evidence of the business practice, the case decision does not move beyond (step 1).

When opening the case, CADE transcribes parts of the of the plaintiff's complaint that almost always has a clearly written theory of harm and sometimes even dismisses theoretical efficiencies. CADE may also open a case stating a plausible theory of harm, obtaining indirect evidence that the defendant may have dominance (not necessarily proven yet) and justify that in order to open an investigation. At the same time, when opening a case, the defendant has the chance of first defense and this document presents possible efficiencies. These are transcribed by CADE in a decision to open the case and replicated in the decision to close the case. We do not consider such preliminary arguments and discussions in the legal standard analysis below. We focus on the latter part of the decision document, as sometimes it can be unclear in the earlier part of decisions or cases as to what CADE's opinion or transparency is in reporting plaintiffs' and defendants' arguments.

Nevertheless, the parties' arguments may provide a learning and signaling mechanism for future cases for CADE to present possible theories of harm to competition or to consumers and to provide hypothetical efficiencies. It is often the case that CADE refers to international case law or academic and international organization literature to build a case investigation methodology.

Last but not least, the classification does not evaluate the appropriateness of the arguments and screens presented by CADE in each step, focusing alternatively on whether an economic screen was used, or a presumption was claimed, in each step of the analysis.

1. Case 1: Google Shopping (*E-Media v Google*)

TE-Commerce Media Group Informação e Tecnologia Ltda., that owns two price comparison sites, Buscapé and Bondfaro represented against Google, Google Inc./Google Brasil. The alleged practice was a preferential position for Google Shopping product when users searched for a product in general search. This would lead price comparison sites that compete with Google Shopping to have fewer clicks and revenues. Google was also accused of denying selling competitors space or only selling if under claimed abusive conditions. Together, the main conduct was presented as a strategy of leveraging using a dominant position to promote its own service and impose restrictions on the competitive environment. Ultimately, according to the plaintiffs, competitors would be excluded from the market leading to higher prices for consumers.

The case was controversial. CADE's commissioners were split evenly with three votes for closing and three votes for concluding the case based on anticompetitive conduct. The final decision was reached by CADE's president additional vote in favor of Google.

The assessment followed a number of steps, each step being subject to some disagreement among the commissioners. The practice was well established: Google did not deny that Google Shopping was in a preferential position on the search results. There was a debate about relevant markets: whether this included only one – the generic search engine market, or two, segregating price comparison sites to another relevant market. CADE finally considered there were two relevant markets: (i) the generic search market; and (ii) price comparison mechanism markets. Regarding the generic search engine market, Google had a huge market share – more than 90%. The analysis concluded it had a dominant position in that market. The dominant position in the second market was viewed as dependent upon the dominant position of the search market. Therefore, the conduct was indicated, and the market power established.

Anticompetitive exclusionary effects from the business practice and possible harm to consumers were considered *though there was no attempt to prove or measure harm.* Most of the commissioners concluded that no actual effects were observed, but potential harmful effects could not be discarded. Finally, CADE's Tribunal was also divided on whether it should consider efficiencies and net effects. This was achieved in a particular discussion. The minority argued that a presumption of harm to competition would be appropriate in this decision, while the majority believed that the costs of overenforcement would outweigh underenforcement in this digital platform market, *overemphasizing the role of possible efficiencies*. The decision was made under the *presumption* that the conduct did not generate a negative welfare impact, with the vote cast by CADE's President, Tribunal Chair, settling the decision. Explicitly pointing to the Easterbrook hypothesis of greater harm to type 1 errors in the decision not to convict Google, the report noted the impossibility of "proportional, solid, effective, and measurable remedies" as an additional argument for a non-interventionist stand.

2. Case 2: Google AdWords (*Bing/CADE v. Google*)

In 2013, Microsoft, the owner of the Bing search engine, filed a complaint against Google, the provider of the internet search service Google Search, as is well known, and of the sponsored search platform Google AdWords (AdWords). Microsoft alleged that an update to the terms and conditions for the AdWord application programming interface (API) would prevent multi-homing, i.e., the ability for an advertiser to display its ads on multiple digital platforms.

CADE started the assessment of the case analyzing the contract clauses. It concluded that the existing clauses in the contract would not prevent the creation of a campaign with the same content on various platforms, whether it was done either manually or automatically. The contract also did not carry any exclusivity agreement with advertisers or any kind of retaliation to encourage complete exclusivity of advertisers on the Google platform. In addition, CADE concluded that there were tools created by competing platforms that enable multi-homing among themselves and other platforms. The agency found that the contract would allow efficiencies by ensuring protection of advertisers' data, which resulted in better-performing advertisements. CADE argued that Google provided tools for optimizing and synchronizing ads, making them compatible with the features of each platform. The decision goes on, claiming that multi-homing was not only allowed, but also encouraged by the search engine. CADE viewed the dominant position by Google to be the result of its efficiencies and cross-network effects. It argued that as the platform with the most users and generating the highest ad revenue, Google would attract more advertisers, which in turn, feeds a cycle in which the platform with the highest financial return continues to innovate and, consequently, is more likely to maintain its dominant position in the market by offering increasingly accurate and targeted results to its users. These free and satisfactory search results for the users generate a certain "loyalty" to the platform. As Google´s dominant position was not enhanced by the API, the anticompetitive effect was lacking, and the case was dismissed.

In addition, there was an analysis of the potential exclusionary impact, which could occur according to CADE if the multi-homing limitation was proven. There was no effective analysis of the theory of harm associated with a potential limitation of multi-homing. Because it was presumed that the exclusionary conduct did not exist (no limitations in multi-homing were found), the analysis did not move beyond this.

3. Case 3: Google Scraping (*Buscapé v. Google*)

The e-Commerce Media Group, that owns the price comparison sites Buscapé and Bondfaro, alleged that Google was engaging in scraping practices, i.e., content appropriation from Buscapé's website to benefit Google Shopping, abusing its market power.

When analyzing the conduct (step 1), CADE concluded that there was little use of third-party content. As the practice of scraping could not be proven the case was closed.

Although the conduct was not proven, there was an analysis of the relevant market – defined as: (i) universal search sites, which are located in the upstream link; and (ii) thematic search sites for price comparison, which are located in the downstream link – and associated dominance. Potential exclusionary impacts resulting from an eventual confirmation of the anticompetitive practice were also considered. However, there was no material evidence of the conduct, rendering the further steps of the analysis moot.

4. Case 4: Universal Streaming (*CADE v. Universal Music*)

The case originally arose from a request from a Commissioner to the SG/CADE, which requested an analysis of a possible abuse of Universal's dominant position in the streaming market (such as Spotify and Apple Music). The major labels, especially Universal Music, would use their market power to impose specifics contractual conditions on streaming services and virtual music stores, thereby harming smaller labels.

After carrying out the investigation, CADE concluded that each contract between Universal and the different streaming platforms had particularities and was constantly reviewed. This was taken as evidence of negotiations between agents. Such negotiations would have shown that the major record companies were not able to impose on online stores exclusionary contract terms that would harm smaller record companies. Other music market players consulted were almost unanimous in viewing that the practices adopted by the recording companies were adequate. CADE also stated that the technology required by digital music could be the possible reason for the existence of these clauses, with no exclusionary intent.

Interestingly that, in addition to concluding that there was no clear evidence of harmful practices to competition, CADE stated that no intervention was deemed necessary because it was a rapidly developing sector with many innovations. The case was dismissed for lack of evidence of the conduct, with no actual analysis of the steps beyond the first one.

5. Case 5: Uber Sham Litigation (*Uber v. Taxi Associations*)

Uber do Brasil Tecnologia Ltda and the University of Brasilia Law Student Union presented a complaint against taxi drivers trade unions and taxi service associations for imposing barriers or acting against the operation and development of competitors as per Article 36 of Law No. 12.529/2011. The complaints alleged: (i) sham litigation by the taxi drivers trade unions; (ii) and threats against uber drivers by taxi drivers with support of their associations. The investigation concluded that the complaints were not observed or had no (potential) exclusionary effects.

6. Case 6: Uber Consumer (*Consumer Protection Commission v. Uber*)

The Brazilian Chamber of Deputies' Consumer Protection Commission presented a complaint against Uber do Brasil Tecnologia Ltda for unfair competition due to the absence of regulation for this activity, i.e., they do not follow the same rulers of cities taxi drivers, do not pay taxes and they are under any fiscal control.

This case was seen as a debate on the legality of Transportation Network Companies (TCN), also known as taxi-hailing companies, such as Uber, that provide services that may compete with traditional taxi services. CADE argued that whether TCN can legally operate was outside the scope of competition law. Also, as a complaint of unfair competition was outside the scope of competition law, there was no ground for a case and, as such, no assessment steps were presented in the decision.

7. Case 7: Uber Unfair (*Taxi Drivers v. Uber*)

Similar to the previous case, a taxi driver association made a complaint to CADE accusing Uber of unfair competition. According to the complaint, Uber did not have the same costs as the city taxi drivers because they did not follow the same legal requirements. Therefore, as they alleged that uber service did not respect the legislation, they argued that it was a case of unfair competition. The case was closed by CADE, without further analysis, as this was not considered an antitrust case.

8. Case 8: Online Travel Agencies (*Booking, Expedia, Decolar*) MFN

The case dealt with the possible anticompetitive effect of the MFN clauses imposed by the online travel agencies (OTA)s when lodging businesses offer rooms through their platforms. The case dealt with *wide/broad vs narrow* MFN. The case was settled with a TCC where defendants agreed not to impose broad MFN clauses. As it was settled in a relatively early stage of the investigation, the decision basically summarizes the international cases (Germany, Italy, Sweden and France) in the discussion. The decision states that wide MFNs were the norm in Brazil (step 1) and describes the potential harm from such clauses, in a short statement. No relevant market was delimited, nor actual harm measured or explored. Efficiencies were stated in a short paragraph based on the literature of the other jurisdictions. Interestingly, CADE states that the TCC does not imply a presumption that narrow MFN are lawful or broad MFN are unlawful, as possibly cases in other markets may be investigated in detail.

9. Case 9: (*AMMA v. Uber*)

The case was a Preparatory Procedure for Administrative Inquiry (PP) Against Uber. The representation was based on a complaint from AMAA, an association of taxi drivers. According to the representation, Uber used dynamic pricing and created a mechanism for independent drivers to coordinate their prices. Therefore, these practices could be translated as the following alleged antitrust conducts: dumping and hub and spoke cartel (a coordinated market practice).

The case analysis did not move beyond step (1). The authority accepted Uber's argument that the drivers were not their employees, nor owned their cars and drivers did not have exclusive agreements with Uber. The hub and spoke cartel accusation was misplaced as it would entail any single firm platform pricing strategy to be classified as a conspiracy. As the conduct was deemed non-existent, the analysis was short.

10. Case 10: SEPRAC (*Ministry of Finance v. City of Rio de Janeiro and São Paulo*)

The Competition Advocacy Unit – Ministry of Finance (SEPRAC) complained at CADE accusing the cities of Rio de Janeiro and São Paulo's free app for registered taxi drivers as predatory price conduct against private ride hailing apps.

The Rio de Janeiro and São Paulo Mayor's Office decided to pay for the development, support and distribution of a *free* taxi-hailing app to city registered regular taxi drivers only. The app introduced advances for taxi-hailing such as calls with discount prices, fare transparency and payments by card. Uber independent drivers (as subscribed by SEPRAC) claimed that the app gave the cities' taxi drivers a competitive advantage, reducing their costs to reach customers. As such the app provides predatory prices against Uber drivers. The argument by SEPRAC was that government action does not carry antitrust immunity.

The SG did not accept SEPRAC's arguments. According to CADE, the accusation assumed that public transport was an exclusive private service. Instead, it was a public service comprising two kinds of suppliers. First, city taxis, a public utility service. Second, a drivers' private service using private apps. The two kinds of drivers could compete in the same market, but they operated according to different rules. The mayor´s office had the mandate to lawfully regulate those distinct services. The regulation includes the pricing and terms of services as well as the costs to the prefectures to create the conditions for service provision.

Therefore, the analysis stopped at (step 1) as CADE had no grounds to investigate the Mayor's Office regulatory power actions.

11. Case 11: (*Rappi v. IFood*)

Rappi, a food delivery app presented a complaint against IFood arguing that the latter was unlawfully abusing its dominant position and excluding competitors by imposing exclusive agreements for restaurants (and others such as supermarkets and food stores) with the threat of fines and contract termination. Rappi and IFood are digital platforms that offer the technology for food delivery on a marketplace of restaurants and produce markets.

The SG technical note considered, based on previous merger cases, that IFood is dominant in the food delivery relevant market, with shares "much higher" than 20%.[42] The analysis used a theory of harm for platform markets – the risk of tipping effects. Nevertheless the analysis did not establish exactly why there would be a high probability of tipping in this specific case. Therefore, the contract clauses imposed by IFood to restaurants, such as exclusivity, might close the market, by increasing barriers to entry. At the same time, the size of IFood was considered (though this is not in principle sufficient in general) to make it a "must have" platform for restaurants to work with. As already settled in previous CADE decisions, SG did not consider the exclusivity clause illegal per se. But considering the characteristics of digital platform markets, (i.e., potential market tipping), the level of dominance and disproportional clauses (degraded search results within the app of non-exclusive restaurants and exclusivity termination fees), the exclusivity clauses were considered by SG as anticompetitive in a preliminary assessment strong enough to support a preventative measure.

In early 2023, IFood and CADE were able to settle the question with a TCC, limiting the extent of restaurants with whom the company could sign exclusive agreements. The TCC established also other requirements to prevent tipping effects and reduced the risk of increasing the competitors' costs, such as the prevention of MFN clauses or discounts linked to the market share of IFood.

This case is a good example of CADE using some anticompetitive effects analysis centered in the platform business characteristics, based on the recent antitrust literature. The conduct was confirmed and the assessment moved beyond a per se analysis.

12. Case 12: (*Total Pass v. Gympass*)

In 2020 TotalPass, an app that provides subscription services for gym users (allowing them to use more than one gym and managing payments and access for independent gyms) presented a complaint against GymPass (another gym app) as it was imposing exclusive agreements with independent gyms and, also, requiring MFN pricing to those non-exclusive gyms across platforms. These vertical restraint practices were considered, by TotalPass, to exclude competitors from the market and damaging competition with significant entry and expansion barriers.

---

42 *See e.g.*, CADE Commissioner Lenisa Prado, SEI/CADE REPORT ON PARAMETERS FOR SUBMITTING EVIDENCE IN LENIENCY APPLICATIONS (Sept. 2021), https://cdn.cade.gov.br/portal/centrais-de-conteudo/publicacoes/guias-do-cade/guide-parameters-for-submitting-evidence-in-leniency-applications-atualizado.pdf. The actual market share is redacted for confidentiality reasons.

CADE confirmed that GymPass contracts imposed exclusive agreements and/or MFN clauses to independent gyms. The market definition for gym apps concluded that the defendant, a leader in this market, controlled 80–90% of gyms (concentration was not measured on the user side). While there were entrants in the gym app market, the solid dominance of GymPass was considered beyond doubt.

The rich discussions in the case when an interim measure was imposed by the SG[43] developed the exclusionary theory for digital platforms and the associated consumer harm from the harm to competitors. The importance of network effects, leveraging the single homing/exclusive clauses (and expected user behavior of single homing a gym app), as well as the MFN pricing restrictions contributed effectively to damaging competitors. It was noted that the defendant imposed take-it-or-leave-it non-compete clauses for gyms that left the platform. Efficiencies were considered, following the idea that exclusive dealings would protect opportunistic behavior from gyms. Yet no specific investments were recognized, rendering the efficiency argument moot. No actual measurement of price increases or quality decreases from the practices was conducted (as expected for an interim measure or a TCC). The CADE Tribunal unanimously voted for the interim measures significantly limiting the exclusive agreements and blocking MFN price restrictions. The defendant agreed to convert the interim measure into a TCC to close the case in late 2022. Essentially here competitor exclusion was used as a presumption to characterize the conduct as harmful.

13. Case 13: (*Google v. Yelp*)

In 2008 Google launched its Local Universal architecture for search results and One Box results box when users searched for local businesses, such as restaurants. It would show some results on a Google Maps box with a list of advertised or search generated results. Google placed such results before the organic search results. Earlier, Google would also present its organic search contents with links to local business catalogs, such as Yelp, Foursquare, Apontador, and Kekanto (Brazilian sites). Yelp argued that the Local Universal positioning was robbing opportunities for users to reach its website, even if Yelp was the first result in the organic search. As an organic search would be the main way that users reached Yelp, it would block the access of side users to the platform, reducing its monetizing prospects from ads and business owners' listings.

CADE confirmed that the Local Universal results appeared on top of results during the period the practice was active. CADE delimited two relevant markets, one upstream market for general search and a downstream market for online

43 The interim measures were later converted to a TCC – cease and desist agreement both sustained at the CADE Tribunal.

searches for businesses (based on business listings platforms, such as Yelp). It concluded that Google was dominant in the upstream market but did not measure market shares in the downstream market.

CADE went on to explore the potential or actual exclusionary effect from the launch of Local Universal. Exclusion rested on concluding that the organic search was an "essential facility" (or an essential way for users to reach the local content listing platforms) and verifying if the Local Universal was introduced with exclusionary intent with no consumer benefit. The report concluded that the Google innovation was not capable of generating anticompetitive harm as there would be other ways for a user to reach the platform (e.g., installing an app). It claimed that there was no causal effect from the Local Universal introduction and competitors leaving the market, such as Yelp itself.

Interestingly, the case report stated that efficiencies were measured as the consumer experience improved after Local Universal was introduced. Such an improvement would have more than compensated for any (unproven) exclusionary effect of the practice. It also argued that sponsored results appearing on top of the search results (as in the One Box) are a required feature of the two-sidedness of the search business model, where one side (search) costs are footed by revenues from the other side (ads), precluding any claims of required search results neutrality.

Finally, the case report closed saying that the Google Shopping (see Case 1) decision principles would be observed, namely that the belief of higher type 1 errors in innovative digital platforms should restrain antitrust intervention only to cases where (observed or potential) harm is clearly proven. It also stated that, given the dynamic competition innovation-led search platform market, interventions would generate significant welfare losses from a chilling effect on innovation, with likely harm to consumers from the missed opportunity of experiencing higher quality products. As such it stated that unless clear harm was observed, the authority would consider the innovation as pro-competitive, even if its introduction generated firm closures. While this strong stand permeates various decisions now, no actual evidence justifying this efficiency presumption was presented in the cases reviewed.

IV. Concluding Comments

Competition law in Brazil states that business practices may be considered unlawful if they harm the Brazilian constitutional concept of "economic order". For unilateral conduct with potentially exclusionary effects, such violations would occur if competitors were harmed, and parties abused their dominant position. Market dominance is not considered illegal per se, as it may be the result of competition on merits. Lastly, the law states that harm may be proven even if it is unintentional and only in potential fashion.

In digital market cases, with new theories of harm and possibly innovation-based competition and non-price competitive levers, the international literature has questioned if competition law would need to be modified and/or what legal standard and presumptions authorities should use.

This chapter explored enforcement in digital markets in the Brazilian case. No change in competition law has been argued for by CADE nor any other legal change. The analysis of digital cases has used the same legal framework as in non-digital cases, a priori.[44] This chapter explored the legal standard used by CADE, the Brazilian antitrust authority, in digital platform abuse of dominance or vertical restraints cases. The analysis contrasts the decision-making process in non-merger digital cases using the Katsoulacos et al. (2019) and Katsoulacos (2023)[45] legal standard classification.

Some patterns do appear. In the Google Shopping case, the majority report by Commissioner Bandeira Maia clearly stands with the Easterbrook hypothesis that the costs of a possible false conviction would generate more harm to consumers and competition than a false acquittal. At the same time, President Barreto's opinion summarizes that, while no potential harm presumption would be reasonable in cases involving digital platforms' abuse of dominance cases (though possible under the competition law), there may be an efficiency presumption, stemming from the innovation characteristics of the platforms (amplified by the Easterbrook hypothesis). This case is a good example of the cautionary approach by the CADE Tribunal – efficiencies were explored but not demonstrated in this case. As a side argument, the presumption seems to be couched in convenience terms, considering that an eventual remedy in case of a decision against Google would be quite difficult to enforce and monitor. This presumption of legality in abuse of dominance cases was also observed in other Google cases such as *Yelp* and *AdWords*.

On vertical restraints, such as exclusive dealings and MFN clauses, in a truncated rule of reason, these are presumed to be illegal, and the assessment is closer to modified per se analysis or the decision rests on the presumption of harm from the exclusion of rivals. In all three cases (*OTAs*, *IFood* and *GymPass*) the authority concluded that the context of the practice and the dominance level of the case defendants suggested support for strict interim measures and, later, cease and desist agreements. These TCC limited the use of exclusive agreements and MFN clauses with one side of the two-sided relevant market of the platform. Digital platform competition characteristics such as network effects and the potential for market tipping contributed to the harm presumption.

Interestingly, sometimes the presumptions are based on the presumed innovation effects of certain business practices that have been examined in Brazil by CADE.

44 *See* Barreto et al., BRICS AUTHORITIES DIGITAL MARKET REPORT (2019), *supra* note 39.

45 *See* Katsoulacos et al., *supra* note 14 and Katsoulacos, *supra* note 8.

A low anticompetitive or a pro-competitive presumption would be associated with innovation and self-preferencing; anticompetitive effects should be considered likely on conducts that restrict multi-homing.

This is an initial study on the CADE decisions in a legal standard analysis in digital cases. A larger number of cases could help give a better idea of the approach that this authority follows.

Alleged practical issues in implementing remedies seem to motivate the efficiencies presumption. Along this line, one could argue that developing countries have problems dealing with digital/Big-Tech cases that are different from jurisdictions such as the US and the European Union, as most of the services are provided from abroad. This has been argued as a motivation for the cautionary (anti-interventionist) approach by Brazilian authorities.

The actual limitations, if any, for the remedy enforcement in developing countries would be an interesting direction for future research. Learning more about cases of similar conducts in different developing countries on these new themes is essential to understanding how digital/Big-Tech antitrust cases will be handled across jurisdictions.

Table of Contents

PART II

Legal Standards in Brazil, China, Russia and South Africa

INSTITUTE of
Competition Law
Antitrust databases and resources

The Institute of Competition Law

The Institute of Competition Law is a publishing company, founded in 2004 by Dr. Nicolas Charbit, based in Paris, London and NewYork. The Institute cultivates scholarship and discussion about antitrust issues though publications and conferences. Each publication and event is supervised by editorial boards and scientific or steering committees to ensure independence, objectivity, and academic rigor. Thanks to this management, the Institute has become one of the few think tanks in Europe to have significant influence on antitrust policies.

AIM

The Institute focuses government, business and academic attention on a broad range of subjects which concern competition laws, regulations and related economics.

BOARDS

To maintain its unique focus, the Institute relies upon highly distinguished editors, all leading experts in national or international antitrust: Bill Kovacic, Mario Monti, Eleanor Fox, Laurence Idot, Frédéric Jenny, Ioannis Lianos, Richard Whish, etc.

AUTHORS

4,000 authors, from 85 jurisdictions.

PARTNERS

- Universities: University College London, King's College London, Queen Mary University, Paris Sorbonne Panthéon-Assas, etc.
- Law firms: Allen & Overy, Cleary Gottlieb Steen & Hamilton, Baker McKenzie, Hogan Lovells, Jones Day, Norton Rose Fulbright, Skadden Arps, White & Case, etc.

EVENTS

Brussels, Dusseldorf, Hong Kong, London, Milan, New York, Paris, Singapore, Warsaw and Washington, DC.

ONLINE VERSION

Concurrences website provides all articles published since its inception.

PUBLICATIONS

The Institute publishes Concurrences Review, a print and online quarterly peer-reviewed journal dedicated to EU and national competitions laws. e-Competitions is a bi-monthly antitrust news bulletin covering 85 countries. The e-Competitions database contains over 23,000 case summaries from 4,000 authors.

www.ingramcontent.com/pod-product-compliance
Ingram Content Group UK Ltd.
Pitfield, Milton Keynes, MK11 3LW, UK
UKHW020220290926
15470UKWH00001B/290

9 781954 750098